A Philosophy of Management Accounting

The book introduces pragmatic constructivism as a paradigm for understanding actors' construction of functioning practice and for developing methods and concepts for managing and observing that practice. The book explores, understands and theorises organisational practices as constructed through the activities of *all* organisational actors. Actors always act under presumptions of a specific actor-world-relation which they continuously construct, adjust and reconstruct in light of new experiences, contexts and communication. The outcome of the actor-world-relation is a reality construction. The reality construction may function successfully or it may be hampered by fictitious and illusionary elements, due to missing or faulty actor-world relations. The thesis is that four dimensions of reality—*facts, possibilities, values and communication*—must be integrated in the actor-world-relation if the construct is to form a successful basis for effective, functioning actions.

Drawing on pragmatic constructivism, the book provides concepts and ideas for studies regarding *actors* and their use of management accounting models in their construction of organised *reality*. It concentrates on researching and conceptualising what creates functioning reality construction. It develops concepts and methods for understanding, analysing and managing the actors' reality constructions. It is intended for people who do research on or work actively with developing management accounting.

Hanne Nørreklit is a Professor at Aarhus University, Denmark.

Routledge Studies in Accounting

For a full list of titles in this series, please visit www.routledge.com

A Philosophy of Management Accounting

A Pragmatic Constructivist Approach

Edited by Hanne Nørreklit

Routledge
Taylor & Francis Group

LONDON AND NEW YORK

First published 2017 by Routledge

2 Park Square, Milton Park, Abingdon, Oxfordshire OX14 4RN
52 Vanderbilt Avenue, New York, NY 10017

Routledge is an imprint of the Taylor & Francis Group, an informa business

First issued in paperback 2019

Library of Congress Cataloging-in-Publication Data
A catalog record for this book has been requested.

ISBN: 978-1-138-93009-4 (hbk)
ISBN: 978-0-367-24288-6 (pbk)

Typeset in Sabon
by Apex CoVantage, LLC

Contents

Figures and Tables

Figures

Tables

Foreword

The aim of this book is to introduce pragmatic constructivism as a paradigm for understanding actors' construction of functioning practice and for developing methods and concepts for managing and observing that practice. The book explores, understands and theorises organisational practices as constructed through the activities of *all* organisational actors. Actors always act under presumptions of a specific actor-world-relation which they continuously construct, adjust and reconstruct in light of new experiences, contexts and communication. The outcome of the actor-world-relation is a reality construction. The reality construction may function successfully or it may be hampered by fictitious and illusionary elements, due to missing or faulty actor-world relations. The thesis is that four dimensions of reality—*facts, possibilities, values and communication*—must be integrated in the actor-world-relation if the construct is to form a successful basis for effective, functioning actions. Drawing on pragmatic constructivism, the book provides concepts and ideas for studies regarding *actors* and their use of management accounting models in their construction of organised *reality*. It is intended for people who do research on or work actively with developing management accounting.

This aim of the book was outlined in a workshop at Klitgården, Skagen, Denmark, summer 2014, with the participation of Will Seal, Lennart Nørreklit and myself. Indeed, the content of the book is not a solo project, but constructed through the activities of *all* authors. The authors are actors in developing the book. Therefore, the creation process has involved the orchestrating of co-authorship through several interactive steps of authors producing manuscripts and reviewers and editor providing "meet-back" comments and suggestions for development of the paper.

So after the meeting in Skagen, the authors were contacted. All the contacted authors have experience working with pragmatic constructivism. Also, they are driven by intentional values of doing innovative academic research of high quality with a view to describing methods and concepts that will help organisational actors in their construction and development of successful, functioning practices. With a point of departure in the aim of the book, the contributors were asked to submit abstracts to be used in the formulation of the book proposal. Based on this, Morten Raffnsøe-Møller and I formulated the book proposal for Routledge. Commissioning Editor David Varely, Routledge and three anonymous reviewers were very helpful in making suggestions for improving the book proposal. The proposal was approved in March 2015.

The approval of the proposal kicked off the manuscript production process, making chapter ideas become factually possible. As we wish to ensure high academic quality and complementary contributions, we had a three-step manuscript production and "meet-back" review process. The first step was specific response to the contributors' revised abstracts. Based on the book proposal, contributors were asked to revise and develop their abstracts. I gave follow-up responses to abstracts during August 2015. The second step relates to the production and discussion of the full papers. Drafts of full papers were delivered during the autumn/winter 2015. Some of the chapters were presented at the conference on Actor-Reality construction at ESCP-Europe, Paris, September 2015. In order to organise the review and meet-back discussion, academic salons were organised in Berlin, January 2016, and at Aarhus University, June 2016. Before the meetings, two other authors and I did reviews of chapters which were used as input for the academic salons. The final chapters were delivered 1 August 2016. The final step includes some minor revisions and editing of the chapters and typesetting of the manuscript. Morten Jakobsen was very helpful in this process. The manuscript was delivered to Routledge in November 2016.

Although the book draws on a large source of already published knowledge on pragmatic constructivism, the conceptual framework and its specific application in management accounting have been extended and developed during the process. Thus, pragmatic constructivism and its applications to management accounting are still in the making, and one of the challenges of a process involving the innovative efforts of multiple actors is to orchestrate coherency across the chapters. Therefore, the communication processes have been organised with a view to establishing conceptual coherence across chapters. However, despite the efforts, we cannot ensure complete conceptual consistency. Also, there is some published knowledge on pragmatic constructivism which we have not had sufficient space to include.

I would like to thank the authors for putting into the book their wonderful vigour, academic thoughts and dedicated work. It has been incredibly enjoyable to work, discuss and interact with all you co-authors. I am looking forward to working with you in the future.

Additionally, I would like to thank the Routledge team for supporting the book project and making it possible. Finally, I extend my thanks to the respective authors' universities for funding travel and conference expenses and, in particular, Department of Management, Aarhus University, for funding workshop catering.

Hanne Nørreklit

About the Authors

Gudrun Baldvinsdottir, PhD, is Professor of Management Accounting, Trondheim Business School, NTNU, Norway. Her research areas primarily include relational aspects, such as trust and accountability in management accounting settings, management accounting change, and changes of the management accounting profession. Her recent empirical research covers accountability issues in banking.

Cristina Campanale, PhD, is Research fellow at the Institute of Management, Scuola Superiore Sant'Anna of Pisa. Her research interests include management accounting, cost and performance management and management accounting change in service-oriented organisations.

Lino Cinquini, PhD, is Professor of Management Accounting at the Institute of Management, Scuola Superiore Sant'Anna of Pisa. Also he is the Editor of *Journal of Management and Governance*. His research interests include cost and performance management in service-oriented organisations, strategic management accounting, management accounting change and accounting history.

Cristian Heidarson is a graduate of University of College London, UK and is a research associate of Gothenburg Research Institute. He has 15 years' professional experience as an industry analyst during which he developed industry forecasting models to support competitive positioning and development of strategic profiles.

Lisa Jack, PhD, is Professor of Accounting, Portsmouth Business School, UK. She is President Elect of the British Accounting and Finance Association. Her research interests lie in management information for decision-making, including accounting communication and education, and accounting and social theory. She has a special interest in accounting in agri-food industries.

Morten Jakobsen, PhD, is Associate Professor of Management Accounting at Department of Management, Aarhus University, Denmark. His primary research interest is cost management with a particular focus on inter-organisational relations. More recently he has done research of cost management in the agricultural sector.

Tuomas Korhonen, PhD, is Postdoctoral Researcher at the Cost Management Centre, Tampere University of Technology, Finland. His research interests lie in studying the potential of management accounting in contributing to various types of managerial work.

Nikolaj Kure, PhD, is an Associate Professor at the Department of Business Communication, Aarhus University, Denmark. His primary research interests include New Public Management reforms, organisational paradox, and organisational change.

Teemu Laine, PhD, is an Assistant Professor of Management Accounting, Tampere University of Technology, Finland. His current research interests include management accounting in service business and R&D management. He is also heavily involved in developing the interventionist research approach.

Ruth Mattimoe, PhD, is lectures in Management Accounting at DCU Business School, Dublin. Her research interests concerns real life issues of decision-making and performance measurement in hotel and tourism firms.

Falconer Mitchell, BCom, CA, is Professor of Management Accounting at the University of Edinburgh. He has been Chairman of CIMA's Research Board. His research interests lie in the areas of managerial accounting with particular reference to cost management and management accounting change processes. He is also heavily involved in developing pragmatic constructivism within the accounting field.

Lars Braad Nielsen, PhD, is project manager at the global consultancy company PwC Strategy& (formerly Booz & Company), London. He has done research on out-sourcing decision-making and principal-agency theory. He has experiences in cost optimisation and restructuring of projects within leading international companies.

Hanne Nørreklit, PhD, is Professor of Management Accounting and Control, at School of Business and Social Science, Aarhus University, Denmark. Her research areas include performance management and control, management rhetoric, and validity issues in accounting and management. She is the coordinator of the research network on pragmatic constructivism.

Lennart Nørreklit, Dr.fil., has been Professor of Philosophy and Management at Aalborg University, Denmark. His research interests are the concept of reality, cross-cultural philosophy, methodology of social science and philosophy of the "good life." He has developed the philosophical basis of pragmatic constructivism.

Morten Raffnsøe-Møller, PhD, is Associate Professor in ethics, social and political philosophy at Aarhus University, Denmark. He is the Vice-chairman of the Danish Research Council of independent research. His research interests are organisational philosophy, recognition and self-realisation, political philosophy and the human turn in science and society.

Daniela Pianezzi is PhD Student at Scuola Superiore Sant'Anna of Pisa. Her research interests are business ethics, social accounting and human rights, corruption, ethics in accounting and accountability.

Will Seal, PhD, is Professor of Accounting and Management at Loughborough University. He is a member of the centre for global service sourcing in the School of Business and Economics at Loughborough University. His main research interests are the relationship between theory and practice in management, strategic control, shared services, supply chain management, and lean operations.

Petri Suomala, PhD, is Vice President and Professor of Profitability Management and Management Accounting at Tampere University of Technology, Finland. He was co-founder of the research centre for cost management at Tampere University. His research interests relate to the versatile utilisation of management accounting in industrial companies and other organisations. He is particularly experienced in interventionist research methodology.

Andrea Tenucci, PhD, is Assistant Professor at the Institute of Management, Scuola Superiore Sant'Anna of Pisa. His research interests include cost accounting & management, strategic management accounting, management accounting in services, accounting for sustainability and accounting history.

Emmi Tervala, MSc., is Consultant at Columbia Road, Finland. In her master thesis, completed at Tampere University of Technology, Finland, she focused on project manager's viewpoint to management control.

Mihaela Trenca, PhD, is Assistant Professor of Management Accounting at Aarhus University, Denmark. Her research interests lie in the areas of performance management with a particular focus on performance management practices allowing the development of actors' awareness of the multiple interdependencies that shape organisational reality.

1 Introduction

Hanne Nørreklit, Falconer Mitchell
and Morten Raffnsøe-Møller

A Problem of Mechanical Scientific Thinking

In the prominent article "Bad Management Theories are Destroying Good Management Practices", Ghoshal (2005) argued that the scientific character of the philosophical underpinnings of modern management theories make them problematic to use in practice. This is particularly evident in the early twentieth-century scientific management methodology of Taylorism, which has expanded from factory shop floor guidance to become a managerial doctrine. According to Taylor (1916, 10–11), "the best management is a true science, resting upon clearly defined laws, rules and principles, as foundation." In a modern managerial context, this doctrine entails the implementation of machine-like, repeatable and homogeneous structures and systems even in complex organisational processes with the aim of making "the management of complex corporations systematic and predictable" (Mintzberg et al. 2003, 305). The methodology is based on partial analysis and deductive reasoning, whereas any moral and ethical responsibilities are ignored. Such mechanical and amoral prescription for management practice is arguably damaging for human beings, organisations and institutions (Ghoshal 2005).

Indeed, the 2008 global financial crisis revealed the contemporary presence of similar inappropriate management theories. The crisis came suddenly and surprisingly. The many theories and research models on management practice proved to be inadequate in anticipating and coping with the crisis. Starting with the doctrine of Taylorism, business scholars have initiated numerous mechanical performance management models providing meta-laws for creating and observing successful business.

For instance, performance-based incentive systems, linking individual rewards to the results of the organisation, have been implemented in companies worldwide at all organisational levels to motivate managers to deliver organisational performance that is congruent with the interests of their shareholders. The governing attitude was expressed in slogans such as: "You get what you measure" and "If you pay peanuts you get monkeys". Nevertheless, the financial crisis can to a considerable degree be ascribed to the high emphasis placed on a reductive corporate incentive-based governance system, leading to the neglect of appropriate risk assessment (Kirkpatrick 2009). Likewise, the Balanced Scorecard advocated by Kaplan and Norton (1996) has been a popular mechanical model prescribing actions for obtaining financial success and foreseeing future results. The accomplishments of the balanced scorecard were supported by other scientifically based empirical studies, such as the one by Davis and Albright (2004), who argued that bank branches implementing the balanced scorecard outperformed the other branches within the same organisation on key financial measures. Nevertheless, some of the companies that failed during the crisis, such as Fannie Mae, Nationwide Financial Services Inc., and Chrysler, were the normative examples of the balanced scorecard before the financial crisis (Nørreklit et al. 2012).

There may be several reasons for the failure of these companies; however, as the balanced scorecard is blind to the financial implications and validity of the beliefs and boundaries embedded in the performance measurements, it should not be applied to decision-making at face value (Nørreklit 2000). Overall, the financial crisis exposed significant problems in relation to the mechanical governance doctrine. The models of mechanical scientific thinking may be appealing to practice, but if the scientific foundation is partial and blind to important issues, these models can seriously mislead those using them.

Aim of the Book

By concentrating on the construction of valid organisational practices, this book is concerned with the development of a more productive and beneficial relationship between research and practice. The aim of the book is to describe ways and methods that will help actors in their construction and development of successful, functioning organisational activities with a special focus on the role of management accounting. It is addressed to people who do research on or work actively with developing management accounting practice. To serve this purpose, it is important for research to suggest conceptual models that can be/are used in the development of successful, functioning practices. As outlined above, some conceptual models that are in circulation can be dangerous or misleading. Accordingly, models for measuring and managing practice performance are relevant as study objects.

Pragmatic constructivism is used as a paradigm for understanding and conducting research on accounting actors' construction of valid practice. This is appropriate given that it is concerned with ways in which to do research on what makes things work in a dynamic, material and socio-organisational context, i.e. what creates sound practice performance.

Pragmatic Constructivism

With a focus on the construction of a successful actor-world relationship, pragmatic constructivism offers some conceptual fundamentals for could develop, operate and innovate together. The result of the managerial approach was poor financial performance.

The turnaround was a result of the efforts of organisational actors at all levels in constructing a joint set of successful relationships to the world in which they operated. This regenerative success of LEGO was based on the multiple groups of organisational actors' ongoing reflective practices leading to the development and establishment of a joint set of functioning activities, producing certain intended outcomes. A successful financial outcome is created through, for instance, an interactive process of innovation involving all hierarchical levels as well as LEGO enthusiasts, an integrated set of effective activities involving suppliers, manufacturing, sales and marketing, and the controllers' production of relevant accounting information for planning and decision-making. In this sense, LEGO acted as a joint venture mustering the coalition of organisational actors and creative, technical and economic resources to create products and services that met or even changed children's, parents' and enthusiasts' values by introducing new forms of playing experiences and qualities in their lives (Robertson and Breen 2013).

Four Dimensions of Reality and Construct Causality

Actors do not act in a void but in the world of human life, constructing their relationships to the world. More specifically, one assumption of pragmatic constructivism is that actors always act under presumption of a specific actor-world relation which they continuously construct, adjust and reconstruct in light of new experiences, contexts and communication. The outcome of the actor-world relation is a reality construction. The reality construction may function successfully or it may be hampered by fictitious and illusionary elements that are due to missing or faulty actor-world relations. The conceptual framework used by an actor or group of actors in their reflection and method to control the reality construction is the *topos*. The thesis of pragmatic constructivism is that *four dimensions of reality must be integrated* in the actor-world relation if the construct is to be a successful basis for effective, functioning actions or form the basis for pragmatic constructivism in the establishment of 'construct causalities'. These four dimensions address, simply speaking: facts, possibilities, values and communication. The topos exhibits the particular perception of how to integrate facts, possibilities, values and communication.

The rationale for the integration of these four dimensions of reality in regard to construct causality is as follows. Facts are a necessary basis for action; but facts alone are insufficient. Thus, there can be no action, if there are no possibilities. However, for the possibilities to be more than only a matter of the actor's imagination, they must be grounded in the facts at hand. For instance, the LEGO Star Wars franchise is a human construction developed by organisational actors through the recognition of new types of possibilities. Projecting actions leading to LEGO Star Wars requires the creation of possibilities. However, the development of the activities to make Star Wars a success was not purely a function of the CEO's imagination. The success of LEGO Star Wars involved many organisational actors' extensive collaborative reflections and analyses, developing the set of factual possibilities required to create a successful outcome. The possibilities were grounded in the factual knowledge about plastic bricks, IT-technology, business partners, LEGO enthusiasts, children's play, parents' behaviour, cost structure, etc.

However, if the factually based possible construction is not within the actors' value range, there will be no action. The LEGO brand expresses the organisational values of building through creativity and imagination. These values govern all organisational activities. Also, in order to motivate people to develop, produce and buy LEGO Star Wars, the product must express the subjective values of these multiple actors. If the actors' values are within the range of their factual possibilities, the actor will act and succeed.

Finally, the integration of facts, possibilities and values must be expressed through communication in order to enable action in a social setting by coordinating a social division of labour. For the organisation to create a set of construct causalities, a pragmatic integration of the four dimensions has to be made for each activity in interaction with other activities, i.e. an integration that makes each activity create a set of construct causalities that work successfully together with other activities. Successful action is the aim of applying pragmatic constructivism. One of the reasons why LEGO faced major financial problems in 2003 was the lack of communication about the establishment of construct causality across organisational activities. Thus, in 2003 the Christmas sales of the LEGO Star Wars product flopped due to a failed marketing plan, because there was no new film in the Star Wars series. Accordingly, the ability to act effectively dissolved, as the integration of facts, possibilities, value and communication was incomplete (Robertson and Breen 2013).

Overall, practice is based on the organisational actors constructing complex outcomes by establishing advanced strings of construct causalities. Enabling construct causality is the integrated environment of reality constructs that make up the conditions for a broad range of possible causal strings to succeed. Only actions that integrate all four dimensions will ensure the relevant effect and hence establish the intended causality. Thus, the quality of the integration of the four dimensions of reality is the condition for valid reality construction, i.e. construct causality. Reductionist perspectives address only one or two of these dimensions and hence systematically create validity problems. Pragmatic constructivism recognises that establishing an integrated world-relation is highly complicated, but at the same time it is also the most ordinary task that organisational actors perform through their ongoing practice. Further, it recognises that this task is the presupposition for successful and effective organisational actions and, hence, for practising action such as management accounting. This means that simplifying management accounting beyond this level of complexity takes place at the expense of its connection with ordinary organisational practice and its reality.

An Integrative Learning Theory of Truth

In order to develop and control construct causality, the organisational actors need a highly detailed and complex representation of knowledge about their business reality. Pragmatic constructivism contends that actors construct organisational activities, simultaneously with retaining realism as the pragmatic criterion of a successful outcome of the organisational actors' construction. Our constructions continuously face the test of meeting (or failing) their projected outcomes, because they are oriented towards an intended future and hence may succeed or fail. In that sense, we are dealing with 'constructivism' in a realist way. To address the realism of a construction, pragmatic constructivism offers an integrative learning theory of truth that enables us to theoretically point to problems of validity. It integrates the following principal ideas of truth: pragmatics, phenomenology, correspondence and coherence. The result is a learning theory of truth where the learning circle, i.e. the interplay between the pro-active truth of whether the projection will hold true, and the pragmatic truth of whether it did hold true, forms the basis of the learning process. Managing organisational activities requires ongoing reflection through which conceptual models are developed and reshaped in order to observe, control and reformulate the construct causality upon which successful management action can be executed.

In principle, any kind of information, data and analysis, and thus any kind of knowledge generating methodological technique, may be applied to pragmatic constructivism. What is essential is the ability to trace the meaning of the information, i.e. its role in the reality construction process. Data in itself reflects states of affairs in the world, but the relevant question is if and in what way specific states of affairs and data are relevant and essential in constructing a successful intended reality. The role of these matters in the reality construction processes is analysed through the application of pragmatic constructivism. How do they picture the integration of the four dimensions? How do they fit in the co-authoring process uncovered so far? How do the causal constructs work?

It is especially important to uncover the problems of the interplay between various integrated systems guiding different organisational actors' reality constructions. These problems are often conflicts between competing topoi or even problems due to some important conditions that are not conceptualised in the operating topoi and, hence, operate at a structural or subconscious level. In order to really uncover and analyse such matters, interactive and reflective methodological tools are recommended, which grant access to actors' way of authoring their reality construction through dialogical interaction with their topos(i) and participation in co-authorship. With proper conceptual analysis, supported by adequate coding, it may be possible to overcome pre-categorized patterns of thinking and penetrate to levels where more or less hidden dynamics can be uncovered and conceptualised.

Relation to Other Paradigms

In its study of human activities, this book connects to the domain of practice theory (Schatzki 2001) rooted in Wittgenstein's language philosophy (1953). Pragmatic constructivism agrees with Wittgenstein that practices are organised around language games, which are the totality of the language and the activity into which it is woven. People use language to create intentional action together within specific areas of activities. But Wittgenstein does not pay much attention to the conditions that are necessary for people to *construct* what they intend to do through their actions. Accordingly, pragmatic constructivism enhances Wittgenstein's ideas by emphasising that in order for language to function and trigger the relevant actions, the relevant intentions and situational conditions for creating construct causality are imperative (Nørreklit et al. 2007, 2010, 2012).

This practice theory provides a rebuttal of the traditional scientific 'realist' subject-world separation, which is assumed by the positivistic methods varying from contingency theory to Taylorism. The scientific 'realist' approaches take objective representations of the world as descriptive points of departure and assume that managers and organisations are parts of the natural world and interpret actions mechanistically. Although pragmatic constructivism acknowledges the existence of facts and some natural laws of the world, it does not subscribe to the idea of natural meta-laws for social practices integrating a multitude of free and reflective actors, and hence it refuses to apply such methods to describe functioning management practice.

Other scholars of practice theory, such as Foucault (1969), Latour (1987) and Giddens (2013), are concerned with the dimension of communication and the social (Nørreklit et al. 2016). The main idea is that meta-structures of linguistic practices, expert systems and/or technology shape the agencies and practices in a certain field such as organisations. For instance, research based on Foucault's thinking is concerned with how linguistic practices produced outside the local activity govern both the local individuals' self-understandings and the techniques by which they act and interact in the organisation (Foucault 1969). This often results in a radical constructivist and critical position in which there is no standard of truth but only global techniques of power. Although it sides with such theories in its critical stance towards a number of dominating organisational theories and practices, pragmatic constructivism maintains that any theory of management and accounting must retain a conceptual apparatus that allows it to understand the success and truth aptness of local practices of reality construction and, consequently, of ways of accounting and management. Hence, pragmatic constructivism adheres to the fact that any actor or group of organisational actors must integrate the four dimensions of reality in a situated and original manner if they are to successfully construct operational organisational relationships (i.e. construct causality), and they must reinterpret and customise global linguistic practices in (varied) ways that fit their local aims and needs of reality construction.

Accordingly, pragmatic constructivism offers a middle ground between the 'realist' scientific mainstream and social constructivism by retaining realism as the pragmatic criterion for the success of the organisational actors' construction. There are some philosophical scholars concerned with how people in local practices produce functioning activities in intentional reflective interaction (Schatzki 2001; Thevenot 2001). They look at how people enact macro-level assumptions of causal rules that are suitable for pursuing their intended ends. Individual human actions are driven by subjective values, but actions are by no means universally linked to 'macro-level' prescription (Barnes 2001, 39). It is not the same practice that is repeated across space.

However, apart from the sociological theories of Boltanski and Thévenot (2000), this stream does not pay much attention to the ways in which reflective human beings develop and create new types of construct causality in communicative interaction with a dynamic environment. Neither do they pay much attention to the conditions that are necessary for people to *construct* what they intend to do through their actions. Indeed, these theories primarily focus on how actors *justify* their actions and goals vis-à-vis other actors, and, hence, how they fit into or justify new practices relative to existing practices (Thévenot 2001). This, however, begs the question why the actors go to the lengths of challenging existing practices. In pragmatic constructivism, subjective values and factual possibilities motivate actors to construct new realities, and justify these to co-authors, in order to establish construct causality that will make them true. In emphasising the four dimensions of integration and the integrative learning theory of truth, pragmatic constructivism contrasts with most research approaches to management and accounting that involve the reduction of dimensions.

Management Accounting

Broadly speaking, management accounting research can be divided into three branches. First, we have the conventional wisdom of management accounting concerned with the technical aspect of producing accounting information for decision-making and performance management. Second, we have the 'realist' scientific approach searching for generic actions leading to success. Finally, we have the sociological branch analysing the role of management accounting in the construction of the human being and the social. Below, we discuss pragmatic constructivism in relation to the established paradigms within these three areas of accounting research with a view to addressing some important neglected research areas.

Conventional Wisdom of Management Accounting

Because financial performance is fundamental for doing business, conceptual frameworks of management accounting and performance measurement concern representation of some vital attributes of the business reality. Management accounting measurements are vital to make appropriate outlines for actions and develop and control construct causalities. For instance, a major part of LEGO's turnaround was the establishment and use of management accounting models and information for analysing alternative supply chain configurations, product and customer profitability, investment activities, etc.

The conventional wisdom of management accounting textbooks is primarily technical and tool based. It is concerned with calculative rationality (Scapens 1985). On the whole, the tools are logical conceptual models aimed at constructing and organising human reality with a view to securing the corporate profitability or organisational financial well-being. In view of pragmatic constructivism, an important task for management accounting research is to develop conceptual frameworks to help practitioners in developing and controlling the activities. When the business context changes, there is a need for developing new conceptual models to manage organisational activities. For instance, Kaplan and Johnson (1987) argued that changing business structures created a need for activity-based costing, while making traditional costing obsolete. Over the last few decades, the business context has been changing as fast as ever. However, academic researchers have neglected the calculative core of management accounting (Baldvinsdottir et al. 2010).

This neglect might be explained by the fact that the calculative rational approach has been heavily criticised for its assumption of one organisational decision-maker: a rational economic man with objective knowledge about actual performance, and alternative courses of action and their future consequences (Cyert and March 1963; March 1978). In real life organisations, there are multiple decision-makers who have subjective goals that might be conflicting, and there is limited and uncertain information about the consequences of historical, as well as future, actions.

Traditional Realist Scientific Approach

In response to the critique, some researchers have advocated systemic rational models as alternatives to solve some of the traditional purposes of accounting such as decision-making. For instance, from the systemic rational approach it is argued that decision-making should be based on principles of sensible adaption to changes in the environment and selection of the rules and routines of the fittest (March 1978, 593; Dane and Pratt 2007). Such a view governs some dominating business research approaches such as contingency theory and managerial scientific management. Positivistic methods are used to search for generic mechanical actions driving successful business performance. For instance, based on a quantitative empirical study it is argued that organisational profitability is driven by certain generic actions such as superior quality and sales growth. The models seem to assume that managers and organisations are part of the natural world and they interpret actions mechanistically (Descartes 1637; Newton 1687) or evolutionally (Darwin 1872). Profitability is considered to be a given condition that can be improved if relevant general empirical laws about optimal actions are found by researchers and transferred by practitioners into their local practices. However, as accounting is a logical phenomenon, analysing the profitability of specific organisational actions requires a logical conceptual model of accounting. Therefore, assuming an empirical causal relationship misconstrues the phenomenon of creating financial performance, because the ability to 'account for' financial performance presupposes conceptually established logical connections between central financial phenomena. Overall, in the systemic rational approach, the nature and role of a logical conceptual model of management accounting is neglected in favour of making empirical generalisations about what makes organisations 'fittest to survive' in a changing environment in which it remains quite open what future capacities will become criteria of fitness.

Nevertheless, pragmatic constructivism is in agreement with the calculative conceptual models of mainstream accounting, which operate on an abstract theoretical level detached from the empirical content of action. However, the logical conceptual models have to work within a complex organisational context of real material and social structures, with multiple actors involved in the establishment of a joint set of construct causalities, and information uncertainty in the observation and control of construct causality. From the perspective of pragmatic constructivism, management accounting only provides valid results in practice if they incorporate all four aspects of the world of human life. This requires methodology that can reflect the four dimensions of reality construction in the use and production of management accounting information. The traditional methodology, based on rationalism or positivism, is reductive because it is concerned with possibility and facts, and therefore does not integrate the resources that lie in the actors' values, nor the information that must be extracted through communication. Lack of integration makes the research community and the actors slip into something unreal and purely abstract. Consequently, such reductionist models may, if applied, create dysfunctional results.

Social Constructivism

Social constructivism is a third dominating approach in the management accounting field. Accounting numbers are argued to be a soft and almost hidden form of confining and taming peoples' self-understanding and actions. They exercise their disciplining power over organisational personnel by measuring, comparing, ranking, differentiating and rewarding—or punishing—the personnel (Miller and O'Leary 1987; Porter 1995). The radical constructivist position states that accounting is not to be used for rational reasons of decision-making and control, but to legitimate power structures and dominate local practices only. Administrative ideals of economic rationality, objectivity by quantification, and fair rewarding dominate the discourse of performance measurement and organisational accountability, but they conceal ideals of a social order serving the interest of the governing power structure (Porter 1995).

To a certain extent, pragmatic constructivism is in agreement with the fact that much of the contemporary production and use of so-called objective financial and non-financial numbers has severe and controversial consequences. Claiming to produce objective representations of the world, the so-called scientific approaches might appear to be concerned with the factual dimension, but they are reductive because this is at the surface level only. If a certain power structure only takes one dimension into consideration, it systematically creates validity problems. The power of the scientific doctrine 'objectivity by quantification' is largely a consequence of normative pressure on the ideal of scientific realism rather than its validity (Porter 1995, ix), and when organisational employees are expected to be passive adaptors to illusionary norms and measures, without consideration of whether they are factually possible and within their value range, they are excluded from being actors.

Nevertheless, pragmatic constructivism does not share a common implication of a radical social constructivist view of management accounting. Pragmatic constructivism maintains that accounting is a central epistemic practice of organisations, which is aimed at evaluating organisational activities with respect to their ability to realise a specific set of factual possibilities. Considered production and use of accounting allows external and internal organisational actors to observe, analyse, manage and account for more accurate integration of factual possibilities relating to specific activities. It also helps identify whether the factual possibilities are within the range of subjective values and organisational goals, and whether communication happens across the coalition of organisational actors. The validity of an accounting statement is not an objective point of reference 'out there', but related to the organisational actors' integration of the four dimensions of reality in the construction. This will be revealed through the pragmatic criteria of a successful outcome of the construction. In this respect, an accounting report may give valid or illusionary statements about the state of the organisation.

Indeed, the validity of a given accounting system and theory is a product of certain actors' intentional values and interests, and part of their power to promote and achieve those values. This is a point of agreement between critical social constructivism and pragmatic constructivism. However, pragmatic constructivism views this condition as a starting point for an evaluation of the validity and deformative power structures of different accounting practices. Evaluating these is a very complex matter that must be analysed relative to the coalition of the subjective goals of the organisational actors.

It is related to whether an accounting practice or theory helps achieve specific purposes, and whether individual and organisational values are factually possible. From the point of view of the local practices, the validity of socially dominating forms of accounting can be evaluated and validated. The meta-topoi of accounting must be constructed and reconstructed through their emergence and justification in local organisational practice. Pragmatic constructivism maintains that any theory or system of management accounting must adhere to the integration of the four dimensions of reality in a situated and original manner, if it is to successfully reflect construct causality.

Research Themes

Overall, from the perspective of pragmatic constructivism there is a need for academic researchers to apply a stronger focus on both the technical calculative core of management accounting and to develop methods that can be used to integrate management accounting models with specific operational practices. Calculative models are at the core of management accounting and need ongoing conceptual development to match contemporary practices. However, the conceptual models of accounting cannot produce valid outcomes in practice without being further developed and adapted to the specific sets of organisational topoi. Both the calculative accounting techniques and the methodological procedures by which they are applied are to be understood and adequately described in isolation and in interaction with each other to produce construct causality for organisational practices. Moreover, as management accounting systems are embedded in social order, there should be some concepts for critical studies to evaluate the extent to which the coalition of multiple actors' values and organisational objectives are factually possible.

Pragmatic constructivism is based on the agreement that any theory or system of management accounting must adhere to the integration of the four dimensions of reality. Therefore, it is not enough to analyse the validity of one-dimensional theories or models but, in addition, to access the integration of the four dimensions of reality embedded in the management accounting research approaches with a view to their possibilities to work in conjunction with pragmatic constructivism. In view of that, this book addresses the issues of developing management accounting methodology for use in organisational practices of management accounting, and of expanding the knowledge about the validity embedded in the reality construction of specific management accounting approaches.

Structure and Contributions of the Book

The book consists of three parts. Part one explains the conceptual framework of pragmatic constructivism. Part two and three show the application of the framework in studying and analysing actor-reality constructs. This structure is intended to emphasise both the philosophical basis and the operational conceptual methods and frameworks for understanding, analysing and managing management accounting practices.

Part I: Pragmatic Constructivism

The chapters in part one, written by Lennart Nørreklit, give an in-depth explanation of pragmatic constructivism. Chapter 2 expounds on the actors' point of view of existence, placed in a world in time and space, facing the problem of producing successful actions in order to create a viable construction that fulfils their engagement, i.e. a functioning reality construction. It explains facets of the four dimensions of reality—facts, possibilities, values and communication—that are involved in the actors' constructions of their relations to the world, establishing that the integration of these four dimensions is unavoidable when aiming to establish construct causality. Chapter 3 provides an epistemology for understanding and analysing the actors' construction of practices in an organisational context of multiple realities. It analyses the construction of concepts and how actors come from subjective experiences to ontological realities.

Overall, we can say that pragmatic constructivism offers a paradigm concerned with understanding and analysing how actors construct personal and organised reality in a dynamic environment with a view to obtaining intentional outcome. Part I gives insight into a comprehensive set of conceptual fundamentals for conducting studies on the *actors* and their use of management accounting models in their construction of organised *reality*. This involves a focus on the quality of the conceptual models and the actors' modes of reflecting and creating meaning when using the models in local practices.

Part II: Decision-Making and Performance Management

By applying a pragmatic constructivist approach, part II explores organisational practices of production and use of management accounting in the decision-making and control of the actor-reality construction. The first two chapters address the topic of planning and decision-making. The next two address the performance evaluation of the top management, whereas the last two chapters examine issues of performance management, focusing on the view of the middle management level.

In Chapter 4, Nørreklit, Mitchell and Nielsen develop a conceptual framework for use in fairly complex organisational planning and decision-making situations requiring accounting information. The production of accounting information involves the co-authorship of the multiple actors' perceptions of what may be factually possible and valuable in the future, although there are no definitive facts to base this on. Regarding production and use of trustworthy information about future consequences of planned actions and activities, it advocates an actor-based procedure of co-authorship and skilful and reflective learning perspective. It gives insight into measurement and communication techniques to challenge the pro-active truth of the actors' business topoi.

Chapter 5, written by Laine, Korhonen, Suomala and Tervala, focuses on New Product Development (NPD) project managers as actors, and, particularly, on management accounting and control as experienced and enacted by NPD project managers within a given organisational context. It conceptualises different NPD project managers' topoi and unveils how they interact with company topoi. Specifically, it identifies management topos, business controller topos, analyst topos and technology topos as project manager archetypes. The archetypes may be used in examining how different project managers work with integration of facts and possibilities within their value range, and how they interact with the company topos. Overall, it contributes to understanding how NPD project managers, as actors, help achieve organisational goals and improve NPD performance.

Chapter 6, written by Mitchell, Nørreklit and Nørreklit, conducts an investigation of the business reality subject to accounting measurement, and the ability of accounting epistemology to provide trustworthy information for performance evaluation. An apparatus for improving accounting measurement for stewardship is also proposed in outline. A learning theory of truth, involving interplay between the conception of pragmatic truth and the more conventional pro-active truth, can form a basis for improving the practice of the accounting profession.

In Chapter 7, Baldvinsdottir and Heidarson apply pragmatic constructivism to a longitudinal analysis of the CEO statements in annual reports published by a municipally owned utility company. A narrative interpretation of strategy reveals efforts by senior management to enlist the municipal owners and national regulators as co-authors of the decision-making process. The topoi of the prospective co-authors are integrated into the strategic profile of the company as internalised topos orchestrated narratives that present strategic initiatives as solutions to resolve topos tension.

Chapter 8, written by Trenca and Nørreklit, develops a conceptual framework for understanding and analysing the quality of an actor's performance management topos. It illustrates how a successful manager, by applying actor-based performance management, creates a functioning supply chain practice through engaging in emphatic and conceptually reflective epistemic methods, orchestrating co-authorship in finding the factual problem and solid constructs for solving the problem.

Chapter 9, written by Cinquini, Campanale, Pianezzi and Tenucci, demonstrates how pragmatic constructivism can increase our understanding and assessment of management accounting in the public sector. The analysis shows that the topoi of top and middle managers are formed by conflicting values that cause a disaggregated reality construction rather than an overarching topos coordinating organisational activities. It implies that the ability of an organisation to provide factual possibilities for providing public services dissolves, and suggests that a pragmatic constructivist approach to

accounting in the public sector can play a leading role in creating an organisational topos and solving problems of ambiguity.

Overall, part II contributes by providing new conceptual frameworks for the
management accounting of the actor-reality construction. It extends our understanding of accounting practices and provides methods for the production and
use of trustworthy accounting information in complex organisational environments encompassing multiple actors and uncertainties. Further, it provides
methods that can be used to integrate and understand calculative techniques of
management accounting in relation to the specific practices. Also, insights are
offered to critically evaluate the extent to which the coalition of multiple actors'
values and organisational objectives is factually possible. Hence, the studies
contribute to management accounting theory by developing management
accounting methods that go beyond mechanistic ones and by critically evaluating the constructions on which management accounting practice is based.
There are many knowledge issues and practices of management accounting to
analyse, and therefore plenty of need and possibilities for the development of
more insight into its calculative practices and the methods by which these are
produced, used and assessed. The chapters demonstrate that pragmatic constructivism can fertilise development of new models and methods.

Part III: Research Approaches and Reality Constructions

Part III scrutinises dominating accounting research approaches with a view
to assessing whether they facilitate a functioning reality construction or a
more illusionary one. Drawing on pragmatic constructivism, the chapters
carry out a conceptual investigation of the validity of dominating research
views of accounting, as represented by scientific realism, radical social constructivism, structuration theory, actor network theory and sensemaking.
Also, it reflects upon whether these research approaches can be used in conjunction with pragmatic constructivism.

More specifically, in Chapter 10 Kure, Nørreklit and Raffnsøe indicate
that management accounting research is dominated by two opposing views
on language: a realist stance and a constructivist perspective. Both of these
positions are imbued with a set of problems that obscure one of the core
tenets of management accounting: enabling actors to construct functioning
activities. By way of an alternative, the chapter outlines the characteristics of
a language game that facilitates a functioning reality construction. This conceptual development can be used to critically analyse whether a performance
management system facilitates the construction of illusions or realities.

In Chapter 11, Jack compares actor reality construction and strong structuration theory, and provides a rationale for using them in conjunction. To
explore this contention, the literature on organised crime groups is examined.
Such groups, ostensibly, demonstrate longevity and institutionalisation of
practice based on what might be regarded as illusory realities. In other words,
elements of structuration and time are introduced to examine why organised

crime networks appear to endure. The construction of individual actors as criminals—by themselves or by those interested in crime prevention—and the co-authoring of topoi based around a network of criminals or crime prevention officers provide a deviant setting in which to test out concepts of fact and fiction in the actor-reality framework.

In Chapter 12, Jakobsen analyses similarities between pragmatic constructivism and the early version of Actor Network Theory used in management accounting research. On an ontological level, pragmatic constructivism distinguishes between the world and reality, whereas Latour only operates with reality. Furthermore, Actor Network Theory seems to assume that non-human actors play the main part, whereas the human actors are rather seen as responsive, supporting actors. As such, the human actors' free will seems rather limited, and they are not equipped with an explicit set of values.

Chapter 13, written by Seal and Mattimore, makes a comparison of a pragmatic constructivist approach to management control and a sensemaking and sensegiving approach. The chapter argues that pragmatic constructivism entails more demanding tests of management control knowledge than approaches based on sensemaking, and that actor-based management already captures many of the characteristics of sensegiving activity.

Finally, in Chapter 14, Mitchell addresses new ways of studying differences and changes in management accounting practices. The chapter points to the potential of using a pragmatic constructivist perspective to undertake novel research on the different forms management accounting practice can take in different organisations, and the manner in which it changes over time. Also, it argues that pragmatic constructivism can be used as part of a mixed methods research design to provide new information on the operation of many of the variables involved in other behavioural theories. For example, pragmatic constructivism can, when used in conjunction with another theory such as contingency theory, provide a complementary approach to enable insight on how and why people respond (or do not respond) to contingent variable stimuli when carrying out the practice of management accounting.

Overall, we can conclude that some dominating research approaches tend to be rather one or two-dimensional. However, this does not mean that these models are obsolete, but rather that they can be used to elaborate certain aspects of the reality construction. Also, pragmatic constructivism can be used to advocate constructive solutions to some problems addressed by the critical sociological approaches. Thus, pragmatic constructivism provides some concepts useful for critically evaluating whether management accounting is based on illusion or reality.

Conclusion and Implications for Accounting Research

The preceding introduction demonstrates how this text is designed to show the potential of the philosophy of pragmatic constructivism as a basis for explaining, understanding and developing human behaviour. The focus of this philosophy is on people as they relate to the real world in which they exist, as a precursor to action. In this case, action takes the form of a professional practice, management accounting, which is commonly found throughout the organisational world.

The potential of pragmatic constructivism for both researchers and practitioners of management accounting is argued for, analysed and illustrated in the chapters that follow. It provides an analytical structure that reveals the often intuitive (and therefore hidden) ways in which the calculative techniques of management accounting are employed within the varied and complex organisational processes and practices that involve multiple actors interacting and operating in a dynamic world. Thus, it has the advantages of (a) identifying the ways in which people successfully (or unsuccessfully) engage with the circumstances in which they exist; (b) providing a basis for designing data gathering methods on this behaviour; and (c) constituting a structured foundation for the analysis and interpretation of empirical data on real world management accounting. These attributes make it a powerful tool for both the empirical researcher aiming to gather, explain and understand data about management accounting practice and for the reflective practitioner striving to improve the truth base for and success of their actions.

However, the potential value of pragmatic constructivism goes beyond these important attributes. The insights gained by applying pragmatic constructivism to the study of accounting practice can help the researcher appreciate the real information needs of the practitioner. This can lead to an understanding of why a long recognised gap exists between research and practice in management accounting, and so it can represent a first step towards developing research that will be useful to practitioners and eventually contribute to closing the gap. Finally, pragmatic constructivism provides a structured basis for logical analyses of practice. These (as demonstrated in subsequent chapters) can involve the definition of behavioural ideals by which actual performance can be assessed, the role of language in real world representation and communication, and development of a conceptual framework for practice.

Pragmatic constructivism is an approach to behavioural analysis that avoids the extremes and shortcomings of the more common approaches of realism and social constructivism. It offers an alternative that can generate novel research of use to both academic and practitioner audiences. This text is aimed at commencing the realisation of this great potential.

References

Arbnor, Ingeman, and Bjorn Bjerke. 1997. *Methodology for Creating Business Knowledge*. 2nd ed. Thousand Oaks, CA: Sage.

Baldvinsdottir, Gudrun, Falconer Mitchell, and Hanne Nørreklit. 2010. "Issues in the relationship between theory and practice in management accounting." *Management Accounting Research*, 21 (2): 79–82.

Barnes, Barry. 2001. "Practice as collective action." In *The Practice Turn in Contemporary Theory*, edited by Theodore R. Schatzki, Karin K. Cetina and Eike von Savigny, 17–28. London: Routledge.

Boltanski, Luc, and Laurent Thévenot. 2000. "The reality of moral expectations: A sociology of situated judgement." *Philosophical Explorations*, 3 (3): 208–231.

Cyert, Richard M., and James G. March. 1963. *A Behavioral Theory of the Firm*. Englewood Cliffs, NJ: Prentice-Hall.

Dane, Erik, and Michael G. Pratt. 2007. "Exploring intuition and its role in managerial decision making." *Academy of Management Review*, 32 (1): 33–54.

Darwin, Charles. 1872. *The Origin of Species*. Lulu.com

Davis, Stan, and Tom Albright. 2004. "An investigation of the effect of balanced scorecard implementation on financial performance." *Management Accounting Research*, 15 (2): 135–153.

Descartes, R. 1637 (2008). *Discourse on Method*. Salt Lake City, UT: Project Gutenberg.

Foucault, Michel. 2002 (1969). *The Archaeology of Knowledge*. Translated by A.M. Sheridan Smith. London: Routledge.

Ghoshal, Sumantra. 2005. "Bad management theories are destroying good management practices." *Academy of Management Learning & Education*, 4 (1): 75–91.

Giddens, A. 2013, *Sociology*. 7th ed. Cambridge: Polity.

Kaplan, Robert S., and H. Thomas Johnson. 1987. *Relevance Lost: The Rise and Fall of Management Accounting*. Boston: Harvard Business School Press.

Kaplan, Robert S., and David P. Norton. 1996. *The Balanced Scorecard*. Boston: Harvard Business School Press.

Kirkpatrick, Grant. 2009. "The corporate governance lessons from the financial crisis." *OECD Journal: Financial Market Trends*, 1: 1–30.

Latour, Bruno. 1987. *Science in Action: How to Follow Scientists and Engineers Through Society*. Cambridge, MA: Harvard University Press.

March, James G. 1978. "Bounded rationality, ambiguity, and the engineering of choice." *The Bell Journal of Economics*, 9 (2): 587–608.

Miller, Peter, and Ted O'Leary. 1987. "Accounting and the construction of the governable person." *Accounting, Organizations and Society*, 12 (3): 235–265.

Mintzberg, Henry, Joseph B. Lampel, James B. Quinn, and Sumantra Ghoshal. 2003. *The Strategy Process: Concepts, Context, Cases*. Harlow: Pearson Education Limited.

Newton, Isaek. 1687 (1999). *The Principia: Mathematical Principles of Natural Philosophy*. Berkeley: University of California Press.

Nørreklit, Hanne. 2000. "The balance on the balanced scorecard a critical analysis of some of its assumptions." *Management Accounting Research*, 11 (1): 65–88.

Nørreklit, Hanne, Lennart Nørreklit, and Falconer Mitchell. 2007. "Theoretical conditions for validity in accounting performance measurement." In *Business Performance Measurement—Frameworks and Methodologies*, edited by A. Neely, 179–217. Cambridge: Cambridge University Press.

Nørreklit, Hanne, Lennart Nørreklit, and Falconer Mitchell. 2010. "Towards a paradigmatic foundation for accounting practice." *Accounting, Auditing & Accountability Journal*, 23 (6): 733–758.

Nørreklit, Hanne, Lennart Nørreklit, Falconer Mitchell, and Trond Bjørnenak. 2012. "The rise of the balanced scorecard! Relevance regained?" *Journal of Organizational and Accounting Change*, 8 (4): 490–510.

Nørreklit, Hanne, Morten Raffnsøe-Møller, and Falconer Mitchell. 2016. "A pragmatic constructivist approach to accounting practice and research." *Qualitative Research in Accounting and Management*, 13 (3): 266–277.

Porter, Theodore M. 1995. *Trust in Numbers*. Princeton, NJ: Princeton University Press.

Robertson, David, and Bill Breen. 2013. *Brick by Brick: How LEGO Rewrote the Rules of Innovation and Conquered the Global Toy Industry*. New York: Crown Business.

Scapens, Robert W. 1985. "The conventional wisdom." In *Management Accounting*, edited by Robert W. Scapens, 7–24. Basingstoke: Macmillan Education.

Schatzki, Theodore R. 2001. "Introduction: Practice theory." In *The Practice Turn in Contemporary Theory*, edited by Theodore R. Schatzki, Karin K. Cetina and Eike von Savigny, 1–14. London: Routledge.

Taylor, Frederick W. 1916. *The Principles of Scientific Management*. New York: Harper & Brothers.

Thevenot, Laurent. 2001. "Pragmatic regimes governing the engagement with the world." In *The Practice Turn in Contemporary Theory*, edited by Theodore R. Schatzki, Karin K. Cetina and Eike von Savigny, 56–73. London: Routledge.

Wittgenstein, Ludwig. 1953. *Philosophical Investigations*. Oxford: Basil Blackwell.

Part I
Paradigm of Pragmatic Constructivism

2   Actor-Reality Construction

Lennart Nørreklit

Pragmatic constructivism (Nørreklit, H. et al. 2010; Nørreklit, L. 2011) considers people as intentional actors. To lead their activities to success they develop overarching ideas of what things are, how they function and when actions succeed and when they fail. This is their concept of reality, which guides them to act intentionally and with success. With this concept they can analyse and reflect on their practice—i.e. their practice is a reality construction influenced by the concepts of reality in use. This concept is an active pre-understanding, which guides the actors' understanding of what to do. Whether the concept is good depends on the successes of their reality constructions. Thus, the reality concept and the reality constructions are evaluated from a pragmatic point of view.

Actors improve the conditions under which they work by creating supportive constructions—tools, production facilities, organisation, controls, learning of skills, etc. These constructions improve the success rate of the actor's activities. These constructions are not only external tools and structures; they are also cognitive constructions, observation schemes, and concepts etc. that operate as infrastructural guides of their activities. To evaluate the concepts and constructions we ask the following: under which conditions do actions succeed, and what concept of reality produces good constructions that lead actions to success? Obviously, the more the conditions change, the more dynamic the environment is, the more important the ability to readapt the reality construction to the new conditions.

Because the reality construction determines the proficiency of intentional actions, it follows that *reality as a construction is a relational framework connecting actor and world* (Nørreklit, L. 2011). If it is a good construction, then it gives the actor a realistic understanding of the world with which she can succeed. A poor reality construction gives misleading conceptions of the world thereby endangering the actor. The actor's concept of reality is a tool the actor can use to influence and reflect her reality construction. However, if her concept of reality is inadequate, if it does not understand reality as anything different from world, if it does not consider the relational complex which frames the actors' interpretation of the difference between real and not real, then it may not help her. The task in this chapter is to develop the concept of reality to illuminate the dynamics of the actor-world relation, when it works and when it does not. It is the quality of this relational complex which determines the trustworthiness of our reality construct.

Actions of construction and activities are in no way synonymous, rather two ways of managing. Activities are processes. They may continue indefinitely. They have no finishing point where a target is reached and work can stop. There is no narrative to people's work, just senseless Sisyphean repetition of activity, and efforts never succeed. Workers are like slaves. Actions, on the other hand, are determined by intentions. There is a narrative behind the actions that have a beginning and an end. It can be determined whether the action was a success or not. When the performance is over, the actors can do other things, reflect and find ways to improve. Employees should be competent actors.

The perspective that life is about doing things differs from passive and static perspectives according to which activities only are instrumental, and the goals are of a passive nature such as feeling satisfied, having something or being something. This difference in perspective not only impacts a person's relation to life, but it is important for all issues of leadership and economy. In the active perspective, the actor gets satisfaction not only by receiving something but especially by doing things.

This chapter outlines the reality construction by outlining concepts of actorship (section 2.1), reality construction (section 2.2), the dimensions of reality construction (section 2.3), multiple realities (section 2.4), construct causality (section 2.5), and finally the philosophical background (section 2.6).

Methodology

Methodologically, the approach is inspired by the late Wittgenstein (Wittgenstein 1953) philosophy. To understand a concept, one must look primary at its use, not its reference's. Wittgenstein uses language games to illuminate the use. His focus on how things work and function rather than on how they are is somewhat pragmatic. Thus, we define the type of constructivism to be presented in this book as "pragmatic" to distinguish it from other forms of constructivism.

To automatically look for the reference instead of the usage to clarify the meaning of a concept is a fallacy, in short: the naming fallacy (Wittgenstein 1953, §1). The difference in meaning of related concepts is not just the phenomena they refer to, but the use and thus the function they serve. Absolutist usage of concepts such as 'facts do not exist' is mistaken. If there is a usage of the concept, one must try to understand that usage before making claims. To do otherwise is speculation. Definitions rarely help in clarifying the meaning of concepts because they do not clarify the usage but the reference. We consider concepts as cognitive structures that are used in our construction of reality. To understand and explain them is therefore to clarify the role they play in our reality construction.

2.1. Actorship

Actors

To live is to be active and to do things. Dead entities do not do things. The term 'actor', in the sense of somebody who acts intentionally, is preferred to terms like 'person' or 'human being'. The activities of actors are not only formed by their given environment and genetic structure, but also by their constructions and other changes of their environment. They then react to these changes by creating further changes. Actors create development and history.

Actions are controlled intentionally, motivated by the actor's values. Actions may succeed or fail in realising the target. As an actor, a person has a place in a broader reality construction where she embodies narrated roles and participates in constructing things according to the script she follows. If she succeeds, then her intentions become real constructions and part of the world. The difference between the play of this actor and that of a stage play is that the constructions and the construction processes are real.

In many contexts, the term "agent" (MacMurray 1957; Giddens 1984) is used to denote the person who is the source of intentional activities. On the other hand "agent" is also widely used as a person who acts on behalf of another person. These usages are at odds. I choose to associate "agent" with the second usage and use the term "actor" in a broad meaning as one who acts intentionally—not only in the theatre and the movies, but on the stages of life (Arbnor and Bjerke 2009). An actor is not only playing a role, she is the source of her intentions and activities, and she needs to be co-author of her roles. She not only accepts and plays a given role based on her interpretation, she also moulds it and participates in construction of the role system and the plot in the construct.

The alternative to being an actor is to lose intentionality—either by becoming passive and not trying to accomplish anything or by doing things as a slave or robot without personal intention. Intentional control makes the action a personal endeavour in which the actor experiences motivation and senses the quality and value of what she does. Even in extreme cases of a recluse, her acts are intentional; otherwise she cannot survive.[1]

An actor's activity is not only an 'outward' going process where that actor tries to express herself and become part of the world by setting her mark through her constructions. It is also an 'inward' going process in which the actor experiences what she does and what the reactions to it are. Thereby she involves herself and makes it her life. Action involves an ongoing circulation between *expression* and *impression*. Action flows as long as impressions reflect expressions and expressions reflect impressions and create an experience of making sense. The inward going process, impressions, is itself active, not something passive. Actors develop a relation to their life. They want to do something, namely to realise some of their values. Satisfying one's needs is a condition of life, realising one's values is a purpose. However, people do become passive if they experience that their activities do not lead to realisation of their intentions or make any difference. Or, the impression-expression circulation flow may break down due to traumatic experiences. If that happens then a part of the actor-world relation breaks down.

There are different types of actors. The basic function of an actor is to intentionally play a role that realises her values and potentials and which constructs whatever the role aims at. In this sense all actors are constructors. I prefer, however, to restrict the use of constructor to actors who construct the framework of the play, i.e. the constructor is the actor in the role of constructing reality. Finally, there is the agent who is the actor acting on behalf of and to support others. Such an agency role makes the actor social and ethical and is a basis of social structures.

Actors play specific roles depending on practice. The practice is run by a narrative in which each participating actor contributes by creating certain constructions. The constructions are all kinds of accomplishments—physical, mental, social, theoretical and practical. The various constructions complement each other so that together they constitute a significant accomplishment (Nørreklit, L. 2011).

Co-Authoring

The narrative of a practice needs to be invented or authored. When it is authored, it may be passed on, adapted and re-authored. The leading ideas of practice—its topoi[2]—are the overarching guidelines for the creation and adaption of the narrative (Nørreklit, L. et al. 2006; Nørreklit. L. 2011). The topoi outlines what the narrative is about and what is good and what is bad. And the very topos of the topoi is the concept of reality which all topoi are supposed to obey. For the participating actors it is important that they at least participate in authoring the script for their roles. To author a narrative is to utilise professional knowledge and insight, which is important not only in the exercising but also in the scripting of the role. Leadership, on the other hand, assembles a team of actors to author the narrative and to conduct the authoring process so that the roles fit the actors and complement each other to create a convincing narrative for the practice. To respect and motivate the actors, they need to be co-authors. Leaders may be, but are not necessarily co-authors. The conduction of the authoring process should balance contributions from participating actors.

The co-authoring process directly connects the intentionality of the actor to her role, giving it meaning to her so she can feel she is part of an exciting narrative that produces significant constructions. Leading by co-authoring enhances motivation and creativity because it makes the actors want to do the best they can. Alternatively, one cannot expect high performance in a practice where there is no co-authorship.

Agents

A special role is that of being an agent, i.e. a person who acts on behalf of another person, organisation or power. By acting on behalf of another person in the interest of that person, we make ourselves social beings guided by empathy and concerns of an ethical nature. In ordinary language games, there is an ongoing cooperation in which one actor supplements another actor. This involves a responsibility to help the other person if she should be in need; even if she is unable to request help or does not know that she needs help. A person thinking: "She needs this help, I must do it", is a person acting as an agent on behalf of that person although the person has not requested the help. This is civilised behaviour and social responsibility exemplified in the case of parent to children, friend to friends, professional to client, leader to employees and other stakeholders.

Acting on behalf of others is a form of role-play. It is a normal aspect in any scene involving actors. Actors are agents. There is an element of agency in every role and every act. We expect that actors are ethical and social so that they can be partners whom one can trust to act on our behalf when we need it. We are each other's agents. Agency forms cooperative scenarios where actors not only play their part but are helpful and supportive. This creates cultural friendliness, which is the basis of civilised behaviour.

Some contexts restrict the use of "agent" to situations where there is an agreement or a contract. In business and in political practice the use of agents is a means to 'outsource' some of the roles of a person to professional actors, making them that person's agents. This enables the person to concentrate on the roles of her specialty or her liking.

In principal-agent theory (Ross 1973; Jensen and Meckling 1976) one set of actors, called the principals who own the business, lets another actor, the agent who knows the business, play the managerial role on behalf of the principal. Here the agent is not presumed to be motivated by a desire to help the principal, by friendship, culture or ethics. She is supposed to act out of egoistic motives in contradiction to the ethical connotation of agency. Contractual regulation of the principal-agent relation aims at protecting the principal from being exploited by rewarding the agent in accordance with her fulfilment of contractual performance goals that serve the interests of the principals. Here the agent is presumed to be driven by opportunistic and egoistic motives, contrary to the social and ethical nature of acting on behalf of other people in order to help them.

In a stakeholder model, the management has the role of balancing the interests of all stakeholders and it does so by co-authoring the narratives. The leaders' endeavour to create a convincing narrative may force them to change the group of stakeholders chosen for the play. Otherwise in the shareholder model, the interests that are served are by contract only those of the managing agent and her principals. Other stakeholders may be unaware of the actual agenda defined by the contract.

The principal-agent model binds principal and agent via a contract for mutual benefit. This implies a logical problem because the principals are often larger groups that can only negotiate contracts with the agents by means of chosen representatives. These representatives are then by definition again agents. Thus, in reality, the contracts can often only be made between different agents and not between principals and agents. Contrary to the stated intent of the theory, the consequence is that various networks of agents advance their own interests and not those of the principals. Thus, it is only to be expected that CEOs may be rewarded despite losses created for principals (Nørreklit, L. 2013a).

To use the concept of acting on behalf of others based on opportunistic egoism creates a problem as egoism by definition conflicts with ethical and social motivation. It calls for new ways to control the egoism of the agent so that the ethical perspective of agency is not transformed to a cover for egoistic misuse. In traditional cultures, internalised social norms install such controls. Capitalist economics is, however, individualistic and opportunistic and thus not controllable by such norms.

2.2. Reality Construction

World

Although reality and world are related concepts and are often used as if they have the same meaning, they do not at all mean the same things and cannot be used interchangeably without confusing theoretical consequences. The world includes all things, events or states of affairs that exist, irrespective of whether we know they exist or not. When something is discovered to exist, then it is added to the inventory of the world. To be is to be in the world. It does not matter what kind of phenomenon it is, whether it is a thing, a relation or property, whether it is material, mental or social, whether it is constructed or produced by nature. Although more and more things in our life-world are constructed, the world itself, i.e. the universe, is still not constructed. It developed by forces. How it started we do not know. It was there before we were born into it. We know only a small fraction of that which it contains, but its existence is a condition for us and for our constructions.

Accordingly, 'world' is an *inclusive* concept. It includes everything that exists. 'World' is also a *realistic* concept meaning that the world and its phenomena, including our constructions, exist independently of our recognition of them.

To define existing as being in the world is too shallow as such definition may seduce one to erroneously consider existence as a passive state where 'to exist' means something like one the following:

- *have* something (skills, properties, specifically wealth or power)
- *be* something or somebody (have a position)
- *get* something (needs fulfilled, achieve satisfaction) etc.

In such a passive perspective, living is like sitting in a cinema looking at the world that passes by on a canvas. Activity is just an instrument that serves the purpose of reaching the passive state of having, being or getting (Arbnor and Bjerke 1975). Even research may be considered as a passive, non-influencing observation, e.g. as "a fly on the wall." Although the 'passive' states are important, they are not really passive. They always involve forms of activity such as perceiving, receiving, resting, sleeping and dreaming. Thus, to live is to do something. To live as a person is to act, i.e. be an actor. Only the dead do nothing. *To exist is therefore to interact* with other people and things in the world. *To be* must be to be in a world; otherwise a given thing cannot *interact* with anything and thus it is not distinguishable from non-existing things.

The difference between existing and imagined phenomena is the interactivity of the existing, a property that non-existing phenomena lacks. Imagined things cannot interact and therefore do not exist; but the imagination of them has consequences and therefore an imagined thing exists. This pragmatic interpretation of existence means that existing things have consequences and therefore that they can be traced. Thus, claims as to what exists can be investigated, no matter whether it is information on a tax sheet or a contract or claims on possession of weapons of mass destruction, it can be checked for fraud and deception.

To improve the performance of our actions, constructions are made. Some of them are physical and social constructions, some are theoretical and some are cognitive and mental constructions. Functioning constructions produce successful actions. There is no incompatibility between a realist approach and a constructivist approach. On the contrary—only real constructions work. They work no matter whether they are physical objects, relations or mental phenomena or abstract structures. Our constructivist perspective addresses the actor's construction of frameworks to improve effectiveness of her action. Actors create a framework by organising interaction and relations in an actor-world relational complex. This complex, which is their construction of reality, guides their activities. It enables them to act, recognise success and failure and improve effectively.

Reality

The concept of reality is an instrument for the actor to guide and control her construction of actor-world relations—her reality construction—and enable her to act successfully in accordance with her values. In the process the concept penetrates all the understanding, the basic narratives and topoi of the actor to automatic guide her activities in all areas.

If the concept, the understanding, and the relational reality constructs are unrealistic and thus misleading, then life is a headwind for the actor. Because the concept and the relations are constructs, the actor may have the possibility to reset his reality construction based on different concepts of reality. Actors reflect their position in the world to open horizons of possibilities concerning places to live, professions, partners, ambitions, tastes and values, etc. But they also reflect how to act, how to analyse possibilities and identify values, how to understand people and relate to them, etc.—i.e. how to understand reality. None of these relations and conceptions are given. They are constructed—chosen, developed and maintained—to become a framework for our activities. A modern person is a mature person, i.e. an actor who chooses her relations and functions and how to act and relate herself to the world.

The social world itself is a great construction that reaches out for people in many directions, offering them participation and support. In participation the actor is a co-author of the scripts that then narrate her life. She cannot be the sole author because she lives in interaction. But without her engagement and the engagement of the other actors, the relations cannot not exist. She is part of co-action which succeeds or fails according to the quality of the reality construction or the cooperation. We conclude, *the actor's way of being in the world has the form of reality construction*. The quality of this construction determines how real or illusive the actor's perceptions are (Nørreklit, L. 2011).

The possible roles of the actors depend on the social constructions. In some cultures certain groups have little say about what actor-world relations in which they are to participate. Norms and leaders may decide work and partners, so they are not allowed to become reality constructors co-authoring the scripts they play. Even in such cases, the reality-constituting relations depend on activities of people. The system would not exist unless people followed the script. Modernity, on the other hand, implies that people function as actors and therefore as co-authors of their lives by participating in creating practices and shaping reality.

Whereas 'world' is an inclusive concept, 'reality' is an *exclusive* concept. Some things are real, others are not. Actors may be mistaken as to whether an object is real or not. Thus, they need the concept of reality with which they can differentiate between the objects that are real and those that are not. The difference between real and illusive is in the functionality: the illusive does not function in the way we expect it to function. Thus, the distinction between real and illusive is pragmatic. Ultimately, there is no other way to distinguish real from illusive.

More specifically, when something appears to be real although it is not, then we are dealing with something that is something other than what it appears to be. Then we deal with phenomena such as delusions, dreams, illusions, deceptions, decoys, fake things, toys, etc. When things are what they appear to be, i.e. when they are real, then actors can use them to act successfully. If they are fake, then this is not possible. With real money you can legally buy things, with a real gun you can shoot somebody. Counterfeit money may put you in jail; a toy gun cannot shoot. The difference between real and not real is pragmatic. If we use fake things, then the actions fail.

The pragmatics of action, i.e. that it leads to the intended goals, presupposes that the actor is not guided by delusions nor uses fake tools.

This construction of the concept of reality accords with ordinary usage. Theories that do not accept this exclusivity conflict with this usage and consequently lose the concept of reality by making it indistinguishable from the concept of world.

Fictive objects, imagined things and stories are important in many contexts where they play indispensable roles without being deceptive. Examples are elements of planning or literary fiction. We know they are fictive. The problem only emerges when we are lead to believe that they are not fictitious.

Language games about dreams, fairy tales or psychotic experiences are excellent illustrations of the exclusivity of the reality concept. For instance, a game where a child talks about a flying elephant and the mother teaches her that it is a dream. Some fictive constructions are unintentional such as dreams; others are intentional such as lies, deception, fraud etc. Some of them are difficult to discover. But all of them can manifest themselves in language games where the difference between real and fictive can be elaborated.

Although some phenomena are delusional constructions, they are still reality constructions and part of certain language games. People live with them although they do not exist. These language games prove that dreams and deception exist, but not that they are true. And they demonstrate that reality games are needed to work with the distinction between real and fictive. We need to distinguish between realistic and deceptive games. When the games blind the actors and prevent them from recognising deceptive claims, then the actors become helpless. There are many strategic games to blind people by inducing fictive constructions based on cocktails of pathos and fake evidence.

The distinction "real versus not real" is a sophisticated structure and despite its either-or logic, it proves bendable in practice. For instance, we expect the things to function for a certain period of time, but not forever. However, there are no clear guidelines showing how long things should function for them to be real. With physical objects we can calculate it. But we do not know how long we can trust the social constructions of society. They change. There are even constructions where it is impossible to apply a pragmatic distinction between real and not real using the weird way they characterise phenomena. Even social sciences such as accounting are sometimes considered void of genuine pragmatic content. The opposing view is that accounting should be inherently predictive. This claim has a pragmatic perspective, although it also fails because it destroys the distinction between predictions and information on the present. Without information on the present, i.e. an account, predictions are not possible.

Conditions for Succeeding

The conditions which a phenomenon must satisfy to be considered real and not fictitious or even fraudulent are pragmatic. It must function as expected, i.e. actions based on it should be able to succeed. If it is fiction, then it has no pragmatic effect. We thus have to establish the conditions for achievement and success. Here one must distinguish between *necessary* and *sufficient* conditions. It is common practice in organisations and politics to focus on necessary conditions in the hope that when they are satisfied, then we succeed. Analysing necessary conditions appears as a more modest ambition than the more ambitious but possibly unrealistic endeavour to analyse the sufficient conditions. But this is a mistake. In order to succeed and reach the target, the actors must fulfil a set of sufficient conditions. There may be several ways to succeed, thus several different sets of sufficient conditions. Thinking in terms of necessary conditions presumes that there is only one way to succeed. One may satisfy all known *necessary* conditions and still be unable to reach the goal and all the effort may be in vain. But although it may sound surprising, one may reach the goal although none of the conditions that one satisfied were necessary conditions because the goal could be reached in many different ways. The conditions that were satisfied may be sufficient without being necessary. It is normal that there are several possible ways to reach a goal. Each of the possible ways represents a set of conditions that are sufficient. None of them represent a necessary condition. The core issue in pragmatic constructivism is therefore the analysis of sufficient conditions for succeeding. The framework for action and practice, i.e. the reality construction that regulates practice and action, needs to realise such conditions (Nørreklit, L. 2011).

Reality Construction by Integration

Pragmatic constructivism claims that for actions to succeed the relational actor-world construction must integrate the four elements or dimensions: facts, possibilities, values and communication. Such integrated structure in the relation makes it a working reality construction. If these four dimensions are not properly integrated in the operative relations, then actions tend to fail (see Figure 2.1).

The argument for the four-dimensional integration of reality is as follows (Henriksen et al. 2005; Nørreklit, H. et al. 2010):

There must be a factual basis for the actions. If there is no factual basis to act upon, then there is a risk that actions do not work. If the basis is fictitious, a guess, a hope or a dream or belief, then the actor cannot expect activities to function. The actor needs to know her factual resources, the factual conditions and her abilities in order to act successfully.

What the actor tries to do and accomplish must be possible. She cannot realise the impossible. Further, the possibilities must be factual possibilities. The possibilities must be embedded in her factual basis, i.e. facts and possibilities must be integrated. If the possibilities are factual, then the action *can* be realised with success. The question is only whether the actor performs the action. It will be realised if she does.

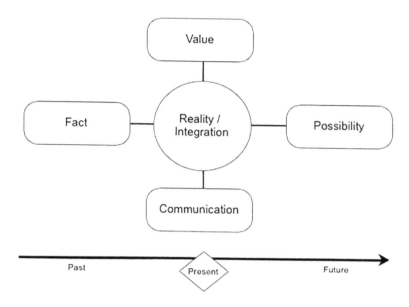

Figure 2.1 Reality as Integration

The mere fact that it is possible to do things is not a guarantee that they will actually be done. The actor must want to do it. But if doing something realises her values, then she will do it. And if it is a factual possibility, then she will succeed. But the action must be based on her personal, subjective values. Social values of wealth, recognition, fame and power are not relevant if they do not accord with her subjective values. If she thinks that her values are outside the range of her factual possibilities, then she is not motivated to act. But if she believes that her values lie within the range of her factual possibilities, then she will act, and if she is correct, then she will succeed. Thus, *by integrating facts, possibilities and values the actor acts and succeeds*. These conditions are sufficient for an actor to act and succeed.

Actors live in social settings where cooperation is necessary for practice and performance. Cooperation is organised through communication that functions as the glue that connects people. For communication to function and enable practice it must convey the integrated fact-possibility-value structure of the participating actors and enable them to form a common narrative as the basis of a common reality construction which realises the values of the actors involved. Communication that integrates the actors' facts, possibilities and values is the final condition.

The integration of facts, possibilities, values and communication is a sufficient condition for actors to perform and to succeed in practice. When they are integrated, then people cooperate, act, and succeed. That is all that is needed. They have the abilities, they are motivated, they understand their function and consequently they act and succeed. Without integrated communication the actors live with multitudes of uncoordinated reality constructions that may cause difficulties in practice.

The four dimensions: fact, possibility, value and communication, penetrate all aspects of the actor-reality relational complex. Each dimension must involve both the actor and the world. This is further explained in the following section.

2.3. Four Actor-World Dimensions

That actors act and succeed or fail is an everyday fact of life. To strengthen the likelihood of success, actors build a relational actor-world framework, which is their construction of reality. Section 2.2 concluded that the reality construction encompasses four dimensions: facts, possibilities, values and communication; their integration is a sufficient condition for actions to succeed. Insufficient integration causes failure. Imperfect integration of the dimensions does not automatically mean that success is impossible; luck and intuition can counter the odds for a period of time. This chapter analyses each of these dimensions and their integration. Because they are dimensions in a relational complex, the analysis must clarify their relational structure. Further, because the concern of our approach is pragmatic and therefore includes relations in time, the analysis should illuminate the 'time structure' of the dimensions.

Communication is by nature a relational concept that involves a relation between communicators and receivers. But the terms fact, possibility and value may not seem to symbolise anything relational. They seem to refer to some type of unit: the fact, the possibility and the value. However, such units are not to be found, which has caused quite some philosophical puzzlement. But remember Wittgenstein's (1953) advice: to look at the use and not at the reference. The use of the concepts of fact, possibility, and value in language games is a guideline with which we can illuminate how these dimensions function in our construction of the actor-reality relationship. Thus, we recognise that facts, possibilities and values are not units that exist in themselves. They exist as dimensions in actor-world relations, where they play important roles in relating actors to the world (see Figure 2.2).

Facts

Fact and Evidence

When we refer to something as a fact, we bestow it special status that tells people it is trustworthy, something they can rely on. Facts are much in demand as a basis for practice.

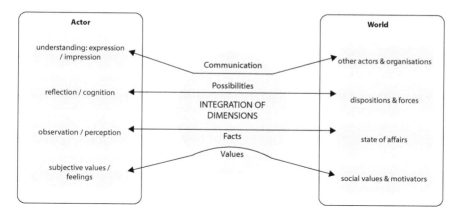

Figure 2.2 Actor-World Relations

A claim that a state of affairs is a fact implies two claims about the inventory of the world: 1) that the state of affairs really exists and belongs to the inventory of the world, and 2) that sufficient accessible evidence corroborating the claim exists. The fact may be something present or past, be accessible or it may be out of our reach. But the evidence must be present and accessible. Thus, the facts and the evidence are two different things and, interestingly, we must have access to the evidence in order to claim the existence of the fact. The fact is that which is stated, whereas the evidence is neither specified nor stated but presupposed. But the evidence can be called for and challenged at any time. One cannot claim that something is a fact without having a good reason, i.e. sufficient evidence, for the claim.

Evidence is necessary to document that a claim not only refers to the subjective imaginations of the speaker, but that it is true because it expresses a real state of the world. In ongoing practice phenomena show themselves, which is sufficient evidence because it demonstrates their existence in the world and not only in the mind of the speaker. However, phenomena and events may be out of the reach of the actor's perception and action, and with time they automatically become past events out of any possible reach. In such cases evidence must be something different from the phenomenon itself in order to be accessible.

What is the relation between evidence and facts? Events generate evidence in the form of traces caused by the event. These traces can be used as evidence for the event if we know how they were produced. The question is whether such evidence can be found and how much information they can provide about the generating cause. Evidence can be strong and conclusive and prove that a certain generating event did in fact exist. But the evidence may also be vague and inconclusive regarding what precisely generated it. In order for a phenomenon to be considered as evidence, it must be available and observable and 'readable', i.e. it must clearly disclose the generating phenomenon.

Facts may be any type of phenomena. 'Fact' is not a special ontological category. There are empirical, logical and mathematical facts; there are objective and subjective facts. Still, the evidence must be observable, testable and readable. This applies to mathematical facts as well. The proof of mathematical facts must be manifested empirically on paper, a blackboard or on something else. The proof is, of course, logical, but all the steps in the proof must have possible empirical manifestations such that they can be analysed and challenged in order to be accepted as proper evidence. Because facts may be any type of phenomena of which we have evidence, any type of methodology—qualitative or quantitative—that is able to produce evidence may be relevant to analyse facts.

Whereas evidence is qualitative or quantitative, facts *per se* cannot be counted because a "fact" is not a special ontological unit. It is a status that is attributed to a phenomenon—due to the evidence—to signal that it is trustworthy. A necessary quality of evidence is durability. Useful evidence consists of traces that are impregnated in durable media. If the traces are unstable, then they disappear and the evidence is lost. Related to this is the issue concerning the way facts may change. It partly depends on the type of description we use. If we use an actor's perspective as in "How is the weather (here and now)", then the facts about the weather change all the time. But if we use fixed positions in time and space, e.g. in "the weather on 1.1.2016 in London", then the weather cannot change. As long as we have the evidence it will be a fact that the weather in London on 1.1.2016 was such and such. But our evidence as to the weather in London at that time may change. This will not change the weather, but it will change the facts. If, for instance, we lose all the records 100 years from now, this will not change the weather, but the facts will disappear.

The Range of Truth

The difference between something that is a fact and something that is a truth but not a fact is the evidence. Many claims are true although our evidence is insufficient to prove them true. We cannot rely on them. They are not facts. We can only guess and gamble. We only have sufficient evidence about a fraction of the world to claim it factual knowledge.

The world's complexity is endless. Everything is full of variations, and structural relations exist and crisscross everywhere. Even with the most detailed descriptions we cannot describe but a small fraction of the complexity of the world. Our knowledge and descriptions are simplifications—no matter how complex they appear to us.

Further, phenomena exist that we cannot even express or describe with the linguistic resources we have because we have not developed the necessary concepts. The range of conceivable truths is limited by our concepts. It is the task of research to penetrate into such areas by developing new theories and concepts. The world is inclusive, larger and more complex than any set of truths we can formulate.

Need

Actors need factual knowledge as the basis of their activities to reduce the risk of failure. They need to be sure that their actions will succeed when the costs of failure are high. They need something they can rely on as a basis of action. To consider something a fact is to give it a special status of reliability because the evidence is convincing. The established status of facts licences them to function as the basis for action in a practice setting, bypassing discussions of who knows what because this is assumed to be common, socially established knowledge. In organised multi-actor settings a common knowledge basis of action, i.e. facts, is needed.

In order to plan and act effectively actors need facts in the sense of claims that they know to be reliable before they act. To obtain these facts, practice establishes evidence-generating information systems. These systems are presumed to improve the degree of reliability compared to a situation where we only rely on subjective impressions, which are unreliable and a risky basis.

Knowledge

Fact and knowledge are related concepts. Knowledge is also based on sufficient evidence and thereby differs from subjective constructs such as beliefs and assumptions, etc. (Chisholm 1966). Fact and knowledge are almost like two sides of the same coin. Knowledge is the presumed truth of that for which one has sufficient evidence.

One difference between fact and knowledge is that they point at different components in the actor-world relation. Knowledge claims bridge the actor-world relation by pointing at a knowing person and at that which the person knows. There seems to be no such bridging in fact claims. Who are the 'knowers' in fact claims, if there are any? If we claim that something is a fact, we imply that it is common knowledge. The group for which it is common may be large or small. Once it has the status of a fact, it is taken for granted by the group.

But opposite, one may imagine something to be a fact without any actor knowing it, as when something is a fact because the evidence exists and is available, although no presently existing actor is acquainted with the evidence. Data collections and libraries produce such facts. One may discover facts by exploring data banks.

Defeasibility

Even when we have the best possible evidence, claims about facts and knowledge are sometimes mistaken. This implies that fact claims are defeasible.

"Fact" is not an absolute concept. A person has the right to call something a fact if—and only if—it satisfies the criteria for sufficient evidence. However, if future evidence should prove the claim to be wrong, then it loses its factual status. And according to its new 'status', it has never been a fact. Thus, by challenging the evidence one challenges the factual status of the claim.

Even the system of evidence can be challenged. The ultimate criterion is that it works in practice. The higher the stakes, the more we expect from our evidence before accepting something as a fact. When we claim that something is a fact, we claim that there is only negligible risk in using the claim as the basis for our actions. Uncertainties imply that a plan-B may be needed, in which case planning is forced to establish the resources needed for a plan-B. Availability of alternative courses of action in the middle of a course of action is not free and reduces the overall efficiency of the performance. A manager must decide whether to reduce the possibility of needing a plan-B by maintaining a high quality basis or whether to take a given risk and eventually need a plan-B. One advantage of reducing risk through high quality is that it can promote development. When we opt for high quality, we also opt for high defeasibility, i.e. that the claims involved in planning are not easily to be defeated. Alternatively, opting for the a priori need for a plan-B is lowering the defeasibility claim by accepting plan-A as insecure due to a weak basis. The problem is that plan-B is also insecure. The policy of not ensuring safety in action by using high standards for facticity burdens business by all kinds of precautions and readjustment costs.

Sceptical scholars sometimes claim that facts do not exist. The claim cannot be based on evidence, because then it would be self-defeating—it cannot be a fact that there are no facts. Such radical rejection of the existence of facts denies practice the tools to make non-arbitrary decisions. It is a functioning language game in practice to formulate factual evidence as reliable as possible a basis for the activities. This language game is needed. And there is no point in the sceptic's denial of the right to use such language game. General rejection of facts is based on a misunderstanding of the concept. This is a "naming fallacy", i.e. the fallacy of not looking for the use, but only for the reference—in the sense of late Wittgenstein.

World of Facts

The discussion of facts is inter alia inspired by the Wittgenstein's early theory (Wittgenstein 1921) that the world consists of facts, not of things. He considered facts as logical relational structures and referred to them as 'logical form'. Although the theory has its merits, it misunderstands the concept of facts by making them a special ontological constituent of the world. This is precisely what facts are not. Anything can be a fact provided that adequate evidence exists. Furthermore, the world is indefinitely more comprehensive than the set of facts as demonstrated. A phenomenon obtains the status of a fact not through its existence or its structure, but through the existence of its evidence. The world is not made of facts, or of knowledge, or of truth, although they are part of the world.

Such 'ontologisation' of facts leads to issues about weird existences. An example is found in negative facts such as the fact that Piere is not in the room (cf. Sartré 1943). However, there is the room with the people and the things it contains. Their factual existence might be evidenced by a photo. But there is no 'Piere not-being-there' anywhere. Piere is simply not amongst the things in the room. Or infinite regress as in the statement that if something is a fact, then it is a fact that it is a fact. This leads to an infinite regress of facts. But there is no ontological regress of facts.

Possibility

Possibilities differ from observed phenomena. They have no direct physical appearance. Neither qualitative nor quantitative studies can observe possibilities directly. We refer to possibilities with words like "can" and "may" in expressions like: "It can be done", "You can do it", "Yes, we can," "It may happen" etc. We notice two types of possibilities: those concerning what actors can do, and those expressing what may happen unrelated to the activities of the actor. These two types are often linked as actors use their possibilities to trigger or to prevent events that are possible.

What are possibilities then? Do they belong to the inventory of the world? How can one study them and use them? We are always concerned with possibilities in action. We cannot do the impossible. We try to find the possible lines of action. Practice is based on using knowledge about possibilities and therefore determination of possibilities is an important part of the actor's reality construction. Because possibilities cannot be observed directly, they must involve cognitive skills of reflection. However, to determine real possibilities, pure speculation will not do. Systematic and thorough thinking, logical analysis, is needed. Possibilities consequently belong to a different aspect of the actor-world relationship than the observation-evidence-fact relation. Although a person may succeed by chance when doing things without knowing the facts, nobody can do things if they are impossible. To an actor the interesting possibility-question is what it is possible—and what is not possible—for her to do. Because possibilities can be influenced, reality construction aims at controlling the possibilities of the actor.

An actor must determine which of her possibilities she wants to realise by her course of action. This is the point of her having the possibilities. She must choose her education, occupation, friends, location etc. amongst the possibilities she encounters in life. To succeed she must be able to judge what choices are possible for her to realise. When she makes such basic choices, then she starts to do something with her life. She constructs herself as an actor who does things, and each of her subsequent choices relate to what she started.

The reason why possibilities cannot be observed is that they refer to something that is not present although the present is claimed to possess powers that can make it real. That something is possible means that it is not part of the present inventory of the world, but the inventory of the world is such that it may become real.[3] Also, 'possible' may pertain to knowledge. To say that something is possible may mean that we do not know whether it is true, but one might find out that it is true. The notion of possibility adds a horizon of possible future states to the set of factual states included in our reality construction. Possibilities may or may not become factual states, depending on the course of events. That something is not possible means that no matter what happens, it will not become real. By the term 'possibility' the present is related in a non-deterministic way to future horizons.

When we perceive things, we automatically perceive them as loaded with possibilities. Whether a thing is real or fictitious mainly depends on its possibilities. There may be no perceptual difference between a real gun and a toy gun, but the possibilities of doing something with the two guns differ: the real gun can really shoot; the toy gun cannot. All our things are defined by possibilities that determine what they are. Their appearance serves only to identify them and if they are fake, then this identification may fail. The real properties of things are defined by what they can affect and do, the possibilities they can realise. Thus, they are defined by their significance to the actor's choices of action. This not only applies to physical objects, guns, computers, etc., but also to social constructs, institutions, laws, contracts, etc., it even applies to subjective phenomena such as feelings, memory, beliefs, etc. They are what they are because of their effects.

Possibilities are relative to the actors. What is possible for some may be impossible for others. The task of reality construction is not to open one but an entire horizon of possible futures enabling the actors to choose which values to realise and how to realise them, which means that the actors can act intentionally. The concept of possibility connects the present to the future and implies the existence of presupposed causalities. It does, however, preclude determinism because it constructs a horizon of possible futures. The actor-world relation interprets causal dispositions that can realise possibilities if triggered by relevant actions. It is not necessary that the physics of the underlying causal dispositions is understood. Possibilities may be recognised by actors before science understands the causal mechanisms behind them. The goal of practice is to achieve control over triggering events to enable intentional action. The question, how to realise future states by enacting triggering events, is basic.

Any actor is surrounded by countless possibilities, but without the actor, the phenomena that constitute the possibilities would be nothing more than mere phenomena; if the actors do not perceive and recognise the phenomena as possibilities, all we have would be processes. As soon as we claim that a specific action or event is possible in a given situation, we introduce a subjective perspective that outlines and defines the possibility. A different perspective outlines other possibilities. Possibility is therefore a dimension in the actor-world relational complex. On the worldly side of the relation, we have the relevant forces and causal powers. On the actor's side, we have the need for the necessary skills to conceive and enact (see Figure 2.3).

Types of Possibilities

There are several kinds of possibility constructs ranging from those that are entirely abstract to those that are entirely specific. Abstract possibilities are theoretical constructs; they claim that something is possible in theory although it may be impossible in practice. In order to be possible in practice, i.e. action possibilities, the possibilities need to be specific in relation to actors who have the relevant competences. When something is a possibility that can be acted upon, then it can be done by some actors under the existing conditions. These are factual possibilities.[4]

Consider a transition of a possibility construct from abstract over theoretical to factual possibility. First, imagine a given state of affairs, For instance: "there are receipts in the box." We have just put them there. It is a fact. But we can imagine that there are no receipts in the box. This is a perfectly conceivable state of affairs constructed by negating the state we know to be true. Thus, it is logically possible that there are no receipts in the box. By the logical operation of negating factual knowledge we produce logical possibilities. Anything imaginable and conceivable is logically possible, provided that it is not self-contradictory. As soon as we have concepts with which we draw—clear or unclear—borders in the world, we have automatically constructed a range of possibilities. By a negation we switch to the other side of

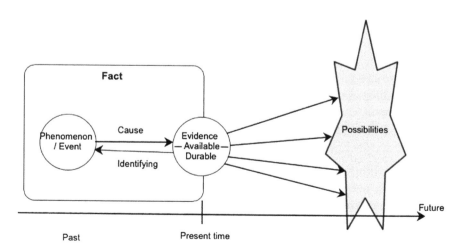

Figure 2.3 Factual Possibilities

the border. If the one side is real, then the other is possible. The possibilities may be possibilities of imagination, they may be unrealistic or they may be fully realistic and factual if we are able to control the events that trigger their realisation.

We can use the logical operation of negation on factual knowledge to construct a large number of logical possibilities. For instance, we observe the door is closed, so we can conceive the logical possibility that it is not closed. Negation opens a horizon of logical possibilities. Although they are initially only logical possibilities, they do allow us to formulate any idea thinkable. Some of the ideas are interesting and exciting. Some may even be or become factual possibilities that can be realised.

That something is logically possible does not imply that it really is possible, only that we can imagine it and think it. It may be impossible for many reasons. For instance, it is logically possible but not technically possible to build a bridge over the Pacific Ocean. It may be technically possible to build a bridge over the Canal but financially impossible, there may be legal obstacles, insufficient resources, insufficient infrastructure or lack of political will to build the bridge. Then it is not factually possible. The technological, economic, social and political disciplines delimit different aspects of possibilities and impossibilities. If something is possible in all these aspects but one, then it is impossible. All these perspectives contain theoretical frameworks of concepts that relate to special aspects of the world, which makes them partly abstract although they define practices that address these aspects. They are abstract because they cannot by themselves guarantee that the possibility they determine is real. They address one aspect of reality only. For something to be possible it must be possible in all perspectives. Practice involves a multiplicity of disciplines. And still it may be impossible although it is possible in all known perspectives, because there may be unknown conditions. All these conditions are necessary, but they are not sufficient.

In a practice setting, reflection is always analysing and developing possibilities in order to generate results by organising strings of events in which realisation of one possibility triggers the realisation of the next. The reflection involves all kinds of inspirational and analytic processes that deepen the understanding of the world's working and how to handle it. The strength of these processes determines the quality and competitiveness of the result.

Factual possibilities integrate fact and possibility. The conceptualisation of the ideas and experience integrates the possible and the factual. Things are characterised not by their appearance but by their causal dispositions, i.e. the possibilities they can create. The difference between the real thing and a fake is not found in the appearance but in the possibilities the things embed. We construct our concepts such that their objects embed certain possibilities and therefore determine possible courses of action. Abstract and theoretical possibilities are not integrated and therefore not factual possibilities. The reflexive activities create a foundation of integrated, i.e. factual, possibilities.

The Possible and the Necessary

Possibility and necessity are related concepts and both are vital in any practice as they integrate factual information as well as future projections. Also, they are interconnected in ways that make them support each other.[5] The *possibility* to do something depends on the *necessity* embedded in the things with which we work to produce the outcome. For instance, the *possibility* of writing messages on the computer depends on the *necessary* causal connection between the activation of keys on the keyboard and the text in the file. The actions of pressing the keys on the keyboard are the events that trigger the causal chains that produce the text file. If that causal connection had been random, the computer would be useless. Necessary connections are embedded in artefacts in order to create possibilities. Such complementary function of possibility and necessity is the backbone of functioning practice as it creates choices for the actors. The computer set-up creates the possibility. The decision of the actor with adequate skills triggers the action which then triggers the causal events that produce the text file. The possibilities for action generate a theoretical need to understand decision-making and the way in which actors form intentions in the reality construction framework.

The role of necessity differs from that of possibility. A basic use of necessity relates to the actor's needs. Needs narrow the free choice opened by the horizon of possibilities. If needs are not fulfilled, then suffering and eventually destruction follows. An actor needs to balance her concern for necessities and survival with her striving to realise what she experiences as exciting and valuable possibilities. Mostly actors try to combine these endeavours: the need for food is combined with the possibilities to make the food attractive and so on. However, the two interests can collide, and actors may have to choose to endure suffering, even death, to realise the things they love.

Value

The Value-Difference

Basic values are the values of an actor. They are subjective. They may be reasonable or not. But they are the real motivators to act. To realise one's basic values gives joy and happiness. To live in a world where they do not thrive is disturbing. Instrumental values complement the basic values. Actors use a lot of energy to obtain adequate instrumental tools—resources, position, knowledge etc.—in order to realise their basic values. This work may be so demanding that the actor oppresses, forgets and gives up her basic values in which case she is lost in life. It may be difficult for her to make a comeback as an actor if she has lost belief in her ability to realise her values.

Values also motivate reflection. Pursuing one's basic values means that one tries to do the best one can, which presupposes reflection. Thus, values are the basis of the actor's development of knowledge and reason, meaning and of achieving happiness and satisfaction. Basic values define what life is about, who one really is and the things in life that have meaning. If the actor believes that her course of action realises her values, then she will do her best. She would cheat herself if she tried to get off lightly.

An actor develops a whole profile of values, both basic and instrumental. The values take turns in motivating the activities of the actor as they vary in strength. The value-profile is not fixed and unchangeable. The person organises her life to achieve the best possible realisation of her values.

The character of the relationship between the actor and the world implies that the actor's values have 'counterparts' in the environment when they are realised. The realised values reflect the actor's personal values. The difference between the actor's basic values and the reality she faces is the *value-difference*. The driving energy to act, the motivation of the actor, is to reduce and overcome the value-difference she experiences, i.e. the difference between the state of the world and the desires of her values. Every endeavour of the actor is about diminishing the value-difference. Empathy enables us to observe and respond to the value-difference of other people, i.e. observe how their values are realised and not realised in their environment, and to form an ethics of support and cooperation on that basis.

Social systems formulate values such as prosperity, social security, fame and power to discipline citizens to act in the way the society wants. These 'social' values are instrumental values to the actor, although to some they obtain the status as basic values. Maintenance of the social system is instrumental as it is a precondition for actors to fulfil their basic values. The factual possibilities and the social systems are instrumental for realising the basic values. Actors strive to achieve control over sufficient instrumental values as the means to strengthen value-difference reduction. Social and technological systems are also a means to help reduce the value-difference of people. Reduction of value-difference is not only about creating and maintaining the relevant values. It is also about influencing the development of the subjective values through learning, experience in action and dominating narratives. The self-narrated history of an actor is the history of how she handled the value-difference. She feels good or bad about herself depending on the success she had in doing so. Thus, the value-difference connects the present and the past in our narration about who we are, our true selves, based on our endeavours to realise our values and handle issues of value-difference.

The values of a person need strength and depth in order to give direction to the endeavours. Socialisation and personal experience through action influence one's values. When the social background is characterised by inconsistent values, then the actor may become confused as to her values. Personal action creates experiences for the person to develop her values. However, if she experiences major defeats in action, she becomes insecure with respect to her values and the direction of her life (see Figure 2.4).

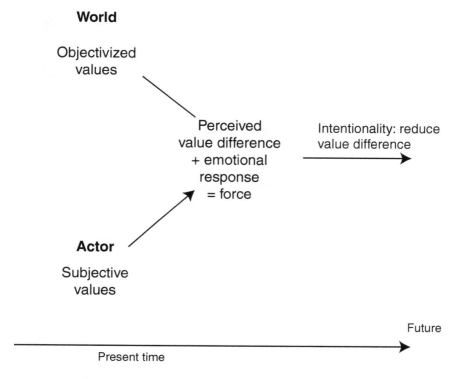

Figure 2.4 Values

Nature of Values

What are values? How do we recognise them? What is their function? (Nør-reklit, L. 2013a). Like possibility and necessity, values are not something that are directly observable.

The basic values reveal themselves in the strivings and preferences of the actor. An actor's values are the people, activities and phenomena that she cares for, and the things and people she wants to protect, promote, strengthen, improve and develop, i.e. basic values involve the desire for endurance of that for which we care. The intended durability of values enables them to give the actor's life direction and meaning. The actor's ability to observe and react upon the value-difference is crucial to her. There is no reason to hurry the enjoyment of realising basic values, because life has nothing better to offer. Things people want to do quickly do not realise their basic values. They are instrumental values or enjoyments.

The value of a relationship of love and friendship grows with the shared history that creates meaning, trust, attraction, joy and the intention to sustain and nourish the relationship in the future. If such value shatters, the actors experience a painful loss of meaning, trust and joy. The polar opposite of this is the pure endeavour to change, consume and destroy. Things we want to avoid, change or destroy are things we consider less valuable or even bad. Change motivated by reduction of value-difference aims for the better, but change just for the sake of change is destructive.

Consider consumption. Things that people consume are destroyed. The value of consumption must therefore be instrumental. Basic values—manifested in relatives, friends, things of high quality, beauty, art, nature etc.—relate to things we do not want to consume. We do not want to consume our loved ones or things we cherish. On the contrary we want to protect them, nourish them, make them strong and successful—support their duration and development. Our deepest values lie in the ability to sustain and develop them over long periods of time.

The focus on consumption in economics is not a focus on basic values but on instrumental values because to consume is to destroy—contrary to *use*, which presupposes some degree of durability. Consumption is necessary because of our needs, whether they are biological needs or caused by social conditions. There is a significant difference between needs and basic values. Fulfilment of needs is an instrumental value. It is a condition of life, but it is a not basic value. Needs must therefore facilitate basic values, the ones that which give life direction and meaning. Actors consequently engage in great projects to make the satisfaction of needs a pleasurable experience, commonly a basic value.

However, we eat in order to live; we do not live in order to eat. Our life is about doing and creating and experiencing things with the friends and partners we love. These are our basic values. Our basic values—i.e. our loving and liking—make us be concerned about our environment. They make us appreciate and care for people and things around us. They are not egoistic, unlike the demand to fulfil needs. They make us human and ethical beings who feel compassion, care and concern. Egoistic modelling of life reduces us to pre-human beings driven purely by needs, whether the necessities are biological needs, genetically determined or a result of economic demand. All these reasons are important, but they are means subordinated and cultivated by the concern for the basic values that give meaning, the love and value we attach to the social and physical world in which we live.

It may be confusing, also to the actor herself, what her values are. An indicator of a person's values is her emotions and feelings. Emotions have a cognitive function in that they inform us about the basic values of a person or even about ourselves when related to events or situations. Positive emotions such as joy and happiness inform us that the event or situation accords with the actor's values—e.g. when the actor sees the things she likes and feels happy. Negative emotions tell us that our values are oppressed—

e.g. when the actor loves children and sees a child being beaten and feels angry. Negative emotions such as anger, frustration, depression, sadness and sorrow are clear indicators of the fact that the values of the actor are threatened or under attack.

The actor's success is—ultimately—the realisation of her basic values. Realisation of instrumental values is insufficient. She may achieve objectives of high social values, but if they do not match her basic values, then she will not be content. She will only be able to realise her values if they are within the range of her factual possibilities. The personal success of her life depends on this. Therefore, she tries to develop her reality construction such that her factual possibilities fit her basic values. If her values are outside the range of her possibilities, then she cannot succeed no matter how many possibilities she has. She may be viewed by others as a success according to generally accepted social values, but as a person she feels deprived of the object of her wishes. For instance, to a person in love there will be little comfort in the fact that there are many other possible partners, if she cannot get the one she loves.

Society advocates a variety of values to guide and support actors in the development of their values. However, the social values advocates change and actors may face problems if they let their development rely too much on social value stability. There are, however, common basic values that are not instrumental and that most actors consider good social behaviour such as friendliness, truthfulness, tolerance, honesty, fairness and helpfulness. These are ethical values that are necessary in a society in which the participants need to trust each other. People want society to be a place where they cooperate without having to fear other people. However, the social system's success values of wealth and profit, fame and influence etc. create a framework with few winners and many 'losers', which undermines trust and solidarity and may inspire actors to break the rules and become winners in alternative games.

Understanding and supporting other people's values is socially important. In particular, leadership should support operative narratives that outline attractive roles that fit and support the actors' values so that the society reality links the values of the actors with those of the society. Social values such as wealth, work, recognition, fame and power are meant to serve the basic values as generated by an actor who acts on love and friendship, and freedom and tolerance. The actual organisation of the culture/the state/the business is not a goal *per se*. Human life, love and happiness are. People do expect something from the organised world, from their leaders, their business and the state in return for them giving them the power to rule their lives.

Communication

The communicative nucleus of integration is the ability to organise topoi around narratives that create roles and plots that in turn motivate the actors. In addition, the topoi are the ideas that guide them in the way they perform their activities. Good communication, good narratives and good topoi are almost self-copying. Actors like to use them. They inspire the actors, create enthusiasm and loyalty and inspire organisational trends. Communication has always been a part of human work. Today it is a major part of work. Sometimes work is almost exclusively of a communicative nature. Physical labour has sometimes become so mechanised and controlled by information processing technology that the actor's part of physical work is to press buttons, to look at monitors and to communicate with co-workers and clients.

The Social Glue

Communication is part of every job and every role we play. It carries bits and pieces of reality constructs around between people. It connects actors and merges their reality constructs to create and maintain practices by encompassing constructs with which they cooperate, understand and trust each other.

Communication is a special type of actor-world relation. Actors connect and create complex organised forms of actorship, practices, in the form of businesses, institutions and societies by means of communication. Communication aggregates individual actors to larger acting entities. It is not just a way of informing, educating and entertaining, but creates impact and social power. High performance presupposes advanced communication—from science to art, and from development to warfare. Thus, communication is the social glue 'between' people. It enables them to understand and support each other. Everything a person expresses, shows and does automatically communicates something—deliberately as well as involuntarily, by body language as well as by style. Linguistic communication is especially versatile, flexible and easy to produce. It can be made to express anything we can think of. By means of communication we can cooperate and organise complex practices. Without communication that would be impossible.

Communication must be integrated in order to function. Imagine communication that is not integrated with anything. It has no content. It may be an exchange of sounds or signs just for the fun of it. In the beginning such 'communication' is un-integrated. It does not convey facts, possibilities or values. It expresses nothing. But it will not take long before it turns into a dialogue in which the participants express themselves to each other. Special sounds are soon recognised as having special meaning, which is recognised intuitively by the accompanying expressions and the emotions they produce, and soon a dialogue starts to explore various possibilities. Even at this stage, communication integrates values and possibilities through the exchange of factual sounds. For communication to function and enable social practices it must integrate and convey states of affairs, possibilities and values, including basic values. Silence does not work. Reductive communication that disregards values or factual possibilities of the relevant actors fails to establish a shared working reality construct. It fails to motivate or to outline actions that can be realised.

Language is an ocean of all kinds of possible organisations. To construct a certain practice a narrative is needed as well as special topoi to guide the various activities (Burke 1945, 1973). Special topoi surround the roles and delimit the essence of each role and show the performance that is expected from the actor. Certain members are especially active in organising the narration by orchestrating co-authorship or by dominant dictation. Consider a family: there is a group of family members, each of whom plays a specific role. The story about the family is captured in narratives about the family and the narratives tell the members who they are and outline the roles they play. The topoi outline the ideals and other ambitions guiding their role-play. By understanding the roles and guiding topoi they can learn how to support and supplement each other. The narrative is mostly the result of a co-authorship that involves all members. Members who are not allowed to participate in co-authoring tend to have a difficult time.

Thus, practice is organised according to narratives, and its activities are controlled by topoi. Narratives position the actors in the encompassing reality construct by assigning roles and defining plots that drive interaction. The acts of the actors and external influences eventually change the workings of the organisation and the narrative must adapt the roles and plots accordingly.

By communicating the actor positions herself in the social world outlining a place where she belongs and a role to play in communicative interaction, so that she and the world are connected. The communication with and around her positions her by merging—or rejecting—her reality construct with the reality construct of the practice she addresses. Her place (Greek 'topos') is characterised by a set of concepts, ideas and topoi of her role. The actor cannot function properly if the relevant parts of her reality construct are not merged and integrated in practice.

Topoi and narratives are complementary instruments. Narratives are the guiding concepts that define what the business, the roles, and jobs will be. The topoi guide the actors' activities and outline ambitions and performance criteria, thereby easing the cooperation amongst the actors.

2.4. Multiple Realities

There are several processes that influence the landscape of reality constructions. Each actor constructs her reality. In 'addition' there are the numerous overarching reality constructs that organise human cooperation and the way we coexist. We live in a world with an indefinite amount of overlapping and differentiating reality constructs of which actors are more or less conscious. In the following we use three distinctions to analyse the issue of reality and multiple realities: integration-disintegration of the four dimensions, merging-diffusion of reality constructs and coherence-incoherence between constructs.

Integration

Reality is an exclusive concept. Accordingly, it involves borders and gate keeping activities. The basic reality construct that enables human beings to function as actors is the four-dimensional integration, which makes it possible for the actor to distinguish between real and illusive. It is a deep and existential structure that is not easily changed because all activities of an actor are based on it. Nevertheless, it is influenced by significant experiences. If the person loses faith in her integrative construct, then she experiences a disintegration that may make her situation chaotic or delusional. The basic reality construct involves the basic narratives and topoi of the actor's life. It is her primary approach to the world based on her most basic experiences. If they do not work anymore, then she is lost.

The basic reality construction of an actor is influenced by already existing social reality constructs. A social dialectics (Arbnor and Bjerke 2009) and structuration process (Giddens 1984; Jack 2017, Chapter 11, this volume). takes place. An actor with a purely individual reality construct is an abstraction. An actor finds herself in a social world and develops her reality construct in interaction with the various constructs around her. Based on her construct she positions herself in the world, but she does more than that. She also positions the others and they position her. Individual actors are people who make up their minds and try to make something special out of their lives through their relations and their values. The possibility of making special choices depends on the culture and on social conditions.

The reality construct is influenced by the social and physical conditions of the actor and it enables her to reflect on her situation and conditions. She can analyse her basis, her possibilities, values and chances. She may do this even when she discusses the issue with herself only. Although actors share a common language, they develop different communication patterns that reflect differences and values, knowledge and possibilities. One quality of a language is its ability to communicate any number of different reality constructs.

There is no logical or a priori way to integrate the four dimensions because logic is a cognitive function in one of the dimensions, the possibility dimension. Thus, dimensions can be integrated and be merged in many ways and can generate many different—more or less consistent—reality constructs. The functioning of practice demonstrates whether the integration is viable. Integrated structures are tenacious, but not static. They change and are instrumental to development. Reality constructs are almost floating and ever changing—sometimes for the better, sometimes for the worse. Antagonistic values and insufficient reflection create risks.

Merging

The process of merging creates a new reality construct from two or more different constructs. It takes place in bottom-up, top-down as well as

Practice is composed of systems of functional units that complement each other and constitute a complex practice. Functionally defined departments of a business are such units, e.g. production, sales, finance etc. Each unit is highly integrated. This is achieved through specialised skills acquired through education and training. The specialised language and the development of the professional topoi of the discipline are a basis for the high integration that is necessary to ensure high efficiency. The price of this high integration of functional units is that they have highly different reality constructs, making it mutual understanding among the units difficult. In addition, the performance goals of the units are naturally different and not fully compatible. Overarching topoi and strategic systems coordinate these units by creating coherence amongst them in the sense that the output of one unit is the input of another unit. Strategic topoi are tools that the management can use to influence the professional departments to give priority to company coherence and subordinate the professional departmental performance to the overall performance.

2.5. Construct Causality

Integration has so far been introduced as a structural feature of the actor-world relational complex that enables actors to perform and succeed. Relevant facts, possibilities, values and communicative processes have to be present and active in an integrated manner. According to the theory of construct causality, the power created by integration is transformed into practice by ongoing causal processes and intentional activities. The structural integration creates power that unfolds in the causal processes.

The link between the structural integration and the realisation of the power that stems from the sequential processes is established by the 'time-structure' of the dimensions: Facts are based on *present* evidence for phenomena that may be *past* or *present*. We see an element of transporting something through time, from past to present. Possibilities are based on the *present* reality that embeds a possible *future*. Possibility also involves simultaneity of a plurality that poses as alternatives. Value involves a 'desire' to produce (*future*) or secure (*present*) the existence and durability of valuable conditions. Communication involves *simultaneity* of message and communicator or perceiver. In the reality construct all the time modes operate in a system.

Structural integration in practice drives the processes by constructing and controlling intentional chains of causal events to realise the various intentions of the parties involved, including the conditions needed by practice to continue. Causal chains involve two types of processes: causation and intentional control. In addition, there are all the processes involved in constructing the causal chains. Whereas causation is concerned with factual possibilities, intentional control is concerned with integrating values. Communication is developing, organising and controlling the chains in a practice.

In a *causal* process, an event, the cause, produces the effect. This production is not intentional. It follows laws that are based on forces of nature. The *intentional acts* are based on the decisions of actors. These acts ignite, i.e. start, the causal chains, control the outcome and adjust the process until the outcome realises the intended values. An intermediate type of process is the influence of socially constructed laws such as economic, political or other social laws. They influence practice. Contrary to the laws of nature, they can be broken as well as changed intentionally in order to influence and control practice. Finally, there are the processes that organise the practice by creating the chains.

We now have the outline of the way in which construct causality generates processes: factual possibilities are causal systems, i.e. systems of causal chains, which are structurally embedded in things. The physically embedded systems are causal systems. They determine what happens if they are enacted, which is the realisation of the possibilities. They are enacted if the first cause in the embedded chain is produced—intentionally or accidentally. The intentional enactment then integrates the factual possibilities with the values, presuming the values are within the range of the possibilities and therefore realisable by the intentional action. Communication controls the intentional activities and creates the reflection and narration that are used when designing the causal system and deciding on the values to be realised. Communication not only interconnects the actors, it also draws on the opportunities given by social structures.

Causal Chains

A causal event is a relation between two events: the preceding cause that generates the subsequent effect. This process of generation is automatic. It is not intentional. It happens every time the cause occurs—provided that the conditions are the same, i.e. ceteris paribus. The cause-effect relation is general and based on natural forces.

When things are factually possible then a chain of causal dispositions for these possibilities is embedded in the things. Artefacts, i.e. any physical constructs such as machines, buildings etc., are made to embed special causal dispositions. The dispositions define the type of artefact. The dispositions come from the structure or system engraved in the artefact. It is an embedded causal system. It is a hypothetical causal event waiting to happen. When the initiating cause is produced, the causal system is activated and produces the effect, which is the realisation of the possibility.

To create complex things, more advanced possibilities have to be embedded. Constructing causal chains achieves this. They are strings of causal events in which the effect of a previous cause functions as a cause that produces a new subsequent effect. The chains are embedded as structural causal systems in our artefacts. All artefacts embed structures of causal chains. They can be ignited and controlled. They are constructed in a manner such that the final effect is the realisation of the advanced intended values that motivated the construction of the chain in the first place. The values are mostly instrumental and in the end they must produce a richness of basic value.

A causal chain is therefore defined as a chain of possibilities in which the realisation of one possibility ignites (causes) the realisation of the next. A chain may exist as an idea or a plan or as a factual possibility embedded in the artefacts, where it 'waits' until it is put in motion. One chain may ignite another. It is ultimately the work of an actor to produce the events that ignite the chain. Some examples: the phone is able to connect to other phones, the hammer is able to drive the nail down in the wood etc. These are factual *possibilities* that define the things. When the phone or the hammer or another thing is not in use, it still embeds the relevant causal structures and systems that are not—but can be—invoked. And if the causal systems and structures are invoked, they necessarily realise the factual possibilities.

Long and complex causal chains can be vulnerable to accumulation of imperfections that have a negative impact on the outcome. Thus, control is necessary to recognise deviations and adjust the process accordingly.

Generality

Causal relations are general—like a rule that can be applied to specific events again and again. Without such generalities there would be no practice.

In the covering-law model, the causal explanation is a deductive argument with one general premise, the natural law, and one specific premise, the causal event. The conclusion is a specific subsequent event, the effect. Simply put without technicalities (Hempel and Oppenheim 1948):

Premise:	An A causes a B	the natural law
Premise:	There is an A	the cause
Conclusion:	There is a B	the effect

In order for the event A to be a cause, it must be an instance of the antecedent of the causal law. The same holds for B being an effect. According to the model, there is no such thing as two events where one is the cause of the other unless they are connected by a natural law that generally applies in space and time, whereas the events take place in a specific place at a specific time. The causal explanation combines the general and the specific in the deductive argument. If we use the alternative method of induction instead of this deductive model, we are still confronted with an element of generalisation: inductive *generalisation*, based on significant correlations found between variables in a sample although the causal relation is stochastic, not deterministic as it was in the covering-law model.

When actors use construct causality to establish the generalities used in practice, they establish them in the causal systems that are embedded dispositions in artefacts that can be activated by actors or incidents. The construction of artefacts is the construction of systems of causal chains. The number of causal relations created in this way by man is endless. There are few known forces of nature—including gravity, the electromagnetic force, the strong and the weak quantum forces—and thus a limited amount of causal laws. They do, however, apply everywhere in the universe and are general in a way that defines the working of the universe. In human practice, however, there are countless different causal relations that are constructed and embedded in our artefacts. Each practice and each technical system embed special systems of constructed chains. For instance, there is a causal chain that enables an actor to produce the letter K on the monitor by pressing the letter K on the keyboard. There is a different causal chain involved when an actor opens the faucet to fill a kettle with water and so on. All the causal chains are constructed although there is no natural law in physics or in social science according to which a press on the letter K on the keyboard produces the letter K on the monitor or a turning of the tap produces a stream of water—although all these things do happen according to the basic natural laws and nothing else. There is, however, a lot of construction needed to create a faucet and a computer based on the natural laws. The chains function in accordance with the laws without which nothing would happen. However, practice must precede our knowledge of basic laws; otherwise they could not be discovered.

Determinism

Modern causal determinism was inspired by classical physics in which mathematised laws in principle enable calculation of the specific effects of any specific causes. Because the effects of given causes are predetermined, it appears as if everything must be predetermined. If this were correct, then there would be no possibilities to choose from, there would be only one possibility and that one would be necessary. Accordingly, factual possibilities, freedom to act, choices and free will would be delusions. The success of physics made it a model for scientific research, inspiring it to search for mathematised laws in each research field.

However, determinism is problematic. It is presumed to apply to the physical world in space and time, although it contradicts our basic experiences of the world in space and time. We experience a world of possibilities and not one consisting solely of predetermined events. The very spatial perception of things and phenomena is a perception of possibilities, forcing the actor to choose among alternative possibilities such as: in which direction do we want to go? Where do we want to be? All the things in space that surround us add to the multitude of possibilities as well as outlining a variety of impossibilities. For instance: doors represent possibilities to enter or leave a room, but the walls are impenetrable and it is impossible to leave the room by walking through them. On the other hand, we can hang a picture on a wall, but we cannot do so on air. The commodities on the shelves in a shop are possibilities for us to buy; the clerks in the shop are not. Possibilities and impossibilities are complementary. Our life-world is loaded with possibilities and impossibilities. And we are forced to choose: where do we go, who do we relate to, what do we do? The very point of spatial perception is the opening of a horizon of possibilities for our choices. Spatial perception presents a multitude of things to us simultaneously and forces us to choose. Simultaneity may be a construct, but it is a construct that gives us our possibilities.

'Being' does not only mean 'being in the world'. It is 'being part of the world and interacting in it'. This makes it impossible for us as actors to apply a fully deterministic perspective. When the world includes other actors, we have an extra element of uncertainty, as the actors do not know what the other actors are going to do as independent individuals. To handle this uncertainty, social institutions are created to facilitate productive cooperation. The integrative power of the communicative dimension is decisive in this respect. If powerful integrative communication is replaced by opportunistic misuse of words, the effectiveness of systems deteriorates.

The importance of the actor—including the scientific actor—aligns pragmatic constructivism with interventionist perspectives, as in the Copenhagen interpretation of quantum physics inspired by Niels Bohr. The very act of observing and measuring phenomena interacts with them and therefore it influences them. A deterministic perspective is impossible (Bohr 1958); to be is not only to be in the world as a 'fly on the wall' but also to interact with things in it.

We explain our cognitive structures in terms of the role they play in our reality construction. We know that the use of possibilities is essential to the existence of actors. The same applies to systems of causal relations embedded in the phenomena without which possibilities would not exist. The enactment of the initial causes 'forces' the possibilities to be realised. Possibilities therefore involve the existence of causal necessities. Causal necessities function as the foundation for possibilities. Thus, if we have possibilities, we have causal relations. With the discovery of physical laws, we also discover how we can construct more and more advanced causal chains to enlarge the horizon of possibilities even further. The causal laws do not eliminate human possibilities by uncovering that they are delusions. On the contrary, they are tools that can be used to create and enlarge the horizon of possibilities, and they have done so successfully.

As regards the social laws of economics, politics etc. these laws are human constructs in a way that the physical laws are not. They are based on culture, legal systems and scientific theories of the disciplines in question. The ability for these laws to function is not given by nature, but depends on social conditions. Such laws only work well for a certain period of time because they transform the society, thereby destroying the conditions under which they function. To avoid this problem they may give rise to the development of increasingly complex structures that in the end defy predictability, making causal determination delusive. To maintain the intentional actorship as a foundation for society and to avoid increasing precariousness for the population, the conditions under which socially constructed laws function must be clarified further. They are not independent of human activity as is the case for the laws of physics.

Causal chains of events have beginnings and ends. These points in time are constructs. In the world as such there is no sharp beginning and end of causal processes. But in practice it is necessary to delimit the events by defining their beginnings and ends when actors control causal chain. This is a constructed time structure needed to establish intentional control. Also, there are all kinds of influencing causes in the world that affect all the events; practice, on the other hand, is able to abstract from such complexity because of the way it constructs and embeds the causal chains.

Intentional Control

To control a system of causal chains, actors must be able to produce the initiating primary causes at will and in such a manner that the chain produces the desired effect. The initiating causes must therefore exist as factual possibilities to actors who possess the necessary skills, have the necessary access to the system and the knowledge of how to produce primary causes and control the chain. The difference between something being a factual possibility and its being a factual possibility for an actor is the skills and the access needed to realise the possibility of producing the primary cause at will. That something is a factual possibility only means that such actors can be assigned. If an actor is *de facto* prevented from producing the primary cause by somebody or something, then it is not a factual possibility for the actor. That something is factually possible to an actor means that it is up to her decision, her will.

The controlling actor directs the activities of the causal system towards a goal that realises the values she intends to realise. The intentionality of the controlling actor integrates the values with the system of factual possibilities of the causal chain. Practice processes complex systems of causal chains with many intentionally operating actors and correspondingly many values in a way that enables the system to maintain its existence. The chains that produce values for customers, users, clients, pupils etc. must therefore be connected with chains that produce value for employees, professionals and the practice organisation itself.

Finally, in order to have intentional control of causal systems involving multiple actors, we need the communicative process that coordinates the actions of actors and integrates factual possibilities and values.

Information Technology

Information technology represents an efficient integration of communication and logical analysis with mechanical causal systems. By integrating communication and information processing in causal systems, new effective planning and control systems have been and are being developed. The systems not only communicate with actors by exchanging information, they also exert intelligent control over machines and other artefacts. They play an important role in controlling actors on behalf of social powers as well.

Integration in information technology is related to the dimensions communication and factual possibilities. Communication is integrated in the technology by combining digital analysis of meaning (the software) with mechanical systems (the hardware).

The digital analysis of meaning originates with the development of formal logic in the beginning of the twentieth century, which inspired the philosophy of logical positivism to pursue a so-called verification theory of meaning, according to which all clear meaning can be expressed in a formalised language of simple and elementary observation sentences, so-called protocol sentences. The elementary sentences are the atoms of meaning. These atoms are combined by logical functions to create complex propositions. A parallel process is the basic formulation of a questionnaire in a survey. The questionnaire consists of a system of possible sentences for the respondents to choose from. These sentences are the elementary sentences from which the researchers' analysis aggregates a conclusion. Especially interesting is Wittgenstein's *Tractatus* (1921), because it combines the atomistic approach to meaning with a digital approach to logic. Specifically, Wittgenstein claims that each sentence shows its own logical form (Adolphsen et al. 1999).

As the identification of elementary sentences seemed impossible, many philosophers—including the late Wittgenstein—switched their focus to the function of ordinary language. But the project of analysing the logical structure of meaning eventually resulted in the methods used in writing software in information technology. Thus, software seems to realise the search for elementary sentences; data files represent informational propositions, whereas programmes execute elementary operational instructions that control the processes of the hardware. The software consists of strings of elementary digital sequences that represent the logical structure of the concepts and operative ideas that are implemented in the programme. In this way the digital analysis of the meaning of words and propositions is transformed into digital information systems. IT systems are complex causal systems with input and output units with which actors can control parts of the processes.

Information technology permeates modern control and management systems. The effects on knowledge processing and the development of resulting possibilities are endless. But there are also negative effects. The vision of life as a language game has essentially been challenged or even rejected. In a language game the communication flows between people in a process of live interaction. This form of life has been replaced by a life in which communication is increasingly controlled by IT-based programmes. Work is no longer about handling professional tasks but has very much been reduced to following programmed instructions. The standards that have been programmed in the systems tend to force communication to become primitive and unintelligent. Furthermore, the authorities' ability to spy on people and to construct control systems that involve huge data collections with highly personal information about employees and entire populations challenges the basis of the democratic society.

This form of logical positivism, which has been rejected by many, has spread to all corners of life at a stunning pace in the form of information control systems. And one cannot help but find it even more stunning when we consider the philosophy of language that Wittgenstein wrote at a later stage in life and which we largely build upon. That philosophy contrasts with Wittgenstein's own *Tractatus*. This philosophy of language games and theory of meaning-as-use has inspired the post-modern set-up that emphasises the importance of communication and social constructivism, and it therefore gives directions that are quite different from those of the formalised world of information technology. One might wonder whether the late Wittgenstein's critique of the young Wittgenstein's philosophy reflects the unfolding critique of modern styles of management and communication.

To pragmatic constructivism one of the greatest issues in the use of information systems is that they only integrate three dimensions. The system has no values. The value dimension can only relate to the system through the actions—input and controls—of the actors. This is bound to have some negative effects on basic values and social interaction. In a language game without information technology, the values of people are reflected in all parts of their communication. When the social game is controlled by information systems, which are dictated top-down, the possibility of integration of the actors' values is very restricted. People who do not find their values integrated in their work-related system must look for other opportunities or perish. The leaders today therefore face almost a real challenge when it comes to finding ways for co-authoring the narratives and spurring productive reflection.

2.6. Philosophical Background

This section describes the development and philosophical roots of pragmatic constructivism.

Wittgenstein and Reappearance of Problems

The philosophy of the late Wittgenstein (Wittgenstein 1953), which plays a central role in the twentieth century's philosophy of language, is the main background of pragmatic constructivism. Like many other language philosophers, Wittgenstein viewed the resistant philosophical problems and untrustworthy speculative theories of pre-linguistic philosophy as a spell of the mind, an 'illness' in cognition, that resulted from being seduced by superficial readings of language and paying insufficient attention to the real usage of words and concepts. His medicine was to analyse language games relevant to the problems. In doing so he illustrated in a pragmatic, down-to-earth manner, the non-problematic functioning of the language as we use it to unfold usage in practice. Hereby the speculative problems withered away. He did not solve the problems, he made them disappear, by showing how the meaning of words in their usage in the language games, i.e. in the worlds of practice, which is composed of actors and actions, cooperation and conflict, control and failure, rules and institutions, sensation and reflection, emotions and feeling, existence and death. This analysis is neither holism nor atomism, but somewhere in between. It is pragmatic and constructionist.

In the 1970s I experienced a social faculty in Denmark working with problem-based research and hence reintroduced the focus on problems, but now not as problems in philosophy but as problems produced in social practice. Although practice solves almost all problems, it simultaneously creates problems that it seems unable to master. Thus, it appears we still need a cognitive social psychotherapy of our time. In other words, Wittgenstein's image of problems as the fly in the bottle that cannot come out reappears to me. The fly always flies in the wrong direction. These problems are created by the very tools with which the actors try to solve them. The very mental bottle we have constructed, i.e. our reality construct, creates the hard problems, and we fly inside unable to find the way out to reality. The way out of the bottle of problems is to ensure that our reality construction is okay and that we are not seduced by simplistic or fuzzy interpretations. Poor interpretations create illusions that eventually can create a worrying abyss. Thus, apparently there exist special dysfunctional language games, where actors cannot find the way out of the bottle.

To come out of such bottles reflection and trustworthy conceptualisation is instrumental. However, a theoretical extension needs to be added to the Wittgensteinian philosophical ladder in order to transcend these problems. As Wittgenstein illustrated the overcoming of philosophical problems by studying the ordinary healthy language games, so we try to illustrate how the problems come and go according to the quality of the reality construction. Thus, we need to understand what real success in action is, and thus what it is to come out of the bottle that creates our problems.

Facing the practical problems there were some philosophical theories about actors and reality ready at hand—two sources of inspiration that gradually merged. Many other contributions of the twentieth century's linguistic turn in philosophy form the basis of analysing the dimension of communication, as for instance by theories of reality-constituting speech acts (Austin 1962a, 1962b; Searle 1969) and of communicative action (Habermas 1981). It is important to an actor to know that she has direct access to reality-constituting activities due to her ability to communicate. Mastering a language enables actors to participate in any language game, i.e. reality construction, of that language. Possession of language enables construction of social institutions. All social processes are mediated through communication with which every actor positions and is positioned in this institutionalised world. However, communication may be intentionally or unintentionally delusive and lead people astray. We need a critique of usage—often it is usage with poor reflection and low degree of understanding and high pathos, but illusions may also be sophisticated.

Finally, a different special source of influence was Niels Bohr's epistemology (Bohr 1958), which already then exerted influence in Danish philosophy.[6] Bohr's arguments that knowledge creation involved influencing the situation and thereby changing it pushed towards considering people as actors and limiting the horizon of possible deterministic predictions. Thus, although 'God does not play dices' (Einstein), future knowledge from the human point of view can only be stochastic. This showed in advance that to achieve control it is necessary to opt for a practice model that is more complex than pure deterministic calculations of alternatives.

Actor—the Constructor of Practice

The philosophy of persons as agents (MacMurray 1957, 6) combined with some sociological trends (Berger and Luckmann 1966) and trends from the Frankfurth School challenged 'passive' perception's existence. The actor's perspective was set in play by a group of researchers at Lund University (Arbnor and Bergkvist 1975). They developed an actor-society structuration model called social dialectics and a related actor-based methodology (Arbnor and Bjerke 1977/2005) further developed at Aalborg University (Nørreklit et al. 1983).

The actor perspective enables a reinterpretation of the Cartesian dictum of the modern awakening (Descartes 1641): "I think, thus I am." This tells some important things to us. First, it tells that to exist is to do something![7] To think is to do something—it is not to have something. Having a thought is not to think, but the result of thinking. Thus, the thinking I is an actor that produces something, namely thoughts. This actor acts even intentionally, because she probably thinks about something. Accordingly, the human being appears to be an actor in the most basic dictum of modern philosophy. This is very different from the classic Aristotelian idea of existence as things/substance that have properties, where the properties may change, whereas the underlying substance stays the same. The combination of activity and thinking, i.e. conscious reflection, is the place where creativity is born. Human beings are creative actors producing constructs to generate development of life styles in a development.

The focus on actors and action imply an inspiration from philosophical pragmatism (Pierce 1905; James 1909). Actions take time. Actors live in a time-span, not in an un-extended moment, a now, but in a present that stretches into the future while retaining something of the past. Similarly, according to a pragmatic approach the meaning of a statement is the expected outcome of possible activities or processes that it implies. This notion of meaning enables language games to function and enables us to conceive the success of action in pragmatic terms.

Dimensions of Reality

The difficulties of identifying non-material phenomena such as value, logic and possibilities in the world and their necessity for practice found a solution in the distinction between world and reality, where reality is considered as a construct that combines facts, values, logic and possibility (Nørreklit, L. 1978; Nørreklit, L. 1987). The reality construct would be very much controlled by the narratives and the conceptual framework of the actors. A reality construction leads to illusions and unsolvable problems if it is determined by an inadequate combination of these constituents/dimensions. The role of communication as fourth dimension occurs a few years later (Nørreklit, L. 1991). With this development the notion of reality as four-dimensional integration which enables the actor to act successfully is established.

With the exclusive character of the concept of reality and the role of conceptual structures as causing fictive constructs, the model of concepts developed, and the notion of conceptual illusions developed (Nørreklit 1987; Nørreklit 2011). Inspirations are found in, amongst other works, critical analysis of the Frankfurth School (Horkheimer and Adorno 1944), antipsychiatry (Laing 1985), and the theories of simulacra (Baudrillard 1981).

Although there is the argument that integrating facts, possibilities, values and communication are sufficient conditions for the actor to act and succeed, one may still wonder: why just these four dimensions? Starting with modernity, the enlightenment and the appearance of modern science, it cannot escape attention that behind the dimensions there are some powerful philosophies. The dimensions of fact and possibility are rooted in two major streams in western philosophy, Anglo-Saxon empiricism and continental rationalism. As to the dimension of value the image is less clear, although there are important efforts of the nineteenth century to cope with values, such as in ethics and existential approaches, amongst others. Finally, the linguistic turn of the twentieth century introducing the philosophy of language is the basis of the dimension of communication.

More specifically, empiricism claims that all knowledge of the world comes from *observation* (Hume 1739/40). Concepts must be derived from and theories proven by observation. This perspective is the basis for the dimension of facts because facts demand empirical evidence; i.e. the connection between actor and world is a connection based on the sense perception. At the turn of the twentieth century, phenomenology emerged as a perspective in continental philosophy in which knowledge is based on experiencing the phenomena (Husserl 1998). Whereas empiricism is concerned with observation and evidence, phenomenology is concerned with the way of experiencing the phenomena. Phenomenology contributes its own methods of analysing experience. All empiricist methods, qualitative or quantitative, as well as methods of careful phenomenological grounding of our observations and concepts, are considered important to pragmatic constructivism.

Rationalism claims true knowledge to be based on logical proof (Spinoza 1677). True knowledge is based on *reflection* through logical analysis and mathematical demonstration. Empirical evidence is an illustration of or a guide to—but not a proof of—knowledge. Especially economics but also to some extent systems approach have rationalist traits. These traits are based on the cognitive capabilities of the brain. Logical truth cannot be tested by perception, only by logical analysis.

To operate with possibilities in the world is to operate with things that are outside the reach of the perception of the present. Possibilities cannot be seen, they can only be thought and imagined. Thus, reflection is needed to analyse possibilities. This is why the dimension of possibility is an actor-world relation anchored in the actor by her rational, i.e. cognitive capabilities, but anchored in the world through the causal dispositions that are embedded in the states of affairs. Rationalism contributes with an arsenal of analytical tools to create theories and proof.

The value dimension is not rich with special methods which are ready to use, unlike the other dimensions of fact, possibility and communication. But it plays important roles in ethics. The existential questions as a reason to live and meaning of life and the notion of existential choice of who we are have influenced our theory of values through a critical argument. Namely, those decisions presuppose a reason. This reason must be a value, and it must be something subjective, because reasons that motivate must be subjective. To the actor values must be the values of the actor herself; otherwise they cannot motivate the actor. They are not just values of a book or a lecture. For a book to motivate an actor, she must first adapt the view of the book as her own. Values motivate the actor because they are her values and thus her *reasons* for doing things. If her actions are not motivated by her values, then it is not her reason that is behind her action. Freedom is the situation where people can act out of *their* personal, subjective values and do it according to their mind.

In the search for basic values and thus the goal of life, the most prominent candidate has been happiness. It is, however, confusing to consider happiness to be one's goal. One can pursue a goal that makes one happy. That goal may be the happiness of others. But pursuing one's own happiness as a goal is likely to make one unhappy. Happiness is not like a need. Happiness is a *reward*, which we, our 'psyche', give ourselves for being faithful to our project of life, i.e. to our values. Thus, it is not happiness that is the value. It is only the reward we give ourselves for pursuing and realising our values. It is also a message to us as to what *our* values are. If they do not make us happy, then they are not really our values. The values on the other hand are that which gives us reason to create and construct in the world. It is our liking, empathy and sympathy, but most of all our loving. They give humans a reason to exist and a meaning in life. Therefore: "I love, therefore I am"—there is no other reason to exist (Nørreklit 2013a).

Incomplete Integration

The modern philosophies of empiricism, rationalism, value, and communicative action are complementary. They need each other. If they are used in isolation, they become reductionist with the delusions that involves. Empiricism may produce scepticism, rationalism may produce abstract models dissociated with reality and communication produces simulacra. Integration is necessary.

Integration is even at the centre of the very concept of philosophy: Philo-Sophia—the integration created by love of knowledge, friendship with wisdom, reason motivated by emotion/value. The difference between a sophist and a philosopher is not the knowledge but the love of knowledge. Thus, there are been important efforts to integrate the dimensions that were separated in empiricism and rationalism.

More specifically, Kant's theory of theoretical reason tries to integrate the empirical and the rational. Thus, he organised empirical knowledge by rational a-priori principles of theoretical reason (Kant 1787) and developed a theory of practical reason where reason is the lawgiver (Kant 1788) that guides us in controlling practice at the expense of subjective feelings. Indeed his work has been an inspiration on how to relate the empirical and the rational, but it fails to make the construction of possibilities intelligible. Also, subjective values are disregarded and therefore not integrated as they are reduced to empirical dispositions.

Kant accepted the typical empiricist position that feelings are needed to motivate reason. He rejects, however, ordinary feelings as mere tendencies. Instead, he claims that reason produces its own special feeling, i.e. *respect* or rather *attention* or *heeding* to (German: Achtung) reason. People discover that using reason creates good results. This generates the respect for reason. Although Kant has a good point, he misses another point. His integration of reason and respect faintly echoes Plato's integration of philo and sophia, which however faces the other way: first, Kant's special feeling is no real feeling. Respect or attention is no feeling. Attention or heeding is a focusing and concentrating on the topic. It is the attention, the ability to focus, that enables us to increase our knowledge and develop reason, not the other way around. And our desire to attend and focus originates from our loving and liking things. It is our loving and liking that make us continue to acquire new knowledge and thus develop insight and reason.

Another stream aiming to integrate some of the dimensions was the Anglo-Saxon philosophy utilitarianism (Bentham 1828; Mill 1901) emerging in nineteenth century. It claims that happiness or pleasure is the basic value. The goal of society is therefore the achievement of the greatest possible happiness or pleasure for its people. The role of reason is to collect knowledge and calculate which actions lead to the greatest possible happiness. Thus, utilitarianism integrates three dimensions, empirical knowledge and rational calculation with achieving the highest values.

A similar form of integration is market economics and the corresponding construction of capitalist market economies. A market consists of rational economic men who are presumed to calculate what is in their best interest i.e. most profitable. She makes choices based on her value preferences, her market knowledge and her calculation how to satisfy her values. Again, this integrates three dimensions: economic values/preferences, knowledge of facts about the market and the rational calculation based on knowledge of the economic laws. The use of cost-benefit analyses in economics is analogous to the calculation of the greatest happiness in utilitarianism.

These approaches are inspired by natural science, in which consequences can be calculated by knowing the facts and the governing natural laws. However, here the ability to calculate consequences is limited for several reasons. For one thing, because the consequences depend on a multitude of decision-makers that influence each other's actions, so none of the action-consequences can be calculated before the others have been calculated, making it a no go. Further, such determinism repeals the role of actors, including the ability of science itself to play a role.

In nineteenth century continental philosophy a dialectical perspective emerged (Hegel 1807), which presents development as the result of a struggle between conflicting elements in the reality constructs of the acting units, the *synthesis*—be they societies or individuals. A synthesis is a historical construct based on integrating conflicting elements such as conflicting social classes. As tensions develop the synthesis gradually changes into its antithesis, i.e. the opposite type of construct, and finally a revolution takes place in which the unit is transformed to a qualitatively different and higher form of synthesis in a dialectical process of development. A dialectical development is a definite law-like sequence of steps of such qualitative jumps in which a synthesis is transformed to its anti-thesis ending with a new higher level synthesis etc.

Although a synthesis may be called a form of integration, the dialectic and law-like process of development is very different from the changing integration which is a much more open structure and has a range of possibilities and a horizon of values. Here development and change proceed in unknown directions. There are no a priori solutions regarding how integration is done. Integrations are floating structures and good solutions are tested in practice.

None of the systems considered so far have genuine actors. Their persons are not driven by values that desire to construct things in loving projects. Let us finally go further back in time to Aristotle's (1998) philosophy of substance and causation, what might be called the most successful philosophy of integration of all time. The basic units of existence are substances—i.e. things in the world. A substance is an object that *has properties*. The substance holds the properties together by integrating them in one unit, so that they do not float around independently of each other in the universe. A substance is defined by the special properties, its essence, that gives it its special nature. More specifically, a substance integrates what he calls *form* and *matter*. The form is the properties of the thing. The matter is that out of which it is made and which determines its *potentials*, i.e. its ability to be used in production of other things. In addition Aristotle operates with the *purpose* of things, depending on the type of thing, especially artefacts. Form, matter, potential and purpose do not float around independently—they are integrated in the substance.

On this basis Aristotle distinguishes between four causes: the teleological, the formal, the material, and the effective cause. The *teleological* cause is the purpose. The *formal* cause is the design of the thing that realises the purpose. The design outlines how to realise the purpose. The *material* cause is the resources that are needed, i.e. that have the potential to realise the design/ form of the thing. Finally, there is the *effecting* cause that sets the production process in motion. This is the actor. The Aristotelian four causes seem to provide a handy planning schema outlining the necessary and sufficient conditions for any construction work to succeed—whether we construct a house or a business. More specifically, consider building a house. The purpose may be to create a living place for a certain family. An architect gives this purpose a form by outlining a house with the relevant facilities. Craftsmen gather the resources needed and assemble the house following the architect's plan. Aristotle's causal schema outlines the necessary and sufficient conditions for activities to succeed, but his theory differs radically from pragmatic constructivism in that the latter is inherently dynamic. First, the absence of the dimension of communication in Aristotelian integration causes the theory to overlook the dynamic influence of social practices. Furthermore, instead of focusing on the substances and their properties to understand human action, pragmatic constructivism analyses reality as an actor-world interface based on a conceptual network to handle a changing world. Finally, concepts are not reflections of eternal Aristotelian essences, but ductile cognitive constructs with which actors organise and control their activities.

Aristotle's great synthesis eventually succumbed to centuries of criticism. As it operates with essences or natures of things, it seems to be fictive and static. In the wake of natural science there is no essence, purposes or potentials existing in anything. There is matter only, which created a radically reductionist background for modern philosophy. Thus, modernity started with the more reductionist—rationalist and empiricist—approaches in the endeavour to grasp human practice.

Overview and Recent Developments

Figure 2.5. gives an overview of the philosophical background of the dimensions to be integrated in pragmatic constructivism.

Nevertheless, also in the new millennium several international as well as local research groups have inspired and contributed to research in pragmatic constructivism in business studies (Henriksen et al. 2005; Nørreklit, L. et al.

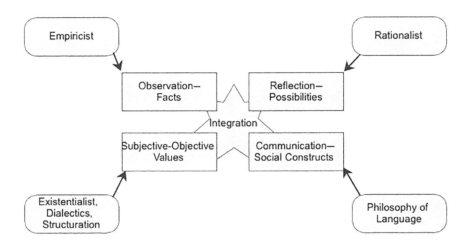

Figure 2.5 Philosophical Background

2006; Jakobsen et al. 2011) and elements of social work and learning (Nør-reklit, L. 2002/3, 2016a, 2016b).

Specific developments include the concept of *topoi* (Nørreklit, L. et al. 2006), the concept of *truth difference* and the *learning theory of truth* (Nør-reklit, H. et al. 2007), the issue of *coherence* between integrated units (Nør-reklit, H. et al. 2007), issues *merging* and *multiple realities* (Jakobsen et al. 2011), the *actor-world relational complex*, the concept of *co-authorship* and *narratives* (Nørreklit, L. 2011), and, finally, the concept of *construct causality* (Nørreklit et al. 2012; Nørreklit L. 2013b).

Notes

1 Both "actor" and "agent" originate from the Latin verb "agere", meaning "to act" or "to be active". Ordinary usage differentiates them: Actors are players on a scene, and agents are people hired to act on behalf of others. Oddly, whereas it seems logical that actors are those who act intentionally, agents are often techni-cally defined as those who do so. To create a coherent usage we stipulate a use. We need four concepts: the source of intentional activity and the player of a role, which we call these 'actors', and the person who acts on behalf of and for oth-ers as well as the person who does so due to an agreement, which we refer to as 'agents'. Other scholars may make alternative terminological choices.
2 Whereas a utopia is a non-existent place, an unattainable ideal, the topos is an existing place, the place of the practice it controls.
3 In modal logic that which is the case is also possible. Such possibilities are point-less for an actor. It destroys the very essence of the concept of possibility, which is to point out things that have not been but may be realised and become factual. Our interpretation accords with the ordinary usage of possibility.

4 Peter Zinkernagel (1962) argued that concepts of things cannot be used independently of expressions for possibilities of action.
5 In modal logic, possibility and necessity are technically defined by each other: What is possible is defined as that which is not necessarily not the case, and vice versa, what is necessary is defined as that which is not possibly not the case. This logic has its merits although it makes one of the concepts redundant. However, it does not clarify the meaning of possibility and necessity because it does not address their function in reality construction, which is our concern.
6 For modern impact of Bohr's philosophy in social science, see for instance Barad (2007).
7 Discussions of this dictum often point out that one can conclude the existence of the person from any of her activities. I sleep thus I am, I read, thus I am etc. are all as valid as I think thus I am. This modifies the rationalist emphasis on thinking. This misses, however, our point that in all these inferences existence is defined as activity—and not as having properties.

References

Adolphsen, Jes, and Lennart Nørreklit. 1999. "Introduktion." In *Wittgenstein: Filosofiske Undersøgelser*, translated by Jes Adolphsen and Lennart Nørreklit, 9–28. Copenhagen: Munksgaard Forlag.
Arbnor, Ingeman, and Tommy Bergkvist. 1975. *Observatör-Aktor*. Copenhagen: Branner and Korch.
Arbnor, Ingeman, and Björn Bjerke. 1977. *Företagsekonomisk Methodlära*. Lund: Studentliteratur.
Arbnor, Ingeman, and Björn Bjerke. 2009. *Methodology for Creating Business Knowledge*. Thousand Oaks, CA: Sage.
Aristotle. 335BC-384BC (1998). *Aristotle's Metaphysics (τὰ μετὰ τὰ φυσικά)*. Translated with an introduction by Hilary Lawson. London: Penguin Edition.
Austin, John L. 1962a. *How to Do Things with Words*. Oxford: Clarendon Press.
Austin, John L. 1962b. *Sense and Sensibilia*. Oxford: Clarendon Press.
Barad, Karen. 2007. *Meeting the Universe Halfway: Quantum Physics and the Entanglement of Matter and Meaning*. Durham, NC: Duke University Press.
Baudrillard, Jean. 1981. *Simulacres et Simulation*. Paris: Éditions Galilée.
Bentham, Jeremy. 1828. *An Introduction to the Principles of Morals and Legislation*. Oxford: Clarendon Press.
Berger, Peter L., and Thomas Luckmann. 1966. *The Social Construction of Reality*. New York: Anchor Books.
Bohr, Niels. 1958. *Atomic Physics and Human Knowledge*. London: Chapman and Hall.
Burke, Kenneth. 1945. *Grammar of Motives*. New York: Prentice-Hall.
Burke, Kenneth. 1973. *Philosophy of Literary Form*. Berkeley, CA: University of California Press.
Chisholm, Roderick. 1966. *Theory of Knowledge*. Englewood Cliffs, NJ: Prentice-Hall.
Descartes, René. 1641 (1996). *In Meditations on First Philosophy: With Selections from the Objections and Replies*. Edited and translated by John Cottingham. Cambridge: Cambridge University Press.
Giddens, Anthony. 1984. *The Constitution of Society: Outline of the Theory of Structuration*. Berkeley: University of California Press.

Habermas, Jürgen. 1981. *Theorie des Kommunikativen Handelns.* Frankfurt am Main: Suhrkamp Verlag.

Hegel, George Wilhelm Friederich. 1807 (1998). *Phenomenology of Spirit.* New Delhi: Motilal Banarsidass Publ.

Hempel, Carl G., and Paul Oppenheim. 1948. "Studies in the logic of explanation." *Philosophy of Science*, 15 (2): 135–175.

Henriksen, Lars Bo, Lennart Nørreklit, Kenneth M. Jorgensen, Jacob B. Christensen, and David O'Donnell. 2005. *Dimensions of Change: Conceptualizing Reality in Organizational Research.* Copenhagen: Copenhagen Business School Press.

Horkheimer, Max, and Theodore W. Adorno. 1944 (1972). *Dialectics of Enlightenment.* Translated by John Cumming. New York: Herder and Herder.

Hume, David. 1739/40 (1975). *A Treatise of Human Nature.* Oxford: Clarendon Press.

Husserl, Edmund. 1998. *Die phänomenologische Methode: Ausgewählte Texte I.* Edited by Klaus Held. Stuttgart: Reclam.

Jack, Lisa. 2017. "Actor reality construction, strong structuration theory and organised crime." In *A Philosophy of Management Accounting: A Pragmatic Constructivist Approach*, edited by Hanne Nørreklit. Chapter 11, this volume. New York: Routledge.

Jakobsen, Morten, Inga-Lill Johanson, and Hanne Nørreklit (Eds.). 2011. *An Actor's Approach to Management: Conceptual Framework and Company Practices.* Copenhagen: DJOEF.

James, William. 1909. *The Meaning of Truth: A Sequel to "Pragmatism."* Amherst, NY: Prometheus Books.

Jensen, Michael, and William Meckling. 1976. "Theory of the firm: Managerial behavior, agency costs, and ownership structure." *Journal of Financial Economics*, 3 (4): 305–360.

Kant, Immanuel. 1787 (1998). *Critique of Pure Reason (Kritik der reinen Vernunft).* Translated and edited by Paul Guyer. Cambridge: Cambridge University Press Edition.

Kant, Immanuel. 1788 (1997). *Critique of Practical Reason (Kritik der praktischen Vernunft).* Translated and edited by Mary Gregor, with "Introduction" by Andrews Reath. Cambridge: Cambridge University Press Edition.

Laing, Ronald D. 1985. *Wisdom, Madness and Folly.* London: Macmillan.

MacMurray, John. 1957. *The Self as Agent.* London: Faber and Faber.

Mill, John S. 1901. *Utilitarianism.* London: Longmans, Green and Company.

Nørreklit, Hanne, Lennart Nørreklit, and Falconer Mitchell. 2007. "Theoretical conditions for validity in accounting performance measurement." In *Business Performance Measurement—Frameworks and Methodologies*, edited by Andy Neely, 179–217. Cambridge: Cambridge University Press.

Nørreklit, Hanne, Lennart Nørreklit, and Falconer Mitchell. 2010. "Towards a paradigmatic foundation for accounting practice." *Accounting, Auditing and Accountability Journal*, 23 (6): 733–758.

Nørreklit, Hanne, Lennart Nørreklit, Falconer Mitchell, and Trond Bjørnenak. 2012. "The rise of the balanced scorecard!—Relevance regained?" *Journal of Accounting & Organizational Change*, 8 (4): 490–510.

Nørreklit, Lennart. 1978. *Problemorienteret Forskningspraksis og den Reale VirkelighedsKonstitution.* Aalborg: Aalborg Universitetsforlag

Nørreklit, Lennart. 1987. *Formale Strukturer i den Sociale Logik.* Aalborg: Aalborg Universitetsforlag

Nørreklit, Lennart. 1991. "Economic management and accounting: A constructivist theory and methodology." In *New Perspectives in Management Accounting*, edited by Poul Erik Sørensen, 155–260. Aarhus: The Arhus School of Business.

Nørreklit, Lennart. 2002/3. "Naturalism and spirituality on the foundation of value and peace." *IUC Journal of Social Work, Theory and Practice*, 6. Retrieved from www.bemidjistate.edu/academics/publications/social_work_journal/issue06/articles/Lennart.htm.

Nørreklit, Lennart. 2011. "Actors and reality: A conceptual framework for creative governance." In *An Actor's Approach to Management: Conceptual Framework and Company Practices*, edited by Morten Jakobsen, Inga-Lill Johanson and Hanne Nørreklit, 7–37. Copenhagen: DJOEF.

Nørreklit, Lennart. 2013a. "Applied ethics and practice ontology." In *Theoretical and Applied Ethics*, edited by Hannes Nykänen, Ole Preben Riis and Jörg Zeller, 143–172. Aalborg: Aalborg University Press.

Nørreklit, Lennart. 2013b. "On complexity and construct causality." In *The Challenge of Complexity*, edited by Gunnar S. Reinbacher, Ole Preben Riis and Jörg Zeller, 59–86. Aalborg: Aalborg University Press.

Nørreklit, Lennart. 2016a. "Precarization and control—delineating a concept." In *Verunsicherte Gesellschaft: Prekarisierung auf dem Weg in das Zentrum*, edited Rolf Hepp, Robert Riesinger and David Kergel, 55–65. Berlin: Springer Verlag.

Nørreklit, Lennart. 2016b. "Pragmatics of learning and participation—a constructivist perspective." In *Partizipatives Lernen zwischen Globalisierung und medialem Wandel*, edited by David Kergel and Birte Heidekamp. Chapter 8, this volume. Berlin: Springer Verlag.

Nørreklit, Lennart, Hanne Nørreklit, and Poul Israelsen. 2006. "Validity of management control topoi? Towards constructivist pragmatism." *Management Accounting Research*, 17 (1): 42–71.

Nørreklit, Lennart, Stig L. Pedersen, Bo Prangsgaard, and Kristian Tuft. 1983. *Aktørsmetoden: En indføring i erhvervsøkonomisk projektarbejde*. Aalborg: Aalborg University Press.

Pierce, Charles S. 1905. "What pragmatism is." *The Monist*, XV (2): 161–181.

Ross, Stephen A. 1973. "The economic theory of agency: The principal's problem." *The American Economic Review*, 63 (2): 134–139.

Sartré, Jean Paul. 1943. *L'Etre et Néant: Essai d'ontologie phe-nomenologique*. Paris: Gallimard.

Searle, John. 1969. *Speech Acts: An Essay in the Philosophy of Language*. Cambridge: Cambridge University Press.

Spinoza, Baruch. 1677 (1996). *Ethics (Ethica: Ordine geometrico demonstrate)*. Translated by Edwin Curley. London: Penguin.

Wittgenstein, Ludwig. 1921 (1961). *Tractatus Logico-Philosophicus*. English translation by D.F. Pears and B.F. McGuinnes. London: Routledge & Kegan Paul.

Wittgenstein, Ludwig. 1953. *Philosophical Investigations*. Oxford: Basil Blackwell.

Zinkernagel, Peter. 1962. *Conditions for Description*. London: Routledge and Kegan Paul.

3 Epistemology

Lennart Nørreklit

This chapter addresses epistemological principles that are involved in the reality construction to gather relevant and trustworthy insight. We focus on knowledge, truth and the role of concepts.

Knowledge Construction

On our journey to discover the meaning of knowledge we distinguish between areas where an actor has knowledge and insight and areas where she only has subjective beliefs and opinions. In broad terms, the basic difference between knowledge and belief is that belief only characterises a state of mind of a person whereas knowledge also carries information about the world. This distinction is crucial to a discipline of knowledge, including that of accounting.

Practical and Theoretical Knowledge

Practical knowledge is basic. A person does something over and over. There is a pattern. She can do something. We give it a name, say, she can walk. We use a concept to specify what she can do. She knows how to walk or cook or something else. She may not be able to explain what she can do. We call this practical knowledge or know-how. In order to act, the actor needs practical knowledge. Practical knowledge enables the actor to achieve her goals intentionally. Practical knowledge is general knowledge that the actor carries with her and that she can use whenever it is needed. It is not knowledge about how to do *one* specific thing at a certain time, but about how to do a certain type of thing whenever one wants to. Furthermore, practical knowledge is knowledge and not belief. What the actor believes is not relevant. If she can walk, then she has the practical knowledge required for walking.

Theoretical knowledge—also called *propositional knowledge* or *knowledge that*—can be defined as knowledge which the actor can formulate or express. For a claim to be a true knowledge claim, evidence is needed. And if the evidence is accessible to a group or to the general public, then it is not only knowledge of a certain actor, it is a fact. Still, knowledge claims are not absolute, rather they are defeasible. Furthermore, theoretical knowledge enables the actors to reflect on things without being involved in doing them. Nevertheless, new theoretical knowledge has an impact on practice if it can be made the basis for new practical knowledge.

The integration of communication in the reality construction intermingles with the distinction between practical knowledge and theoretical knowledge. Practice is itself a system of language games in which actors communicate their practical knowledge to each other by means of theoretical knowledge claims. Consequently, there are theoretical knowledge claims that express practical knowledge. The reflective processes in practice—planning, strategy and development—produce theoretical knowledge that can be used as new practical knowledge. It is an issue among researchers whether theoretical research knowledge can be used as practical knowledge. If it is not usable, we are facing a theory-practice gap (Pfeffer and Sutton 2000; Tucker and Parker 2014).

The pragmatic approach to knowledge implies that theoretical knowledge must ultimately be interpreted as a form of practical knowledge. One example: "It is raining." This is a theoretical knowledge claim. A pragmatic interpretation might be something like: "If you go out, then you will get wet." This practical causality claim can be used to test the truth of the theoretical claim. A theoretical claim may, however, be tested by means of a wide range of practical implications. For instance, "it is raining" may be tested by "you get wet," "it gets slippery outside," "plants get water (they needed that)," "you can hear the raindrops fall," "the vision is impaired (drive carefully)," "you may freeze," "we can get water." A theoretical knowledge claim has a range of practical implications that can be used for testing it or to perform various types of intentional action. This means that theoretical statements can be seen as a kind of generators of possibilities for action. Therefore, they can be part of numerous forms of practices. One of the reasons for this is that—contrary to practical knowledge—theoretical knowledge is defined by its informational contents and not by specific intentions or achievements. "It is raining" is defined as the falling of raindrops and not by the many practical implications that can test it.

Theoretical knowledge is especially developed within scientific disciplines at research institutions, where it is not directly related to practical usage. This distance to practice may cause a loss of practical relevance because no practical implications can be identified.

Critical and Sceptical Concerns

To avoid costly mistakes, it is advantageous to base actions on factual knowledge. Opinions, beliefs or presumptions are not knowledge. They inform us about cognitive attitudes of the person who holds them, but not about states of the world they concern. Knowledge claims and fact claims, on the other hand, are supposed to provide information about the parts of the world they concern. To obtain this status they must be based on adequate evidence.

A person with a scholarly and scientific attitude inspects knowledge claims with a critical eye, looking for weak points that justify criticism and possibly a general scepticism towards a project. It is possible that an entire system of ideas is based on weak and unconvincing evidence and thus has to be dismissed. A philosophical scepticist may even go further and reject all knowledge claims as being based on inconclusive evidence. One argument against such scepticism is the existence of practical knowledge. Sceptical arguments only address theoretical knowledge. But in practice, theoretical knowledge is involved in practical knowledge partly because actors need to communicate. The general sceptical arguments can therefore only concern theoretical statements that are not validated in practice. Some disciplines have been subject to special scrutiny by sceptical eyes, for instance psychoanalysis and accounting, as scepticists suspected their knowledge claims were fictitious because they presuppose impossible evidence such as evidence of the unconscious, the self (Popper 1963; Torrey 1986) or of economic value of tangible or intangible things (Tinker 1991). We address this issue pragmatically by reference to functioning language games. Although some of the definitions of mental units such as the unconscious or economic units such as value seem metaphysical, an ability to create coherent usage by means of observable evidence counters such critique. The sceptical argument, that there are no such objective units in the world that ascribe economic value, is a clear naming fallacy. We must look for the use to know what we mean by economic value. And there is a huge usage with plenty of criteria that are more or less consistent. That economic values are constructs is no proof that they to do not exist—on the contrary. The very point in calling something a construct is that it does exist because it is accomplished—it is not just a fiction, an idea, a plan or a project.

Knowledge Fields

The difference between knowledge and belief may depend on the skills and the efforts with which the actor studies the topics. However, the difference may also depend on the nature of the area that the actor is studying. We will denote such areas of study as *epistemic fields*. These fields are cognitive constructs. The fields may be studied in a scientific or professional discipline or they may be delimited by a philosophical perspective. For instance, empiricist philosophy outlines the field of sense perception as the field of all knowledge. Physics, medicine, accounting, law and so on all outline their specific epistemic field, i.e. the fields of physics, medicine, law etc.

The interesting question is whether and under which conditions an epistemic field is indeed a knowledge field, i.e. whether it is able to produce evidence that justifies knowledge claims. Obviously, the knowledge claims of the field must not presuppose evidence that cannot be produced within field. Metaphysical objects are consequently outside the range of justifiable knowledge claims because they, by definition, are outside the range of observable evidence. We thus have to accept the existence of some epistemic fields that are not knowledge fields but merely fields of belief.

We noticed above that when we make a theoretical knowledge claim, then we implicitly presume that a horizon of evidence claims is true. These evidence claims are themselves knowledge claims. Consequently, theoretical knowledge must be part of an epistemic system that links the various knowledge claims together in networks of evidence. This seems to imply that the knowledge field to which a knowledge claim belongs is a special type of epistemic field in which the elements of evidence are interrelated in certain ways. The principles of such interrelations are the rules of evidence. Knowledge does not exist in the form of isolated and atomic knowledge units. It exists in a knowledge field as part of a system of knowledge claims that are interrelated by rules of evidence. The evidence must exist and be available. Thus, there is an encompassing system of knowledge in a knowledge field through which phenomena are linked with evidence that is linked with other evidence and so on in complex networks. Our entire body of knowledge consists of interdependent elements of knowledge in various knowledge fields.

Still, our knowledge claims are fallible. Sometime we err. And if we can make one error, then we can make many. We must therefore address a crucial question: how do we know when we err? Maybe we always err? Maybe there are no credible knowledge fields? This line of argument is a generalisation from that fact that because we have made one or more erroneous knowledge claims in a certain epistemic field, it is possible that all our knowledge claims in the field are erroneous. To counter this sceptical generalisation we need to look into the structure of the epistemic field. The interrelated structure of the evidence has the consequence that the only ways to demonstrate that a knowledge claim is erroneous is by using other knowledge claims that are presumed not to be erroneous according to the rules of evidence. We therefore need to possess knowledge within the field in order to demonstrate an error within the field. If there are conflicting knowledge claims, one follows the evidence, hoping that it is conclusive. Thus, the sceptical generalisation, that we may always err, is invalid. The opposite is true: in order to know that we made an error, we must have knowledge in the field. If the evidence is inconclusive, then we do not know which claim is true although we may know that one of them is true—which is still knowledge within the field. Thus, a knowledge field determines its own criteria for assessing when evidence is inconclusive. Furthermore, the knowledge field is a functioning practice and hence it produces practical knowledge irrespective of occasional theoretical errors. For instance, the broad field of sense perception is a knowledge field because an erroneous perception is proven by better perception, according to the rules of perceptive evidence.

Disciplines such as maths and physics delimit knowledge fields because an error in maths can only be demonstrated by better maths, and an error in physics can only be demonstrated by better physics. These disciplines are so well established that it is absurd to imagine that we would let a layman check the physical measurements or complicated mathematical demonstrations.[1] In contrast, consider astrology. Astrological predictions are predictions which cannot be tested by astrological rules of evidence because they make predictions in everyday language and can therefore only be verified by everyday experience. Astrology is therefore not a knowledge field but a field of opinion and belief and, consequently, it is not a discipline that produces scholarly knowledge. Now consider the discipline of accounting, which is concerned with measuring performances and values, especially economic value. In complex projects and businesses, a layman has no way in which he can estimate the credibility of a financial statement. Only experts within the field can do so, which points in the direction that the epistemic field of accounting should be a genuine knowledge field. In some cases, however, reality conflicts with the professional accounting analysis, when for instance a company that is well consolidated according to its financial statements, suddenly goes broke. Such cases make the accounting discipline look more similar to astrology. It is a task for any science and for any scholarly discipline to overcome such issues and establish its field of study as a knowledge field. If this is not possible, then one might try to combine the field of study with other disciplines in the endeavour to construct a more comprehensive knowledge field. Alternatively,- one may need to abandon the field and replace it with something that does function.

There are many interrelations and overlaps between the fields, and their borders are not clear, but subtle and blurred. Nevertheless, the systemic features function. The grand ambition of unifying science is to unify all fields into one. Lower levels of unification aim at perceiving fields as complementing each other in an interdisciplinary way.

Finally, actors do not and cannot always know what they know. Knowledge is not automatically self-reflexive. As long as they know how to do things, they have knowledge, even if they may be unable to express this knowledge. Knowledge starts as knowledge of how to do things. We know things even without knowing what knowledge is. Nevertheless, a knowledge field guarantees that the actor, who masters the basics of a knowledge field, also has theoretical knowledge, although it may be uncertain what it is that she knows (compare 'meaning holism', Hempel 1950; Quine 1951).

Construction of Dogma

The exclusive nature of the concept of reality is manifest in the construction of knowledge fields. Fields that are based on evidence and defeasibility create knowledge fields with which we can overcome errors and deception. A knowledge claim within the field may be demonstrated beyond doubt— but it is never a dogma, it can be challenged, and only evidence can prove it right. On the other hand, epistemic fields that reject defeasibility and therefore install dogma produce delusions. The dynamic development of knowledge fields is a result of systematic reflection, a concept that took off in Greek philosophy and eventually resulted in the development of science and the secular society with an advanced economy and technology. Unfortunately, the use of dogmas in practice control is a defensive tactic which may be used to strengthen the power and dominance of management. Transforming social knowledge production so that it takes place in epistemic fields that are not knowledge fields but fields of dogma, belief and superstition, weakens the secular and tolerant knowledge society.

If we remove the feature of defeasibility from the epistemic systems of practice, we are left with a system in which there will be dogmas that are treated as absolute truths that cannot be questioned. Evidence rules in such an epistemic system are biased to produce answers that are pre-set by the ruling dogmas. The dogmas transform the evidence rules and thus the entire epistemic field into a paranoiac system, because all evidence is read to support the dogma, no matter what the evidence is. The dogmas function as *a priori* axioms for all knowledge claims. The very notion of knowledge is destroyed. Leadership must respect knowledge or it will destroy it; knowledge cannot obey leadership. A procedure that instals dogma can be used strategically to strengthen a given power structure, but it weakens the overall performance of the system by rejecting its own insight. Furthermore, instalment of dogma is easily combined with communication strategies based on pathos to create emotional responses which overpower understanding and undermine the demand for proper evidence. To counter such negative media tendencies, it is imperative that our rhetoric is improved by strengthening the cognitive aspects in communication to cultivate the judgement of the actors.

Truth

Knowing Truth and Falsity

A theory of truth addresses questions like: what is truth and how does it differ from falsity? How can we know the truth? And what types of things can be true or not true? Truth deals with representations, such as for instance theories, claims, suggestions, beliefs, ideas, hypotheses, memories and thoughts. A representation is true if it adequately reflects that which it represents, otherwise it is false. A representation may also be too vague or fictitious to be either true or false. There are different usages of the term: truth as a quality and truth as a true and fair view. A person, a report or a medium may be truthful in the sense that it endeavours to present the truth. The true and fair view means that one is not misguided by the presentation. Such usages presuppose, however, the basic notion of truth as adequately reflecting that which the representation claims to reflect.

Practical knowledge may be a skill that does not include any verbal representation and may therefore not involve any truth, only the skill. Theoretical knowledge, on the other hand, is representational and therefore it must be true in order to be knowledge. Practical knowledge needs not to be representational. For instance, the knowledge of how to walk is practical knowledge residing in acquired reflexes. It may not involve representation of what walking is. The proof that a person possesses this knowledge is that she actually walks. Only people who have a concept of walking as a tool in their toolbox can formulate representations of the act.

When we consider the complexity of the world and compare it with our limited communicative resources and the need to draw borders that mark the distinction between what is true and what is not, then we face a problem of truth. How are true representations possible under such conditions? Truth relates to representational constructs that can only be simplified representations of certain aspects of the world they represent.

Truth as a representation makes a claim, which is a simplification in relation to the complex conditions it concerns. No representation can reflect the immense complexity of the world. For a representation to not automatically be false, it must make abstractions from the complexity. Consider a line. We study it and conclude that it is straight. We need straight lines in practice. Buildings and material technology amongst other things use them. However, there are no straight lines in physical matter; matter is composed of atoms that move and do not line up in straight lines. Still, we produce representations of straight lines for the purposes of planning and communication, as well as to construct artefacts. This always involves a certain abstraction from the reality of the atomic, chaotic, moving "lines" of the world.

When we improve our system of evidence, we improve our representations and reduce the level of abstraction, but that is not sufficient to put us in a position to claim any absolute truth. The level of necessary abstraction depends on our knowledge, technology and purpose. A truth claim therefore only makes sense as a claim in relation to a specific epistemic system. The distinction between truth and error is a distinction within a knowledge field.

Pro-active and Pragmatic Truth

Tradition distinguishes between correspondence and coherence theories of truth, correspondence (Austin 1950; Searle 1995) relating to the fact dimension, coherence to cognitive relations (Putnam 1981; Young 1995), i.e. the dimension of possibility. According to the correspondence theory a true representation signifies a feature of the world. This is in accordance with the concept of truth as adequate representation. For instance, "it is raining" is true if raindrops are indeed falling. According to the coherence theory, on the other hand, a true representation coheres with other accepted representations. For instance, "it is raining" coheres with the representation "raindrops are falling".

The correspondence theory has been criticised because it seems to make no sense to compare linguistic representations with the world. They have no similarity. "Raindrops are falling" is just another representation. However, we need to relate representations to the world. If we cannot do so, they have no practical meaning. Correspondence means that the world is what the representation claims it to be. To find out what the world is, we need to study it and not the representations of it. On the other hand, the coherence theory correctly points out that representational claims are interconnected. Concepts are interconnected, and the rules of evidence in the knowledge field connect the claims of the system. In reality, correspondence and coherence complement each other. Both are needed. When analysing a study, we look for evidence that establishes correspondence as well as for coherence amongst the claims of the study. We integrate correspondence and coherence. The integration of correspondence and coherence constitutes what we call pro-active truth meaning it is the presumed truth, the presumed factual basis, as we see it before we take action.

The pragmatic approach to truth, on the other hand, concerns the expectations of the future that a truth claim involves (James 1909). It is pragmatically true if the expectations it generates in relation to future observations become fulfilled. Pragmatic truth must be distinguished from a forecast or a prediction because the former concerns the present, which the latter do not concern. The latter only concern what will become the case in the future.

Thus, we integrate two perspectives on truth, namely the historical here-and-now perspective of pro-active truth that is based on existing evidence and the pragmatic or post-active truth that is based on the future fulfilment of the expectations that the truth claims produce. For instance, "it is raining". The claim is based on our observations. This is correspondence. In addition, the claim coheres with many other pro-active claims, for instance what some people tell us. Therefore, it is a pro-active truth. In addition, "it is raining" makes us expect that we will get wet if we go out. This concerns the future. If it holds true, then the claim is pragmatically true. We thus have two interpretations of the truth of the same claim, one that is historical and one that is oriented at the future and carries information that is relevant to the formation of intentional actions. Both of them are based on evidence— existing evidence and possible future evidence.

Truth Difference and Learning

We normally expect pro-active truth evidence and pragmatic truth evidence to yield the same result, but because of the time difference, this is not a matter of course. However, the claims that express our factual possibilities must not only be pro-actively true but primarily pragmatically true if we are to succeed as actors. When we construct technologies, our expectation as to the functionality is based on pro-active calculations. Extra security may then be added to the constructs to compensate for the possibility that the pro-active truth of the performance of the design deviates from the pragmatic realities of the performance. In practice, planning is based on calculation of pro-active truth. The actual results represent the pragmatic truth. The skill of producing a pro-active truth that is matched by the pragmatic truth is crucial.

The difference between the pro-active and the pragmatic truth is the *truth difference* (Nørreklit, H. et al. 2007). If the difference is vital for the planning of activities, then we have a *truth gap*. Any defeasible knowledge claim can function as a pro-active truth claim that invokes expectations which can be tested pragmatically. The pragmatic truth is pragmatic in relation to the preceding pro-active truth. It may, however, be used as new pro-active truth to calculate new expectations so actions can proceed. If, however, the test 'defeats' them, we face a truth difference or even a truth gap. A truth gap provides ample reasons to learn how to improve the system instead of just continuing with the system as it is.

In times of change, truth differences are constantly generated and an organisation must therefore cope with this reality. It is necessary to observe and control the truth difference in a way that prevents it from growing into a truth gap if we are to maintain the ability to control operations. It is consequently important to keep an eye on the truth difference on an ongoing basis and when it increases, one needs to analyse why this happens. The observation and analysis must be used to generate a learning process that results in improved evidence, more realistic calculations and better judgement.

Practice operates in accordance with available information within certain fields of action that thus constitute its epistemic fields. Practice needs to estimate the credibility of its information to avoid troublesome truth gaps. It therefore needs to ensure that the fields are indeed knowledge fields and that it understands them. The field must contain criteria with which the actors can estimate the quality of the evidence. A learning system based on the analysis of changing truth difference is an instrument for improving the understanding and evidence collecting system of a business. It is also an instrument for improving the evidence principles of the knowledge system in use when estimating the evidence. A knowledge field is not a static structure; therefore the evidence and the principles of the field must be constantly re-evaluated.

Concepts

Without concepts, constructions would be incomprehensible and beyond intentional control. Cooperation would be impossible and there would be no difference between real and fake, function and dysfunction.

Concepts are not something in an abstract transcendent reality or something floating around us in a mysterious socio-linguistic superstructure. They are something we have, namely acquired cognitive skills that reside in our bodies, especially the brain (e.g. L. Nørreklit 1973; Dummet 1993; Bennett & Hacker 2008; Kenny 2010). They function as a part of the pre-understanding with which an actor approaches her world. They are constituents in her reality construction. They relate the actor to the world by identifying phenomena, outlining possibilities and values, and *thereby they enable intentional action*. They connect actors and enable cooperation through communication (e.g. Cummins 1998; Weinberg et al. 2001; Williamson 2005). They are developed through experience and reflection, and thus redefine the actor-world relation (Carruthers 2000; Millikan 2000). They are not fixed and stable but change and develop and they are more or less clear and precise or fuzzy and ambiguous (Quine 1951).

Due to the complexity of the world we need a reality construct based on concepts so that we can simplify things in intelligible ways to enable intentional courses of action. To create trustworthy simplifications, concepts have to be carefully "phenomenologically grounded". The process of concept formation involves constructing systems of concepts that outline practice ontologies of the reality construct (L. Nørreklit 2013).

The concepts are relational constructs that relate the actor to the world by being 'about' something—their 'objects' in the widest possible meaning. These objects may exist or may not exist in the world. There must be a difference between the objects of a concept and other things. This difference creates a boundary encircling the concept's extension, i.e. the group of existing objects of the concept, leaving all other things on the other side of the border. If one cannot draw such borders, one cannot distinguish between the objects to which the concept applies and those to which it does not, and the concept would have no practical application.

Concepts are constructs that combine communicative skills, perceptual skills, analysis and reflection and a sense of value, i.e. the four integrated dimensions (L. Nørreklit 1973, 2011; Davidson 1975; Brandom 1994). When a concept is constructed, then it is real and exists in the world as a cognitive model that applies to a group of objects.

It is complicated to draw the borders. For one thing, the world has few—if any—absolutely sharp borders. Its borders are fuzzy when we look at them close up in order to achieve precision. There are gradual transitions everywhere. Second, the world is an unending complexity of changing differences (Urry 2005). However, in order to act intentionally, the actor needs relative conceptual simplicity to structure her actions. She also needs concepts that draw clear demarcation lines such that she can perceive if she is doing what she intends. The fuzzy and floating nature of the world therefore poses a challenge to the actor's skills in concept formation, without which she would not be able create a practice in this hyper-complex world. To be of any use a border must embody a reason so that it can play a role in organising activities. The criterion of a functioning border is, therefore, pragmatic.

Thus, concepts have an exclusive character, too. They draw a line between those phenomena that fit the concept and those that do not. This line may be sharp or blurred, but it must be there. This exclusivity enables concepts to link and form systemic groups that support the drawing of conceptual borders. This spurs the development of a knowledge field from an epistemic field.

In this way, the actor-world relationship can be more or less organised and controlled by an actor's concepts. The concepts enable the actor to reflect on her relations and understand things that reach beyond that which can be perceived directly. Concepts are the vehicles of thought (Wilson 1969; Fodor 1998).

Concepts have a history in which they change according to the needs of our practices. To understand the meaning of a concept is to understand the role it plays in our reality construction including the construction of our knowledge fields. It is this role and not the definitions that explain why we have the concept.

A Conceptual Triangle

Concepts are constructed by combining three elements: they are anchored in the actors by their cognitive side, we call it their *content* or, alternatively, it is called their idea, meaning or intension. The content is a cognitive construct of the actor and thus it changes and varies from actor to actor. Concepts are anchored in the world by their worldly correlates called their *object*, alternatively called their referent or (collectively) their extension. The objects may be constructs or natural objects. They exist independently of the concepts of specific actors. Finally, concepts are anchored in language by a *symbolic representation* in the form of words or symbols with which actors can share concepts, and thereby share understanding and cooperation. These constituent elements generate a triangle (compare Ogden's triangle, Ogden and Richard 1923) as shown in Figure 3.1.

There are three corners in this triangle: 1) a social corner of symbolic representation, which makes the concept shared and public, 2) a cognitive corner containing its cognitive content, and 3) the corner of the object comprising the objects in the world that fall within the concept.

The triangle represents three relations. First, the conceptual content determines what the concept *is about*. It is the idea with which the actor *conceives*,

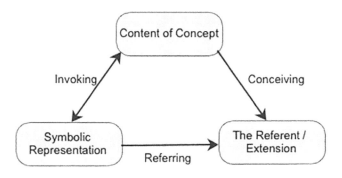

Figure 3.1 Conceptual Triangle

i.e. identifies and understands its object. This content is automatically associated with the symbolic representation as well as with the objects identified. There are other expressions for the relation between content and object such as: the object *falls within* the concept, is an *exemplar* of the concept, and we may say that the objects are the *extension* of the concept. A concept may have any number of referents, including nil. It is in principle the content of the object that should determine whether an object falls within the concept or not. Second, the symbolic representation is a conventional way to *refer to* the object. Actors develop shared concepts by developing the meaning of the symbolic representations together. Third, the symbolic representation *invokes* similar content in the actors so that they conceive of similar things. A verbal expression may be used as symbolic representation for several different concepts. Thus, ambiguity and vagueness of the meaning of words and phrases must be reflected and used with care to avoid confusion.

This double relation to the object, one by reference and one by conceiving, opens the door for one type of emerging conceptual illusions, namely if the concept is used to refer to something that does not accord with the conceptual content, which happens in authoritarian environments. In an authoritarian culture the content may be determined arbitrarily by reference, according to the will of the authority, whereas in a non-authoritarian culture the objects are determined by the content, leaving it to discussion, understanding and practice to clarify differences. When actors do not in the communication reflect the concepts they use, then they may verbally seem to use the same concept although their concepts are in reality different.

Development of practice involves change and development of the controlling concepts and therefore actors not only need common education to acquire a common conceptual background, but also need the ability to participate in reflecting and developing the conceptual systems that control their practice. The criteria for the adequacy of the concepts, which are to be worked out by this reflective practice, are pragmatic. The concepts must be able to provide their service in practice.

In addition to the content with its layers and the impact of authoritative communication, one must also consider the use of conceptual criteria to illuminate the use of concepts (Nørreklit, L. 2011).

Content

The conceptual content with which we conceive and understand can be analysed as having layers parallel to the dimensions of integration: a perceptual layer, a systemic layer and a value layer.

The Perceptual Layer

To perceive things, the actor needs a pattern or a schematic imagination of the object so that she can recognise whether the object she observes falls within the boundary of the concept or not. The conceptual objects are not identical in appearance, rather they resemble each other. Thus, the observation pattern is based on resemblance. It allows a range of variations in form, all of which make the object an instance of the concept. The perceptual patterns are integrated in the actor's perception, enabling her to recognise things automatically when she sees them. The pattern may be a series of vague or overlapping forms, like family resemblance (Wittgenstein 1953), or well-defined forms, the presence of which can be tested, measured and documented.

The Systemic Layer

It is important to distinguish between, on the one hand, perceptual *classification* and *identification*, which is based on appearance, and on the other hand, understanding and knowing *what* something is. Things are normally not defined by their appearance, but by the possibilities they embed. The nominalist principle of perceptual resemblance can only be used to make a preliminary, defeasible identification of things. We need to consolidate our identification by checking the embedded possibilities.

The possibilities are embedded in the conceptual content in the form of a layer that comprises relations to other concepts in a network of concepts that is more or less interconnected to make a conceptual system. These relations constitute the conceptual logic and are used to explain and define the concept. How developed an actor's conceptual system and understanding of conceptual logic is depends on the learning and reflective work put into her concept formation (Hempel 1950; Quine 1951; Carey 1985; Gopnick and Meltzhoff 1997).

The systemic layer positions the concept in clusters of associated concepts including by logically linking it to certain other concepts that express the defining possibilities, for example: 'phone' to the possibility 'to make a call', 'cup' to the possibility 'to contain liquid', 'to drink', 'to quench one's thirst' and 'money' to the possibility 'to buy' etc. Each concept is related to the actor's conceptual system which determines what the concept is about. Contrary to empirical systemic relations, conceptual relations cannot be tested empirically because a negative correlation would 'by definition' not be an instance of the concept. For instance, money that could not be used to purchase anything would not *be* real money but, for instance, toy money as is used in a game. However, discovery of new empirical correlations is often used to change the logic of the concept by being integrated into its systemic layer. The interconnectedness of the concepts enables the actor to reflect about things. The more complex the interconnectedness between the concepts, the more sophisticated the reflection it enables. Thus, 'concepts are vehicles of thought.'

A system of concepts is in no way stringent. All concepts are part of smaller clusters of concepts to define them by their conceptual logic, but the system as a whole appears open and vague with endless possibilities for identifying new transverse relations. Through reflection, one may discover many new conceptual relations that appear in the form of unexplored logical possibilities.

The perceptual and the systemic layers must be connected.[2] The alternative is almost inconceivable. Such a concept would be totally inconsistent. The connection between these layers establishes the perceptual evidence needed to apply the concept. The prima facie perceptual evidence is still defeasible and a test of the embedded possibilities may be needed to demonstrate that the concept applies, for example to avoid mistaking a toy gun for a real gun because they resemble one another. Psychological illusions of perception are other such illusions. On the other hand, it is not possible to use concepts in a non-arbitrary way without the assistance of the patterns of perceptual recognition.

To imagine how the systemic relational content can emerge, imagine a concept starting with a layer of perceptual recognition only. It delimits a border. We perceive an object lying within this border. As we have the ability to reflect, we automatically generate alternative possibilities of the perceived object by negating some of its qualities by imagining them to be different. In this way, we construct alternative possibilities by the simplest logical reflection, the negation. These alternatives are just logical possibilities. With those alternatives we can generate worlds of fantasies. At the beginning they are just logically possible worlds, but we can continue to work with the real objects and see what we can do with them, and sometimes we succeed in obtaining control over the changes we produce and become able to intentionally produce imagined changes. Then the alternatives are no longer only logically possible worlds, now they are factual possibilities engraved in the systemic layer of our concept. Such developments of concepts are part of dynamic practices.[3]

The construction of new alternatives and new factual possibilities involves using some artefacts to do something other than the intended use for which the artefact was created. The creative process challenges and transcends the accepted interpretation of the artefacts and their concepts. Things can always be used to do something other than for which they were meant. They have other possibilities than those they conceptually embed by tradition. Thus, it needs critical reflection that challenges traditional usage to unlock creative development. Conceptual relations are historic and changing. Criticism of the existence of fixed conceptual entities is well founded. There are no absolute conceptual relations. Concepts are not entities, but cognitive constructs reflecting our understanding. However, without concepts, thinking is association and arguments are attempts to persuade. A given thesis in the field of empirical social research becomes a trivial statement or an analytical statement in disguise. Why do we need an empirical study about whether bachelors are unmarried men? Or whether satisfied people are—in a sense—more loyal than unsatisfied people? We construct the concepts in certain ways, and we may reconstruct them too. If we construct them very differently, then we are unable to understand each other (Quine 1951).

The Value Layer

Still the conceptual content lacks something: why do we have the concept? What is its purpose? Which values—basic or instrumental—does it serve? The concepts are there for a reason, i.e. the value it serves. These values are or should be part of the content of the concept. This part is the value layer.

The value layer is the reason why we have constructed the concept with this perceptual and systemic layer. The value is, however, compatible with a range of different systemic and perceptual solutions. It may be realised in many ways. When we analyse a concept and come to understand the underlying value, we can use our reflection to seek more creative solutions than if we start from the perceptual or the systemic layers by accepting them at face value. Thus, the value layer enables actors to think of new solutions that go beyond the limitations of the layers of logical possibilities and perceptual form. Creative processes should first of all be anchored in the value layer to enable new and more innovative solutions. Although this is more creative, it is also more demanding to the developmental process. By determining things through the value they serve, innovative solutions can be discovered to accelerate development.

An example: if a blackboard is defined systemically by a conceptual logic such as: "it is a flat thing put on a wall upon which one can write and re-write things with chalk or a marker," then it is defined as a thing with certain properties. This prevents one from solving the problem of writing and re-writing things publicly in different ways such as by using the wall itself as the blackboard. The desire for creative solutions should focus on the value layer first. The instrumental value of the blackboard is to have a flexible place to write or draw which is public to a group or class. This value does not have to be realised by a special thing. Creativity is set free to conceive the solution in any way that serves this instrumental value.

Each layer outlines a specific boundary that separates the things that are objects of the concept from those that are not. These boundaries are not identical, as illustrated with the observation that illusions occur due to discrepancies between the perceptual and the systemic content. In addition, there may be advantages in focusing on the value dimension when looking for innovation because it differs from systemic border drawing. How we prioritise the borders is a question of convention and strategy. All layers are necessary. The perceptive layer is needed to relate to the surrounding world. The systemic layer is needed to enable thought and reflection. The value layer is needed in order to motivate and innovate.

In any concept these three layers can be made distinguishable and their integration is important for the concept to function. Although the systemic layer defines the concept through logical relations to other concepts, the other layers may also be characterised by a description made by means of other concepts. Thus, innovative processes do not destroy the conceptual system; they redefine some of the relations.

Criteria

There are other mechanisms that can influence the border drawing. It is unavoidable that we sometimes face complications when we use layers in conceptual content to delimit the group of objects that fall under the concept. Different layers outline different borders. The standard convention is that the systemic layer should outline the conceptual border supported by the perceptual recognition—which, however, is defeasible. In other situations it may be advantageous to change priorities. Borders may be vague in situations where we need sharp borders, and borders may appear subjective in that different actors outline the borders differently although common border drawings are needed. In such cases, criteria that delimit the border may be convenient. Control and thus practice almost always need operative criteria. An example: colours. The perception of colour varies amongst actors. This has resulted in the construction of simple criteria: a procedure using Ishihara plates to identify various types of colour perception. Instead of arguing over the subjective perception of colours, the criteria enable one to objectively subdivide people according to their colour perception.

A criterion is a test procedure, i.e. a sequence of actions, that provides an objective answer to the question of whether an object falls within a concept or not—any competent person can take or administer the test, and the result does not depend on the person who makes it. Consider again colours: one may define colours technically by reference to the length of the light waves they reflect. After measuring the light waves, one can determine the colour by looking it up in a table that defines the colours by light waves—long waves being red, short waves being blue to violet, with the other colours in between. Here, we see how criteria are based on creating evidence, in this case measuring wavelengths that are translated to colours by means of established colour charts. The whole system of operating with evidence is established through advanced working with concepts.

The demand for precision in technological control triggers an extensive use of criteria in technological concepts. Similarly, the modern state's desire to control the population and its activities has generated a boom of conceptual criteria for enabling bureaucratic control. The criteria range from powerful criteria for contractual bonuses to "dumbed down" criteria for the work procedures of blue collar workers. Due to lack of conceptual analysis, these criteria are often highly problematic. Technological criteria have to withstand a pragmatic testing, whereas there seems to be lack of testing of the reasonability of the criteria in the state's apparatus for administrative performance control. Additional research in managerial accounting and control is needed to prevent the state from making itself absurd by additional decoupling criteria and conceptual content in its operations. Criteria need a reason in order to not be arbitrary. This reason is their relation to the systemic or the value layer. If the reason is unclear or missing, the criteria change and develop according to biased interests at odds with acceptable legitimisation.

Communicative Tradition

In an educated and enlightened world the symbolic representation of the concept is presumed to relate to the objects via the understanding provided by the conceptual content or their associated criteria. However, this may not be the case. Autocratic willpower or traditional communicative practice may relate the concept to things that are not in accordance with the conceptual content.

The layers, the criteria and the communicative tradition can all outline different borders. The differences may be anything from insignificant to radical. We need a cognitive strategy to handle these differences and guide their integration such that practice can function in an intelligible way. This strategy influences the formation of the very concept of concepts and thus the cognitive culture. How borders are handled should depend on the context. The enlightened way is normally to determine the borders by the systemic layer. In everyday contexts, simple and sharp borders may be irrelevant and confusing. In scientific analysis and discussion, clear perceptual and systemic content involving clear ideas about borders is important. In operation and control contexts, criteria are essential for creating the necessary sharp borders. In innovative contexts, new perspectives involving possible new borders are inevitable, as shown in Figure 3.2.

Working with Concepts

Definitions

Concepts are defined in a variety of ways. In *demonstrative* definitions one points at typical exemplars and leaves it to the pupil herself to make the abstractions needed to construct a perceptual pattern (Rosch 1978). Remembering that concepts are exclusive, it must somehow be clear how the exemplar chosen differs from other things. It is complicated to introduce the relevant possibilities in a demonstrative definition, amongst others because pointing out specific exemplars does not suffice, one needs to illustrate how possibilities are realised.

In *verbal* definitions a concept is explained by means of other concepts and phrases. Verbal definitions outline the relations between concepts as in the systemic layer. In everyday practice, it is expedient to combine demonstrative and verbal definitions.

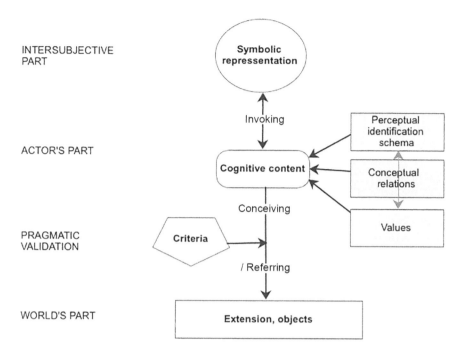

INTERSUBJECTIVE
PART

ACTOR'S PART

PRAGMATIC
VALIDATION

WORLD'S PART

Symbolic
repressentation

Invoking

Cognitive content

Perceptual
identification
schema

Conceptual
relations

Values

Conceiving

Criteria

/ Referring

Extension, objects

Figure 3.2 Elements of a Concept

Theoretical work generally relies on definitions pertaining to the systemic layer, whereas empirical work concerns the use of perceptual patterns to organise observations and data collection. It is, however, generally presumed that the systemic determinations of the theory can be *operationalised*, i.e. be translated to perceptual patterns to enable observation of the conceptual objects. Such operationalisations are necessary for the system of concepts to constitute a knowledge field.

None of the definitions explain why we have a certain concept or why we need it, although that is the most important thing about a concept. The definitions seem to be focused on establishing a way to introduce the concept by drawing the boundary and identifying the objects contained within the boundary, but they give the actor no understanding of her concepts. The inability of definitions to include the value layer causes technical concepts to have no inherent relation to values, and the theories therefore to become reductionistic, making them existentially uninteresting and alienating.

In addition, explaining a concept by defining its object is a mistake. Wittgenstein's dictum: 'look for the use', also applies here. The meaning of a concept and its basic value is the role it plays in reality construction (see also Fodor 1998). Once this is understood, the work with the other aspects of the concept, such as how to define it and mould its boundaries, makes sense.

Practice is based on the use of generalisations. The source of these generalisations is the concepts with which the actors organise the set-up and control of intentional activities. In a static society, the concepts will be static, too, and the conceptual layers will be moulded to create 'harmonious' concepts. In developing societies where knowledge and technologies always change, the concepts constantly change as well. Their internal structure is challenged and the layers point in different directions. Although exciting, such process involves confusion and arbitrariness and consequential insecurity. Skills to advanced development of operating concepts are much needed instruments to transform confusion to organisation of dynamic development.

Developmental dynamics cannot be realised without adequate conceptual development. When we involve people in the development of practice by training them in the analysis, development and changing of concepts, we make those people competent actors who participate in the development rather than people who are victims of it. The skill of working with concepts, to analyse the possibilities of the various layers and their interplay under new conditions, can be enhanced by advanced learning, education and training. If the actors' skill of conceptual reflection is not developed, then change produces chaos.

Conceptual Illusions

Working with conceptual borders can create conceptual illusions in several ways. The illusion does not exist in the concept itself. However all the border-outlining elements do outline different borders. Thus, it is easy to see that statements that are based on one type of border—for instance traditional reference—are understood as being based on a different type of border—for instance the systemic border. Such statements create the illusion that they pertain to the systemic content. Such errors may be intentional. To avoid such errors it is necessary that the parties reflect the way the concept is used. The concepts only produce illusions if the actors tacitly assume that there is only one border, to which all users adhere. Without training in conceptual reflection, actors may find themselves in a situation where it is difficult for them to maintain the exclusivity of concepts and they become unable to distinguish cognitively between those objects that do and those that do not fall within a concept. Then the distinction becomes opportunistic, and knowledge tends to reduce to issues of belief and political correctness.

Reflection

A scientific approach for creative development of concepts and theories is based on reflection and insight, and hence rejection of dogmatic attitudes.

The conceptual logic used to introduce the concepts is based on creating clusters of concepts that complement each other, as for instance the concepts of a family hierarchy, the service on the table or types of clothing etc. These clusters of conceptual relations function in ordinary language games. However, we are confronted with problems that are much more complex. Things must have meaning; they must make sense to our values and therefore many types of overall conceptual structures are needed to interconnect the various parts of our conceptual framework. The development of conceptual structures presupposes skills in working with concepts and conceptual understanding. The logical relations in the conceptual network are dynamic and not fixed. They develop with ongoing reflection and help provide answers to increasingly difficult questions. The discovery of a question is the beginning of a series of empirical and conceptual discoveries because the question itself is a first conceptual discovery, before observations and theorising. It is a discovery that there may be an answer to that which the question calls and looks for. Without conceptual reflection we cannot learn and get wiser.

Notes

1 Compare Piere's thesis that science is self-correcting (cf. Mayo 2005).
2 Compare Kant's (1787) statement: concepts without precepts are empty; precepts without concepts are blind.
3 Compare Deleuze's analysis of concepts (1994).

References

Austin, John L. 1950 (1979). *Truth*. Oxford: Oxford University Press.
Bennett, Maxwell, and Peter Hacker. 2008. *History of Cognitive Neuroscience*. Oxford: Wiley-Blackwell.
Brandom, Robert. 1994. *Making It Explicit: Reasoning, Representing, and Discursive Commitment*. Cambridge, MA: Harvard University Press.
Carey, Susan. 1985. *Conceptual Change in Childhood*. Cambridge. MA: MIT Press.
Carruthers, Peter. 2000. *Phenomenal Consciousness: A Naturalistic Theory*. New York: Cambridge University Press.
Cummins, Robert. 1998. "Reflections on reflective equilibrium." In *Rethinking Intuition and Its Role in Philosophical Inquiry*, edited by Michael DePaul and William Ramsey, 113–127. Lanham, MD: Rowman and Littlefield.
Davidson, Donald. 1975. *Inquiries into Truth and Interpretation*. Oxford: Oxford University Press.
Deleuze, Gilles, and Félix Guattari 1994. *What Is Philosophy?* New York: Columbia University Press.
Dummet, Michael. 1993. *Seas of Language*. Oxford: Oxford University Press.
Fodor, Jerry. 1998. *Concepts: Where Cognitive Science Went Wrong*. Oxford: Clarendon Press.
Gopnick, Alison, and Andrew Meltzhoff. 1997. *Words, Thoughts and Theories*. Cambridge, MA: MIT Press.

Hempel, Carl G. 1950. "Problems and changes in the empiricist criterion of meaning." *Revue internationale de Philosophie*, 41 (11): 41–63.

James, William. 1909 (1979). *The Meaning of Truth*. Cambridge, MA: Harvard University Press.

Kant, Immanuel. 1787 (1998). *Critique of Pure Reason (Kritik der reinen Vernunft)*. Cambridge: Cambridge University Press.

Kenny, Anthony. 2010. "Concepts, brain, and behavior." *Grazer Philosophische Studien*, 81 (1): 105–113.

Mayo, Deborah G. 2005. "Peircean induction and the error-correcting thesis." *Transactions of the Charles S. Peirce Society A Quarterly Journal in American Philosophy*, 41 (2): 299–319.

Millikan, Ruth G. 2000. *On Clear and Confused Ideas*. Cambridge: Cambridge University Press.

Nørreklit, Hanne, Lennart Nørreklit, and Falconer Mitchell. 2007. "Theoretical conditions for validity in accounting performance measurement." In *Business Performance Measurement—Frameworks and Methodologies*, edited by Andy Neely, 179–217. Cambridge: Cambridge University Press.

Nørreklit, Lennart. 1973. *Concepts: Their Nature and Significance for Metaphysics and Methodology*. Odense: Odense University Press.

Nørreklit, Lennart. 2011. "Actors and reality: A conceptual framework for creative governance." In *An Actor's Approach to Management: Conceptual Framework and Company Practices*, edited by Morten Jakobsen, Inga-Lill Johanson and Hanne Nørreklit, 7–37. Copenhagen: DJOEF.

Nørreklit, Lennart. 2013. "Applied ethics and practice ontology." In *Theoretical and Applied Ethics*, edited by Hannes Nykänen, Ole Preben Riis and Jörg Zeller, 143–72. Aalborg: Aalborg University Press.

Ogden, Charles K., and Ivor A. Richard. 1923 (1989). *The Meaning of Meaning*. Orlando, FL: Harcourt Brace Jovanovich.

Pfeffer, Jeffrey, and Robert I. Sutton. 2000. *The Knowing-Doing Gap: How Smart Companies Turn Knowledge into Action*. Boston: Harvard Business School Press.

Popper, Karl R. 1963. *Conjectures and Refutations: The Growth of Scientific Knowledge*. London: Routledge, Psychology Press.

Putnam, Hilary. 1981. *Reason, Truth and History*. Cambridge: Cambridge University Press.

Quine, Willard V.O. 1951. "Two dogmas of empiricism." *The Philosophical Review*, 60: 20–43.

Rosch, Eleanor. 1978. "Principles of categorization." In *Cognition and Categorization*, edited by Eleanor Rosch and Barbara Lloyd, 27–48. Hillsdale, NJ: Lawrence Erlbaum Associates.

Searle, John R. 1995. *The Construction of Social Reality*. New York: The Free Press.

Tinker, Anthony M. 1991. "The accountant as partisan." *Accounting, Organizations and Society*, 16 (3): 297–310.

Torrey, Fuller E. 1986. *Witchdoctors and Psychiatrists: The Common Roots of Psychotherapy and Its Future*. New York: Harper & Row Publishers.

Tucker, Basil, and Lee D. Parker. 2014. "In our ivory towers? The research-practice gap in management accounting: An academic perspective." *Accounting and Business Research*, 44 (2): 104–143.

Urry, John. 2005. "The complexities of the global." *Theory, Culture Society*, 22 (5): 235–254.

Weinberg, Jonathan, Shaun Nichols, and Stephen Stich. 2001. "Normativity and epistemic intuitions." *Philosophical Topics*, 29 (1–2): 429–460.

Williamson, T. 2005. "Armchair philosophy, metaphysical modality and counterfactual thinking." *Proceedings of the Aristotelian Society*, 105 (1): 1–23.

Wilson, John. 1969. *Thinking with Concepts*. New York: Cambridge University Press.

Wittgenstein, Ludwig. 1953. *Philosophical Investigations*. Oxford: Basil Blackwell.

Young, James O. 1995. *Global Anti-Realism*. Aldershot: Avebury.

Part II

Decision-Making and Performance Management

4   Reflective Planning and Decision-Making

Hanne Nørreklit, Falconer Mitchell and Lars Braad Nielsen

Introduction

This chapter is concerned with the production and use of management accounting in organisational planning and decision-making. Conventional wisdom of organisational planning is dominated by the cybernetic paradigm of control (Beer 1959; Anthony and Govindarajan 2007; Merchant and van der Stede 2007). More specifically, the planning and decision-making process involves the successive step-by-step process of goal formulation, identification of alternative plans of achieving the goals, and decision-making to select a specific plan. Subsequently, the plans decided upon are implemented and their progress is monitored. The organisational levels are linked together by deploying strategic goals hierarchically i.e. top-down from the strategic level to the management level and then to the level of tasks. The basis of the cybernetic approach to planning and decision-making is that the management has correctly formulated the company strategy and when deployed hierarchically and top-down, the system of goals is coherent with the company strategy. Also, the human brain is perceived as a self-regulating machine, which implies that the goal setting and linking of negative/positive feedback to the goal achievement will trigger human corrective actions to ensure that results conform to the goal (Beer 1959).

Additionally, the conventional approach to planning and decision-making includes the production of accounting information (Anthony and Govindarajan 2007; Merchant and van der Stede 2007). Thus, developing and deciding on alternative opportunities require knowledge of alternative courses of action and information on their consequences (March 1978, 587). To support the attainment of information for decision-making outputs, the cybernetic planning and decision-model has been complemented and supplemented by economic, statistical and operational techniques to enable forecasting based on historical data (March 1987; Scapens 1991; Nielsen et al. 2015). It is assumed that trustworthy information about alternative actions can be obtained through a scientific process.

However, research documents that the human capabilities to formulate alternative courses of actions and estimate their future consequences are limited and uncertain (Simon 1986; March 1987). In practice, planning and decision-making is thus based on subjective anticipation and estimation of the alternatives and their future consequences (Merchant and van der Stede 2007). In particular, when faced with strategically important and complex organisational tasks, information uncertainty can be high. Moreover, the problem of uncertainty in respect of the production of alternative decision plans and the accounting information regarding their implications are activated in the organisational context of multiple decision-participants. Most organisations comprise coalitions of decision-makers who hold subjective and potentially conflicting preferences or values which can be fuzzy and change over time (Cyert and March 1963). Consequently, the employees may manipulate their data production in accord with their own values and in conflict with organisational values. Also, strategic planning and decision-making can be complex social activities that might take place in different departments and situations, where the reflective managers might be strategizing in an ongoing process of social doing and becoming (Carter et al. 2008). Thus, organisations involve a number of human aspirations and ongoing activities that need to be juggled and balanced (Parker 1979). Finally, as planning and decision-making are integrated with execution, these might not be physically separated from the processes of implementing and monitoring as suggested by the cybernetic paradigm.

The shortcomings of the cybernetic approach to planning and decision-making do not imply that the management accounting tools for such purposes are obsolete. Indeed, management accounting might contribute to the establishment of connected structures of intentionality across organisational activities that mobilise the individual's actions towards the achievement of what is perceived as organisational objectives (Ahrens and Chapman 2007). However, there is a need for developing the organisational planning and decision models to make them match the complexity of practical reality involving a high degree of information uncertainty and a coalition of decision-participants. Drawing on the practice paradigm of pragmatic constructivism (Nørreklit et al. 2006, 2007; Nørreklit 2011; Nørreklit 2017, Chapter 2, this volume), this paper outlines a framework for how organisations, when confronted with a complex planning and decision situation, can structure their planning and decision analyses and incorporate management accounting information into it.

The paper is structured as follows: in the next section, we outline the core concepts of a pragmatic constructivist approach in order to understand organisational planning and decision-making in a dynamic organisational context of multiple actors working with strategic important tasks; in relation to this, core dimensions of a conceptual framework for planning and decision-making that incorporates accounting information is established; following this, two case studies demonstrate how the conceptual dimensions unfold in competent practices; finally, we conclude the analysis and point to needs for further research.

Planning and Decision-Making Framework

Multiple Actors' Creation of Construct Causalities

Pragmatic constructivism acknowledges that individual and organisational actors construct their relationship to the world. When making plans and decisions, the actors project different configurations for future actions and constructs. Whether the configurations projected and considered by an individual or a company are illusionary or feasible depends on their relation with reality. To create a successful basis for undertaking actions, the four dimensions of reality—facts, possibilities, values and communication—need to be integrated. Thus, for the actors to make their plans work in practice, i.e. for creating construct causality, the projected constructs must be integrated with facts—i.e. factual possibilities not speculative ones. Furthermore, the plans must express the subjective values that motivate the people involved and be within the range of the factual possibilities. Finally, communication must convey this integrated structure of facts, possibilities and values among the people involved.

The individual actor's or group of actors' specific structure of integration forming construct causality is labelled topos. However, an organisation does not run by a single topos, but by a set of topoi. Different types of knowledge topoi such as technological, social, business and financial are involved in the establishment of construct causality in the various activities. For the organisation to create a set of construct causalities, a pragmatic integration of the four dimensions has to be made for each activity in interaction with other activities, i.e. an integration where each activity creates a set of construct causalities that work successfully together with other activities. Thus, the actors operating in the various organisational units must create construct causalities that fit rather well together on all levels. They must complement or support each other to function and cooperate effectively. This fitting together is termed practical coherence, which constitutes the cooperation of larger integrated units. Practical coherence should be expressed conceptually in the communication that connects the units. Thus, there is an overall topos embedding a conceptual coherence between the concepts of the operating actors that enable them to establish practical coherence.

In this analysis, strategy is considered to be about creating and enacting an overarching topos that aims to make specialised departmental topoi create construct causality together in interaction with their environment, i.e. to create practical coherence among operating actors over time. It comprises a business topos that concentrates on practical aspects of creating an overarching form of construct causality throughout the whole value chain to make the set of interrelated topoi running the company successful together. Also, a part of creating an overarching form of construct causality is that the financial topos is integrated into the strategy topos running the organisation and, thereby, implying that the financial consequences of the different configurations considered are taken into account.

Uncertainty in Accounting Measurement

For planning and decision-making, management accounting includes various conceptual models and techniques for calculating the financial consequences of future actions. Aiming to cohere with the institutional construction of economic reality, the accountants require relevant costs for the purposes of planning and decision-making. However, relevant costs are conditional, depending on the decision context. Accordingly, there is a need for a method to conceptualise an accounting model, structuring the financial consequences of the specific business topoi. The business topoi frame the planning and decision-making problem and, hence, should shape the accounting planning and decision-making model. Companies need to structure their planning and decision analyses in relation to a specific practice and incorporate management accounting information into it.

Additionally, planning and decision-making relate to the actors' perception of what may be factually possible and valuable in the future. In some contexts, construct causality can be established, implying that rather deterministic calculations of action and future consequences can be made from facts. However, in more dynamic organisational settings where factual possibilities and human values are changing, information uncertainty about construct causality is always present. That is, when calculating the financial consequences of the alternatives, information is uncertain due to the actors' insufficient knowledge about the practical and financial dimensions of creating construct causality. Also, the actors' values may conflict with the organisational values, thus potentially incentivising the actors to manipulate the data production to the benefit of their own values (March 1987).

Accordingly, the challenges of the planning and decision-making models are to have a trustworthy accounting model that shapes the company's business topos and to produce trustworthy information about the company's creation of construct causalities.

Pro-active, Pragmatic and Learning Theory of Truth

From the perspective of pragmatic constructivism, uncertainty in the accounting model and information for planning and decision-making is related to whether actor expectations hold in the future (pragmatic truthfulness). However, because no actor can access the truth of his expectations before events have happened, only a pro-active truth can exist at the point of decision-making. A truth gap is created between pro-active true information (expectations) and pragmatic true information (actual outcomes), which leads to uncertainty (Nørreklit et al. 2007; Mitchell et al. 2013). This uncertainty in pro-active information for decision-making is triggered by insufficient knowledge about the structure of integration forming construct causality in the set of activities; i.e. the lack of pragmatic truth is related to uncertainty in facts, factual possibilities, values (goals) and communication.

Uncertainty can be managed by working on the dimensions of integration forming construct causalities.

This pragmatic view of information uncertainty related to the management of construct causalities differs from the traditional calculative-based rational choice view concerned with uncertainty in relation to issues such as observing and predicting events, actions, cause-effects and preferences in relation to a utility maximisation decision problem. The traditional calculative choice model neglects the human reflective aspects of constructing factual possibilities and human values.

As a result, conceptualisation of the business topos and anticipation of future consequences of planned actions and activities require a skilful and intelligent practice concerning observation and assessment of the level of integration, i.e. construct causality. A reflective learning perspective, where the pro-active perspective on planning and decision-making meets the pragmatic perspective, is required. Such a learning theory of truth involves numerous stages of problematisation, diagnostics and conceptual development that starts from a pre-understanding of the planning and decision-making situation, continues with the creation of a deeper understanding of the possibility of creating construct causality in relation to the phenomenon, and ends with a post-understanding providing sound insights into the construction of construct causality. To generate valid pro-active statements about the construct causalities, the conceptual apparatus used must be based on the three criteria of phenomenological grounding, correspondence, and complete coherence. The phenomenological aspect ensures sufficient empirical grounding of accounting information in well-defined data to avoid subjectivity and lack of validity. Finally, in the absence of analysis of coherence, no statement can provide any reliable expectations about real world phenomena. The difference between pragmatic and pro-active truth constitutes the truth gap. Knowledge creation is an iterative and reflective process in which the actor(s) undertake(s) conceptual development to continuously improve the level of insight and diagnostic certainty in order to establish a pragmatic truth construct causality. In this way, the truth gap is diminished (Nørreklit et al. 2007).

Orchestrating the Co-Authorship of Multiple Actors' Planning and Decision-Making

The presence of multiple topoi implies that the creation of knowledge to establish construct causality is not an entirely individual matter of integrating facts, possibilities and values. Rather, it is a social process in which the actors' individual efforts to create construct causalities are interconnected to co-authorise a complex set of functioning construct causalities. Thus, establishing cooperation among multiple actor efforts directed towards creating construct causalities that work successfully together presupposes that management is involved (co-authorship).

Following an actor-based procedure, co-authorship involves a social process comprising three integration processes: subjectification, externalisation and objectification (Arbnor and Bjerke 1997, 175–178). Initially, each actor brings to the table his expertise, observations and experience from previous engagements, all of which represent his *subjective* view of the factual possibilities. In interaction with other actors, a process of *externalisation* subsequently occurs in which the various understandings of valuable factual possibilities are *communicated*, and challenged individually and against each other. In this way, the individual actor's understanding of the situation is advanced through dialogue and reflection. Systematic observations of facts form a basis for the actors' observations and reflections on the degree of construct causality and their learning process to continuously improve the knowledge system and develop language. The participants are creatively and logically challenged to describe issues and search (together) for the re-creative development of conceptual models that will increase insights. As a result, information is *objectified* as the set of beliefs and model estimates that 1) correspond with factual observations, individual actor expertise and experience, and 2) cohere across executive areas (social acceptance). When plans and decisions are made, the objectified plans are to be integrated with material things, and human and social processes. During this process, it becomes clear if the pro-active true objectified plan is pragmatically true.

As on the individual level, this analysis leads to a framework of practical validity and truth, which can be applied to accounting in the form of a learning model that continuously improves the validity of pro-actively true accounting information.

Company Cases on Planning and Decision-Making

In this section, we will demonstrate two cases of how companies draw on pragmatic constructivism methodology to create trustworthy information in a context of multiple actors. The concern of the cases is the managers' topoi and their relationship to the management of uncertainty in pro-active information initiated by the lack of pragmatically true knowledge about the dimensions of integration forming construct causality. The two empirical cases[1] illustrate methodological aspects in relation to structuring the planning and decision-making process, and the creation and use of accounting information with a view to analysing how uncertainty can be addressed. The first case illustrates how a division manager evaluates the local managers' budgets. Thus, the case is about co-authorship between two topoi placed at different hierarchical levels. The second case illustrates how a company structures decision-making on product development from the early stages of idea generation through concept development to the final stages of full-scale production and business evaluation. This case focusses on co-authorship across different functional topoi.

Case A: Validation of Local Managers' Budgets[2]

Consider a division manager of a division selling a wide range of building materials to professional customers. The division consists of 45 units organised as autonomous investment centres, each with its own local manager. Each investment centre is strategically limited to its business area, i.e. its products and market segments. Apart from that, however, it enjoys considerable freedom as regards sourcing, sales, choice of product mix, and day-to-day management. The division has realised strong financial results in recent years and the local managers are very satisfied with the division manager's performance.

The division has a fairly comprehensive and formalised planning and reporting system with budgeting and planning organised as bottom-up processes. The divisions are measured as investment centres on the basis of EVA. In addition, the market share and the monthly turnover rate of accounts receivable and of stock are measured. The division manager's measurement philosophy states that it is necessary to have sufficient information in order to feel confident when assessing how things develop.

The Budget Validation Scheme

The division manager's validity assessment of the local managers is mainly effected through managerial communication at budget meetings in which the division manager and the local managers participate. Meetings are held regularly and the agenda includes items such as debate on the business plan, follow-up on the plan, and motivation to strive for efficiency and performance. When evaluating the local managers' budget, the division manager analyses their business topoi. The local managers' business topoi include their reflections on how to infer the activities necessary to go from the existing reality construction to another future reality construction. Any reasoned or well-argued budget is based on valid business topoi, which implies that they have to express a solid understanding of the nature of integration in order to successfully guide organisational action.

In validating the business topoi, the division manager assesses the pro-active truth of the local managers' action plans and budgets. Thus, his view is that budgets must be realistic. The targets are consciously set by the local managers at an achievable level (i.e. factually possible), while guarding against budget targets that are too optimistic or pessimistic. The division manager tries to assess the pro-active truth of the budget data and plans for each local manager through a dialogical communication strategy which enables him to assess the integration of the local manager's business topoi. Below, we explain core elements of his validation of pro-active truth.

Validation of the Pro-Active Truth of the Budgets

Pragmatic True Facts

It is fundamental for the division manager's assessment that he can rely on local managers to communicate openly, honestly and clearly. Thus, he checks whether the facts claimed are consistent over time and thereby pragmatically true. More specifically, the division manager writes down major points of agreement in a "little black book" i.e. the factual basis of the budget. When the division manager visits a local manager to discuss an agenda previously agreed, the division manager consults the "little black book".

An example of how honesty is checked is the control of the investment centres' accounts receivable. Once, when the division manager was paying a visit to a local manager, the local manager mentioned a customer with an accounts receivable balance of €50,000, saying "but it's still below the €60,000 we agreed upon last time". The division manager opened his black book, looked at it and said, "Yes, that is true". Also, he checks that the company's policies are followed. For example, he regularly checks the debtors of the investment centres and any centre with unapproved debtors has to submit an explanation.

In checking the consistency of the information provided by the local manager, the division manager checks whether he can trust the factual information included in the local manager's topoi. By assessing to what extent the company rules are respected, the division manager checks whether the local manager's topoi imply that the values and social topoi outlined by the headquarters are understood and followed.

Integration of Factual Possibilities and Local Values

In evaluating the factual possibility of the plan, it is important to try to assess the local manager's judgement and, in particular, to assess how confident he is in the integration embedded in his own plans. Especially in a situation in which the structure of the division includes autonomous investment centres, the assessment is critically important because responsibility and control have been decentralised. If the manager in charge of the centre exercises poor judgement, it will, ceteris paribus, decrease the performance of his unit.

During budget meetings, the division manager listens to the local manager's budget proposal expressing values, possibilities and the factual conditions. Then, he challenges the proposal partly by disclosing the subjective judgement involved, and partly through the negation of factual assumptions:

> "When I meet with the local managers, they have described their plans and I ask them what they have not described. What are you afraid of? If there is a problem, I ask them what they feel like doing about it, and then they find the solution."

Thus, the division manager attempts to uncover the local manager's perception of the extent to which the budget topoi will work in practice and, consequently, the extent to which facts, possibilities and values are integrated. The division manager questions weak factual possibilities and value support in the plan. If there is a problem, the division manager's enquiries induce the local manager to find solutions which may negate the non-supporting fact, weak possibilities and values.

In applying his communication model, the division manager not only checks but also strengthens the judgement of the local manager and so improves his ability to control the centre. Specifically, if the local manager is uncertain about how to create integration, then the division manager applies his communication strategy in an attempt to *encourage* him to find ways to build integration. In a way, this resembles the hermeneutic method used by Socrates to make his pupils find the truth themselves. The division manager asks questions and lets the local manager search for answers or recognise sustainable topoi through his own reflections. This is very different from a leadership style by which the decisions are made on behalf of the local manager because this induces him to continuously *learn* by doing. In this Socratic way of orchestrating co-authorship, the division manager helps the local manager strengthen his business topoi and his judgement of the factual, as well as the possibility and value, dimensions. Contrary to this, the absolute decisions made under a top-down leadership style weaken the business topoi and the judgement of subordinates.

Integration with Divisional Topoi

Part of evaluating the integration is to match the local topoi of the local managers with the social or overall company expectations (the topoi of the division). The division manager emphasises that the firm has a goal, which is embedded in the plan for the next few years. "We are men at work", as he puts it. He wants the local managers to produce better results each year; and if, for some reason, this is not possible, he demands three reasons for the stagnation or lack of target fulfilment, and three ways of improving the results. Accordingly, the local manager´s subjective values need be aligned with the core social values of the division.

This is why the division manager assesses the extent to which the external conditions of a particular investment centre fit the factual possibilities embedded in the business topoi used by its manager. Specifically, the division manager tries to make the centre managers see their factual possibilities from a different perspective, thus inducing them to develop the business topoi:

> "All investment centres have elderly customers, but the elderly customers are not the ones who bring in large orders and new growth opportunities. For example, a local manager sold primarily to elderly customers. I asked him to stake more on new customers. I know what is going on."

In essence, the division manager tries to influence the local manager to change his plan of action and budget assumptions, meaning the division manager tries to change the local manager's perception of factual possibilities. The division manager was not able to mobilise the will and energy of the local manager to attract new customers. The local manager did not have the requisite values and would not attempt to catch the interest of new customers. Therefore, his business topos was not sufficiently integrated with company values and hence the topos was not valid. As the division manager considers it important to motivate local managers to try new factually based possibilities and realise them, he replaced this particular local manager.

Historical Abilities to Create Pragmatic True Results

The division manager grounds a great deal of his total assessment on the local manager's previous results. The successful managers can look for new, although risky, possibilities that may create more value to the company. As most local managers like a high degree of autonomy, the division manager motivates them to pursue their own values. However, his trust and confidence in the local manager's business topoi are proportional to the local manager's historical ability to generate sufficient profit. Overall, if an investment centre is doing well, it will not get much attention; but if a local manager is not performing, the division manager will intensify the dialogues with the local manager in an attempt to strengthen his business topoi. It is apparent that the historical ability to meet profit targets may be used as a significant indication of the pro-active truth of the local manager's business topoi. Hence, the ability to create pragmatic truth is used as an indication of pro-active truth. A truth gap gives rise to an intensive learning process driven by the division manager.

Sub-Conclusion

On this basis, we can conclude that the evaluation of the integration of the local managers' business topoi is crucial when the division manager validates the local manager's action plan and budget. Evaluating the integration of local manager's business topos, the division manager assesses the extent to which the local managers: 1) are trustworthy in their communication of facts (i.e. pragmatically true facts); 2) believe in the factual possibilities of *their own plans* (i.e. integration of factual possibilities within the local managers' values and the overall strategy of the company); 3) integrate divisional values; and 4) have demonstrated the ability to create financial results meeting the targets (i.e. pragmatic truth). This constitutes the consideration of the pro-active truth of the budget presented. If the integration is weak, the division manager may not accept the budget as pro-active truth.

In brief, the division manager, when judging the local managers' plans, considers the financial results and the extent to which the managers are trustworthy and integrate the outlined company strategy. Teaching subordinates to make pragmatically true plans based on their own judgements is important, but avoiding too many wrong decisions is equally important (as is avoiding any lack of decisions). When the division manager, through dialogical and knowledgeable communication, challenges the local manager's business topos, it becomes obvious to what extent the local manager accepts the construct causality of his own plans and budget. Through a Socratic way of questioning, the division manager becomes co-author of the local managers' business plans.

Case B[3]: Planning and Decision-Making

MED is a large Danish company with approximately 7,500 employees selling products and services to people with medical problems in more than 65 countries. The company is structured around the executive areas of Research and Development (R&D), Manufacturing Operations, and Marketing and Sales. For more than half a century, the company and its employees have developed core competences and technologies around the key value of making daily life easier for people with the particular illness in which they specialise. In addition, sustainable profitability and operational stability are key strategic values. The core values are an integrated part of the communication and reflection at all levels in the company.

In what follows next, we will elaborate on how the creation of construct causality in relation to new product development is organised in MED, and, subsequently, how accounting information is produced and used in support of the planning and decision-making processes.

Organising the Creation of Construct Causalities

Innovation Stream Funnel

The planning and decision-making process is structured around an Innovation Value Stream (IVS) funnel (see Figure 4.1). The IVS is a funnel that structures product development from the early stages of idea generation through concept development to the final stages of full-scale production, sales and business evaluation. Specifically, a new development project starts on the basis of ongoing value propositions driven by the core competences, matching the company's overall strategy and the needs and potentials identified in the market by Marketing. These value propositions are transformed into Target Product Profiles, which specify the needs and potential that the products are expected to satisfy/target if manufactured. Subsequently, the selected product profiles enter a so-called "Accelerate Ideas to Market process" within IVS, which divides the product development into several reflective stages. The aim throughout the various stages of the funnel is to reach successively higher states of knowledge certainty about technologies, players and activities and, hence, functioning construct causalities.

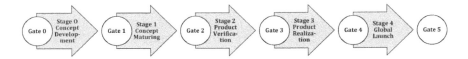

Figure 4.1 Innovation Value Stream Funnel

At the initial stages of the funnel, great uncertainty exists with respect to product specifications on both the supplier side and the customer side. The uncertainty relates to possible products and not to existing products. However, core competences formulated by the management group are a given denominator that drives the construction of realistic possibilities throughout the entire IVS process. Hence, the number of product possibilities is confined. At decision gate 1, a maximum of three concepts is selected for further maturing. At the subsequent stage 1 of the funnel, great uncertainty exists with respect to product specifications, thereby leaving many open-ended questions on both the supplier side and the customer side. At decision gate 2, the number of concepts is narrowed down to one, and the design specifications and tolerances are frozen while parts of the supply chain are put in place. The product design is verified from a technical as well as business perspective. After gate 2, the process specifications for manufacturing are finalised. At decision gate 3, all product and manufacturing process specifications are locked in, equipment for in-house production is procured and supplier contracts not already established at decision gate 1 or 2 are settled. In this respect, decision gate 3 represents the point of no return. It is where the techniques and money are committed. At this gate, there is an integration of what is factually possible and valuable at the product and machinery side and the supply chain side. At the final stage 4, the full launch of the product takes place, where the real customer demand and sales become factual. The business project is closed and evaluated at decision gate 5.

Overall, it is apparent that as the innovation project proceeds, the product, the productions processes, and the market conditions etc. change from being mainly a matter of possibilities and values to become increasingly factual. The IVS funnel produces integration of facts and possibilities in new constructs fulfilling the core values. In short, during the stages, the functioning causalities are constructed.

Evaluation of Progress in Integration

Product development comprises several stages of reflective activities in which the employees involved aim to construct alternative realistic possibilities in accordance with core values and exclude potential non-realistic possibilities. To ensure ongoing monitoring of progress in construct causality, every stage is succeeded by a decision gate, at which the project is reviewed by a cross-functional group of senior staff members from each executive area. Here, it is critically evaluated whether the technical product requirements, financial objectives and core values are in accordance with what has been set out as objectives. Overall, it is about making a pro-active evaluation of whether the expectations to the development project will hold in the future and become pragmatic truths.

As profitability is a core value, accounting information is produced throughout each of the innovation stages of the IVS funnel. The production of valid accounting information for use in decision-making about the financial feasibility of product alternatives is an integrated part of producing construct causality. If a project does not meet the financial objectives at a decision gate, it will not move forward to the next stage. Either the project is terminated or it returns to an earlier stage for further development/refinement. Also, the objectified information at earlier stages is questioned at later process gates.

Due to project uncertainty, a major challenge is to establish credible information for decision-making at each gate. At the initial stages, the accounting data is very uncertain, but as the project takes shape, the data becomes increasingly definite and factual. The commitment to product specifications and manufacturing facilities at all stages results in increasingly factual expenses and costs whereas the revenues are rather uncertain until the last stage. Therefore, handling the time gap between the commitment to costs and the knowledge of the market is one of the major challenges of MED. Accordingly, it is challenging to evaluate whether the expectations of the projects will hold in the future and become pragmatic truths.

Multiple Topoi

The IVS funnel is all about multiple employees making a product work. Thus, the activities are organised around cross-functional teams, in which the individual actors' expertise and reflections in interaction with others become involved in the construction of possible products fulfilling the core values. There are various types of specialist topoi involved such as the technical, the supply chain, sales and marketing and the financial topoi. Throughout the entire planning and decision process, the focus of the team is on the assessment of both operational feasibility and financial feasibility of possible product constructs. Each stage contains a number of coordinated activities designed to optimise the conceptualisation and manufacturing of the product solution while fulfilling customer needs as well as legal and business requirements. The technical topos and the accounting topos interact with each other to construct technically possible and financially feasible products within the value range. The focal point of the teams throughout the innovation process is the construction of profitable products in interaction with other topoi.

Below, we outline how multiple interacting actors through the entire IVS funnel, simultaneously with constructing technically feasible products, produce and use accounting information with increasing diagnostic certainty for use in decision-making about the financial feasibility of product alternatives.

Multiple Actors' Production of Pro-Active and Pragmatic True Accounting Information

In the IVS funnel, the team draws on accounting information at each of the innovation stages. At the initial intake of product concepts for the concept development process, only a rough business case is constructed. Thus, decisions on product concepts are based on an early evaluation of attractiveness that focus on a preliminary sales forecast, the resources available for R&D and a narrative expression of how the Target Product Profiles fit with the overall corporate strategy. As the product passes through the subsequent stages, team members prepare more detailed plans and information on the possible costs and revenues of the business case to provide an early indication of whether the concept at hand can ever become profitable. A financial model developed by the accounting unit is used to calculate the financial implications. The model outlines three alternatives: 1) the proposal, 2) the "as is" situation, and 3) the best alternative proposal. The model includes key accounting figures such as changes in revenues and direct costs, impact on cash flow, net present value and rate of return, as well as incremental gross profits. Through the various stages of the IVS funnel, the team of actors produce and use pro-active true accounting information for the financial model through a social process facilitating co-authorship.

Co-authoring Pro-Active Truth during the Research and Development Stages 0–2

More specifically, during stage 0, prototypes of the product concept and the required manufacturing machinery are constructed and tested for each alternative. The results from these prototypes are used to revise and elaborate on the business case in order to describe the revenue and cost implications as bases for the performance expected for each project. The evaluation criterion is a target cost profile determined at a higher level in the organisation, specifying the contribution margin required in order to ensure profitability.

When determining the revenue side of the business case, Marketing cooperates with the sales regions to prepare early country-specific forecasts of the expected sales volume if the product concept were to be marketed. Thus, sales estimates are produced by local sales personnel (subjectification). Also, a group of statisticians and market modelling experts repeatedly assess and challenge these estimates for every country using quantitative analyses based on historical market trends for similar products (subjectification). Two planning topoi drive the sales forecast: 1) one based on historical facts of what has been factually possible in the past, and 2) one based on future anticipation of what might be factually possible in the future. The two views are fused and the sales forecast is advanced through reasoning and reflection (externalisation) intended to produce a forecast that can be agreed as realistic (objectification). The reflective interactions between the two are used to make a synthesis of the two ways of making pro-active judgement of whether the projected sales possibilities integrate with facts. This form of triangulation is used to increase the strength of the pro-active judgement of the revenue information used for decision-making. However, the pragmatic truth of the revenues estimates cannot be judged before they are factual at gate 5.

Following the same procedure, the volume estimates are updated as the concept passes through the research and development stages of the IVS funnel. Also, to ensure that the forecasts provided by Marketing meet the organisational values related to realism, incentives are provided through the employee compensation structure so that bonuses partly depend on how accurately the forecasted sales mimic the actual sales. In this way, the employees in Marketing are held accountable for their actions and have no incentive to deliberately manipulate the estimates.

In relation to the cost side of the business case, direct cost estimates are largely determined in collaboration with the engineers at the Technical Competence Centres. They develop the machinery for manufacturing the concepts as they hold extensive knowledge about output per hour as well as the number of people needed to operate the machines and handle the product throughout the manufacturing process. The accountants are involved as sparring partners when cost estimates are made for the various prototypes. Two different costs are usually calculated to imitate both the early phase where the product is manufactured in small numbers at dedicated facilities, and the final phase, when production is moved abroad to large-scale facilities. Furthermore, Manufacturing Operation in interaction with Engineering simulates several configurations of the supply chain to understand which parts of production could potentially be contracted out. Simultaneously, the Supply Chain department obtain offers from alternative suppliers for each non-core item considered for out-sourcing. In this respect, the target cost profile and the estimated cost price of the concept play important roles. Qualitative strategic aspects are also emphasised in an attempt to ensure that the company maintains control of its core competences.

It is apparent that at least three interacting topoi are involved in constructing the product: 1) an engineering topos driving the construction of the prototype and the machinery; 2) a supply chain topos driving the sourcing of the product; and 3) an accounting topos driving the cost calculation of the product. Each of the topos contributes with highly specialised knowledge in the development of the product (subjectification). The engineering topos and supply chain topos drive the construction of factually based possible products, machinery and sourcing within core values. Confronting the two with the costing side, the accounting topos highlights the importance of making profitable constructions. The reflective interaction (externalisation) among the three topoi is used to create a synthesis (objectification) of the various aspects of constructing a feasible product, i.e. a product that is factually possible to produce in an economical way. The interaction between the actors allows for a meaningful reduction in the uncertainty and complexity of the decision parameters under consideration, as the parameters are reflected upon from different angles and weighted against each other.

The business case developed on this basis for each product concept is assessed at decision gate 1. A concept that is not profitable is cancelled or is sent back to stage 0 for further development. Essentially, stage 0 is repeated during stage 1 and 2 as the concepts are refined and matured to provide better and more realistic estimates of the factors in the business case, including the calculation of the financial implications.

The financial model is revised on the basis of updated specifications and estimations. Again, if the design is unprofitable, it is either cancelled or sent back to an earlier stage for further development.

Managing Uncertainty in Pro-Active Truth at the Investment Stage 3

Decision gate 3 coincides with stage 3, when actual production capacity is purchased, supplier contracts are made, and product manufacturing is started. The project expenses and costs are integrated with what is factually possible and within the acceptable value range. However, realised sales remain unknown and estimated sales remain uncertain. To reduce the risk of selecting an improper supply chain set-up inaccurately scaled for actual demand, MED deliberately delays the "full-blown" investment decisions at decision gate 3. The company keeps the possibilities open and hence extends the integration of factual possibilities.

Thus, although extensive preparations and analyses precede decision gate 3, MED remains cautious and risk averse. In order to handle the uncertainty, semi-manual manufacturing and out-sourcing of some product parts are considered while the investment level is increased gradually. Overall, in dealing with the time lag between costs and revenues, employees intervene by postponing major investment decisions to further improve the precision of sales estimates as product samples are tested on customers. In other words, the company aims to obtain a high degree of factual information in the sales estimates before the investment decisions are made. Possibilities at the manufacturing side are kept open through constructing a flexible manufacturing and sourcing platform. Postponing the scaling of manufacturing creates higher direct costs but reduces the possible risk of major investment failures.

Pragmatic Truth after Full Launch at Stage 4

The full launch of the product takes place at decision gate 4. Because most of the product specifications have been frozen and the supply chain has been established at stage 2, information production for the financial model is basically reduced to mechanically updating cost and sales estimates as the final product specifications and supplier quotation prices become known. At stage 4, an information system closely monitors factual sales as MED, in collaboration with its suppliers, has installed a system in hospitals around the world to track the products sold in order to improve operational planning.

Finally, decision gate 5 marks the end of the IVS funnel and functions as a feedback mechanism that helps improve the planning and decision-making for future innovations. Consequently, the market position achieved is evaluated and compared to the forecast position. Moreover, information on actual sales is reported back to the respective executive areas where it can be used for future projects, as described above. The forecasts are based on available historical information for similar products. In other words, at this stage, the company considers whether the production of pro-active true information matches the pragmatic true information as the outcome. The truth gap gives rise to a learning process.

Sub-Conclusion

Generally, the case study illustrates that several topoi interact to create construct causality. The innovation of construct causalities, the construction of alternatives, and the production of accounting information are defined as part of multiple actors' reflective and interactive learning process. An actor-based method orchestrates the co-authorship of the multiple actors' topoi. Thus, their way of interacting follows the social integration processes of subjectification, externalisation and objectification. The reflective interaction between the specialised topoi creates a synthesis of the various aspects related to constructing a feasible product in an economical way.

There is a continuous interchange between pro-active and pragmatic truth in the method that proves valuable and reinforces the learning process, as the models and databases used for costing and forecasting have been repeatedly tested and refined by previous projects. The information produced in the initial stages does not represent facts in a very strict sense, because correspondence to already established facts is impossible to establish due to the lack of a physical product and actual customers. Nevertheless, through the individual actors' experience and expertise and the practical coherence established across disciplines, the information produced is broadly anchored in the company's business reality.

The interaction between the actors allows for a meaningful evaluation of the uncertainty in relation to the various highly specialised aspects of the project. It thus partially assures the feasibility of the consequences envisaged. This precision is further strengthened by the incentive system put in place as it holds the employees accountable for the estimates produced and encourages them to strive for "realistic" costs and revenues. Finally, it should be noted that the company handles uncertainty when establishing pro-active sales volume by keeping possibilities at the manufacturing side open through constructing a flexible manufacturing and sourcing platform.

Conclusion

Drawing on the ideas of pragmatic constructivism, this paper has developed a conceptual framework for use in complex organisational planning and decision-making situations requiring accounting information. We have emphasised that complex planning and decision-making relate to organising the co-authorship of the multiple actors' perception of what may be factually possible and valuable in the future (for which there are no definitive facts). For the production and use of trustworthy information about future consequences of planned actions and activities, we have advocated a skilful and reflective learning perspective aspiring to make the actors' pro-active perspectives meet the pragmatic perspective. Such a learning theory of truth considers knowledge creation as an iterative and reflective process in which the actors obtain increasingly higher insight and diagnostic certainty when establishing pro-active true statements. As a result, the truth gap between pro-active and pragmatic truth is diminished. Organising multiple actors' perception of what may be factually possible and valuable in the future requires an actor-based procedure of co-authorship involving dialogical interactive integration processes. Accordingly, the pragmatic constructivist way to produce and use accounting information differs substantially from the cybernetic paradigm involving mechanical approximation, coordination and adaption.

Also, the study has used a conceptual framework to illustrate, analyse and explain how two organisations, each faced with a complex planning and decision situation involving a high degree of information uncertainty and multiple decision-participants, organise their planning and decision process and incorporate accounting. Both companies draw upon conventional management accounting information and techniques to produce accounting information to calculate the consequences of the alternatives constructed. However, in both cases there is a continuously dialogical interaction between several specialised actors to produce co-authored pro-active and pragmatically true accounting information. The cases give insight into measurement and communication techniques to challenge the pro-active truth of the actors' business topoi. Also, it reveals that holding actors accountable for realising pragmatically true planning and decisions is important to ensure they establish trustworthy pro-actively true information that reduces the truth gap.

Overall, the chapter provides more insight into the interactive dimension of management control (Simons 1995). It provides methodological insight to be applied by the reflective practitioners' interacting across functional specialities and hierarchical level (Trenca 2016), and hence contributes to extending the technical toolbox of the accounting experts (Laine et al. 2016).

Finally, it provides tools for generating "realistic" accounting information for planning and decision-making and, thereby, uncovers ways of managing uncertainty in accounting information.

Further research is required to obtain additional insights into a variety of techniques for establishing and working with pro-actively true accounting information in the context of multiple actors. Further case studies are required to reveal other ways of working with the problem.

Notes

1 The case materials have been collected through two qualitative studies (see Nørreklit et al. 2006; Nielsen et al. 2015). This chapter makes a novel conceptual development based on the cases.
2 The description of case A contains excerpts that are "Reprinted from Nørreklit et al. (2006) with permission from Elsevier."
3 The description of case B contains excerpts that are "Reprinted from Nielsen et al. (2015) with permission from Elsevier."

References

Ahrens, Thomas, and Chris S. Chapman. 2007. "Management accounting as practice." *Accounting Organizations and Society*, 32 (1): 1–27.
Anthony, Robert, and Vijay Govindarajan. 2007. *Management Control Systems*. Boston: McGraw-Hill.
Arbnor, Ingeman, and Bjorn Bjerke. 1997. *Methodology for Creating Business Knowledge*. 2nd ed. Thousand Oaks, CA: Sage.
Beer, Stafford. 1959. *The Cybernetics of Management*. New York: John Wiley.
Carter, Chris, Stewart R. Clegg, and Martin Kornberger. 2008. "Strategy as practice?" *Strategic Organization*, 6 (1): 83–99.
Cyert, Richard M., and James G. March. 1963. *A Behavioral Theory of the Firm*. Englewood Cliffs, NJ: Prentice-Hall.
Laine, Teemu, Korhonen Tuomas, Petri Suomala, and Asta Rantamaa. 2016. "Boundary subjects and boundary objects in accounting fact construction and communication." *Qualitative Research in Accounting and Management*, 13 (3): 303–329.
March, James G. 1978. "Bounded rationality, ambiguity, and the engineering of choice." *The Bell Journal of Economics*, 9 (2): 587–608.
March, James G. 1987. "Ambiguity and accounting: The elusive link between information and decision making." *Accounting, Organizations and Society*, 12 (2): 153–168.
Merchant, Kenneth, and Wim A. Van der Stede. 2007. *Performance Measurement, Evaluation and Incentives*. Harlow: Pearson Education.
Mitchell, Falconer, Lars B. Nielsen, Hanne Nørreklit, and Lennart Nørreklit. 2013. "Scoring strategic performance: A pragmatic constructivist approach to strategic performance measurement." *Journal of Management & Governance*, 17 (1): 5–34.
Nielsen, Lars B., Falconer Mitchell, and Hanne Nørreklit. 2015. "Management accounting and decision making: Two case studies of outsourcing." *Accounting Forum*, 19 (1): 64–82.

Nørreklit, Hanne, Lennart Nørreklit, and Falconer Mitchell. 2007. "Theoretical conditions for validity in accounting performance measurement." In *Business Performance Measurement*, edited by Andy Neely, 179–217. Cambridge: Cambridge University Press.

Nørreklit, Lennart. 2011. "Actors and reality: A conceptual framework for creative governance." In *An Actor's Approach to Management: Conceptual Framework and Company Practices*, edited by Morten Jakobsen, Inga-Lill Johanson and Hanne Nørreklit, 7–37. Copenhagen: DJOEF.

Nørreklit, Lennart. 2017. "Actor reality construction." In *A Philosophy of Management Accounting: A Pragmatic Constructivist Approach*, edited by Hanne Nørreklit. Chapter 2, this volume. New York: Routledge.

Nørreklit, Lennart, Hanne Nørreklit, and Poul Israelsen. 2006. "Validity of management control topoi — towards constructivist pragmatism." *Management Accounting Research*, 17 (1): 42–71.

Parker, Lee D. 1979. "Divisional performance measurement: Beyond an exclusive profit test." In *Readings in Accounting for Management Control*, edited by Clive Emmanuel, David Otley and Kenneth Merchant, 551–568. New York: Springer.

Scapens, Robert W. 1991. "Researching management accounting practice: The role of case study methods." *British Accounting Review*, 22 (3): 259–281.

Simon, Herbert A. 1986. "Rationality in psychology and economics." *Journal of Business*, 59 (4): 209–224.

Simons, Robert. 1995. *Levers of Control*. Boston: Harvard Business School Press.

Trenca, Mihaela. 2016. "Tracing the becoming of reflective practitioner through the enactment of epistemic practices." *Qualitative Research in Accounting and Management*, 13 (3): 350–369.

5 New Product Development Project Managers as Actors

The Viewpoint of Management Accounting and Control

Teemu Laine, Tuomas Korhonen,
Petri Suomala and Emmi Tervala

Introduction

This chapter focuses on management accounting and control in supporting managerial work (Hall 2010), especially new product development (NPD) management, which has not been adequately examined from a managerial-work viewpoint (see e.g. Jørgensen and Messner 2010). Research already acknowledges the presence of multiple, sometimes competing, objectives in NPD projects (Davila and Wouters 2006). These objectives would require the employment of multiple mechanistic or organic controls (Ylinen and Gullkvist 2014). However, the roles given to or taken by individual NPD management actors are not sufficiently understood (for control system challenges, see e.g. Tervala, Laine, Korhonen et al. In press).

In order to address this research gap, this chapter provides a detailed account of one actor group that clearly identifies and influences many possibilities in organisations and enacts management accounting and control for NPD—namely, *NPD project managers*. This chapter concentrates on how the production and use of NPD project management accounting and control are experienced by NPD project managers through interacting with other manager groups. There is considerable uncertainty in the interaction of factual possibilities and multiple actors in NPD. Essentially, by employing the pragmatic constructivist perspective, this chapter reveals NPD project managers' viewpoints on how pragmatic truth statements of management accounting and control are produced in their business context (see Nørreklit et al. 2017, Chapter 4, this volume). Naturally, in many business contexts—the NPD context included—validating pragmatic truth is a question of delimiting some aspects outside of one's thinking. Oftentimes, it is difficult to say whether a past decision actually provides positive or negative impacts or, if it does, to what extent it influences the impacts compared to other topical aspects. Hence, whether one invests in an NPD project or certain technology are likely to be ambiguous decisions with regard to pro-active and pragmatic truths (Nørreklit 2017, Chapter 2, this volume).

This chapter delves into NPD project managers' organisational realities through the concept of *topos*. In this approach, an individual actor's *subjective topos* refers to 'an individual actor's particular way of understanding acting in the world' (Nørreklit et al. 2017, Chapter 4, this volume). When multiple actors are involved, the concept of topos needs a social dimension. Therefore, a *social topos* is 'the common way of understanding acting shared by a group of actors' (in Nørreklit et al. 2017, Chapter 4, this volume). When these multiple actors are working for a company, then a certain *company topos* becomes relevant. Company topos refers to the overarching way of coordinating different functional groups of actors, interpretations of organisational circumstances, accessible possibilities and values to create collective progress (Jakobsen et al. 2011; Nørreklit et al. 2017, Chapter 4, this volume). This topos is a construction that aims at integrating and balancing individual actors' topoi within the company (Jakobsen et al. 2011). Regardless of the viewpoint taken (actor, social or company), the integration of facts, possibilities, values and communication is important.

Addressing the construction of the company topos is especially important because the reality of an NPD project manager is affected by different actors' requirements or viewpoints that are related to the success of a new product, the budget and schedule of the project, the technical characteristics of the new product and the fit of the new product to the existing operations of the company, which (together) constitute the business impacts of the new product. Related actors, together, are to form a factual possible product within value range and thereby establish the pro-active true statements about a future product, e.g. what assumptions about business success they are committed to and what technical goals they accept (Nørreklit et al. 2017, Chapter 4, this volume). The fundamental role of management accounting and control is to support the construction of a product based on pro-active true statements about what would expectedly be functioning in practice; thus, whether values and possibilities integrated with facts need to be considered and communicated within a company across organisational activities (Jakobsen et al. 2011). This chapter asks the following research questions:

1. How can we conceptualise different NPD project managers' management accounting and control topoi?
2. How can project managers interact with the company topos?

To answer these questions, in-depth empirical insight was needed. To acquire this insight, the chapter draws on in-depth interviews of nine NPD project managers in Finnish R&D intensive companies. The NPD project managers were interviewed within a larger study of 23 NPD project stakeholders— namely, project managers, product managers, R&D managers and business controllers.

The emphasis in this examination was placed on the potential of accounting information in supporting decision-making (Nielsen et al. 2015) and, more widely, in supporting the management of the factual possibilities embedded in NPD projects (Nørreklit et al. 2010; Mitchell, Nielsen and Nørreklit, this volume; see also Hall 2010 and Rodney and Müller 2004 for accounting information supporting managerial work). Altogether, the employment of pragmatic constructivism enables the current roles and limitations of management accounting and control for NPD management to be examined.

Literature Review

NPD Project Managers' Organisational Context and Working Environment

NPD is typically undertaken in projects with interfaces to different business functions (from purchasing and operations to sales and marketing). An NPD project aims at transforming an idea into a commercialised product (Davila 2000). The Project Management Institute (1996) defines an NPD project as a temporary activity for creating a unique product or service, and project management refers to the adoption and use of knowledge, skills, tools and techniques to fulfil the stakeholders' (i.e. actors') needs and expectations (Project Management Institute 1996). The role of an NPD project manager is of great importance because the management and implementation of an NPD project significantly affect NPD project success (or failure) (Tatikonda and Rosenthal 2000a, 2000b). Quite typically, companies set several competing objectives for NPD projects (Rozenes et al. 2006); those objectives include product features, quality and cost efficiency, accompanied by several other aspects related to a company strategy.

From the viewpoint of pragmatic constructivism (Nørreklit et al. 2010; Jakobsen et al. 2011; Nielsen et al. 2015), the NPD project portfolio, and single projects within that portfolio, represent a multitude of *factual and illusionary* possibilities. Hence, NPD project managers and other related actors are supposed to assess which of these possibilities are factual, desirable and actively contribute to realising the possibilities perceived most desirable. For these purposes, companies have means and practices for NPD project portfolio management, as well as for managing individual NPD projects. Essentially, NPD projects usually have a specified project manager, who is responsible for project implementation and performance. An NPD project manager typically has a dual role because 1) he/she is controlled by the overall organisation with his/her NPD project objectives and 2) he/she controls the project execution and project stakeholders, respectively, in order to ensure project performance. Typically, top managers or R&D managers have chosen the means to control NPD projects; whereas, NPD project managers practically affect control decisions within single NPD projects (Tatikonda and Rosenthal 2000a; Ylinen and Gullkvist 2014).

Stage-gate models (Cooper 1990) are typically used in NPD project management. The innovation process is managed through gates, in which the innovation needs to fulfil the goals and requirements (Lewis et al. 2002; Ylinen and Gullkvist 2012, 2014). The formal checkpoints of a formal model intend to provide desired support for an NPD project manager (Lewis et al. 2002). At the same time, formality may hinder resource flexibility, which can again hinder project performance under uncertainty when new possibilities emerge (Tatikonda and Rosenthal 2000a; Sethi and Iqbal 2008). However, project management autonomy is not always desired because it requires an NPD project manager's ability to solve emerging problems (Lewis et al. 2002) and also to use organic controls instead of/besides mechanistic ones (Ylinen and Gullkvist 2012, 2014).

Management Accounting and Control Do Support NPD Project Managers

Even if there is a lot of potential in using financial control for NPD, the practice is not necessarily understood well enough in research (Nixon 1998; Jørgensen and Messner 2010). Thus, there is a need to obtain knowledge about the integration of factual possibilities in NPD. Indeed, NPD projects have been seen as a challenging context for management accounting and control, as uncertainties embedded in NPD activities challenge the adoption of management accounting and control tools. Still, there are several studies that highlight the importance and positive consequences of using financial control in product development (e.g. Nixon 1998; Davila 2000; Davila and Wouters 2004; Suomala 2004; Laine, Korhonen and Martinsuo 2016; Laine, Korhonen, Suomala et al. 2016). In particular, Suomala (2004) highlights the need for NPD performance measurement, stating that there are at least two meaningful motivations for financial control in the NPD context: 1) financial controls should provide information about the current NPD project statuses and enable decisions accordingly; and 2) financial control should provide information and scenarios that would enable long-term learning and development efforts. Both of these motivations are important and can be solved by mechanistic or actor-based approaches to management accounting and control.

However, the actor-based approach relates to realising what is factually possible (Jakobsen et al. 2011; Nielsen et al. 2015). Accounting information could be used not only in seemingly rational decision-making, without interaction among actors involved, but also in extending the awareness of and building a shared understanding about central business phenomena (Hall 2010). This idea is well in line with pragmatic constructivism and the actor-approach for decision-making (Nielsen et al. 2015) and seems to have potential for better understanding management accounting and control in NPD project managers' work.

Empirical Findings

The Research Process, Data Gathering and Analysis

Our field study was conducted among R&D intensive medium- or large-sized companies in Finland between November 2011 and June 2012. Interviews of nine NPD project managers in seven companies serve as the primary data source of this chapter (bolded in Table 5.1). Six among the seven companies represent mechanical engineering, and one represents the ICT sector. All the actors interviewed to accompany the NPD project managers are listed in Table 5.1, covering 23 managers in total. Also, all the other actors interviewed work directly in R&D or have a clear connection to R&D activities (R&D directors, business controllers, product managers). Altogether, the NPD project managers' perceptions of financial control were gathered and supplemented by the other actors' viewpoints.

NPD project management, in general (company topos), as well as the individual NPD project managers' identities (topoi), were the primary units of analysis. The interviews, which were semi-structured, were recorded and transcribed. We used Atlas.ti software for the purpose of analysing the interview material. The researchers' interpretations of the data were coded according to the topics under examination. The list of codes included, for instance, overall controls for R&D, project objectives, project stakeholders and their viewpoints, facts, possibilities, values and communication. Furthermore, the researchers' access to in-depth case studies in some of the interviewed companies was used in validating the conclusions.

Table 5.1 The Interviewed Organisations and NPD Project Stakeholders

Organisation	Industry	Interviewees
A	Machinery and services	R&D director, two business controllers, **project manager**, product manager
B	Manufacturing systems and services	R&D director/**project manager**, business controller, product manager
C	Machinery and services	R&D director/**project manager**, business controller, **project manager**
D	Production machinery	R&D director, two business controllers, **project manager**, product manager
E	Production machinery	Business controller, **two project managers**
F	Machinery and services	R&D director, **project manager**, product manager
G	ICT products and services	R&D director/**project manager**

To answer its research questions, in the following sections, this chapter first presents different NPD project manager archetypes and then gives exemplars of each of these archetypes. This chapter then illustrates project managers' interactions with the company topos before forming conclusions of empirical findings. Accessing project managers' topoi, both with regard to their specific role and their interaction with the company topos, will help obtain knowledge about the integration of factual possibilities in NPD. Indeed, in order to better understand the interviewed NPD project managers' roles and the roles they desire from management accounting and control, one needs to understand the company topos under which a certain NPD project management operates. When this understanding is acquired, research and practice can better reach the pragmatic prerequisites for and means of integrating different actors' topoi to build a shared understanding about the key business phenomena and functioning practice.

Results on the NPD Project Managers' Topoi Affecting Management Accounting and Control

First, it is important whether the organisation (or the actor himself/herself) considers NPD project managers primarily as actors under control or as actors who, due to their responsibility, actually control the project organisation. In fact, our empirical data shows that both viewpoints of control simultaneously coexist, but NPD project managers' role under control seems to be much more apparent. Second, it is important how an actor works with facts and possibilities. Table 5.2 illustrates NPD project managers' different identities by presenting certain archetypes of NPD project managers' topoi.

The NPD project managers, who interpret themselves as being primarily under control and do not (by themselves) produce financial calculations, typically represent the *Technology topos*, with a clear focus on the engineering and technology aspects and project practicalities. These project managers focus on being technological 'hubs' by solving technical and sourcing-related problems and coordinating technical development work tasks for other actors. NPD project managers with this type of technology topos can have limited, although sometimes critical, interest toward business aspects; their facts and possibilities lie particularly within the domain of technology. These NPD project managers can also crave more support

Table 5.2 Different Topoi of the NPD Project Manager Archetypes

	Primarily under control	*Also in control*
Primarily uses calculations	Technology topos	Management topos
Actively also produces calculations	Analyst topos	Business controller topos

from business people, possibly highlighting their critical view toward current support that, for them, is inadequate.

The NPD project managers that interpret themselves as being primarily under control but are actively involved in producing (and possibly communicating) the calculations hold, in this typology, an archetype of *Analyst topos*. This involvement also means that these project managers' relationships with other actors and their facts and possibilities are also in the domain of business, supplementing project management or technology substance. The analyst topos refers to the execution of a project according to given requirements but with limited interest or involvement in or responsibility to actively control other stakeholders.

Those project managers that are also in control (but naturally not only in control) can be seen to hold the archetype of *Management topos* when taking advantage of calculations produced by other project stakeholders. The project managers with the Management topos see their facts and possibilities, respectively, within a wider domain. Because these project managers are also in control of how 'things get done', this nuance is also reflected in how these project managers interact with other actors.

Alternatively, the NPD project manager can hold the archetype of *Business controller topos*. In this archetype, the NPD project manager interprets himself/herself as being (also) in control while taking responsibility for producing the calculations according to project control needs as well. In this topos, the element of 'how things get done' is accompanied by facts and possibilities in producing calculations.

Exemplars of Different NPD Project Manager Topoi

An Exemplar of the Technology Topos

In this section, we provide examples of different NPD project managers' topoi in our empirical findings. To start with, we exemplify the technology topos. The interviews suggest that some project managers with the technology topos are primarily senior designers and only secondarily business managers of the NPD project. Financial facts might be linked to certain technological specifications, component lists etc.; thus, the project manager relies on these given economic facts and is reluctant to estimate otherwise (e.g. in Organisation A):

> I have noticed that the more you are an engineer [you have purely technical education], the more difficult it is for you to give estimates [about financial aspects with uncertainty]. It is a way of thinking, there is uncertainty and it can be very difficult to give a rough estimate.

The technology topos in this example implies that establishing pro-active truth, in relation to the integration of factual possibilities, is challenging.

These project managers focus on historical facts and not possibilities. For some more technologically-oriented managers, giving an estimate actually seems like giving a promise for which they are then responsible, thereby making them reluctant to try to estimate what is anyway uncertain.

An Exemplar of the Analyst Topos

In our interview data, the formal project model was one clear frame that controls NPD project managers' activities. It can be interpreted that NPD project managers are there to ensure effective project execution with limited flexibility and power. However, also within this model, some of the interviewed NPD project managers, classified as *Analyst topos*, saw the possibility for top-down and bottom-up communication and, especially, the possibility to bring up uncertainties and surprises during project execution. A project manager (Organisation D) described their project model enactment, underlining its formality in bringing problems up:

> [the project model] forces us to report, follow certain issues very carefully. And at the same time, it provides us a formal route to bring up problematic issues. These issues escalate [and will be managed] quite naturally, if we follow the project model.

In this quote, some emerging project-related facts bring forth the possibility to avoid problems. Therefore, our empirical findings show the positive stance toward formal project models, although they might also be considered burdening in their bureaucracy.

An Exemplar of the Management Topos

As a contrast to the analyst topos, and to clarify the difference between different NPD project manager identities, a project manager (Organisation F), illustrating the *management topos*, criticised the overemphasis on project budgets and highlighted the importance of active product costing in NPD projects:

> Product cost is more essential; it is the mechanism for future profits. It enables keeping the contribution margin. . . . The project cost is paid only once, and it will pay back typically in months or in few years, and it should not be that strict, but the product cost is the important one, it will accumulate the profits or losses.

This person in the management topos, hence, exemplifies the shortcomings of the formal project model. The project model does not necessarily allow wider optimisation but, rather, might even encourage sub-optimisation or focus attention to suboptimal control mechanisms. In this topos, possibilities arise from defining functioning practice (see also Laine, Korhonen and Martinsuo 2016): what should the company focus on? What is meaningful? What further bottlenecks need to be removed? A person that asks these questions needs to have not only good negotiation and reasoning skills to be able to influence the current company practices but also routes to acquire needed calculations to back up their ideas.

An Exemplar of the Business Controller Topos

Sometimes, the wider profitability impacts were discussed (Organisation E), reflecting the *business controller topos* among NPD project managers:

> I think that [a business impact analysis] responds more to that project as an investment, and we expect income from it, and we look at the pay-back time.
>
> Project manager 1

> We look at those issues, but our analysis includes also all the potential cannibalisation, after sales expectations, total business impacts, and there are different scenarios . . . what do we expect, best case and worst case scenarios. And the project should provide input according to the current status.
>
> Project manager 2

These project managers expect a lot from NPD accounting and control and have positive expectations, laying fertile ground for constructing pro-active truth in NPD. However, they also see the ambiguities related to producing the needed calculations. Their facts and possibilities are manifold; thus, they need to decide what aspects are consciously left out of a certain decision. These project managers need to have the relationships to influence decision-making practices and the perseverance to continuously scope the relevant facts and possibilities in different NPD-related decisions.

Project Managers' Interactions with the Company Topos

In this section, the chapter presents insights about how project managers interact with the company topos. The section builds upon the understanding that, in the NPD project management practice, different types of objectives need to be balanced and prioritised. A company needs to execute the projects according to the division of tasks between different managers (as either adaptors of calculations or actors involved in producing those calculations). Understanding the process of structuring and prioritising the facts mechanistically related to NPD projects is not enough to understand NPD management. One needs to involve different stakeholders' viewpoints (Laine, Korhonen and Martinsuo 2016) and bear in mind the values and other aspects affecting different stakeholders' topoi and, thus, company topoi, in general (Jakobsen et al. 2011). In particular, this section first presents project managers' interactions with the company topos through acquiring competitive advantage, project objectives and the usefulness of accounting information.

Acquiring competitive advantage: in most of the companies interviewed, the company topos includes the values of innovativeness and business renewal in sustaining competitive advantage. These values are translated in different ways into NPD project objectives and, respectively, into NPD project managers' expected roles.

If the possibilities related to NPD projects include a huge amount of potential business impacts, there can be clear differences between companies in how clearly actors are able to explicate factual possibilities and how much of NPD project managers' active work is required. As some elements of competitive advantage clearly are constructed in NPD, project managers are in a key position to integrate facts, possibilities, values and communication. Whether a project manager is an active producer of accounting calculation, or whether he/she can be in control, can determine the extent to which the values of innovativeness and business renewal are involved or compromised in NPD project management. Less empowerment can easily mean a narrower decision-making scope and vice versa.

Project objectives: in some organisations, the interviewed project managers considered that the immediate project objectives and also the expectations set for NPD project managers' roles are quite clear after project acceptance. However, the project manager in Company A, for example, admitted that several additional NPD project objectives seem to stem from external sources. These objectives are not clear enough for NPD project managers. Thus, NPD project managers need to put a lot of effort into refining and communicating NPD project objectives among project stakeholders as expected NPD project impacts.

Among NPD project business impacts, cost efficiency/reduction and project budgets were brought up several times during the interviews. Some project managers actively review the project budget; whereas, in other companies, NPD controllers compare budgeted and actual figures. The emphasis on project cost issues, in comparison to other accounting issues, varies from one company to another. For project managers with management or business controller topoi, there are several other important business impacts (in addition to the project budget) to be planned and controlled, such as expected sales volumes, pricing scenarios and after sales possibilities. In fact, one can interpret NPD projects as investments with certain project costs, future product prices, volumes and costs. These investments would also have several types of indirect effects, representing overall business impacts as aspects of pro-active truth. The aspects are not necessarily carefully defined or actively managed in every NPD project, but they do represent one starting point for valuating and communicating possibilities in

NPD. Conversely, some NPD project managers with technology or analyst topos, i.e. primarily under control, seem to be willing to focus on project costs, as well as technological solutions, product features and project schedules, as project objectives. One interviewed project manager had the impression that, in their project model, the formal process is overemphasised, and the decisions are sometimes made formally (at the cost of the *de facto* business possibilities). Therefore, it seems that pro-active truth is not necessarily followed but overshadowed by the formal project model.

Usefulness of accounting information: although the scope, content and interpretation of management accounting and control varied across the interviewed companies, most of the interviewed NPD project managers considered accounting information beneficial. Some of the interviewed project managers described that they were satisfied with the financial support, which quite typically consisted of the economic facts delivered to project managers and the clear performance measures in project models. These aspects relate to project managers as adopters of accounting information. Besides using economic facts for management, NPD project managers are supposed to identify and analyse a variety of possibilities, with values related to the products that are under development. Some of the interviewees discussed the actual role of financial control related to those possibilities. For example, a project manager (Company A) highlighted the fact that financial control should play a crucial role in the beginning of an NPD project, i.e. when the economic possibilities are estimated under a relatively high uncertainty and the managers make, perhaps, the most important new product decisions. Some interviewees highlighted the need for freedom and flexibility in research projects and concept development, where new possibilities are developed. At this stage, there was not that much need for accounting and control as restrictions, but rather, there might be a need for using calculations as a source of inspiration. We expect that those project managers primarily in control, in particular, will be able to influence how companies use accounting information as a source of inspiration, although much technological development is needed in early NPD stages as well.

Conclusions of Our Empirical Findings

Altogether, the perceived support from financial control can vary based not only on the characteristics of different company topoi but also on individual project managers' needs and preferences. It may also depend on individual actors' topoi as to whether business possibilities are primarily interpreted as financial, technical, operational or quality-related aspects. In response to our research questions, we found out that organisational realities are affected by the overall R&D organisations, NPD project models in use (e.g. formality), project characteristics (e.g. uncertainty) and roles given to and actually taken by NPD project managers (e.g. autonomy and flexibility). These roles are also affected by NPD project managers' experiences and personalities. Therefore, it is of great importance to understand the interactions between a company topos and the topoi of the individual NPD project managers within that company.

The identity of the NPD project manager, as a managerial actor, varies from one company to another and among the individual project managers within the organisations. There is no common identity or topos that is better than the others for an NPD project manager (even in a certain context). However, importantly, the role of an NPD project manager should be in line with the overall company topos and with the tasks given to project management.

Conclusions

Answers to Research Questions

This chapter asked two research questions: *1) how can we conceptualise different NPD project managers' management accounting and control topoi?* and 2) *how can project managers interact with the company topos?* The findings of this chapter are based on how NPD project managers experience the notions of facts, possibilities, values and communication (Nørreklit et al. 2010; Jakobsen et al. 2011). These notions represent the fundamental viewpoints of company topoi and individual topoi, and through these notions, it is possible to examine management and control practices in the NPD context. In NPD project managers' organisational realities, facts, possibilities, values and communication need to be acknowledged, examined and integrated. If this integration is successful, NPD project managers can have a role with meaning, possibly leading to higher willingness and capability to contribute to meeting overall company objectives.

This chapter shows that it is important to examine the role of the project manager in relation to the use of management accounting in NPD. Moreover, the chapter presents some of the NPD management aspects that pragmatic constructivism brings forth. Indeed, leveraging a company topos in NPD project management requires adjusting the topos according to individual NPD projects (Jakobsen et al. 2011; Laine, Korhonen, Suomala et al. 2016). More importantly, and as an answer to the first research question, we can conclude that one needs to seek a balance between the requirements set by 1) NPD project management models, 2) the characteristics of an individual NPD project and 3) the topos of an individual NPD project manager. The division of tasks in analysing and controlling NPD projects should be made case-by-case, and learning between projects needs to be organised.

Our results show that the roles given to and taken by NPD project managers vary from one company or project to another. We identified *management topos*, *business controller topos*, *analyst topos* and *technology topos* as archetypes, but these archetypes do not even attempt to comprehensively capture the versatile practice of management accounting and control in

NPD. Rather, they are archetypes that facilitate understanding the different topoi between different actors with ostensibly similar responsibilities, i.e. managing an NPD project. By acknowledging the existence of different topoi, and by balancing and adjusting management accounting and control in cooperation, companies can attain better management accounting and control support for NPD managers. This is in line with Hall's (2010) idea on accounting information extensively supporting managerial work outside of decision-making (see also Nielsen et al. 2015). Therefore, this chapter adds a sound viewpoint of pragmatic constructivism to this particular line of research. In practice, when finding the balance between the company topos and the topoi of individual NPD project managers, thinking about the identity archetypes outlined above could be helpful in finding ways to adjust the management accounting and control practice in a given NPD project context. The archetypes can provide a tool for conceptualising how facts and possibilities work in different NPD project managers' practice.

As a response to the second research question, the maturity of communication culture, which is central in the interaction of individual project managers and the company topos, seems to vary from one organisation to another, along with the scope and content of management accounting and control in use (in line with the observations by Laine, Korhonen and Martinsuo [2016]). The actual support for managerial work from management accounting and control requires acknowledging differences between different actors' topoi in the NPD context and making management accounting and control help define pragmatic truth in a given business context, i.e. what is factually possible (Nørreklit et al. 2017, Chapter 4, this volume). Also, in the NPD context, the construction of common topoi that integrate different actors' topoi is important yet difficult (see Trenca and Nørreklit 2017, Chapter 8, this volume). Therefore, enhanced communication among NPD management actors would mean (or require) co-authorship and increased attention to intentional (joint) construction of these company topoi. When using the archetypes of this chapter, one can see how different project managers interact with the company topos with regard to competitive advantage expected from projects as impact, project objectives which direct action and accounting information that support these project managers' work.

Contribution

The contribution of this chapter is twofold. *First*, the chapter examines the identity of an NPD project manager as an organisational actor and advances knowledge on NPD project managers' topoi. In all, the scope and content of financial control vary from one organisation to another. Some organisations strictly follow the rules of a project model with only limited project manager autonomy. NPD project managers seem to only rarely initiate discussions among project stakeholders about wider business impacts, i.e. discussions about wider impacts are not sufficiently supported by the *de facto* financial NPD project control. Some NPD project managers, on the other hand, see the project model as a mechanism supporting their work with substantial flexibility (cf. Tatikonda and Rosenthal 2000a). This finding provides more understanding about management accounting and control actually supporting managerial work in practice. The involved NPD project managers' ideas and expectations were explicitly related to the wider notion of NPD performance. Thereby, the chapter reports co-authorship in management accounting practice in action and, thus, highlights the need for supplementing seemingly rational decision-making with more pro-active, actor-based features in both research and practice (cf. Nielsen et al. 2015; see also Hall 2010).

Second, the chapter shows how NPD project managers, in their current roles, can desire enhanced interaction and communication (with regard to NPD project objectives and execution) in order to attain better support in their work that easily relates to wider business impacts. As NPD project managers are, by definition, in charge of an NPD project, they are in the position of making decisions and choices towards realising related possibilities. In the terminology of pragmatic constructivism, this requires both identifying underlying values in the company topos and examining different factual or fictional possibilities (Jakobsen et al. 2011) in order to attain or extend the benefits of an NPD project (Laine, Korhonen and Martinsuo 2016). In analytical decision-making, described by Nielsen et al. (2015), financial control should informationally support an NPD project manager's decision-making. However, as NPD projects are activities that deal with emerging possibilities with remarkable uncertainty of their potential value, such an analytical approach, i.e. seemingly rational decision-making without interaction (or co-authorship) among the actors involved, is not enough to understand the current or desired role of financial control in NPD (see also Korhonen et al. 2016).

Attaining NPD project objectives requires acknowledging the differences between different actors' topoi in the NPD context. This means making management accounting and control help define pragmatic truth in a given business context. It is essential to acknowledge the presence of different topoi that relate to each other and should be integrated and leveraged to make things actually work. Different topoi can (either intentionally or unintentionally) lead to varying accounting and control practices inside companies, e.g. in terms of division of tasks between actors, formality of management accounting and control utilisation and different procedures adopted. Hence, this chapter provides new knowledge about the integration of different actors' topoi in a context with a high uncertainty and plenty of opportunities (see Jakobsen et al. 2011; Laine, Korhonen, Suomala et al. 2016; Nørreklit et al. 2017, Chapter 4, this volume). Altogether, the requirements set for an NPD project manager in a given business context should be in line with the company topos and intentionally adjusted according to the characteristics of an NPD project manager or task, i.e. the particular

NPD project. This chapter contributes to understanding how NPD project managers, as actors, help achieve organisational goals and improve NPD performance. Advancing this understanding facilitates interactions between the company topos and individual actors' topoi in NPD projects.

More precisely, in a highly mechanistic view, one could assume that the top management priorities are merely translated into NPD project priorities and objectives and then realised by NPD project managers and other project personnel. This chapter shows that NPD projects offer a dynamic context with uncertainty; it is essential that NPD project managers are able to cooperate with different NPD project stakeholders and understand both technical and economic new product aspects (Tatikonda and Rosenthal 2000a). Moreover, an NPD project manager himself/herself may have, for instance, a technological or economic orientation and may possess more or less interactive character.

Finally, calculations may provide social structures and means of communication among different actors (Nørreklit et al. 2010; Laine, Korhonen, Suomala et al. 2016). In NPD project managers' organisational realities, actors should be comprehensively understood (Nielsen et al. 2015) while acknowledging their significant influence on NPD project performance and wider business performance. Moreover, communication among different NPD stakeholders needs to be taken into account (Laine, Korhonen, Suomala et al. 2016), and the potential support from management accounting and control to NPD should be designed and utilised accordingly. Management accounting and control practices could, in some cases, be based on the activities taken primarily by an NPD project manager himself/herself. To be effective, choosing the person responsible for enacting management accounting and control should be aligned with the company topos, division of tasks and related individuals' topoi.

Further Research

Based on our results, NPD project managers' overall roles and responsibilities are well acknowledged, and there have been clear attempts to enhance the role of management accounting and control to support NPD projects and project managers. However, much work is still needed in order to provide NPD project managers with the means to control and support project execution. Currently, management accounting and control for NPD is primarily interpreted as a set of mechanistic tools; whereas, this chapter highlights the need for supplementing seemingly rational decision-making with more pro-active, actor-based features to actually realise the factual possibilities in NPD. This aspect could be examined in various different (industry) contexts in the future to understand their possible similarities and differences (see Messner 2016).

As observed in this chapter, NPD project managers have a challenging role featuring several interactions with (and co-authorship among) other

NPD project stakeholders. This chapter underlines how NPD project managers, as actors, can help achieve organisational goals and improve NPD performance. Indeed, management accounting and control enactment requires finding a proper balance between a company topos and NPD project managers' topoi; moreover, both of these need to be adjusted in different projects through interaction between related NPD managers.

Acknowledgements

The research projects resulting in this chapter have been funded by the Centre for Technology and Innovation in Finland (TEKES) and the Academy of Finland. The authors also wish to thank the interviewees for their valuable contribution to this study.

References

Cooper, Robert G. 1990. "Stage-gate systems: A new tool for managing new products." *Business Horizons*, 33 (3): 44–54.

Davila, Antonio, and Marc Wouters. 2004. "Designing cost-competitive technology products through cost management." *Accounting Horizons*, 18 (1): 13–26.

Davila, Tony. 2000. "An empirical study on the drivers of management control systems' design in new product development." *Accounting, Organizations and Society*, 25 (4): 383–409.

Davila, Tony, and Marc Wouters. 2006. "Management accounting in the manufacturing sector: Managing costs at the design and production stages." In *Handbook of Management Accounting Research*, edited by Christopher S. Chapman, Anthony G. Hopwood and Michael D. Shields, 831–858. Amsterdam: Elsevier.

Hall, Matthew. 2010. "Accounting information and managerial work." *Accounting, Organizations and Society*, 35 (3): 301–315.

Jakobsen, Morten, Inga-Lill Johansson, and Hanne Nørreklit (Eds.). 2011. *An Actor's Approach to Management — Conceptual Framework and Company Practices*, 160. Copenhagen: Djøf Publishing.

Jørgensen, Brian, and Martin Messner. 2010. "Accounting and strategising: A case study from new product development." *Accounting, Organizations and Society*, 35 (2): 184–204.

Korhonen, Tuomas, Teemu Laine, Jouni Lyly-Yrjänäinen, and Petri Suomala. 2016. "Innovation for multiproject management: The case of component commonality." *Project Management Journal*, 47 (2): 130–143.

Laine, Teemu, Tuomas Korhonen, and Miia Martinsuo. 2016. "Managing program impacts in new product development: An exploratory case study on overcoming uncertainties." *International Journal of Project Management*, 34 (4): 717–733.

Laine, Teemu, Tuomas Korhonen, Petri Suomala, and Asta Rantamaa. 2016. "Boundary subjects and boundary objects in accounting fact construction and communication." *Qualitative Research in Accounting & Management*, 13 (3): 303–329.

Lewis, Marianne W., M. Ann Welsh, Gordon E. Dehler, and Stephen G. Green. 2002. "Product development tensions: Exploring contrasting styles of project management." *Academy of Management Journal*, 45 (3): 546–564.

Messner, Martin. 2016. "Does industry matter? How industry context shapes management accounting practice." *Management Accounting Research*, 31: 103–111.

Nielsen, Lars Braad, Falconer Mitchell, and Hanne Nørreklit. 2015. "Management accounting and decision making: Two case studies of outsourcing." *Accounting Forum*, 39 (1): 64–82.

Nixon, Bill. 1998. "Research and development performance measurement: A case study." *Management Accounting Research*, 9 (3): 329–355.

Nørreklit, Hanne, Falconer Mitchell, and Lars Braad Nielsen. 2017. "Reflective planning and decision-making." In *A Philosophy of Management Accounting: A Pragmatic Constructivist Approach*, edited by Hanne Nørreklit. Chapter 4, this volume. New York: Routledge.

Nørreklit, Hanne, Lennart Nørreklit, and Falconer Mitchell. 2010. "Towards a paradigmatic foundation for accounting practice." *Accounting, Auditing & Accountability Journal*, 23 (6): 733–758.

Nørreklit, Lennart. 2017. "Epistemology." In *A Philosophy of Management Accounting: A Pragmatic Constructivist Approach*, edited by Hanne Nørreklit. Chapter 3, this volume. New York: Routledge.

Project Management Institute. 1996. *A Guide to the Project Management Body of Knowledge*, 176. Sylva, NC: PMI Publishing Division.

Rozenes, Shai, Gad Vitner, and Stuart Spraggett. 2006. "Project control: Literature review." *Project Management Journal*, 37 (4): 5–15.

Sethi, Rajesh, and Zafar Iqbal. 2008. "Stage-gate controls, learning failure, and adverse effect on novel new products." *Journal of Marketing*, 72 (1): 118–134.

Suomala, Petri. 2004. "The life cycle dimension of new product development performance measurement." *International Journal of Innovation Management*, 8 (2): 193–221.

Tatikonda, Mohan V., and Stephen R. Rosenthal. 2000a. "Successful execution of product development projects: Balancing firmness and flexibility in the innovation process." *Journal of Operations Management*, 18 (4): 401–425.

Tatikonda, Mohan V., and Stephen R. Rosenthal. 2000b. "Technology novelty, project complexity, and product development project execution success: A deeper look at task uncertainty in product innovation." *IEEE Transactions on Engineering Management*, 47 (1): 74–87.

Tervala, Emmi, Teemu Laine, Tuomas Korhonen, and Petri Suomala. In press. "The role of financial control in new product development: empirical insights into project managers' experiences." *Journal of Management Control*.

Trenca, Mihaela, and Hanne Nørreklit. 2017. "Actor-based performance management." In *A Philosophy of Management Accounting: A Pragmatic Constructivist Approach*, edited by Hanne Nørreklit. Chapter 8, this volume. New York: Routledge.

Turner, J. Rodney, and Ralf Müller. 2004. "Communication and co-operation on projects between the project owner as principal and the project manager as agent." *European Management Journal*, 22 (3): 327–336.

Ylinen, Mika, and Benita Gullkvist. 2012. "The effects of tolerance for ambiguity and task uncertainty on the balanced and combined use of project controls." *European Accounting Review*, 21 (2): 395–415.

Ylinen, Mika, and Benita Gullkvist. 2014. "The effects of organic and mechanistic control in exploratory and exploitative innovations." *Management Accounting Research*, 25 (1): 93–112.

6 The Validity of Financial Statement Measurement

Falconer Mitchell, Hanne Nørreklit and Lennart Nørreklit

Introduction

The analysis in this chapter starts from the presumption that the role of financial statements is to provide primarily financial information that is based on trustworthy evidence for multiple purposes including stewardship, planning, decision-making, rewarding and controlling. In accordance with this presumption, one common position taken in the literature of accounting is that mainstream accounting theory and practice should emanate from the paradigm of realism (Sterling 1972; Abdel-khalik and Ajinkya 1979; Tinker et al. 1982; Chua 1986a, 1986b; Tinker 1991). For example, Solomons (1991a, 1991b) argues that accountants should see themselves as providers of unbiased information to facilitate social and economic activity undertaken by others. Whereas perfect neutrality in information provision may be impossible, accountants should still seek to achieve it. Thus, from this perspective, in mainstream accounting the assumption has to be that empirical reality is objective and external to the subject (the accountant) and that an objective, representational truthfulness of it can be translated into valid information by using accounting measurement methods.

However, the abilities of existing accounting models to provide such information in practice have frequently been challenged. In particular, the realism assumption has been heavily criticised from the perspective of social constructivism. There can be no representational faithfulness because no objective economic reality exists to which representation can be faithful. This implies that the search for representational faithfulness is futile (Tinker 1991, 303–304). Furthermore, the meaning of accounting signs may change with the speaker, situation and "traces" of previous articulations (Tinker 1991, 303–304). Rather than representing some form of objective reality, accounting serves as a ceremonial means for symbolic demonstration of an organisation's commitment to a rational course of action (Meyer and Rowan 1977). Additionally, various forms of company scandals and financial crises demonstrate the problematic challenge of achieving trustworthy accounting information.

The theoretical critiques and the practical failures of accounting justify the questioning of accounting information's link to reality in a sufficiently trustworthy manner. Addressing the question of creating trustworthiness in accounting measurements requires a paradigm. Thus, in analysing the validity of accounting measurement methods, the phenomenon subject to accounting measurement, i.e. the business and economic reality, must be ontologically specified and the epistemological apparatus of accounting measurement also needs to be addressed. In this paper, pragmatic constructivism is considered as a paradigm for understanding and developing accounting methods for practice. It involves a middle ground approach to ontology by integrating dimensions of both the realist and constructivist view referred to above (Nørreklit et al. 2007, 2010, 2012; Nørreklit 2017, chapter 2, this volume). From this foundation, an investigation of the business reality subject to accounting measurement and the abilities of accounting epistemology to provide trustworthy information are conducted. An apparatus for improving accounting measurement is also proposed in outline.

The chapter is structured as follows. First, drawing on pragmatic constructivism, the business reality subject to accounting measurement is conceptualised. The phenomena of doing business and financial units are explored. Second, the application of the performance measurement ideas of pragmatic constructivism to accounting are used to outline criteria for accounting measurement validity. In doing this, the twin concepts of correspondence and coherence are established as underpinning measurement practice and the integration of the narrative linking measurement to action. This is achieved through these concepts facilitating the operational meaning and validity of the measurement practices used by accountants. Next, the dimensions of pro-active truth and pragmatic truth are used to analyse the integration of the four dimensions of pragmatic constructivism and so establish an *integrated learning based theory of truth*. The interplay between pragmatic truth and pro-active truth forms the basis for an ongoing improvement of the ability to generate accounting information. Subsequently, the extent to which there is trustworthiness in the dominating financial statement model is reviewed. The trustworthiness of the historic cost based approach is discussed. It is suggested that the conventional model of measuring income and value is trapped between the conflicting intentions of producing objective accounting information founded on past transactions and being more economically credible by using subjective future-oriented management information. Conclusions are drawn on the need for a learning theory of truth to establish trustworthiness in what are becoming increasingly hybrid accounting statements.

Business Reality

Doing Business

Business and organisational processes are based on 'construct causalities'. These are grounded in a mixture of gifts of nature and constructions used in the complicated process of organising. There is no natural law that for instance, pressing a button makes a person sell 1000 cars, or creates a financial accounting report, or develops a financial accounting regulation. As in these actions, technology is based on constructing causal relations. There is no natural law in physics that for instance pressing a button starts a car. The causality is constructed. The construction works because of natural laws, whether we know them or not, but the technological system of causes and effects is constructed. Whereas there are few natural laws, the causal relations constructed in technology are enormous. Nature is given, not technology and human activity.

From the perspective of pragmatic constructivism, for activities to be fulfilled i.e. for establishing construct causality, there must be an integration of four dimensions involved in the endeavour: a factual observational basis; a set of possibilities that are integrated with the facts; values and goals that express the subjective values that motivate the people involved and are within the range of the factual possibilities; and finally, communication must convey this integrated structure of facts, possibilities and values to the people involved. *If* these conditions are fulfilled, then people will act and the acts will succeed. Essential to modern business are the continuous processes of change and development. Business ideas and practices are not static but are always changed and reformulated to cope with the new future. This means that construct causalities are constantly subject to scrutiny, adaption and change.

A viable company must be an integrated unit, i.e. a unit capable of acting in a way that ensures it is a *going concern*. The idea of a going concern is ontologically based on the notion of an economic unit with a functioning integration which enables it to operate as an organised actor able to establish profitable construct causality in the market economy. The functioning integration uncovers a unit that is able to act intentionally and thus operate rationally to formulate competitive goals and achieve them. When this ability breaks down, i.e. disintegration occurs in that facts no longer create sufficient possibilities and the possibilities available have insufficient value or cannot be understood and communicated, then the firm ceases to be an able actor in the market, i.e. it is no longer a going concern. Thus, the market as a competition mechanism tends to automatically eliminate the organisations that become poorly integrated constructs.

Financial Units

To facilitate trade, objectified monetary values are essential. Without a functioning financial currency institution, a modern business economy would be impossible. In broad terms, the subject of accounting is to determine the monetary values of various activities, objects and organisational units. Monetary and financial value therefore is one of the basic concepts involved in accounting practice.

Financial units are integrated units par excellence. They always occur in a factual form in some physical medium but these factual appearances integrate a meaning, a set of possibilities and a specific value. Traditionally, coins and paper money are the instruments used to carry financial value. According to the realist, Searle (1995), monetary units are constructed by applying a rule to a physical phenomenon according to the following scheme: the physical phenomenon X counts as the social phenomenon Y in the system C'. For instance, certain coins with the words "one pound" printed on them count as the financial value of one British pound in the global economy, and are usable for making payments in the UK. Thus, Searle considers money as constructed by the integration of a physical phenomenon, the coin and a social phenomenon, the financial value (one pound) by means of a rule. What Searle's rule tells us, therefore, is that social regulations define the physical monetary units and their values. However Searle's theory does not tell how financial or any other social values are constructed. On the contrary, by presupposing the social value it makes their construction incomprehensible in his realist philosophy.

According to pragmatic constructivism the financial value of, say one pound sterling, is a reality if and only if it integrates all four dimensions. First of all, it has a linguistic side. There is the meaning of the expression "one pound sterling". Everybody living in the UK knows the meaning of it otherwise they could not function in the UK society. Without the linguistic meaning, financial information as well as financial institutions would cease to exist. Financial values are socially constructed and can only exist as expressed in financial information. The financial value would not exist without linguistic expressions that facilitate communication within society.

The financial value has a factual side, as noticed by Searle (1995). Thus, the financial meaning carried by words does not by itself have any monetary value. However, when words occur on special physical units, coins or notes, legal documents or in electronic media, they express the financial value of this unit. The special characteristics and qualities of such physical units are important because there is always a matter of possible fraud to be considered. The distinction between the real and the fake (not real) is, in this case, not a distinction between having or not having the right function, but a matter of having the right origin. The origin of the money is a condition for the functioning of the institutional financial system. It would not exist without this distinction between real and fake. Anybody could make up their own money without this distinction. Monetary value is defined by the currency only. The value of bonds and shares differ from the value imprinted on their documentation. Thus, the concept of financial value develops as necessary to compare the financial value of all the physical units that can be used as payments in trade.

The dimension of possibility and logic connected to a monetary unit constitutes the possibility of buying anything in the market with the use of the specific currency. By introducing money one greatly enhances the possibility of trade because then one can trade with anybody and not only those who want the special products which one can provide. This means that financial units are not only integrated units par excellence, but are, in addition, a socially implemented method for a vast improvement of the possibilities for an actor to create powerful integrations by creating the universal tool of the price mechanism for facilitating exchange. Financial currencies thus open a wide horizon of future possibilities to the actors.

Values per se are related to the desires, interests and needs of people. How they are fulfilled is primarily expressed in people's emotions and feelings. Society organises social values in order to promote and coordinate the efforts to realise the many different values of people. Monetary units and financial institutions are precisely such social constructions. A financial currency value is an objectified and almost universal instrumental value. The point in this value construction is the ability to facilitate all forms of economic transactions thereby greatly enhancing the ability to coordinate the production and realisation of values in society for all citizens operating in a given market.

Values are subjective in the sense that they are relative to those who possess them. All trade, all market-based economic transactions are the result of exchanges of values that occur on a voluntary basis because it is considered beneficial by both parties. To the seller the subjective value of the monetary payment is higher than that of the item, whereas for the buyer the subjective value of the item is higher than the monetary price he has to pay. The difference in the estimate of the subjective value drives all trade and economic transactions. This is possible only by attaching financial value to all things in order to enable the comparison of values. In order to create a sense of fairness, which is a condition of trust, to the objectified financial value it is necessary to give the same things similar financial value in the market. If the same things are traded at vastly different prices, then people feel cheated and mistrust the system. A well-functioning market economy is necessary to preserve fair values.

The financial units represent a buying power, which can function as a universal substitute for value as long as their buying power is stable. However, if the value of the currency changes frequently due to high inflation, then annual financial statement expressed in that currency lack meaning. An underlying currency of some stability is a condition for its use in generating meaningful financial information.

Criteria of Valid Measurement

In order to observe and create construct causality practitioners need to create a highly detailed and complex representation of knowledge about their business reality. Conceptual frameworks of measurement are tools for the actors to develop and control construct causality. They are about making representations of some attributes of the business reality that are at the core for creating functioning practice (Nørreklit et al. 2007).

Conceptual Criteria of Correspondence and Coherence

The grounding of knowledge in the phenomenon to be reported on is crucial for the development of functioning practice (Husserl 1913; Heidegger 1927). However, direct observation of phenomena are subjective and often vague, distorted by memory and frequently imprecise. Therefore, concepts are at the core of creating and controlling construct causality. Business processes require ongoing reflection in which concepts and conceptual structures are developed and reshaped in order to observe, control and reformulate the construct causality (Nørreklit et al. 2007, 2012).

Conceptual qualities of correspondence and coherence are basic for all type of conceptual frameworks including those of accounting. A conceptual definition of the validity of information depends on two complementary ways of determining the meaning of the concepts in use. On the one hand, the concept can be defined demonstratively (by directly pointing out the phenomena) by formulating criteria for observing and measuring the phenomena under consideration, i.e. by establishing rules and procedures for observation and measurement. On the other hand, reference to reality in itself means nothing. For a concept to have meaning it must be integrated in a coherent conceptual framework, model or system, i.e. it is structurally defined by its relation to other concepts. If there is a mismatch between these two forms of definition—the demonstrative and the conceptual—then the measurement framework is incoherent and the data cannot be used to draw any valid accounting and performance measurement reports. For example, when ROCE is defined as earnings before interest and tax (an operational entity measurement perspective) divided by capital employed, it would be a mismatch if capital employed is taken as equity capital (a proprietary measurement perspective) rather than total assets (an entity measure).

Integrated Measurement Narrative

Accounting measurements are especially related to the observation of the factual dimension of the world. Whereas it may not be possible to measure possibilities and their values, narratives and indicators of them can be created. Nevertheless, construction of concepts and conceptual models are not simply schemata to identify things although they may start as such. Properly developed concepts go a step deeper to project action-related possibilities and values derived from facts. What identifies a factual 'thing' may be its appearance, but what makes it the type of thing it is, is related to what we can do and not do with it. 'Things' in the real world are not simply 'brute' facts, they are loaded with possibilities and impossibilities. In some cases what 'things' can do are defined in a way that is tightly integrated to facts. This implies action becomes a matter of necessity and, hence, we can make deterministic calculation. In a dynamic human context there can be many possibilities linked to facts and the deterministic calculation of actions is problematic. Also, our concepts have to take into account the value of the 'thing' and what it can do for people. What makes the 'thing' and what it can do relevant to the human actors is the fact that the possibilities it offers are a way to realise human values. Finally, to be a socially functioning construction it must communicated in a language understandable by the actors.

Measurements are one-dimensional in relation to reality and, therefore, they need to be supplemented with a narrative. Thus, a unified part of the measurement framework should be a narrative telling how to construct the relationship of the thing to the world. In identifying and developing the measurement system, the narrative comes to play a crucial role in reasoning and justifying the choice of certain measures and how they should be linked to action. Overall, for the measurement framework to have validity it must both fulfil conceptual criteria of definitions and establish the narrative telling how to link measures to human action and intention in an integrated way.

Pro-active, Pragmatic and Learning Theory of Truth

Criteria of conceptual definitions of measurement and the narrative linking the measurement to action are thought models that can help us to create some control over our practical world. However, the concepts are abstraction only. It is only through their pragmatic use that we can find out whether the measurement and the narrative express reality that is not fictitious or illusionary. In other words, to be practically valid the narrative governing the use of performance measurement should be integrated in reality. The practical validity of the measurement narrative is always linked to whether the future action holds true.

For that reason, we also need a pragmatic theory for evaluating the quality of our performance measurement. It is through the pragmatic aspect of our performance measurement model that we find out whether there is integration in reality. According to a pragmatic theory of truth a statement is true, if it leads to successful actions, i.e. if its future predictions hold true (Pierce 1905; James 1909). This principle can be applied to all relevant information. It is based on the consequences of what one can do. Because one cannot usually wait for truth verification but needs information in order to operate in the current time period, one needs an idea of truth based on the present so that it can serve as a basis for action. This is termed *pro-active truth*. It involves adequate analysis and reality checking of both the integration and the intended results in the measurement narratives. If the expected results are realised in action, then the statement is pragmatically true. *Pragmatic truth* can only be judged ex-post as experience of success or failure becomes apparent. The difference between pro-active truth and pragmatic truth can be termed the *truth gap*. The truth gap should become a basis for a continuous *learning* and improvement process. Without this, pro-active truth will become unreliable.

The Validity of Financial Accounting Models

The Nature of Accounting Measurement Models

The role of financial statements in the construction of social reality is to provide the informational basis necessary to support the financial markets' request for market economies to function. The apparent elusiveness of financial values makes it important to create an institution, which guarantees that people can trust companies reporting on their financial situation. Financial accounting should provide trustworthy information to all parties about the financial performance of the market actors (players) to improve fairness in trades and contracts. Fairness means that the value determined should not depend on subjective conditions such as friendship or family relations, bribery, power and influence, fraud or other hidden and undisclosed matters. Fair determination of the financial value of an item does not involve an absolute truth but a conceptually based evaluation process that excludes economically irrelevant and objectionable factors.

Generic accounting models are logical conceptual models where concepts such as assets, liabilities, revenues, expenses, costs and cash flow are linked together in a logical and coherent conceptual framework. The logical conceptual frameworks are based on an a priori rationalistic form of coherence without an empirical point of reference of its results. The rationalistic coherence theory of truth (Blanchard 1929) focuses on a priori conceptual relations, definitions and the analyses of inference and consistency. It is not an empirical reference that makes a statement true, but its coherence with other statements (Blanchard 1929). In accrual accounting, a payment of a managerial salary is a revenue expense not simply because of the statement that it is an expense that can be referenced to a payment event in the real world, but also because accountants use the term "revenue expense" about a certain type of financial transaction which contrasts with "capital expenditure". To refer to it as capital expenditure would be incoherent with respect to conceptual accounting logic. In contrast, under a cash flow model the significance of this distinction would change to reflect the use of operating and investing cash flows.

Traditionally, accountants have created and used financial statements that are based predominantly on historic cost measurement. This approach has emerged from the experience of practice over many years. Numerous alternatives exist (e.g. replacement cost, current purchasing power, fair value, deprival value and economic value) but none have usurped the primary position of historic cost.

A traditional paradigm of realism suggests that a choice can be made between alternative accounting models by an assessment of how truthfully they correspond to the real world. However, because accounting models do not exist in complete independence of human consciousness it is not possible to test them empirically in respect of whether their financial results and measurements are true. Accounting models are logical models that generate information on variables such as assets, liabilities, revenues and costs and logic cannot be positively observed, as it is not part of the physical world. Their truth cannot therefore be found by empirical correspondence. Logic (and therefore accounting models) can only be proved or rejected by logic. It is only through logic as opposed to recourse to realism that accounting models can be assessed in terms of their usefulness in the real world. Therefore, empirical testing of the accounting model based on proxies of earnings quality such as earnings persistence and smoothness generates misleading evidence. Thus, to clarify whether persistence and smoothness happens because of earnings management or other reasons requires the application of accounting logic (Ewert and Wagenhofer 2010). Also, using the investors' responsiveness to earnings as a proxy for earnings quality presupposes the accounting logic. Finally, an argumentation for the use of fair values in accounting statements has been that these correlate with the shareholder value. However, this is not surprising as both types of measurements are related to market expectation and hence are logically measuring similar phenomenon.

Historic Cost Accounting

The Measurement Model

Conventionally, accounting statements serve the traditional stewardship function of corporate financial accounting (Littleton 1953; Chua 1986a). Stewardship involves, "monitoring and reporting on the custodianship of resources" (AAA 1966) in order that agents (company directors) can be held accountable by their principals (shareholders). Its rationale is based on producing accounting information for controlling the managers' actions. Accountability is based on measuring the income and value of the company in order to identify bankruptcy, facilitate performance evaluation and rewards and support investors, creditors, shareholders and other stakeholders.

To achieve these purposes financial statements are intended to be "real world phenomena represented by numbers" (Ijiri 1978) and to be constituted as "aggregate statements which reflect, and do not distort the underlying reality" (Sidebotham 1970, 32). If accounting information were to be considered fictional, then its suitability for the stewardship function becomes compromised.

Consequently, accountants have sought objectivity for the financial statements that they produce through the measurement of an entity's income and value. Objectivity is considered to comprise "independence of judgement" and therefore a "freedom from bias" that "means that facts have been impartially determined and reported" (Paton and Littleton 1964; AAA 1966). Objectivity also implies that accounting information is capable of verification i.e. "essentially similar measures or conclusions would be reached if two or more qualified persons examined the same data" (AAA 1966).

Due to these requirements, accountants have traditionally advocated and used the system of historic cost accounting which, for much of its content, strives for a referential observational system that allows verification from past transaction records and documentation. Thus, governing the observational system are original purchase costs and revenue recognition.

In achieving financial measurement, management are also required to give narratives reviewing their understanding of the financial situation and prospects of the company. There is a regulatory requirement for relevance and trustworthy or faithful representation, but, given its nature, this requirement is inevitably somewhat lax.

There are different narratives for applying historical accounting measurement. One type of narrative is deterministic where measures are linked mechanically to action. An example of this is when a management contract links rewards directly to the accomplishment of accounting targets. However, a narrative may also be of a more holistic and reflective nature. It uses historic cost accounting information as one element in a more complex knowledge and judgement system. An example of this is when management evaluations are linked to some more detailed business knowledge and to the prospects of the company. Reviews by members of the board of directors include disclosures that concern information, which provides a more holistic and reflective narrative.

Historical accounting is a conceptual model structurally linking together particular items of measurement through logical relationships. The conceptual system is designed to measure managers' abilities to create financial wealth. Governing the referential observational system is the establishment of observations that correspond to objective financial transactions. The accounting model aims to fulfil the measurement criteria of both correspondence and the coherence theory of truth. However, historic cost accounting's limitations as objective referential observational system have long been recognised (e.g. MacNeal 1939; May 1972). Attempting to defend it as such is, therefore, problematic (Solomons 1991a, 1991b). The crucial issue for historical cost accounting lies in the degree to which the referential system is problematic. Below, the referential aspect of historical cost accounting is analysed from the perspective of pragmatic constructivism.

The Validity of the Historical Accounting Model

The problems of historical cost accounting have been attributed to difficulties in relating information to the real world that it is meant to represent, "the primary problem of accounting is that our figures do not have empirical referents" (Sterling 1979, 213). There is a lack of ontologically objective reality in the accounting measurements used. In particular, the monetary unit utilised by accountants in their measurements does not exist independently of human consciousness (Ryan et al. 2002) and therefore it has no physical referent.

However, from the perspective of pragmatic constructivism the lack of physical referent is not the major problem of historical accounting. Doing business is based on human constructs and hence all accounting phenomenon are human constructs. Although some of the historical cost accounting transactions relates to physical phenomenon such as raw material, land, buildings and equipment, societal actors including the accounting profession construct historical accounting measures. These are therefore institutional constructs e.g. observable market prices used by accountants, the adoption of currency as a measurement basis and the time period used as a basis of reporting. The existence of these facts depends on their construction being agreed by societal groups such as the business and investment communities, the legal profession and the accounting profession as a means of functioning. In this way they get a language and become institutionalised. However, the fact that accounting draws on institutional phenomenon and hence does not exist in an ontologically objective way in the world does not necessarily imply that there is no factual reference. Not only physical phenomenon, but also institutional and subjective phenomena have a referent. Crucial for trustworthiness in accounting is whether the referent is real or illusionary.

A financial accounting statement can be considered to be founded in reality if, and only if, it integrates all four dimensions of pragmatic constructivism. Many, but not all of the contents of historic cost-based financial statements are based on references to factual financial transactions. However, these are not 'brute facts', but facts based on constructs integrated with possibilities and human values which determine their selection. Financial statements are based on what it has been factually possible to do. Much of the linking to possibilities is historically based, e.g. inventory is based on historical evidence of its existence and that it has been factually possible to produce a certain item at a certain historic cost.

The historic cost accounting model implies that value measurement is restricted to assets that have been subject to accountable transactions. Thus, purchased goodwill is included in the balance sheet whereas non-purchased goodwill has generally been excluded. The self-generated wealth inherent in the creation of firm reputation, research in progress and employee expertise and motivation is, therefore, largely ignored although these factors may have required heavy investment. Whereas it is a possibility that these type of attributes will have great value, it is not factual.

Also, there are practical flexibilities concerning issues (such as the depreciation of fixed assets, the valuation of stock, the establishment of provisions, the recognition of income, variation in the purchasing power of the measurement currency and the segregation of capital and revenue expenditure) that make it difficult to produce indisputable factual information (Chambers 1966; Sterling 1979). Some of the measures involve the need to make future estimates, e.g. asset lives, consumption patterns and residual values, debtor receipts and stock selling prices. The reporting is based on what is assumed to be factually possible to do. "Facts" of this type are not susceptible to claims of truth on a directly observable correspondence basis. The use of future information inevitably makes accounting information moderately subjective. Overall, financial accounting statements are based on assumptions involving human judgement and some of the estimates made may be conjectural rather than factual (Paton 1962). Reinforcing these problems are the "incorrigible" cost allocations that pervade financial accounting (Thomas 1974, 1976). Whereas the establishment of regulations and standards can increase uniformity in accounting by developing rules for measurement and disclosure, it is unlikely that prescriptions of this type will eliminate flexibility. At best they restrict but do not uniformly define the realities upon which accounts are based.

Nevertheless, accounting practices draw on elements of pro-active and pragmatic truth when making judgements. Thus, guiding the subjective judgement in financial statements are principles of going concern, conservatism, consistency and reliability. For example, the evaluations of debtor receipts and stock selling prices are reflectively based on a judgement of whether the debtors will pay and whether the goods in stock will sell for that price. The pro-active judgement is an integrated part of a pragmatic observation of whether the debtors are paying and the stock is selling. In this way, the assumption about what it may be factually possible to do and the values to be employed in reporting are linked to the conservative projections of historically rooted business.

Consequently, historical financial accounting has a partial factual basis. However, the trustworthiness of some of the referent shaping the foundation for the historical accounting is problematic. In particular, there are the problems in relation to the financial consequences of the uncompleted chains of action that extend beyond the time of measurement. Accordingly, there are not only the measures that relate to what it has been possible to do and which possess value, but, also, the measures that relate directly to assumptions about the future. Historical accounting does not emphasise many of the elements which have no documented historical referents and do not have explicitly cost value. As validity presupposes the observational system matches the conceptual structure, the consequence of referential problems is that the measurement system becomes abstract in relation to company realities. The historically based conservatism of accounting principles governs considerations on pro-active and pragmatic truth. However, in a dynamic world the historically based conservatism could be misleading for the judgement of what is factually possible and valuable in the future.

Conclusion

Historic cost accounting, in its contemporary form, is an incomplete model of measuring managers' abilities to use resources to generate financial value. This approach, traditionally developed as a stewardship model of income and value aimed at ensuring the preservation of money capital, is trapped between the conflicting intentions of producing objective accounting information (based on past transactions) and being more economically credible (but less objective) by incorporating more subjective current values. The latter development is advocated as better supporting the investment decision-making purpose of financial statements and this aim has gradually begun to subsume stewardship as the primary function of financial statements. However, movement in this direction has meant that the paradigm of realism has become even less relevant as a justification for and defence of accounting practice.

It is the contention of this chapter that the development and adoption of a paradigm of practice, based on the framework of pragmatic constructivism can provide a solution to this accounting dilemma. First, due to the existing subjectivity (e.g. in provision setting) and estimation (e.g. in the determination of depreciation) required in contemporary financial statement preparation, the validity of accounting information should be maintained through the application of a learning theory of truth. In this way, an interplay between the conception of pragmatic truth and the more conventional pro-active truth can form a basis for the accounting profession's practice improvement. Practice can focus on reducing the "truth gap" that exists in applying these two truth concepts. As a result the accountant's claim to produce true information becomes more credible.

Second, the methodology of pragmatic constructivism can be employed to generate a paradigm to replace realism. This can take the form of a new conceptual framework that accountants can use as a bulwark to justify and defend their practice as valid. This can be achieved by the application and integration of the four dimensions of pragmatic constructivism to the reality of accounting practice. Then, a factual basis for practice can legitimately be claimed. Recognised facts and their inherent possibilities provide a basis for the substance and boundaries of practice. The search for revising the facts and possibilities provides the means to develop practice. Professional values that are societal, ethical and technical can be established to provide a basis for selection of possibilities. Finally, the process of communication will be a primary concern for practice. How communication is to function and who are to be the recipients of accounting information are questions to which the adoption of the pragmatic constructionism perspective necessitates answers. The framework also requires an integration of the four pragmatic constructionism in a way that ensures correspondence with the reality of each and coherence between them. A conceptual framework of this type will enhance the accounting profession's credibility by providing a logical basis for explaining, justifying and developing practice.

References

AAA. 1966. *A Statement of Basic Accounting Theory*. Evanston, IL: American Accounting Association.

Abdel-khalik, A. Rashad, and Bipin B. Ajinkya. 1979. *Empirical Research in Accounting. A Methodological Viewpoint*. Sarasota, FL: American Accounting Association, Accounting Education Services.

Blanchard, Percy B. 1929. *The Nature of Thought*. London: George, Allen and Unwin.

Chambers, Raymond J. 1966. *Accounting Evaluation and Economic Behaviour*. Englewood Cliffs, NJ: Prentice-Hall.

Chua, Wai F. 1986a. "Theoretical constructions of and by the real." *Accounting Organizations and Society*, 11 (6): 583–598.

Chua, Wai F. 1986b. "Radical developments in accounting thought." *The Accounting Review*, 61 (4): 601–632.

Ewert, Ralf, and Alfred Wagenhofer. 2010. *Earnings Quality Metrics and What They Measure*. mitsloan.mit.edu/groups/template/pdf/Ewart-Wagenhofer.pdf.

Heidegger, Martin. 1927 (1977). "Sein und Zeit." In Heidegger's *Gesamtausgabe*, edited by F.W. von Herrmann, 2 (XIV): 586.

Husserl, Edmund. 1913. "Ideen zu einer reinen Phänomenologie und Phänomenologischen Philosophie." In *Allgemeine Einführung in die reine Phänomenologie*, 1–323. Freiburg: Universität Freiburg.

Ijiri, Yuji. 1978. *The Foundations of Accounting Measurement*. Houston, TX: Scholars Book Company.

James, William. 1909 (1997). *The Meaning of Truth: A Sequel to "Pragmatism."* New York: Prometheus Books.

Littleton, Ananias C. 1953. *Structure of Accounting Theory*. Urbana, IL: American Accounting Association.

MacNeal, Kenneth. 1939 (1970). *Truth in Accounting*. Lawrence, KS: Scholars Book.

May, George O. 1972. *Financial Accounting a Distillation of Experience*. Houston, TX: Scholars Book.

Meyer, John, and Brian Rowan. 1977. "Institutionalized organizations: Formal structure of myth and ceremony." *American Journal of Sociology*, 83 (2): 340–363.

Nørreklit, Hanne, Lennart Nørreklit, and Falconer Mitchell. 2007. "Theoretical conditions for validity in accounting performance measurement." In *Business Performance Measurement — Frameworks and Methodologies*, edited by Andy Neely, 179–217. Cambridge: Cambridge University Press.

Nørreklit, Hanne, Lennart Nørreklit, and Falconer Mitchell. 2010. "Towards a paradigmatic foundations of accounting practice." *Accounting, Auditing and Accountability Journal*, 23 (6): 733–758.

Nørreklit, Hanne, Lennart Nørreklit, Falconer Mitchell, and Trond Bjørnenak. 2012. "The rise of the balanced scorecard! Relevance regained?" *Journal of Accounting and Organizational Change*, 8 (4): 490–510.

Nørreklit, Lennart. 2017. "Actor reality construction." In *A Philosophy of Management Accounting: A Pragmatic Constructivist Approach*, edited by Hanne Nørreklit. Chapter 2, this volume. New York: Routledge.

Paton, William A. 1962. *Accounting Theory*. Houston, TX: Scholars Book.

Paton, William A., and Ananias C. Littleton. 1964. *An Introduction to Corporate Accounting Standards*. New York: American Accounting Association.

Pierce, C.A. 1905. "What pragmatism is." *The Monist*, XV (2): 161–181.

Ryan, Bob, Robert W. Scapens, and Michael Theobald. 2002. *Research Method & Methodology in Finance & Accounting*. Padstow, UK: Thomson.

Searle, John. 1995. *The Construction of Social Reality*. London: Penguin.

Sidebotham, Ramon. 1970. *Introduction to the Theory and Context of Accounting*. Oxford: Pergammon Press.

Solomons, David. 1991a. "Accounting and social change: A neutralist view." *Accounting, Organizations and Society*, 16 (3): 287–295.

Solomons, David. 1991b. "A rejoinder." *Accounting, Organizations and Society*, 16 (3): 311–312.

Sterling, Robert R. 1972. *Research Methodology in Accounting*. Houston, TX: Scholars Book.

Sterling, Robert R. 1979. *Theory of the Measurement of Enterprise Income*. Lawrence, KS: University Press of Kansas.

Thomas, Arthur L. 1974. *The Allocation Problem: Part Two*. Sarasota, FL: American Accounting Association.

Thomas, Arthur L. 1976. *The Allocation Problem in Financial Accounting Theory*. Sarasota, FL: American Accounting Association.

Tinker, Anthony M. 1991. "The accountant as partisan." *Accounting, Organizations and Society*, 16 (3): 297–310.

Tinker, Anthony M., Barbara D. Merino, and Marilyn D. Neimark. 1982. "The normative origins of positive theories: Ideology and accounting thought." *Accounting, Organizations and Society*, 7 (2): 167–200.

7 Orchestrating Strategic Co-Authorship

Gudrun Baldvinsdottir and
Cristian Heidarson

Introduction

The communication and implementation of organisational strategy is traditionally seen as the role of senior management—typically led by the CEO. The annual report represents one way of creating a narrative to support the organisation's strategic profile and is recognised as an important means of communicating corporate strategy (e.g. Foreman and Argenti 2005). The CEO statement is the most widely read part of a company's annual report and it is seen as highly indicative of framing strategies used (e.g. Fanelli and Grasselli 2006). It presents an opportunity for senior management to communicate the company strategy to business stakeholders on an ongoing basis.

The ability of this communication to foster stakeholder cooperation is critical to the efficient execution of the company strategy. The public nature of the CEO statement requires that the concerns of all stakeholders be addressed, although individually stakeholders may hold opposing values, understand facts differently and foresee disparate possibilities. In other words, the topoi of senior management must integrate a multitude of external topoi that may be in conflict with one another. Such significant divergence presents a communication challenge for the CEO. At a bare minimum, the statement should avoid invalidating any progress already made during discussions with individual stakeholders, but a more ambitious statement may go further and offer overarching narratives which simultaneously reconcile multiple concerns.

Strategy based on pragmatic constructivism considers business as a backdrop against which co-authors construct a common narrative. The CEO statements enable an analysis of the CEO's motivations from a distance, suggest a certain leadership quality and provide important governance and investment signals to the broader spectrum of stakeholders (Craig and Amernic 2011). The CEO's ideas have consequences for key corporate decisions because words are powerful, especially when expressed strategically in support of organisational practice or in order to counteract opposition to it. Ideally, managers will attempt to coordinate the backdrop of perspectives and create storylines aimed at unifying participating co-authors behind the strategic profile.

Accordingly, the CEO statement serves as an opportunity to recognise the multiple topoi interacting with senior management as well as being a negotiation tool to solve potential conflicts. Thus, the CEO statement is primarily geared towards resolving the tension between the many topoi of the business stakeholders. Against this background, the following research question is stated:

How is strategic co-authorship orchestrated through CEO statements?

Theoretical Framework

When senior management develops the strategic direction for a company, their decisions will stem from their understanding of the facts relating to the company, on logical possibilities that arise from those facts and the values of the individual team members. A management topoi will thus emerge through ongoing conversation between the team members, culminating in an agreed upon set of facts, possibilities and values. The factual possibilities that align with the values of the topoi represent the real strategic options available to the team.

As an organisation grows larger, it will become too complex to sustain a single topoi where all employees share the same vision of values, facts and possibilities. Senior management, the sales organisation, the engineering organisation etc. will each have their own individual topoi. However, as employees from multiple topoi communicate across the company, consensus may emerge on some facts, possibilities and values thereby establishing an overarching company topoi. (Nørreklit 2017a, Chapter 2, this volume; Nørreklit et al. 2017, Chapter 4, this volume.)

Strategy as Narrative

Prevalent strategy literature is primarily concerned with matching a company's external environment with its internal structures and resources (e.g. Chandler 1990; Miles and Snow 2003). Ogilvy et al. (2014) argue that the literature can be structured into two major streams, one focusing on the external environment such as Porter's approach to competitive strategy (e.g. Porter 1985) and the other focusing on the alignment of internal resources, as in the resource-based approach to strategy (e.g. Prahalad and Hamel 1990). Within this paradigm, the strategic profile is understood as the structural relations between a company's internal structure and its external environment. Senior management's role is to examine the fit of these relations and ensure decisions that best achieve this fit (Mitchell et al. 2013). An acknowledged challenge for management is the asymmetry between the two of them, where external conditions are at most indirectly controllable and internal are more controllable.

Recent literature suggests that the traditional view of strategy as the property of the organisation needs to be complemented with a view of strategy as something that people do (e.g. Jarzabkowski 2004), because theoretical reasoning needs to be qualified by practical experience and good judgement, i.e. practical wisdom (Ogilvy et al. 2014). Activities can be traced through conversations, talks and text, and this further justifies the inclusion of a narrative approach to strategy, where the narrative is defined as "thematic sequenced accounts that convey meaning from implied author to implied reader" (Barry and Elmes 1997, 431). This is in line with the definition of strategy presented by Fenton and Langley (2011) and is applied within this chapter:

> Strategy manifests itself through patterns of action that have significance for the organisation's overall direction and in particular for its relationship for its environment.
>
> (1192)

Strategy is seen here as a set of actions and activities that relate to strategic outcomes; they are always related to a desired future, a way forward from the past through the present and represented by narratives of real events to be developed and implemented. As such, the purpose of a strategic narrative is to motivate future action, rather than justifying prior decisions. Strategies are thus neither true nor false, but serve as invitations towards a desired future (Ogilvy et al. 2014). These invitations are extended as a response to the asymmetric levels of control over internal and external conditions. This does not mean that organisations are without means to influence external parties, however; on the contrary, the organisation can intentionally use its control of internal capabilities and resources to mould its external environment (Mitchell et al. 2013).

In this chapter, the CEO statement is looked upon as a strategy text (Fenton and Langley 2011). The statements typically contain observations of facts about the company as well as the applicable industry. They also express company values, either stated explicitly, or implied through the justifications for company initiatives, which means that they contain a narrative of the real strategic options available to senior management. Seen from this perspective, the statements' communication of facts, possibilities and values may be understood as an expression of the company's strategic profile to its stakeholders (Mitchell et al. 2013). The statements serve as a conversation in which the narratives from various stakeholders are integrated (Robichaud et al. 2004). The CEO statements can indicate how management seeks to find coherent narratives that allow coexistence and synergy between the multiple topoi of stakeholders.

A Pragmatic Constructivist View on Strategic Profile

Co-authoring the Narrative of the Strategic Profile

Leadership involves the authorship of the main activities of the organisation. At the core of pragmatic constructivism is the recognition that effective organisational practice is the outcome of the actions, constructions and integration of external and internal actors. The strategic profile of the organisation therefore includes the actors as co-authors. The narrative created by the strategic profile is composed, re-composed and actualized by the management and in this process the co-authorship of other actors is integrated by assigning them a role that fits their skills and motivations. Without this integration, an actor's own sense of meaning, belonging and participation in the strategic profile cannot be achieved. It is indeed an advanced skill to manage a co-authoring process! In such a process, the management writes the outline of the business in cooperation with other actors and by doing so they are made co-authors. This process of co-authorship needs to be organised to ensure the inclusion of the specific factual conditions, possibilities and values of the participating actors. This in turn creates a narrative and a set of related topoi to ensure that each actor will contribute in the best interest of organisational practice.

To be effective, the co-authored narrative of the strategic profile needs to be communicated both internally and externally. This is the 'social function' of the narrative which creates a coherent reality for the actors involved. Communication of the strategic profile thus satisfies the condition of positioning the organisation within the social world where it operates.

Communication is usually a combination of two processes, the expression and interpretation of messages. However, deeper communication also requires an active exploration of subsequent reciprocal expressions by the various actors during an ongoing conversation. The strategic profile of an organisation is communicated through intentionally chosen expressions. Heuristics and bias—or pre-understandings—inform the interpretation of expressions creating the framework on which a valid reality construct hinges. It guarantees that organisational targets are within reach of factual possibilities and as such, pre-understanding determines the impression, reaction and reciprocal expression. (Nørreklit 2017a, 2017b, Chapters 2 and 3, this volume; Nørreklit et al. 2017, Chapter 4, this volume)

The Reality Constructs of the Strategic Profile

The constructed reality representing an organisation's strategic profile takes into account a variety of different possible futures each permitting the realisation of governing values through the choice of actions. This means that the actors' actions are not only dependent on their pre-understanding, but also on linking their impressions and subsequent expressions through an assumption of causality between events. The concept of possibility can connect the present to different possible futures, but the linking of impressions and expressions is done through the identification of causal chains which can be intentionally organised and acted upon.

In practice, causal relations are constructed by the actors involved, who can enact some of these causal relations to realise a specific possibility. The choice of a specific possibility is embedded in a system of intertwined casual chains that together represent not only the specific goal, but also the personal and organisational values which need to be fulfilled. In the absence of certainty regarding the future, management is limited to developing its strategic profile from an understanding of such causal links grounded in existent truth. The causal links identified are supported by thorough analysis of future possibilities and the resources needed to achieve the goals are reflected in the strategic profile. Integration of possibilities and values is made by the actors' interpretation and moulding of the system of causal chains. Consequently, practice is based on 'construct causalities'—causalities that are the results of social constructs in the unique business practice of each organisation.

Through the construction and reconstruction of causal chains in the light of pre-understandings, new experiences, context and communication, this reality construction is subject to continuous scrutiny because endeavours may not turn out as expected. A process of monitoring, analysing and correcting is the basis for continuous learning and improving processes that lead to constant revisions of the reality constructs. When management is able to detect the missteps of explorations of previously identified possibilities, and can deal with the consequences by identifying new causal chains to realise modified possibilities, the reality construct is adequate.

The distinction between a functioning reality construct and an illusionary one is nevertheless not distinct and has to do with the uncertainty of both future possibilities and the causal chains constructed in respect to them. Illusions may be difficult to detect, and even intentionally created as social gaming due to various strategic reasons. A functioning reality construct however, is based in sincerity and allows for flexibility. It can be tested and adjusted if possibilities once declared factual, are found to be illusionary. The construction of a strategic profile can therefore be seen as a guideline on how to build a flexible practice under changing conditions.

The Validity of the Strategic Profile

Only in practice can a specific organisation prove whether a reality construction is valid for the organisation in question. Its validity is proven through an iterative process where pro-active and pragmatic truth are continuously compared and the inevitable truth gap monitored carefully. The distinction between the two is of particular interest when it comes to the strategic profile of an organisation. CEO statements represent iterative milestones that are subjects to truth gaps as soon as the last word is written. Yet, when creating a strategic profile, the management needs to have an idea of truth based on the present, in absence of certainty regarding the future. The projected causal links are grounded in thorough analysis of future possibilities and the resources needed to achieve the goals implied in the strategic profile. This idea of pro-active truth serves as a basis for current action. If the actions that are decided upon the causal links related to the pro-active truth lead to the intended results, pragmatic truth is in place. Pragmatic truth only holds if the predictions of pro-active truth hold, because it can only be evaluated ex-post when the management knows for sure if the intention of the strategic profile has been fulfilled.

In practice, the gap between the two is evident. It is, however, imperative to take measures to keep the truth gap as small as possible, because if it grows too large, the pro-active truth becomes a misleading tool in the decision and planning process. Systematically monitoring the difference between pro-active and pragmatic truths increases the likelihood of the identification of a truth gap. It can thus be analysed and traced to its origin. This process of monitoring, analysing and correcting is the basis for continuous learning and improving processes that lead to constant revisions of the strategic profile which aim at decreasing the variance between the two. (Nørreklit 2017a, 2017b, Chapters 2 and 3, this volume.)

Empirical Context

Swedish Electricity Market Reforms

The quest for deregulation of the energy sector in the 1980s signified a departure from previous political and economic consensus. The main argument for the deregulation—competition as positive force in the development of infrastructure—challenged the predominant monopoly-oriented policies of regulators. Such a line of reasoning questioned the need for state ownership of network utilities and reconsidered long-standing notions about natural monopolies and related regulatory interventions (Högselius and Kaijser 2010). It was argued that a deregulated industry would lead to greater competition, spurring energy companies to offer their customers a variety of new and innovative services aimed to facilitate long-term customer relationships and generate sustainable energy and energy-related sales. Against this background, the move towards market liberalisation in Sweden was initiated in 1991 (Riksdagsförvaltningen 1991a, 1991b).

Municipal actors largely supported deregulation as they expected to benefit from lower electricity prices and greater flexibility and freedom by avoiding dependency on their traditional regional suppliers. Like the large power companies, they saw that the possibility of increased wholesale competition could lead to lower electricity prices. Yet, at the same time, they were uncertain about their own role on a future deregulated retail market and feared that they might be too small to act successfully (Högselius and Kaijser 2010).

The Case Company—Göteborg Energy

Between 1990 and 2007, Göteborg Energy (GbgE) was the largest utility company in Gothenburg. It was owned by the municipality of Gothenburg and employed about 1200 people. Historically, it had good profitability and solvency but of all its utility products, district heating was its feather in its cap, and had been so since the mid-1950s. The prohibitive cost of switching to a different supplier meant that in practice, it operated as a monopoly.

At the beginning of the period electricity transmission accounted for over 50 percent of company revenues and district heating for the another 40 percent—the rest made up by a mix of natural gas and energy services (Annual Report (AR) 1990). At this time, GbgE lacked its own electricity production. The ongoing debate regarding deregulation of the electricity market, and its anticipated implementation, initiated discussions and initiatives within the company about how it should adapt to a liberalised market, and resulted in the company being incorporated in 1990. Several actions were taken in subsequent years to secure GbgE's role as a leading utility company in West Sweden, mainly through acquisitions of utility companies in the surrounding municipalities of Gothenburg. Furthermore, the regional reach of the district heating system was expanded and several contracts were signed with local industry to ensure the recycling of waste heating into the district heating system. At the end of the period, the company had the largest interconnected district heating area in Europe (AR 2007).

GbgE also cooperated with main industry actors in West Sweden in order to decrease and even eliminate their carbon emissions. Costly investments were made in facilities where biogas was upgraded to the more environmentally friendly natural gas and large-scale wind turbine projects were initiated south of Gothenburg. The year 2006 saw the inauguration of the Rya Combined Heat and Power Plant (CHP) fuelled by natural gas (AR 2006). The CHP plant had the capacity to supply 30 percent of the electricity needs of Gothenburg as well as about 35 percent of its district heating requirements. In 2007 the main revenue streams were from the transmission of electricity (23 percent), district heating (52 percent) and electricity sales (8 percent) (AR 2007).

Methodology

The CEO statements used in this study are from 1990–2007. This period was chosen because it follows a particularly long-term strategic initiative to build the CHP plant, first mentioned in 1990 but only completed in 2006. The statement of 2007 contains the last effort to justify the project. The long time-horizon allows an evaluation of the development of strategies over the tenures of three CEO's, revealing consistent patterns in what might otherwise appear as dramatic back-tracking and strategic shift.

A note on the terminology used in the analysis: The word *topoi* is from classical Greek and is the plural of *topos*. However, within the framework of pragmatic constructivism, *topoi* has a more specific meaning than simply the plural of *topos*. Within this framework, a *topoi* is the set of multiple *topos* on which several actors agree in their communication, especially when communicating about actions. So, whereas a single *topos* represents the thematic integration of a set of values, facts and possibilities, a *topoi* also includes communication. Therefore, these words will be used to refer to their respective concepts both in the singular and plural:

- *one topoi, several topoi;*
- *one topos, several topos.*

The analysis of the empirical material was conducted in three phases. In the first phase, the authors read through the CEO statements, independently assessing which outside actors had a stake in the company's actions. The combined assessment was reviewed by two consultants who had a history of working with GbgE. In the second phase, each sentence was considered separately, asking the question: "how does this sentence help justify the company's actions?" The answers were then assigned to thematic groups which corresponded to interests of stakeholders as understood through the first phase of analysis. These groupings were interpreted as a number of topos, and each sentence was individually tagged with the topos it touched upon. In the third phase, the two authors together analysed the pattern of topos on a paragraph-by-paragraph basis. In paragraphs that addressed multiple topos, the interaction between the topos were categorised as either simply recognising the importance of each topos individually; describing a causal relationship between the topos; describing a conflict between the topos; or the mobilisation of one set of topos to resolve a conflict between another set of topos.

CEO Statements

Statements of the First CEO

The first CEO led the organisation from 1990 to 1996, overseeing the transition from a municipal utility to a business-oriented company as the electricity market was liberalised in 1996. From the outset, senior management expressed optimism about the task.

> GbgE has the ambition to play an important role in establishing the dominance of western Sweden [within the transforming power industry].
> (Translated from the Annual Report 1990)[1]

Although the CEO statements express satisfaction with financial results, there is a concern regarding how these results can be maintained and improved. The municipal owners are experiencing financial pressures and are considering divesting a portion of its shares. The statements repeatedly stress the size of dividends returned to the owners. At the same time there was a commitment to keeping energy prices low for households and local industry. The statements present efforts to improve utilisation of assets as a solution that will protect the interests of both owners and customers.

> Our ambition is to increase our financial results further through internal efficiency programmes and without raising customer prices. [. . .] we have had the goal to increase our profitability without increasing customer prices.
>
> (AR 1993)

The Abandoned First Proposal to build the CHP Plant

The deliberations over the CHP plant ran as a common thread through the first 17 years as a privatised company. During the tenure of the company's first CEO, the plant was seen primarily as a guarantee for the independent supply of energy to the region:

> Our long term strategy includes the building of a combined heat and power plant in order to minimize our dependence on others, and thereby increase security of long-term energy supply. [The CHP plant] can be expected to become an important part of our long-term ventures.
>
> (AR 1992)

The statements present the decision matter-of-factly, without any overt efforts to convince the reader to support the proposal. The benefits of the plant are summarised with:

> long-term profitability, environmentally sound, needed as replacement for aging facilities and to ensure a secure supply of energy.
>
> (AR 1993)

However, against a context of uncertain rules for the taxation of energy production, the expected decision was abandoned after 1993. In the 1996 statement, the outgoing CEO suggested that the dismantling of the country's nuclear power production capabilities would make the CHP plant a priority for his successor.

Early on in the period, the statements pointed out that the CHP plant application had been conditional on meeting environmental targets. For the next couple of years, the CEO statements outlined a growing role for sustainability in the company's profile.

> Over the last years we have actively promoted effective energy utilisation by our customers, [offering them] environmentally friendly services. To improve our employees' environmental awareness, we have carried out an internal campaign [and] employed an environmental controller to strengthen our profile as a sustainable company.
>
> (AR 1994)

The new business in energy-efficiency services (EES) consultancy was central to the developing profile. The services were positioned as a way to shift energy use to more efficient forms such as district heating and cooling, as well as improving the energy utilisation of properties and equipment.

Statements of the Second CEO

The second CEO led the organisation from 1997 to 2001, overseeing a period during which the organisation was shaped by competitive forces and fought to retain its independence in a consolidating industry. Throughout the period, the statements emphasised growth.

> We want to grow in size and strength. We have the capacity and competence. And we will always strive for more.
>
> (AR 1997)

Early on, the statements proposed that whereas the newly competitive market had meant a loss of market share (from 100 percent), these losses could be offset through expansion into new markets. The case was made for doubling the volume of electricity sales, which resulted in spinning off the business into a joint venture together with the largest national player. This allowed the company a stronger focus on expanding its infrastructure for district heating, an area where it enjoyed a monopoly.

Whereas the role of EES consultancy services was deemphasized, the statements continued to bolster the company's sustainability profile. The professed environmental benefits of district heating were central to developing this profile.

> Environmental awareness is one of our keywords. The goal of our district heating system is to feed it with waste heating from other processes, collected from local industry. This is in line with our resource management.
>
> (AR 1999)

The statements reported mostly satisfactory results while reiterating the company's determination to keep prices low. Instead, positive results were to be achieved through improvements in internal efficiency such as the decision to reduce a substantial part of the workforce through early retirement. Indeed, when the results lower than expected this was attributed to the company's refusal to raise customer prices despite a spike in fuel costs. In his last statement, the CEO observed that even municipal companies must be profitable in order to fund investments and expansion. However, he stressed the need for a municipal company to balance the goal of profitability with the interests of stakeholders, and the continued importance of social and environmental goals for the organisation.

Making a Passionate Plea for the CHP Proposal

In contrast to the first CEO, the arguments for building the CHP plant were made forcefully and with the intent of convincing the reader. Under the tax system at the time the plant would not have been financially viable, which prompted the second CEO to focus the last two statements of his tenure on a passionate argument for reforming the system. The argument rested on the pressing need to build the plant to support the growing demand for district heating, and possible risks of not being able to satisfy that demand.

> We will continue with our supply guarantee even if the temperature falls in western Sweden. [. . .] Let us hope we have seen the end of cold winters for now, so that we can manage for a little longer. But who dares to trust [the weather]? The parliament and government? We do not want to take a chance. [. . .] we stubbornly continue to work on getting the natural gas taxed in a way that makes it profitable to use.
>
> (AR 2001)

He also elaborated on the environmental benefits of the CHP plant, positioning it in direct competition with Danish coal power plants. The CEO described the challenge GbgE and other energy industry actors had in order to harmonise global energy taxes, arguing that sustainable solutions such as the CHP plant could not compete with Danish and German imports. Whereas the matter was not resolved during his tenure, the statements do note that the company's efforts had received support among the political parties.

Statements of the Third CEO

The third CEO started his tenure in 2002 just as the municipal owners had agreed to the construction of the CHP plant. By then, the organisation was firmly entrenched in the market, and the statements during this period emphasised technological innovation. The strategic focus on developing value-added services was illustrated by "new customers who purchase more complicated products [are developing the capabilities of GbgE]." By 2006, the CEO statement declared that the company was "building the future", and listed multiple infrastructure investment and customer engagements that achieved cost savings and a reduced environmental footprint through new technologies. Sustainability pervades the statements of the third CEO, with almost all initiatives in some way motivated by a reduced environmental footprint. The statements demonstrated a renewed focus on the development of the EES consultancy business, and discussed cooperation with major corporate customers to reduce their energy usage.

Efficiency continued to be in focus. The efficiency programme "Effekten" was discussed at length, and cost reductions were brought to the fore.

"Effekten" was completed with results that exceeded the goal [resulting in] profits beyond expectations, and we are now able to continue our investments with a sound proportion of equity.

(AR 2004)

The Construction of the CHP Plant

The CHP plant was built despite uncertainties about carbon taxes and emission allowances. The statements give credit to the owners of GbgE who were willing to trust political intention regarding fiscal regulation—the new system would not take effect until 2008. New issues arose around the plant, such as the Swedish contribution to the Kyoto protocol, and the statements made the case for a fair distribution of CO_2 emission quotas.

During this time, there was a noticeable shift in tone towards evangelising the CHP project and positioning it as a springboard for other initiatives. For example, the size of the investment was used to justify the layoffs resulting from the "Effekten" programme. Also, as the CHP plant could use both natural gas and biogas as fuel, a new major facility for refining biogas was proposed:

> If the gas used in the power plant came from biofuels, the positive climate impact would be even greater. This presupposes that we can gasify wood fuels economically and we have now initiated research to find out the feasibility of a larger biogas plant.
>
> (AR 2005)

The rationale for these actions rested on the expected value of the CHP plant. The CEO justified the decision as ensuring uninterrupted supply of energy, as well as a reduction in emissions.

> To increase the security of supply in Gothenburg, we are building the new CHP plant, producing electricity and heating simultaneously. About a quarter of the electricity and heating consumption in Gothenburg will be met with the new plant. It can also cover for supply of the city's most important functions in the case of major national electricity disruptions. With both efficient technology and using natural gas as fuel, it will minimize all emissions.
>
> (AR 2003)

The statement of 2007 reflected on the first full year of operation for the CHP plant. It was noted that profitability was hit by the unfavourable current tax system. The coveted change to the tax system was due to take place the following year and was expected to result in tax and fee savings between 100 and 200 million Swedish Krona.

Discussion

The Company Topoi

The Overarching Company Topoi: the Topos of Infrastructure

In the first annual report produced by the newly reincorporated company, the statement emphasises that:

> The question of our future power supply is of fundamental importance.
> (AR 1990)

The importance attributed to power supply can be understood as an expression of an overarching company topoi. Common facts, values and possibilities for a utility company such as GbgE are most likely to relate to the infrastructure, production assets and their analogous economics, as well as the recognised role such a company plays in national energy policy. The assets that remain the most significant to the company throughout the period include the electricity grid which relied on external sources, and the infrastructure for district heating which included its own production facilities.

In the CEO statements, the company topoi manifests itself as a set of thematic sequenced accounts that is distinguishable as a discrete topos: the *Infrastructure* topos. The topos includes updates about infrastructure acquisitions, maintenance and upgrades. The values of the topos are employed to motivate investments in order to achieve supply independence and ensure an adequate supply of fuel.

The Topoi of the Senior Management Team: the Topos of Differentiation, Growth and Innovation

In addition to the *Infrastructure* topos, the CEO statements display a consistent sense of optimism and pro-active attitude towards change. This sentiment can be understood as an expression of the senior management team's personal topoi. Each CEO expresses a unique approach to leadership corresponding to the maturity of the company and the market, to support their take on organisational practice and to contravene external opposition to key decisions. The first CEO highlights the need to differentiate the products and services in order to ensure competitiveness ahead of market liberalisation; the second CEO indicates the opportunities for growth in the newly liberalised market; and the third CEO emphasises the need for innovation to provide a new direction for a company that is now firmly entrenched in the market. Each approach represents a topos—*Differentiation*, *Growth* and *Innovation*. Whereas emphasised to different degrees by the three CEOs, all topos can be identified throughout the entire period.

All of these topos are employed to champion the construction of the CHP plant. The topos of *Infrastructure* can be identified in warnings that existing facilities are approaching the end of their lifecycle as evidenced by increasing failures. The topos of *Differentiation* justifies having both heating and electricity generation; the topos of *Growth* is employed to rationalise capacity investments supporting business expansion; and the topos of *Innovation* supports investments in new production technologies to provide more efficient fuel to the CHP plant.

Initiating a Conversation with Stakeholders

The proposal to build the CHP plant required approval both by the municipal owners as well as by national regulators. Finding common ground between the owners and the legislators required a conversation that moved them towards a shared understanding of the facts and expectations that suggested the factual possibility of the plant, as well as an agreement on some of the values that justify its construction. The CEO statements represent an opportunity to recognise both parties as co-authors of the company's strategic profile and to present possible avenues towards mutually beneficial solutions. Within the discussion of strategy in the CEO statements, these stakeholders are only rarely addressed explicitly. Instead, their concerns are integrated into the strategic narrative as topos—facts, possibilities and values that consistently repeat as thematic sequenced accounts.

The Topoi of the Municipal Owners; the Topos of Social and Finance

The topoi of the municipal owners are recognised in the statements as the topos of *Social* and *Finance*. The company remained wholly-owned by the Gothenburg municipality throughout the period covered by this analysis. The owners of the company had a broader set of interests beyond financial returns. As the transition to market competition began in 1995, the CEO stresses that the municipal ownership restricted the possibilities available to the company, and that price levels will be held artificially low during the transition to protect customers. As market prices rose in 1996, the CEO framed the decision to keep prices low as a "political" decision. The statement further describes how the company lobbied regulators for changes to remove barriers of exit for smaller customers—i.e. make it easier for customers to leave the company.

However, the rules imposed by the market liberalisation reform required that the company be run in a business-oriented manner, i.e. it had to compete in the market as a for-profit enterprise. Whereas it did not pursue a profit-maximizing strategy, there was still a fundamental requirement that all investments show a positive return. Furthermore, during the company's first years the CEO points out that the municipal owners were experiencing budget issues themselves and so were in need of dividends from the company.

*The Topoi of the Regulators; the Topos of Sustainability,
Security and Competition*

The topoi of the regulators are recognised in the statements as the topos of *Sustainability, Security* and *Competition*. The concerns of the regulators are first recognised in the statement of 1991, which describes the political debates that resulted in the decision to ween the country off nuclear power and liberalise the energy industry. The debates were defined by a strong environmental movement that sought to replace nuclear power with more sustainable alternatives—the topos of *Sustainability*. Without new power production, the dismantling of nuclear power capacity would make the country increasingly dependent on imports. This created concerns about national security as well as a potentially negative impact of high energy prices on the domestic industry—the topos of *Security*. The liberalisation of the energy market was proposed as a strategy to ensure continued low prices and efficiency gains through market innovation—the topos of *Competition*.

Recognising Stakeholder Tensions

Senior management can pro-actively engage another party to find overlapping values and a shared understanding of facts and possibilities. Convincing several other parties to engage in such a conversation with one other requires a more complex form of persuasion. This becomes a critical task when decisions rely on multiple company stakeholders, as conflicting interests may prevent cooperation and hold up decisions. As opposed to more private communication channels, the CEO statement publicly facilitates awareness of different party interests within the company's strategic profile through a narrative where the different topoi are represented as topos in tension with each other.

The complicated situation surrounding the taxes and quotas represented a major hurdle to the company's efforts to get the CHP plant constructed. Confusion about the tax on district heating was one of the issues that postponed the decision on the proposal during the tenure of the first CEO. This issue becomes a priority for the second CEO who presses the concern throughout his tenure. His argument can be analysed as examples of reality construction in practice. Consider the following statement:

> [Most] electricity production is also a heat-generating process. However, most of this heat is disposed into the sea [while] we import electricity from Danish coal power plants. Importing electricity is relatively cheap and occurs to some degree all the time. However, this is a major drain on the environment due to the emissions involved and the problem is a global one. [. . .] We must find a fair alternative to the current situation where the warm water that is produced through electricity

generation is free to dispose into the sea but taxed when employed in a district heating system.

The arguments in this paragraph take three forms. First, they present a series of construct causalities between international trade and global emissions; taxation and international trade; and taxation and wasteful disposal of useful warm water. Second, they construct a reality in which the multiple topos of individual topoi are inconsistent with each other. The topos of *Competition* is presented as inconsistent with *Sustainability*, as competitive energy prices favour emission-heavy imports over solutions that make use of existing waste energy in the system. Furthermore, the continued use of nuclear power and the resulting disposal of waste heat reminds the reader of the conflict between *Sustainability* and *Security* that was at the centre of the energy policy debate in the 1980s.

Third, they highlight the conflict between topos belonging to different topoi: the financial requirements of the municipal owners that all investments provide a positive return, regardless of the benefits to society. The statements present a negative construct causality where the inconsistent topos of regulators are forcing the municipality down a path where its topos of *Finance* conflicts with its topos of *Social*. Over the next years, the tension between *Finance* and *Social* is repeatedly emphasised in the statements, as the delays in building the CHP plant threatens to cause major issues for the region's citizens and industry.

The paragraph clearly argues for regulators to review the current tax system. However, an analysis of the topos in the text reveals that the argument is as much addressed to the company's owners as to the regulators. The narrative invites the municipality to participate in negotiations with the regulators and to consider the conflict when reviewing the company's proposal to build the CHP plant.

Resolving Tensions through Strategic Initiatives

Several strategic initiatives were announced by the CEO statements, beyond the construction of the CHP plant. The first CEO sought to broaden the company's portfolio through the addition of energy-efficiency consultancy services (EES). The second CEO pursued massive expansion of the electricity sales operation through a joint venture. The third CEO sought to follow up the CHP investment with a proposal to build a bio-fuel refinery, another large-scale, multi-year project. Each initiative can be understood as a possibility that establishes coherence between the topos of *Infrastructure* and the preferred leadership topos of the CEO: *Differentiation*, *Growth* and *Innovation*. Tension and inconsistency among topos creates cognitive dissonance and constrains decision-making capability because it is unclear which facts, possibilities and values are most relevant.

The second CEO pushes through the decision to build the CHP plant by presenting it as critical

- For the country's efforts to find a commercially viable power production solution that is also environmentally sustainable.
- To ensure continued low prices for local industry and enough capacity to keep the city's most important functions running in the case of a national grid failure.
- To support the expansion of the company's district heating business.

By addressing each of these issues, the statement achieves coherence between *Security, Sustainability, Social* and *Growth*. As the third CEO starts his tenure after the CHP proposal has been accepted the statements during his term focus on the topos of *Innovation* as a direction for future company development. There is a noticeable assumption of agreement between stakeholders in these statements, especially around the arguments for building the CHP plant. The third CEO typically employs the CHP plant as an argument for initiatives. For instance, when proposing a biogas refinery as the next big investment for the company, the statement merely points to how the use of biogas will make the plant more environmentally friendly, will reduce costs even more and make the supply of energy to the region even more secure. Thus, the coherence achieved when the CHP plant was accepted, appears to have become institutionalised.

However, achieving topos coherence is not only important to ensure cooperation among stakeholders; the narrative created also has the power to fix the strategic direction of senior management. As an example of this, consider the EES initiative during the tenure of the first CEO. Among the primary concerns for the company during this time was increasing energy prices brought on by new environmental taxes, a national freeze on new power production—also motivated by environmental concerns and a growing demand outstripping supply. This threatened the economic viability of the local industry. These concerns were repeatedly addressed in the statements by narratives highlighting tension between the topos of *Sustainability*, *Security*, *Competition* and *Social*. In 1993, the EES initiative is presented as a pro-active solution that resolves these tensions ahead of the imminent market liberalisation:

> It is our conviction that we are entering a period when management of finite resources is necessary. Investing in this direction will be a competitive differentiator that will bring improvements to the environment as well as reduced costs. For a power utility such as us, in practice this means the effort to help our customers manage their power usage in a sensible way [through EES].

(AR 1993)

By expanding into EES consultancy the company would become more competitive, achieve lower costs for its customers and respect the freeze on new power production. The coherence provided senior management with a narrative that aligned the interests of the company with both its owners and regulators and became the cornerstone of the company's strategic profile for many years. However, a truth gap existed between the company's strategic narrative and the pragmatic truth. By the time the second CEO took the helm the company had amassed some experience of actual market competition. The attempt to hold on to the company's customers through differentiation with EES services was unsuccessful and by 2007 the company's market share had dropped to 50 percent from its 100 percent monopoly position before market liberalisation. Identifying the truth gap between this pragmatic truth and the pro-active truth that held that EES services would reduce customer costs, the new CEO refocused efforts on achieving competitive pricing through economies of scale.

Conclusions

GbgE's strategic profile can be seen as a structural relationship between its infrastructure and a changing energy industry (e.g. Miles et al. 1978). However, this relationship has been far from a static one. Acquisitions and divestures transformed the company's competencies and capabilities, and changes in the industry meant each CEO grappled with significantly different environments.

Each CEO held their own pre-understandings and experiences which—together with those of their respective management teams—resulted in a unique set of construct causalities illustrated in the strategic narrative within the CEO statements, and which were intended to 'invite the desired future' (Ogilvy et al. 2014). These CEO statements also revealed idiosyncratic leadership styles (Armenic and Craig 2010) and over time, the statements showcase the company's evolving strategic profile.

By combining the structural and narrative approach to strategy, we sought to answer the research question:

How is strategic co-authorship orchestrated through CEO statements?

Reading the CEO statements as strategic texts which integrates stakeholder perspective within the company narrative, reveals an effort by senior management to invite external parties to co-author the company's strategic profile. Stakeholder support for company initiatives is sought by deconstructing external party topoi into a number of topos, which are then integrated into the internal topos and subsequently used in the narrative to justify those initiatives.

Co-authorship is complicated by conflicts arising between the topoi of external parties but can be partially mitigated by highlighting them within the narrative as tensions between the internalised topos. By identifying tensions between the topos of individual topoi, the company is also able to present strategic initiatives as solutions to multiple tensions within and between topoi. This produces a grand narrative that aligns the interests of the company, its management and its stakeholders around the success of the strategic initiative.

We've identified three techniques within the narratives of the CEO statements aimed at orchestrating the strategic co-authorship of its stakeholders: recognising the topoi of external actors as internalised topos; recognising conflicts between topoi as topos tension; and presenting strategic initiatives as resolutions to such tensions. There is arguably evidence of increasing sophistication in the use of the last two techniques.

During the tenure of the first CEO, these tensions are referenced but not used as any overt justification to follow a particular direction. During the tenure of the second CEO, the statements present narratives which cite multiple tensions to passionately argue for a particular strategic initiative intended to resolve them. These narrative techniques were also incorporated in the statements by the third CEO, who employs them in a more neutral and formulaic manner to argue for reviews of CO2 emission quotas and other regulatory systems, as well as using them to justify further infrastructure investments over and above the CHP plant.

Overall, a review of GbgE's CEO statements reveals a highly strategic response to the asymmetric levels of control over internal and external conditions (Mitchell et al. 2013). By shaping the strategic narrative to leverage stakeholder cooperation, senior management extended its control to the external environment through the power of narrative (Ogilvy et al. 2014).

Note

1 All quotations are from the Annual Reports and are translated by the authors.

References

Amernic, Joel H., and Russell J. Craig. 2010. "Accounting as a facilitator of extreme narcissism." *Journal of Business Ethics*, 96 (1): 79–93.

Annual Reports, Göteborg Energi. 1990–2007. Copies of hardcovers available on request.

Barry, David, and Michael Elmes. 1997. "Strategy retold: Toward a narrative view of strategic discourse." *The Academy of Management Review*, 22 (2): 429.

Chandler, Alfred D. 1990. *Strategy and Structure: Chapters in the History of the Industrial Enterprise*. Cambridge, MA: MIT.

Craig, Russell, and Joel H. Amernic. 2011. "Detecting linguistic traces of destructive narcissism at-a-distance in a CEO's letter to shareholders." *Journal of Business Ethics*, 101 (4): 563–575.

Fanelli, Angelo, and Nora Ilona Grasselli. 2006. "Defeating the minotaur: The construction of CEO Charisma on the US stock market." *Organization Studies*, 27 (6): 811–832.

168   *Gudrun Baldvinsdottir, et al.*

Fenton, C., and A. Langley. 2011. "Strategy as practice and the narrative turn." *Organization Studies*, 32 (9): 1171–1196.

Foreman, Janis, and Paul A. Argenti. 2005. "How corporate communication influences strategy implementation, reputation and the corporate brand: An exploratory qualitative study." *Corporate Reputation Review*, 8 (3): 245–264.

Högselius, Per, and Arne Kaijser. 2010. "The politics of electricity deregulation in Sweden: The art of acting on multiple arenas." *Energy Policy*, 38 (5): 2245–2254.

Jarzabkowski, Paula. 2004. "Strategy as practice: Recursiveness, adaptation, and practices-in-use." *Organization Studies*, 25 (4): 529–560.

Miles, Raymond E., and Charles C. Snow. 2003. *Organizational Strategy, Structure, and Process*. Stanford, CA: Stanford University Press.

Miles, Raymond E., Charles C. Snow, Alan D. Meyer, and Henry J. Coleman. 1978. "Organizational strategy, structure, and process." *Academy of management review*, 3 (3): 546–562.

Mitchell, Falconer, Lars Bråd Nielsen, Hanne Nørreklit, and Lennart Nørreklit. 2013. "Scoring strategic performance: A pragmatic constructivist approach to strategic performance measurement." *Journal of Management & Governance*, 17 (1): 5–34.

Nørreklit, Hanne, Mitchel Falconer, and Lars B. Nielsen. 2017. "Reflective planning and decision-making." In *A Philosophy of Management Accounting: A Pragmatic Constructivist Approach*, edited by Hanne Nørreklit. Chapter 4, this volume. New York: Routledge.

Nørreklit, Lennart. 2017a. "Actor reality construction." In *A Philosophy of Management Accounting: A Pragmatic Constructivist Approach*, edited by Hanne Nørreklit. Chapter 2, this volume. New York: Routledge.

Nørreklit, Lennart. 2017b. "Epistemology." In *A Philosophy of Management Accounting: A Pragmatic Constructivist Approach*, edited by Hanne Nørreklit. Chapter 3, this volume. New York: Routledge.

Ogilvy, Jay, Ikujiro Nonaka, and Noboru Konno. 2014. "Toward narrative strategy." *World Futures*, 70 (1): 5–18.

Porter, Michael E. 1985. *Competitive Advantage: Creating and Sustaining Superior Performance*. New York: Free Press.

Prahalad, C.K., and Gary Hamel. 1990. "The core competence of the corporation." *Harvard Business Review*, 68 (3): 79.

Riksdagsförvaltningen. 1991a. "Proposition 1990/91:87." http://www.riksdagen.se/sv/dokument-lagar/dokument/proposition/om-naringspolitik-for-tillvaxt_GE0387.

Riksdagsförvaltningen. 1991b. "Skrivelse 1990/91:49." http://www.riksdagen.se/sv/dokument-lagar/dokument/skrivelse/19909149_GE0349.

Robichaud, Daniel, Hélène Giroux, and James R. Taylor. 2004. "The metaconversation: The recursive property of language as a key to organizing." *The Academy of Management Review*, 29 (4): 617–634.

8 Actor-Based Performance Management

Mihaela Trenca and Hanne Nørreklit

Introduction

Performance management[1] is about influencing employees to make decisions and carry out actions that are in the best interest of the organisation (Otley 2003; Anthony and Govindajaran 2007; Merchant and Van der Stede 2007). In order to implement the organisational goals and strategies, the performance management literature advocates performance measurement as a vital tool. But as "it is people in the organisation who make things happen" (Merchant and Van der Stede 2007, 8), the understanding of human behaviour in relation to performance measurement becomes profound for making effective performance management.

The mainstream performance management literature tends to explain human action as determined by natural laws. In particular, some behavioural research focuses on how factors within and/or outside the human being determine their specific actions (Covaleski et al. 2006; Ittner 2014). However, despite the fact that some actions of human beings do follow a pattern of deterministic stimulus-response regularity, natural law causality cannot explain *all* human action. Repeatedly, research documents that mechanical performance measurement systems have problems producing the intentional effects (see e.g. Merchant and Van der Stede 2007). Overall, the problem embedded in the assumption of determinism in human conduct is that it underestimates the extent to which the individual's freedom to choose, reflect and interact is a fundamental element shaping human practice (von Wright 1983; MacIntyre 1990). There are more dimensions involved in understanding human action than the force of natural law.

Research with a more constructivist leaning claims that people are governed by globally developed cultural or social practices that determine their outlook or self-understanding. Concurrently, leading sociological scholars (Foucault 1976; Latour 1987; Bourdieu 1990; Giddens 2013) point to the fact that human actions are governed by the techniques and practices of power installed by social and material structures outside their local practices (Schatzki 2001). However, individual human action is not omni-suitable, linked to meta-procedures formulated at 'macro-levels' (Barnes 2001, 39). People enact and develop their local practices drawing on existing knowledge, but it is not the same collective procedures that are repeated by human beings across time and space. People are acting human beings in the construction of organisational activities including performance management activities (Nørreklit et al. 2016; Nørreklit 2017, Chapter 2, this volume).

Pragmatic constructivism emphasises the importance of the actor when creating functioning practices. Organisational actors do not only construct the performance measurement instruments and norms; indeed, they construct and undertake the actions required for making functioning practices and hence the actual performance outcome. For the actor's or group of actors' construction to be successful as a basis for effectively functioning actions, the four dimensions of reality need to be integrated (von Wright 1983; Nørreklit et al. 2007, 2010). Thus, successful actions require factual possibilities within motivational value range and coordination of communication across activities. The actors' conceptual structures of reflecting and creating knowledge about integration are at the core of creating successful action and hence performance. The actor's specific conceptual structure of integration, forming the relationship to the world, is labelled topos. In view of that, the validity of the manager's topos governing collective efforts of constructing functioning activities is vital for effective performance management.

The purpose of this paper is to develop a conceptual framework based on pragmatic constructivism to analyse an actor's performance management topos, with a view to enriching our insight into how to develop more successful constructions. It illustrates the framework by analysing the performance management topos of an organisational successful supply chain manager, applying actor-based performance management. The manager creates a functioning supply chain practice through empathic engagement and conceptual, reflective epistemic methods, orchestrating co-authorship in identifying the factual problem and developing solid constructs for solving the problem. Hence, the analysis of the manager's topos contributes to the performance management theory by developing performance management techniques that go beyond mechanistic ones. In particular, we show how a manager's interactive and reflective epistemic practice can lead to the emergence of a participatory social practice (Dachler and Bernhard Wilpert 1987) involving multiple actors' topoi in the creation of construct causality.

The chapter is structured as follows. First, a conceptual framework for understanding and analysing the individual's practical reasoning or topos, as we prefer to label it, is introduced. Second, the conceptual framework is employed in analysing the practice of an American supply chain manager, to understand how she constructs her topos. Finally, some conclusions are drawn and ideas for future research are presented.

Conceptual Framework for Analysing Topoi

A topos is a person's or group of people's specific ways of reasoning, which they apply when constructing their relationship to the world. It drives the actor's action, departing from an integrated reality of which it forms part, to a future integrated reality of which it also forms part. In conceptualising an actor's performance management topos, we concentrate on the dimensions of intentionality and epistemic method applied to achieve the intentional outcome.

Intentionality

One force working for the individual's action is grounded in the values driving change towards a future integrated reality, i.e. the actor's intentionality with respect to the future construction (von Wright 1983; Nørreklit et al. 2007, 2010). The values driving the individual human actions can be analysed through the actor's wishes and wants for herself and the other—i.e. her projection of the future construction. We can access this dimension in relation to the actor's perception of core dimensions of the future construction, such as 'things', persons, rules, activities and relationships between individual topoi and an overarching collective one. In view of pragmatic constructivism, the actor should strive for a future reality construction where an integration of the four dimensions of reality has to be made for each activity in interaction with other activities.

Epistemic Method

An important aspect of the epistemic method is the actor's thoughts on the forces shaping actions and hence future construction. It is related to the actor's perception of the forces of the existing construction, and how to make intentional changes to that construction. The changes are to be constructed through a set of more or less implicit principles and methods according to which one set of value and possibility loaded facts leads to another set of value and possibility loaded facts through a set of specific courses of action. In order to function according to intention, they should create construct causalities through the integration of facts, possibilities, values and communication. We can access these through the actor's perception of the current reality situation and the type of actions or intervention required to go from one situation of reality to another situation of reality.

The actor's perception of the existing reality construction and the course of actions—interventions—required to cause change from this situation to the intentional situation takes form as a conceptual logic (von Wright 1983) or, as we prefer, the epistemic method (Cetina 2001; Nørreklit et al. 2007, 2010). The epistemic method is shaping the relational idiom between the actor's intentionality and the four dimensions of the world—i.e. the actor's relation to the world. The epistemic method includes those human activities that have as a central purpose the creation of valid knowledge about a phenomenon with a view to establishing successful action. Coordinating with the intentional and epistemic methods of multiple actors is a particular aspect of an actor's epistemic method.

The epistemic method of an actor involves two levels. One level relates to the knowledge model the actor uses in her operational practices to produce intentional results, i.e. the operational level. The second level connects to the knowledge models the actor uses to develop and validate the robustness of the epistemic method she applies in her operational practices, i.e. the development level. Below, we explain the actor's epistemic method from these two levels.

Operational Level

Concepts are at the core of creating and controlling the local practices. Valid knowledge requires the conceptual framework to be grounded in the factual phenomenon in focus. Conceptual qualities of correspondence and coherence are essential to establishing a factual observational ground for thoughts and action. Thus, concepts must be defined both demonstratively by formulating criteria for observation and measurement, and structurally in relation to other concepts. The two forms of determining the meaning of the concepts in use must be complementary. However, properly developed concepts and conceptual models are not simply principles to identify factual things, but also about linking facts to action-related possibilities and values and to the other actors' understanding. Thus, additionally, we need a conceptual narrative to integrate factual observation with actions and intentions and hence facilitate the operational meaning of the concepts used (Nørreklit et al. 2007; Nørreklit 2011).

The epistemic narrative is not shaped as formal logic involving a deductive logical relationship, building on the conclusion from premises. Such a rationalist approach towards understanding human action through a set of premises and deductive reasoning has proved not to be trustworthy in regard to predicting action in a real life context. Rather, the conceptual connection made by the individual, between the forces shaping action and the intentions, takes form as a semi-logical relationship, which is a practical form of argument taking into account a complexity of material and human aspects of a situation and judging the potentialities for action leading to results. It is an epistemic model of perceiving factual ground, deriving possibilities and interacting socially with a view to creating successful actions fulfilling the values. Various types of experiences, logical reasoning, emotions, social authorities, etc. may shape the semi-logical relationship. We can access the type of semi-logical relationship through the epistemic method shaping the observational ground and the actions assumed to lead to intentional results. In constructing a set of actions functioning through interconnection, the actor will have to draw on a string of semi-logical relationships. Together, the string of semi-logical relationships shapes the actor's paradigm for action.

The actor's epistemic method is not a purely individual development (Barnes 2001). Actors accomplish the construction of the system of functioning methods through analysis and reflection on the situation, as well as reflection on the applicability of existing available methods. Existing methods can enter as vehicles for the actor's reflection and analysis (Nørreklit, Nørreklit, and Mitchell 2016).

Development Level

Conceptual frameworks are thought models only. It is only through the pragmatic use that we can find out whether the epistemic method expresses a reality construction that can be used to achieve the intentional outcome. Adequate analysis and reality checking of the integration of the epistemic method creates a pro-active true construction. If the expected results are realised in action, then the epistemic method is pragmatically true. Reduction of the truth gap requires a learning process based on ongoing reflection and improvement of the ability of the epistemic method to generate trustworthy results (Nørreklit et al. 2007). Given that the lack of success in meeting intentional outcome can be caused both by illusionary intentions and malfunctions in the epistemic method, both aspects of the topos should be reflected upon in the learning process. Such an ongoing dialectical learning process should not only be a part of the individual actor's epistemic method, but must also be mirrored in the establishment of a collective organisational topos.

However, the phenomenological grounding of our concepts and reflective learning happens only if the individual engages in an empathic relationship with the phenomenon of inquiry (Trenca 2016a). In operational routine situations, the relational idiom between the actor and the phenomenon can be passive, although when confronted with problems or new situations, the relational idiom between actor and phenomenon has to become active. These situations require that the actor consciously draws upon relational resources that help them overcome this actor-phenomenon separation, and becomes engaged in or 'being-in relation' to the phenomenon in order to be able to define and continue their activity. Oriented towards the phenomenon, the relational resources are engaging in some form of empathy in the phenomenon (Cetina 2001). At the same time, the understanding of the problem has to become enhanced and enlarged through the actor's visualisation, reflections and conceptualisation of it and its context (Heron 1992).

Empathy requires the affective mode of feeling, which is the person's mental capacity to engage with, or place themselves in relation to, the differentiated other or the phenomenon (Heron 1992). It differs from the affective mode of emotion, which relates to the individual's experience of affect (joy, anger, etc.) that arises as a result of the frustration or fulfilment of needs and values. Whereas emotions are separating the actor from the other, feelings activate the participatory function towards others. In order to have a balance between the individual's values and those of others, the two polarities of the affective mode should be in a dialectic interaction. Whether the knowledge creation takes a participatory or a disconnected form depends on the personhood.

The pragmatic constructivism advocates an interactive dialogical procedure in which there is the possibility of co-authoring both empathic and conceptual reflective insight. The interactive dialogical procedure requires the actors to share their empathic and factual insight, intentionality and epistemic method (Raffnsøe-Møller 2015).

Method for Accessing the Actor's Topos

Actors' topoi can be accessed through their micro-stories; hence, discourse analysis forms the basis for their conceptualisation. Through their specific choice of language, i.e. speech genre, the actors express their way of understanding and acting in the world, and hence they reveal the form of construct they strive for and how to obtain it (Wittgenstein 1953; Ricoeur 1983). Thus, speech genre and practice form are intertwined. The engaged and embodied human beings' speech genre says something not only about their understanding of their existence, but also their motivation for and epistemic way of changing that existence. A certain practice field is constructed through a large and complex set of speech genres expressing a set of topoi, which are produced through the actors' sequence of more or less tightly connected micro-stories (Ricoeur 1983).

In identifying the speech genre, we look at the textual features of the actor's network of micro-stories (Ricoeur 1983). In focus are the micro-stories expressing the reality construction the actor strives for and those on how to achieve the intentional reality construction departing from the current, perceived reality construction.[2] In the textual analysis of the micro-stories, we are concerned with the argumentation, narratives, semantic and syntactical features that frame the situation, events, persons, tools and knowledge procedures (Toulmin 1974; Ricoeur 1983). Based on textual analyses, we interpret the types of practice forms embedded in the actor's genre of constructing a functioning relationship to the world as expressed in the network of micro-stories. As we are concerned about the soundness of the actor's topos, we conceptualise practice in relation to the types of knowledge procedures governing the epistemic method. In other words, we aim to identify the paradigm in use and its ability to create integration. The analysis of integration forms the basis for a pro-active assessment of whether the epistemic method can lead to the construct causality projected. However, revealing whether the topos is pragmatic truth requires the observation of whether an actor's epistemic method is effective in creating successful outcomes and whether intentions are real.

Analysing a Manager's Topos

In this section, we analyse the topos of an American supply chain manager. The analysed material is part of a case study of a large Danish-owned multinational company, undertaken by one of the authors of the paper (see Trenca 2016b). The interview with the manager took place in the form of a dialogue with a focus on how she manages her supply chain team.

The manager is employed in a Danish-owned subsidiary in the US. The company is within the energy manufacturing industry. According to HQ, things are going fine in the supply chain manager's unit. The supply chain manager has a new, quite young team who is trying to make things work. Below, we analyse the supply chain manager's topos when she tells about the performance management of service level. First, we present, the analysis of the micro-stories shaping the manager's projections of a future reality construction, and subsequently, the analysis of the set of micro-stories shaping the manager's epistemic method driving the construction of the projected reality.

The Manager's Intentionality

The overall intention of the supply chain manager is to meet the target of 85 percent *on time delivery*, which is set for her unit by the organisational manager. The 85 percent *on time delivery* outlines the conceptual content and criteria for organisational objectives, an intention to which the manager subscribes. Otherwise, she does not have much focus on measurement targets, but more on the employees' perception of what is the right state of affairs. Thus, the manager aligns the measurement concept of on time delivery to a narrative conceptualisation of the implication of on time delivery for organisational action and end results:

> So how do I know that *BU* is *satisfied*? If *I* have *components and stocks*, if I *have what they need*, and they can get it in a *timely manner*, and they can get their *things fixed*, *they're happy*, *I'm happy*. That's how I measure my job. And if so, I'm doing a good job—that's how I measure myself. And that is also how our *team* does it—it's the same way actually. Thus, does *Laura* have *everything covered* for *Turkey* and *Australia* and stuff? That's how we're measured. And we have different *platforms*, so I have to make sure that there is stock in *Denmark* to cover some of *Laura's region*. And vice versa, as one of the platforms that *Laura* covers is affecting my stock over here.

In the quote, we see that there are multiple organisational units or *platforms* involved in the production of on time delivery. The employees' perception of the objective of doing a good job is about making other units satisfied. The focus of the supply manager and her team should be on whether her units have the *components and stocks* and are *getting things fixed*; whether the other units *have what they need in a timely manner*; and whether her unit has *everything covered* from other organisational *platforms*. When everybody has what they need in a timely manner, the values of organisational actors are in a good state of affairs—the employees are *satisfied* and *happy* and the organisational target is achieved. The intention of a functioning delivery practice is formulated in an affective conceptual language, which links abstract measurement with a narrative expressing the practical meaning of the objective. Shaping an affective state of emotional happiness when the other obtains what they need, the supply manager advocates a practice emphasising empathic social values.

The supply chain manager emphasises the importance of the actors' orientation towards each other in another micro-story:

> I'm trying to help service *understand* the SBU (Sales Business Unit) side, and the SBU side *understanding* SPR (Spare Parts & Repair) and the supply chain side. And I'm also *trying* to make that *buffer and* say when I'm working with the SPR side and the supply chain side. You have to *understand* their side of sayings, so it's really a matter of opening the door and presenting both sides.

Again, we witness that multiple, mutually interdependent units are involved in the production of on time delivery. The actors' mutual *understanding* of each other's work processes and the managers *buffering* the actors against each other are at the core of creating a functioning practice of on time delivery. The organisational actors should be conceptually reflective and empathically oriented towards the others' topoi.

Overall, the manager strives for the construction of an organisational employee who is intrinsically motivated to fulfil the other organisational members' needs, hence meeting the organisational objectives. Indirectly, it is stated that opportunistic values should be moderated or oppressed. Also, the employees should have an orientation towards the others' way of making a successful construction when reflecting on their own way of making a successful construction. Thereby, the manager advocates a sort of altruistic and cooperative practice rather than an opportunistic and autonomous practice.

The Manager's Epistemic Method

The epistemic method applied by the supply chain manager to construct a functioning collective practice is based on a string of observations and reflections on working with problems. Overall, she applies procedures for creating factual observational ground, managing motivational values, orchestrating pro-active, true problem solving and observing pragmatic truth and learning. Below, we explain these knowledge procedures in more detail, leading to a conclusion on conceptualising the manager's epistemic method.

Creating Factual Observational Ground

Important for creating multiple understanding is the observation of the factual performance and finding the reasoning for poor performance. The following quotes exhibit the focus on *facts* about performance and finding the *root cause* creating lacking performance:

> It's all about presenting the *facts* . . . [We build trust] by knowing the *facts* and only presenting the *facts*. It's what it is, and I can have my opinions, and I can turn off my microphone, and I can say my opinions out loud to myself, but it's a delicate situation. [I ask:] *How come that you don't have my components for me?* You have to dig all the way down to what is the *root cause.*

The root cause of missing components is hindering construct causality, which is the reason it is crucial for the manager that they do something about it. Also, the quote indicates that questioning is pivotal when searching for the root cause. An elaboration of the manager's way of using questioning and observational facts in the search for root causes can be found in the following:

> . . . We have a target of 85, so if we got 99 we are doing very well. If we got a 60 or 40 [on time delivery], then we *dig* in to see what the issue was. *Was it* a transportation issue, was it that there was no stock? *Was it* too short the lead time from the customer? You know that type of things . . . I'm *not blaming* transportation, I'm *not blaming* the service side. . . . The ultimate is not to place blame, but to *figure out what happens.* When you do the analysis you present the facts. And then [during the digging] someone may say "Ok, we only had 45 % on time to require this week, this is the analysis that's been done." But it comes down to that SBU put down the same day for delivery, on their main component. . . . And I *dig* back in and do the analysis on that and I say "Ok, but I had a stock there when the order came in, so I'm not sure *why it didn't get* to Turkey on time." Some of it is simple as, they put an order today, and they say they want it delivered today. Then it's on the SBU. Then it's on the service side, because they didn't do their job correctly. Or I have it on the warehouse but the warehouse didn't ship it for two days. That's on the warehouse. But it's still on our group to figure out why it didn't happen . . . Ok, so you have to start *digging* backwards. But, in the middle of that, one time you might go left, and one time you might go right. Depending on what the results are and your findings. . . . It's not knowledge, because I obviously do not know everything. It's *interpretation or understanding* what you're finding when you're doing that analysis that leads you to the next step . . .

We witness that the observation of poor factual performance is the point of departure for a search process *digging* for root causes. There are many possibilities to consider when digging for a root cause, but it is the factual, possible one that has to be detected. The root cause is the missing action for creating construct causalities. In searching, the manager is asking for information on factual actions in the network of organisational actors: *Was it . . . ? To fig- ure out what happens, and why it didn't get to . . . ?* Through the manager's conversation process with the other actors, the factual actions are revealed, and whether these can be the cause of poor performance is reflected upon. The searching process follows a scheme of discovering the facts and develop- ing diagnostic understanding. During the search process of questioning, the manager's knowledge is moving to an increasingly higher level of diagnosing the problems, and it goes on until the collected factual information provides a sufficient conceptual *interpretation* for *understanding* the phenomenon of poor factual performance. At this stage the root cause is found.

Overall, insight is shaped through knowing and discussing the factual course. Searching for facts, the supply chain manager is opening up the problem area until a sufficient understanding of the problem and what causes it is found. The actors are the source of information for finding the root cause. But the factual observations, and the plausible argumentation on how to relate these to problem creation, become the binding elements for the objectification of the problem.

Managing Motivational Values

In the quote above, the manager mentions that the search process is about *not blaming*. This is further emphasised in the following.

> . . . I do find that people on the supply chain side come to me and complain about the people at the SBU. So I have to try to buffer that. And when I go to the SBU, I have to say: *"Ok, we've got an issue, and we need to know your opinion,"* instead of the tone of voice, or what- ever I got from the SPU. You know, you try to buffer and make it "We really need your help" instead of "We've got a problem" (in a tough voice). . . . You have to be the Mister Nice Guy in the middle, so *I see it from the SPU, from the service sides* as well. . . . And when you do that, I think that creates confidents from the both sides. That says, you know what you do is breaking down to what is the issue, and then you break that down and say: "Ok but that really means this and this and this." . . . I'm trying to be the middle person that takes the angry SPR email and says you know, what is going on, and then you tone it down, and you email somebody else and say: *"Ok, here's the issue, what can you do to help us?" You want to make them feel like they are in control,* whether it's going from the service side to the SPR or the SPR to the ser- vice side. *You want to make them feel like they are in control,* like they have the input and they're helping with the outcome . . .

The manager aims to transform factual claims loaded with negative emo- tions into factual claims calling for empathic insight: *"Ok, we've got an issue, and we need to know your opinion,* "*instead of the tone of voice, or whatever I got from the SBU*"; and "*Ok, here's the issue, what can you do to help us?*" By being factual and not activating the angry emotions through blaming or communicating complaints, the manager takes away the separating force of the message. Instead, she creates empathic attention to the problem, hence shaping the actor's participatory function. The explicit, formulated intention is to construct employees with a problem-solving ethos: *You want to make them feel like they are in control.*

The construction of the employees as problem solvers is important because the pivotal point of finding the root cause of a problem is solving it. Some problems are to be solved by making the employees internalise existing knowledge on what is the right action. Effective production of on time delivery requires skilled and informed employees. The company has job and process documentation on what is the right thing to do, which can be useful for new employees and service technicians. However, effective, functioning practices advance far beyond process instructions; they require acting employees with work *experiences and knowledge*:

> [H]ow do you document *work ethic*? You know, you can't. It comes from, you *know* . . . If you were to take how to document something that I'm doing, and all those connections, and all those little things that you do. I don't know how you can document that and give it to a brand new person coming in, and say: "You can do this job." . . . It's just got to be *learned*. I think, it's work ethic . . . It's *experience*, past *experience*. It's *working knowledge*.

The quote points to the fact that work processes are to be enacted by the actors and hence shaped by the actors' work knowledge and personal ethics. Work processes do not pass unchanged from individual to individual, but require the actors' empathic and reflective 'being-in relation' to the phenomenon. When enacted, work processes are infused and become the carriers of each actor's values and knowledge.

Overall, in her interaction, the manager aims to positively influence the actors' mode of affect, which separates her from the other, so that she activates their participatory function. She aims to construct the employees as problem solving actors rather than angry, self-centred bodies. Because the questioning and interpretation takes place in interaction with the network of actors, the process also contributes to increasing the employees' knowledge and understanding of what is good and poor action. Thus, the manager's questioning is not only about revealing the facts, but also about making the actors think about what is the right action and hence construct a practice that will function in the future. In that, she is formulating the epistemic and ethical codes to which the organisational members should accommodate their topos (Foucault 1976).

Orchestrating Pro-Active, True Problem Solving

Whereas some problems are about making the employees internalise existing knowledge on what is the right action, other problems will require the discovery of new knowledge. Discovering new solutions, the manager is digging for knowledge among the network of actors:

> Sometimes it's a matter of me *knowing who* to go to *ask* who can resolve it. It's all about the *contacts*. I got *contacts* everywhere. I don't claim to know the answers but I do know people that I can say "*I don't know what the answer is, this is what I am looking for, can you help me?*" It's about me accepting that I don't know everything . . . I have to *ask the questions* . . . I randomly start to send emails to people and say "Hey, I think that you're *maybe the contact* for this. If you're not, who is it?" And I get a name and then I *go to that person*. So that's how you dig to the bottom, that's how you try to *establish those connections* and stuff. It's just like *growing a tree and you know, just more*, more, more. So a lot of people come to me and say "Hey I don't know the answer, but I think I know who does. Let me contact them for you."

Thus, the manager's way of searching for solutions is governed by questioning and interacting with the other actors. Unlike in the questioning above, detecting facts, the possible solutions are found in the knowing and understanding of those with whom she is speaking. The manager's strategy thus seems to rely on the competent organisational actors in establishing solutions. It is about finding the actors who know something about solving the problem. In order for her to be able to engage in such an investigation, she needs to adopt an open and humble attitude, which means that she has to be able to present her inquiry openly and to nurture a state of psychological comfort with the idea of not having the ready-to-use answers to the problem (Yanow 2009).

Sometimes, finding a resolution requires the collaboration of multiple actors. If so, the actors are brought together in a meeting to find solutions.

> You have to bring the *stakeholders together*, it has to be a meeting, and we have to initiate a whole new process or make an adaptation to a current process. . . . You call them down and say "*Ok this is the situations we need to discuss*," . . . you try to have an agenda and try to stick to it. And from that there might be another meeting because maybe all the points weren't there or whatever. But you have to *make sure that you know whether something is missing or whether the right people are not involved*. . . . Maybe *somebody else knows something* that I don't and they get in the meeting and they say "Oh yeah, we should be talking to (?), or (?) should be involved in this." . . . And sometimes it is finance, sometimes it is legal and I wouldn't even have thought of that . . . [When

I can't figure things out] it is really good trying to *involve everybody to make sure that the process is complete.*

We witness that the solution to the problem is not given by the manager but by the employees. The manager asserts the problem situation and invites other key actors into a process of co-authorship. Again, factual observations, questioning and reflection drive an interactive communication process. The collective reflective discovery process goes on until a possible solution is conceptualised by the collective of actors. During the discovery process, the manager's knowledge is moving to an increasingly higher level of diagnostic understanding of the possible solution to the problem. The binding element of the understanding seems to be the plausibility of the employees' argumentation on how to solve the problem. Thus, the validation of whether the solution is pro-actively true seems to be based on faith in the actors' knowledge and willingness to solve the problem.

Observing Pragmatic Truth and Learning

Orchestrating problem solving, the manager is giving the actors time to develop factual functioning solutions (construct causality):

> I figured out that this is what the root cause is, and this is what they're doing about it. Now we have to be patient, and *let that resolution take effect.*

The manager communicates to the actors that the problem solving process may take time. However, the phrase *let that resolution take effect* indicates that at some point or another there will be a check of whether the resolution is pragmatic truth. Thus, eventually there will be an evaluation of whether the actor's idea for problem solving is pragmatically true. If the projected solution is not pragmatically true, it will display itself in lack of construct causality and hence initiate a new learning search into finding the root cause.

Sometimes there is not an immediate resolution. Then as a final attempt, in closing the gap between pro-active truth and pragmatic truth, the manager might use the technique of questioning a more experienced person, Soren, at a higher organisational level:

> Sometimes I present the facts to Soren and say "Ok, this is the issue. I've got my orders in, I've done what I was supposed to do and I'm not getting an end result" . . . then he will take the information, the facts that are in the email, and say: 'We have an issue here, what are we gonna do about it? Where is our order? Where is this material? When did the material come to the repair facility?' " . . .

The quote reveals that the success of a local activity relies on the combination of different functions within the value chain. Accordingly, the validation of the pro-active truth becomes challenging, because the effect of an action can rely on multiple interfering actors and can take time to materialise. Although the process and methods are in place locally, and hence the pro-active truth has been constructed rigorously, the pro-active truth is impeded from becoming a pragmatic truth because failure occurs in other activities along the value chain. Nevertheless, taking the collective learning approach to the gap between the pro-active truth and the pragmatic truth opens an avenue for digging across functional activities to detect the failure and hence to co-author a solution for solving the problem together with managers at higher organisational level. Thus, the epistemic method of the manager involves a reflective approach developing the organisational method of controlling the specific operational practice.

Also, the manager is working with a learning theory of truth at the personal level:

> And sometimes your professional judgment is wrong and you hit a dead end or someone says "Oh my God, what are you talking about?" and you're "Ok, I'm gonna go back and I'm going to take to the right now because the left wasn't the right answer" . . . so a lot of that it's just learning from mistakes.

We witness an evaluation of whether the manager's professional judgement becomes pragmatically true. And if there is a truth gap, she makes corrections. Mistakes are unavoidable and the challenge is how to learn. Accordingly, the epistemic method of the manager involves reflective learning at two levels. One relates to adjusting the epistemic method controlling the specific practice; the other relates to the personal knowledge system governing the creation of knowledge about controlling the specific practice.

But the manager is not born into an empathic and humble enquiring management approach. She has developed her knowledge procedure over time through a self-reflective learning process:

> I'm not a very patient person, especially when people are yelling quite loudly. But over the years I found that it's best to wait until you have all of the information that you need and then reply . . . [Before], I wanted results right now. And then you find out that you get better results when you put something out there nicely than when you are demanding.

We see that the development of her empathic and reflective management process involves the self-management of her personhood governing her knowledge creation process.

Conclusion on the Manager's Epistemic Method

The supply chain manager is driven by the intention of creating a reality construction of a functioning practice through a network of actors who are motivated and cooperative, in order to achieve the organisational objective of on time delivery. The epistemic method applied to construct a functioning supply chain practice is dominated by her use of an actor-based method involving questioning, understanding and reflection. Through the interactive questioning and reflection, the manager uncovers the facts regarding actions creating poor performance, makes the employees understand the problem situation, and searches for factual possible solutions for problem solving among the network of actors. During the search process, the manager's knowledge is moving to an increasingly higher level of diagnostic understanding of the problem, pragmatically related to the possible solution to the problem. The search process goes on until the collected factual information provides a sufficient conceptual interpretation for understanding the phenomenon of poor factual performance. Subsequently, a trustworthy conceptualisation of a possible solution is found by the actor or group of actors.

The manager has a high awareness of the fact that in order to come to a real understanding of the phenomenon, she needs to integrate multiple perspectives, coming from different actors. Her ability to facilitate the creation of a community of enquiring is a tool in the process of orchestrating the co-authorship of an organisational topos. She does not rely on her own understanding of root causes and problem solutions, but invites and relies on the employees to identify root causes of problems and to develop construct causalities. Through questioning, she leverages the employees' knowledge and engages them in co-authorship, in the search for the factual root cause hindering construct causality and a viable solution to the problem. Through her interaction, she infuses the mini-community with her own values of empathic engagement and thoroughness, so that the different stakeholders can come together in constructive interaction aimed at finding solutions instead of engaging in a blame game. Finding and solving the problem are the binding elements for the mini-community created around it.

However, the questioning does not always take form as a dialogue between equal partners. In particular when searching for reasons to the problems, the manager's questioning seems to be a one-directional inquiry into the factual root cause hindering construct causality. The factual ground, together with questioning, is used to manage both the employees' cognitive understanding and emotional affective mode. Thereby, she seems to create and build a social acceptance of a world of facts and the importance of constructing functional activities that meet the objectives of on time delivery. Contrary to problem solving, she gives the actors autonomy to find factual possible solutions fulfilling organisational values. The manager is orchestrating the various employees into co-authoring the solution to the problem. They are assumed to have the knowledge and motivation to search for the factual possibilities of problem solving, as well as make judgement of whether their solutions are pro-actively true. However, the ultimate test for the employees' solutions is whether they meet the criteria of pragmatic truth. And if pragmatic truth results are not achieved, she will start an enquiry into the factual situations with a view to reducing the truth gap. By collecting a more comprehensive set of facts, and reflecting upon them, a solution is achieved through which the four dimensions of reality are being increasingly integrated to facilitate a functioning practice through a complex set of interlinked construct causalities.

In the manger's communication, she recognises the reciprocal expectation in creating an atmosphere of trust and altruism. The manager is striving for the actors to share their information, topoi and, in general, their diagnosis of problems and possibilities, thereby constructing a common diagnosis of the situation. Nevertheless, the specific goal was the realisation of efficient supply to an external demand identified by the top management, and, hence, the goal of the epistemic method was the identification and diagnosis of problems or barriers to the realisation of this goal. The altruism, humility and openness of the actors were in the service of common problem solving, and hence in the service of the effective realisation of the common goal, so to speak!

In sum, we find that in striving for the establishment of a practice producing on time delivery, the manager draws on various methodological techniques to access all dimensions of reality. We know that the HQ consider the supply manager to be quite successful in meeting organisational objectives and hence that her management topos has a pragmatic true effect. Also, we know that the manager is concerned about whether her methods and judgements are pragmatically true. She takes a learning perspective in relation to both adjusting the epistemic knowledge system controlling the specific practice and the knowledge system governing her creation of knowledge about controlling the specific practice.

However, it should be noted that the manager's method presupposes a collective acknowledgement of the common goal of creating functioning activities, and hence that functioning activities are a motivational ground for participation in the community of inquirers. We do not have narratives from other organisational employees on how the supply chain manager's conduct is influencing their motivational value and actual doing.

Conclusion and Discussion

This chapter has provided a conceptual framework for understanding and analysing the actor's or group of actors' performance management topoi shaping their integration of the four dimensions of reality, and hence their reality construction. The actor's intentionality and epistemic method are at the core of conceptualising the topos. Whereas the actor's intentionality helps us to understand something about the future reality construction she strives for, the epistemic method helps us to understand something about the way the actor aims to achieve the intentional construction. It is related to the actor's perception of the forces of the existing construction, and how to make intentional change to that construction in interaction with others—with a view to achieving the intentional construction. For the epistemic method to express a feasible reality construction, it should be conceptually grounded in the phenomenon in focus and include a semi-logical conceptual narrative integrating factual observational ground with actions and intentions. Whereas the ex-post analysis of the integration of the epistemic method creates a pro-active, true construction, the ex ante checking of whether the actual results match the expectation demonstrates whether the epistemic construction is pragmatically feasible. Reduction of the truth gap requires a learning process based on ongoing reflection on and improvement of the ability of the epistemic method to generate trustworthy results. Such an epistemic process requires an interactive, reflective and empathic actor.

We apply the framework in analysing a successful manager's performance management topos. Through this analysis, we reveal the active role of the manager who, through sophisticated methodological techniques, executes performance management. Through reflective interaction, the manager orchestrates the collective identification of series of facts and pro-active, true possibilities, which become the building blocks for envisioning and creating construct causalities fulfilling the intentional reality construction. We point to the fact that such a successful performance management process relies heavily on both reflective and personal empathic abilities. In particular, the manager's ability to facilitate the creation of a community of enquiring is a tool in the process of orchestrating the co-authorship of organisational problem solving. Creating conceptual coherence and correspondence in her epistemic method relies on her being able to facilitate the development of a community of reflective dialogical questioning. But fundamental to a reflective dialogical process are feelings of trust and interdependence amongst organisational members. Such relational reality construction relies not only on intellectual capabilities but also on the affective attitudes of the subject, like empathy, openness and a humble attitude. Both are preconditions for an epistemic performance management method that facilitates the creation of construct causalities. However, it should be noted that the successful and apparently altruistic epistemic method seems to presuppose a unity or consensus about the intentional topos, given that a collective acknowledgement of the common goal or good seems to be the motivation for participating in the community of inquirers.

We have analysed the epistemic method in a context where the intention seems to be achievable. But this is not always the case. In such situations, one has to consider in which areas the intentional reality construction is too ambitious or the epistemic method is poor. Further research is required to provide more insight into such situations and how to reduce the gap between intention and epistemic method. Also, it would be beneficial to study other cases of supply chain performance management and other more complex cases of organisational performance management. Finally, there is a need for further research on employees' topoi in interaction with organisational management.

Notes

1 Following Otley (2003), we use the terms performance management and management control equivalently. Performance management comprises various tools such as result controls, action controls and personnel controls. However, the mainstream literature gives far more attention to result controls and hence performance measurement.

2 There is intention embedded in all utterances. Nevertheless, this paper makes a distinction between micro-stories with utterances on overall objectives and micro-stories with utterances on how to achieve these objectives.

References

Anthony, Robert, and Vijay Govindajaran. 2007. *Management Control Systems*. Boston: McGraw-Hill.

Barnes, Barry. 2001. "Practice as collective action." In *The Practice Turn in Contemporary Theory*, edited by Theodore R. Schatzki, Karin K. Cetina and Eike von Savigny, 17–28. London: Routledge.

Bourdieu, Pierre. 1990. *The Logic of Practice*. Translated by Richard Nice. Cambridge: Polity Press.

Cetina, Karin K. 2001. "Objectual practice." In *The Practice Turn in Contemporary Theory*, edited by Theodore R. Schatzki, Karin K. Cetina and Eike von Savigny, 175–188. London: Routledge.

Covaleski, Mark, John H. Evans, Luft Joan, and Michael D. Shields. 2006. "Budgeting research: Three theoretical perspectives and criteria for selective integration." *Handbooks of Management Accounting Research*, 2: 587–624.

Dachler, H.P., and Bernhard Wilpert. 1987. "Conceptual dimensions and boundaries of participation in organizations: A critical evaluation." *Administrative Science Quarterly*, 23 (1): 1–39.

Foucault, Michel. 1976 (1990). *The History of Sexuality (Histoire de la Sexualité)*. Translated by Robert Hurley. New York: Random House.

Giddens, Anthony. 2013. *Sociology*. Cambridge: Polity Press.

Heron, John. 1992. *Feeling and Personhood — Psychology in Another Key*. London: Sage.

Ittner, Christopher D. 2014. "Strengthening causal inferences in positivist field studies." *Accounting, Organizations and Society*, 39 (7): 545–549.

Latour, Bruno. 1987. *Science in Action: How to Follow Scientists and Engineers Through Society*. Cambridge, MA: Harvard University Press.

MacIntyre, Alasdair. 1990. *Three Rival Versions of Moral Enquiry: Encyclopaedia, Genealogy, and Tradition* (Gifford Lectures, 1988). Notre Dame: University of Notre Dame Press/London: Duckworth and Co.

Merchant, Kenneth, and Wim A. Van der Stede. 2007. *Performance Measurement, Evaluation and Incentives*. Harlow: Pearson Education.

Nørreklit, Hanne, Lennart Nørreklit, and Falconer Mitchell. 2007. "Theoretical conditions for validity in accounting performance measurement." In *Business Performance Measurement*, edited by Andy Neely, 179–217. Cambridge: Cambridge University Press.

Nørreklit, Hanne, Nørreklit, Lennart, and Falconer Mitchell. 2010. "Towards a paradigmatic foundations of accounting practice." *Accounting, Auditing and Accountability Journal*, 23 (6): 733–758.

Nørreklit, Hanne, Lennart Nørreklit, and Falconer Mitchell. 2016. "Understanding practice generalisation — Opening the research/practice gap." *Qualitative Research in Accounting and Management*, 13 (3): 278–302.

Nørreklit, Lennart. 2011. "Actors and reality: A conceptual framework for creative governance." In *An Actor's Approach to Management: Conceptual Framework and Company Practices*, edited by Morten Jakobsen, Inga-Lill Johanson and Hanne Nørreklit, 7–37. Copenhagen: DJOEF.

Nørreklit, Lennart. 2017. "Actor reality construction." In *A Philosophy of Management Accounting: A Pragmatic Constructivist Approach*, edited by Hanne Nørreklit. Chapter 2, this volume. New York: Routledge.

Otley, David. 2003. "Management control and performance management: Whence and whither?" *The British Accounting Review*, 35 (4): 309–326.

Raffnsøe-Møller, Morten. 2015. "Dimensions of freedom: Axel Honneth's critique of liberalism." In *Recognition and Freedom: Axel Honneth's Political Though*, edited by J. Jakobsen and O. Lysaker, 101–123. Leiden: Brill.

Ricoeur, Paul. 1983 (1984). *Time and Narrative*, vol. 1 (*Temps et Récit*). Translated by Kathleen Blamey and David Pellauer. Chicago: University of Chicago Press.

Schatzki, Theodore R. 2001. "Introduction: Practice theory." In *The Practice Turn in Contemporary Theory*, edited by Theodore R. Schatzki, Karin K. Cetina and Eike von Savigny, 1–14. London: Routledge.

Toulmin, Stephen. 1974. *The Uses of Argument*. Cambridge: Cambridge University Press.

Trenca, Mihaela. 2016a. "Tracing the becoming of reflective practitioner through the enactment of epistemic practices." *Qualitative Research in Accounting and Management*, 13 (3): 350–369.

Trenca, Mihaela. 2016b. *Actorhood and the Construction of Epistemic Practices in Management Accounting*. Kolding: Southern Denmark University.

von Wright, Georg H. 1983. *Practical Reason*. Oxford: Basil Blackwell.

Wittgenstein, Ludwig. 1953. *Philosophical Investigations*. Translated by G.E.M. Oxford: Anscombe, Basil Blackwell.

Yanow, Dvora. 2009. "Ways of knowing: Passionate humility and reflective practice in research and management." *The American Review of Public Administration*, 39 (6): 579–601.

9 Discovering and Understanding Performance Measurement in a Context of Ambiguity

Lino Cinquini, Cristina Campanale, Daniela Pianezzi and Andrea Tenucci

Introduction

The objective of this chapter is to demonstrate how pragmatic constructivism (PC) can enhance our understanding of accounting in the public sector and strengthen its role, with particular reference to the issue of ambiguity. The usefulness of PC in supporting the understanding of accounting stands on its epistemological assumptions that establish a base to evaluate the validity of existing performance measurement systems in avoiding ambiguity. Traditional management accounting theories often seem to be concerned with only one or two dimensions of human life. For example, positivistic management and accounting research focus on facts, principal-agency theory on logic-possibility and radical social constructivism on communication and language (Nørreklit et al. 2006) In mainstream management accounting research, the values of everybody within an organisation are assumed to be the same, and the role of communication is neglected. By contrast, PC recognises that management accounting provides valid results in practice only if it incorporates all four aspects of the world of human life. In this chapter, we refer to accounting in broad terms as a "collection of practices such as budgeting and product costing, whose systematic use supports the achievement of some goals" (Chenhall 2003, 129).

The validity of accounting in the public sector has been subjected to intense debate (see, for example, Humphrey et al. 1993; Lapsley 2001; Kurunmäki and Miller 2006; Arnaboldi and Palermo 2011). A major concern relates to the adaptation of accounting tools traditionally implemented in private organisations to the public context (Puxty 1993; Otley 1999; Lapsley 2001). A recurrent issue pointed out by several scholars is *ambiguity* (see, for example, Brignall and Modell 2000; Modell 2004; Pandey and Wright 2006; Vakkuri and Meklin 2006; Arnaboldi and Lapsley 2009). In accounting studies, ambiguity originates from the bounded rationality perspective (March and Simons 1958). The ambiguity aspect of decision-making refers to a situation with lack of clarity and consistency in reality, causality and intentionality in organisational decision-making (Vakkuri and Meklin 2006). In fact, the social world of decision-making and performance measurement is not completely rational (Davis and Hersh 1986) because it is filled with conflicting interests, uncertainties, paradoxes and ambivalences. Despite these complexities, activities still have to be coordinated, decisions have to be made and performance has to be measured. In other words, decision-makers have to cope with ambiguity.

Ambiguity has different facets. First, there is goals ambiguity which refers to the existence of "vague, multiple and mutually conflicting goals" (Rainey 1993, 123). Goals ambiguity is strictly correlated to role ambiguity (Wright 2001, 2004) which refers to lack of clarity about the types of behaviours that are appropriate and functional (Rizzo et al. 1970) and creates uncertainty about the roles of the various organisational actors in organisations. A few key characteristics of public organisations heighten the problem of ambiguity. First, public sector organisations serve society by providing social services and goods that cannot be exchanged in the economic market (Rainey 1983; Baldwin 1987). As a result, "the economic indicators of efficiency and effectiveness, such as prices and profits, that help to clarify goals in the private sector are often unavailable in the public sector" (Pandey and Wright 2006). Second, in public organisations, there are conflicting cultures: several internal and external actors, who are dominated either by professional or political issues, have conflicting interpretations of accounting (Simons 1991).

Consequently, similar accounting techniques may lead to different results depending on different interpretations by organisational actors (Hopwood 1972). When multiple cultures give multiple meanings to performance measures, these meanings can conflict (Matland 1995): for example, middle and line managers search for accounting and control systems tightly coupled with actions (Covaleski and Dirsmith 1981), whereas top managers often tend to use accounting and control to ally with political bodies (Brignall and Modell 2000; Klott 2002; Modell 2003; Modell 2004). This also makes public organisations similar to 'political arenas' in which different groups of actors strive to determine organisational performance criteria according to their own interests (Scott 1995). Third, in public organisations, delegation of a few significant aspects of decision-making from policymakers to administrative arms and public agencies (Pandey and Wright 2006) fragments authority, creates complex organisational structures and creates the need for coordination among multiple decision-makers.

Ambiguity in the individuation, implementation, use and effects of accounting can arise when an organisation has fragmented authority, unclear goals and responsibilities, lacks traditional market information and conflicting cultures. Embracing the conceptual insights of PC, this paper investigates both the *topoi* of business actors and the validity of accounting in a regional authority (Tuscany Regional Authority: TRA). This case is particularly helpful because it is an example of a complex public organisation where accounting validity is lacking and ambiguity is high owing to the coexistence of a complex organisational structure, multiple decision-makers and conflicting actors and *values*. In this context, the need for coordination among multiple *topoi* and the integration of these *topoi* through accounting is important to achieve a common organisational strategy and avoid ambiguity.

This chapter focuses on three key issues. The first one is how actors construct their *reality* in relation to the world by integrating *values*, *facts*, *communication* and *possibilities*. The second is alignment of different actors' *values*. The third is the pragmatic true nature of performance measurement systems, that is, the ability of such systems to express the reality of actors by integrating facts, values and possibilities. Hence, a case analysis is developed that allows readers to see how PC can be operationalized through discourse analysis.

The remainder of this chapter is organised as follows. The second section explains the research context, the third section explores a few theoretical constructs underlying PC that are useful for our analysis, and the fourth section describes our methodology and methods. Our findings are summarised in the fifth and sixth sections. The former describes actors' topoi and their level of integration, whereas the latter describes the validity of accounting in terms of its ability to represent *reality*, to coordinate multiple *topoi* and avoid ambiguity. Finally, a discussion and our conclusions are provided.

Research Context

The Tuscany Regional Authority represents the regional community. It safeguards the fundamental rights (such as healthcare, work, family etc.) of the region's citizens by defining priorities, managing funds, planning services, stipulating contracts with external providers (such as municipalities or agencies) and controlling external providers. Three main aspects determine the complexity of the work in TRA: organisational structure, relationships with external entities (municipalities, agencies, service providers and companies) and influence of politicians. TRA employs about 2,300 people, of which about 130 are managers (top or middle).

TRA has an articulated organisational structure with decentralised responsibilities organised in six main divisions called Directions, managed by top managers with competences in broad fields (for example, infrastructure, environment and healthcare.). Top Managers are appointed by politicians and are accountable to them. The Directions are further organised into lower levels, 18 Coordination Areas first and then 22 Sectors, managed by middle managers with competences in specific and more detailed fields. Middle managers are appointed by public competition and are accountable to top managers. Below this level, there are employees with lower responsibilities.

The number of relationships with external entities (municipalities, agencies, service providers and companies) is another element that increases the complexity of TRA's work. In fact, the Region does not directly provide services but assures service provision. Hence, even if the Region is not directly in charge of providing services to citizens, it oversees efficient and effective development of service delivering.

The influence of politicians is the third element contributing to the complexity of TRA's work. Citizens elect politicians, and politicians are therefore accountable to citizens: politicians' mission is to answer citizens and get their consensus to be re-elected and have a long career. Capabilities to be flexible are particularly required because of the unpredictable changing environment of government rules, for instance new communitarian directives, disasters caused by natural events, which warrants continuous re-adaptation of priorities. TRA is accountable to politicians and is subject to the same changes in priorities as those of politicians. Top managers are particularly influenced by politicians who appoint them.

TRA introduced a performance measurement system in 2010. The system was implemented to legitimate TRA rather than for managerial purposes. In fact, the system is compliant with national (Law 150/2009) and regional (Law 57/2010) regulations requiring 'performance evaluation systems' in public administration. The 'performance evaluation systems' of TRA, implemented according to Regional Law 57/2010, is supported by two main documents, namely, 'Strategic Plan' and 'Plan of Performance'. The Strategic Plan is a triennial document that defines long-term strategic goals in terms of outcome, for example 'sustaining research', 'diffusing education' and 'increasing tourism'.

The strategic goals are deployed annually throughout the organisation by using a 'Plan of Performance'. More specific goals are assigned first to top managers, then to middle managers and, finally, to the other employees. An indicator is associated with each goal. 'Trees of goals' (and indicators) are defined to illustrate the cause-effect relationship between strategic long-term goals and annual goals of the various organisational positions. The majority of the goals of both top and middle managers are in terms of output (e.g. number of documents, number of laws, etc.) or efficiency (e.g. percentage of time savings). Additionally, top managers have a few goals in terms of outcome, and these are measured over a longer period such as two or three years.

Annual evaluation of the employees is based on a complex process that includes different parameters: contribution towards achievement of strategic goals, achievement of individual goals and behavioural evaluation. All managers and employees receive a monetary reward proportional to the percentage of goals achieved.

Accounting within Pragmatic Constructivism

Whereas the reader can refer to Part 1 (Nørreklit 2017a, 2017b, Chapters 2 and 3, this volume) for the main concepts of PC, in this chapter, we recall key issues regarding accounting in PC that are relevant to the research conducted in TRA. The first key issue is the concept of *communication*. In PC, *communication* is the way to access *reality*: actors, through *communication*, express their own *reality* that would otherwise remain confined to the actors. Actors use language for *communication*, but accounting is also a specific language whose aim is to integrate the dimension of actors' *reality*.

The second key issue is that of validity of accounting in PC. In fact, PC considers accounting a practice concerned with making statements that express matters regarding the construction of reality and assesses the validity of accounting in terms of its capacity to make pragmatic true statements about organisational *reality*. According to PC, accounting systems are valid when they are consistent with organisational *realities* (Nørreklit et al. 2010) even if not with every aspect of *reality*. Otherwise, accounting systems cannot work in practice (Nørreklit 2014). From this perspective, when studying the validity of accounting, one cannot ignore preliminary investigation of organisational and social contexts (Puxty 1993; Otley 1999).

PC suggests that to investigate the functioning of accounting, it is first necessary to investigate the actors' construction of *reality* and the condition to succeed in action. An actor should construct an adequate representation of the world to act successfully. Otherwise, we have fiction, illusions, dreams, hopes and so on. The condition for human action is that there must be a *factual basis* upon which to act. If the basis is fictive, the actor cannot act. Second, the actor can realise only what is factually possible. In other words, the *possibilities* must be embedded in *factual basis;* thus, *facts* and *possibilities* must be integrated. Third, the actor should be motivated to act. If the actor thinks that his/her *values* are outside the range of *factual possibilities*, then he/she is not motivated, but if his/her *values* are within the range of his/her factual possibilities, and he/she believes so, then he/she will act and succeed.

Management and accounting information contributes to the construction of reality if it is *valid*, that is, if the actions that are decided on its base are related to pro-active truth and lead to the intended results. Then, such information incorporates all four aspects of the world of human life and has pragmatic validity.

The third key issue is the role that accounting can play in complex organisations. In fact, PC recognises that in an organisation, each unit or organisational level has a specific professional *topos* and that coordination of actors' *realities* is required to run the organisation under a common organisational strategy driven by shared *values*. PC recognises the role of top managers in enabling the coordination of actors' *realities* into management and control *topoi*, and top managers adopt change implementation strategies to motivate lower levels (middle and line managers, and employees) (Poister and Streib 1995; Weiss 1996; Kaplan 2001; Cavalluzzo and Ittner 2004; Modell 2004; Wright 2007). Furthermore, PC recognises the support provided by accounting to coordinate actors, stimulate cooperation and enable convergence of different *topoi* into 'an overarching business *topos*' (Seal and

Mattimoe 2014). Hence, within PC, accounting represents a key element that facilitates the creation of a shared *reality* and cooperation for addressing critical issues that characterise public organisations such as complex organisational structure, multiple decision-makers and conflicting actors.

Methodology and Methods

As *communication* is the way to access *reality*, this chapter attempts to discover *reality* by analysing *communication*. To that end, a qualitative analysis of actor's argumentation appeared as a suitable way of accessing actors' *topoi*.

Hence, this chapter proposes the adoption of Toulmin's model of argumentation (2003) as a tool to interpret actors' argumentation and to derive the dimensions of *reality*. Starting from the analysis of arguments made in lawsuits (Kim and Benbasat 2006), Stephen Toulmin proposed a model to analyse *all* argumentations that can express the complexity of day-to-day communication. As explained by Toulmin, "it is impossible in the last resort to divorce the criticism of 'reasoning' and 'decision-making' entirely from an understanding of the people giving the reasons and making the decisions" (Schmidt 1986, 508). By describing linguistic logic as 'generalised jurisprudence' (Schmidt 1986, 502) rather than as a highly formalised and abstract a priori system, this perspective discovers and highlights the pragmatic dimension of language. Its focus on the ordinary use and social dimension of language makes this methodology especially suitable for our analysis, which attempts to show how language mirrors actors' reality.

Qualitative approaches are particularly useful not only for gathering and understanding in-depth information about the dimensions of actors' *reality* (*facts, values, possibilities* and *communication*) but they also contribute to the definition of future research questions and to assessing the feasibility of a certain theory (Yin 2013). Therefore, to perform Toulmin-based analysis of actors' argumentations, we collected qualitative data, specifically interviews, because they can provide useful insights for investigating the actors' *topoi* through analysis of what the actors communicate. Interviews involved top managers and middle managers in the Regional Authority and concerned 1) actors' argumentations, including what top managers and middle managers *communicate* about their own *topoi*; and 2) accounting, as a means of creating trustworthy information about *reality* and coordination of multiple organisational *realities*.

Specifically, we relied on different data: 1) interviews with the six top managers (the heads of the six Directions) and 2) interviews with 12 middle managers (the 12 heads of the 18 Coordination areas belonging to the Directions). Between November 2011 and February 2013, we conducted 8.5 h of interviews with top managers and 17.5 h with middle managers. The interviews were audio taped and transcribed. The interviews focused on the activities of managers and on their perspectives about the existing performance measurement system. In addition, we conducted a document analysis to understand the performance measurement system and the characteristics and processes of budgetary and political negotiation. Documents included organisation charts, "Strategic Plan", "Plan of Performance" and linked rewards.

In a second stage of the analysis, we preliminarily analysed interviews and focus groups to identify and code recurrent topics. Then, we used a software application (NVivo) for qualitative analysis to codify and categorise the quotations of interviews into the identified topics. This software package for qualitative research offers a set of tools that allow for a sophisticated, time-efficient and rigorous data coding and analysis process (Ozkan 2004). After having imported all the documents into NVivo, each of us independently coded text into the topics identified in the first phase, thus creating what are called 'nodes' in NVivo. These nodes are collections of references resulting from codification. The aim of this analysis was to organise and categorise contents according to our theoretical constructs (Auerbach and Silverstein 2003). Together, we reviewed, revised and supplemented the first draft of the analysis (including identified topics and nodes) until we reached an agreement about the codification results and the key actors' arguments (key nodes) to be analysed further.

We then applied Toulmin's model to the selected actors' arguments to discover the dimensions of the actors 'realities. According to this model, arguments comprise three main components: *datum (D)*, *claim* (C) and *warrant (W)*. *Datum* is the explicit data or *facts* upon which an argument is based, *claim* is the conclusion that can be inferred from the *datum* and *warrant* is the implicit rule or assumption that makes the inference possible. *Warrants* are not explicit but may be interpreted by the observer (Henriksen et al. 2004).

This model may be adopted to understand the dimension of PC from the analysis of language. In particular, it can help investigate the *facts* recognised by actors and the *values* that sustain their *warrant* and *claim*. In particular, the *datum* of an actor's argumentation represents the dimension of *fact* of the actor's *reality*. The interpretation of how actors derive conclusions (*claim*) from *facts* allows for the identification of the *warrant*. *Warrants* and *claim* are influenced and hide *values*. Comparing *values* with *facts* helps understand whether an actor has the *possibility* to realise his/her *values* with the available resources (*facts*). In other words, it helps understand whether *possibilities* are *factual*.

The following section shows how Toulmin's model was used herein to analyse actors' argumentations and to describe the actors' *topoi*. In this respect, it should be noted that when a researcher investigates actors' *reality*, he/she may easily identify explicit elements (such as *facts*) but should interpret actors' argumentation and language to trace other elements (such as *values*, *communication* and *possibilities*). This, as in all qualitative research, brings the problem of reflexivity: the researcher's background and position affect what he/she chooses to investigate, angle of investigation, methods judged to be most adequate for this purpose, findings considered most appropriate and framing and communication of conclusions (Malterud 2001, 483–484).

Actors' Topoi

We explored what middle and top managers communicate about 1) the resources they have at their disposal (money, people, procedures, laws etc.) to realise their objectives (*facts*), 2) their personal motivations behind their work and goals (*values*); and 3) the "triggering conditions" they consider important to realise their *values* and create *factual possibilities*. A comparative analysis of the two topoi (middle managers' topos and top managers' topos) allowed us then to explore whether an organisational topos exists. The following sub-sections will discuss the top managers' *topos* and the middle managers' *topos*, as well as their integration (or non-integration).

Top Managers' Topos

As regards the top managers, *facts* are communicated explicitly and their investigation is easier. For example, this top manager explains the changing and variable working environment as a *fact*.

> The problem is that there is high variability in the work: in daily work, offices perform activities that change every day according to new goals.
> (Direction "Organisation and Resources")

Another top manager explains, as a *fact*, that one of the reasons of this changing and variable environment is the role of politicians.

> Politicians have a very invasive role in our decisions. This is the main and the most delicate point of indirect influence of politics. Because a politician may even say "I want the motorway connection between those two towns", then I go out the meeting and the politician stops me saying, "make sure you do not to do that. . .". But, I cannot say that the motorway connection should not be made. This is something that happens every day.
> (Direction "Competitiveness and Development")

Politicians may rapidly change priorities according to urgencies and new needs. Top managers appointed by politicians and, in turn, the entire TRA organisation, are particularly affected by any route change. In this specific case, top managers seem uncertain about how to behave, whether to oppose politicians or comply with them. In fact, complying with politicians may contrast with the necessity of the population (for example the need for a motorway). By contrast, opposing politicians can be very difficult because the top managers' organisational position is subordinated to politicians' will. These contrasting feelings lead to a situation with ambiguity about goals and roles.

When explaining his working environment, another top manager says what, in his mind, is required to cope with such an environment.

> In an organisation where we handle emergencies bigger than us to solve huge problems every day, we need people who respond on a daily basis—we need available and helpful people.
>
> (Direction "Presidency bureau")

According to Toulmin's model, this sentence shows *datum* and *claims*, whereas *warrant* is implicit. The *datum*—the *fact* in the PC framework—comprises unexpected events and urgencies related to a changing environment. This top manager claimed that helpful and flexible people can cope with this environment. The *warrant* that establishes the link between *data/fact* and *claim* is that helpful and flexible people are necessary for creating *factual possibilities* (i.e. to cope with a changing environment). The implicit *value* behind *warrant* and *claim* is the *value* of flexibility: the skill of people to change work and tasks, collaborate with other people and change thinking to adapt themselves to the (new) needs of the organisation. *Factual possibilities* of this actor are conditioned by having flexible people to reach goals (triggering condition), i.e. flexible people would be required to face unexpected events. This sentence also suggests that top managers feel that the preferred behaviour is to be flexible in order to comply with the changing environment determined by politicians.

The position and tasks of top managers in the organisational structure may explain their *values*. They are appointed by politicians who may change priorities rapidly and are involved in strategic non-routine decisions. Accordingly, they ask for flexibility and fewer rules.

Middle Managers' Topos

Middle managers confirm the changing and variable environment as a *fact* in their reality construct. Moreover, they feel that coping with political instability makes their work tough. They call for separation between their autonomy and that of politicians, so that sudden changes in politicians' priorities do not affect their ability to perform daily tasks and attain their performance objectives:

> Today politicians assign certain goals, for example, to produce a document in six months. I write the document within the deadline, but then politicians change their goal for certain reasons and they do not need the document any more. I should be considered successful in attainment of the goal. For this reason, I would like separation between my autonomy and the autonomy of politicians, and the responsibilities of politicians and technicians.
>
> (Coordination Area "Infrastructures and Mobility")

The *datum/fact* on which this argumentation is built is a changing and variable working environment governed by political influence, causing ambiguity in the definition of goals and the evaluation of performance as a consequence of the overlap between the political and the administrative spheres of action. When claiming that there is the need to separate the administrative function from politicians, the middle manager claimed independence from politics as a *value* that should be pursued and protected. The role of politicians, who change goals frequently, contributes to creating "goals ambiguity"—e.g. goals assigned in advance are replaced with new conflicting goals—and "task ambiguity"—e.g. to produce a document or not—and makes the work of middle managers difficult. This manager opined that the condition to create *factual possibilities*, that is, being considered successful in his work and avoiding ambiguity, is to create independence from politicians.

Middle managers, when explaining their work—how it is performed and verified—reveal a *value* substantially opposite to that of the top managers.

> Once we know that the car should arrive in Pisa, for us, control means substantially to determine which road brings us to Pisa and periodically compare the number of kilometres we have driven with the itinerary defined in advance. I recognize that this seems too simple but this is what we need.
>
> (Coordination Area "Presidency")

The implicit *warrant* that can be derived from the above quote by a middle manager is that to reach an organisational goal (e.g. to go to Pisa), they need a procedure (e.g. the itinerary). In the above sentence, the middle manager addresses implicitly the triggering conditions to create *factual possibilities*, that is, creating the condition to work: advance definition of clear objectives (i.e. to go to Pisa) and expected behaviours/tasks (itinerary to arrive to Pisa). The implicit *value* of this warrant is compliance with clear rules and goals. The tasks of middle managers in the organisational structure may explain their *values*. They are involved in operational and routine activities. Accordingly, they ask for clear indications of the tasks expected (and recognition of the tasks performed). However, their position in the organisational structure contrasts with their *values* because they are accountable to top managers who ask for flexibility. Consequently, in this category of managers, ambiguity (of goals, roles and behaviours) is high.

Lack of an Overarching Organisational Topos

Results show that top and middle managers have diverging *values*. Thus, top managers call for greater flexibility because of their need to please the politicians that influence their appointment and professional career. Accordingly, they perceive the problem of lack of flexibility of middle managers and other employees as the main constraint to productivity:

> A critical cultural problem is the tendency to "stay in our own back-yard: . . . People say "I'm ok when I have done just my own tasks". The great problem is that people are not autonomous; they do not take decisions out of their pre-defined tasks and do not collaborate.
>
> (Direction "Organisation and Resources")

However, this call for flexibility contrasts markedly with middle managers, who call for pre-defined rules and tasks and do not feel comfortable with flexibility. From the perspective of middle managers, the flexibility required by their bosses only increases the ambiguity about the tasks they should perform:

> Flexibility is a great thing but I feel the need to know what I have to do. I have heard that people must be able to do everything. This is not possible. Instead, we need to know our role and tasks. I do not agree with this issue of flexibility.
>
> (Coordination Area "Culture")

Top managers felt the lack of *factual possibilities* to address successfully an unstable environment dominated by the changing requirements of politicians because middle managers are not flexible. Middle managers believed that their *factual possibilities* are limited by the shortage of clear rules and are in contrast with top managers to whom they are accountable. What emerges is a paradoxical situation: top managers perceive flexibility as a *value*, whereas middle managers perceive flexibility as a source of ambiguity.

The reasons for the emergence of this situation may lie in the different positions and tasks that managers occupy in the organisation. Particularly, top managers are more devoted to strategic decisions and political compliance, tasks which require flexibility. By contrast, middle managers are more engaged in operational tasks and look for clear rules, even if this contrasts with their bosses, to whom they are accountable.

These conflicting *values* made impossible the integration between top managers' *topos* and middle managers' *topos*, and created an organisation without *possibilities for the actors*. Hence, a question arises about the role of the existing performance measurement system in supporting integration of the different *values* and creation of an overarching organisational *meta-topos* to avoid the ambiguity described above.

Validity of Performance Measurement System as Perceived By Actors

Our findings show that the formal performance measurement system does not function because it does not incorporate the four dimensions of actor's *realities*. In depth, the dimensions of *facts* and *values* constructed by the actors are not incorporated in the formal performance measurement system. As a result, the system is not pragmatic true because it produces a fictive reality that is blind to the needs of the actors and is unable to bring about the desired outcomes.

The perception of top managers is that the formal performance measurement system does not represent their *value* of flexibility and existing *facts*. For example, despite the importance of flexibility for *top managers*, this *value* is not represented in the performance measurement system. The top managers, when discussing unexpected events and urgencies, underline a gap between working practices and performance evaluation systems, and the resulting ambiguity in goals and roles:

> New key influences and events loom (or dominate) over formal objectives and create new objectives; [. . .] these new objectives are not captured by the performance measurement system.
>
> (Direction "Territorial policies")

After having declared the need for helpful and flexible people, another top manager (the Direction "Presidency Bureau") continues to argue that the performance measurement system does not change in accordance with the unstable and complex environment *(fact)*.

> I continuously send e-mails to my subordinates, asking things out of the formal objective, things that are not measured (and measurable) by the performance measurement system. This is of vital importance to cope with politicians.
>
> (Direction "Presidency bureau")

The *fact/datum* emerging from this quote is that some things are not measured (or measurable) because the existing performance measurement system is not able to capture this fast-changing environment or because of the impossibility of translating some tasks into measurable indicators. Therefore, this top manager claims that his subordinates should perform activities out of the formal objectives—in other words, he asks for an informal system. Top managers suffer the invalidity of the system because it is unable to help them measure and obtain the flexibility to comply with politicians.

Middle managers also feel that the formal performance measurement system does not incorporate their *facts and values* in the information it provides. They confirm that they operate in a complex and changing environment dominated by uncertainty that the static performance system is unable to capture, thus contributing to ambiguity:

> The problem of all performance measurement systems is their fast obsolescence with respect to the changing context.
>
> (Coordination Area "Strategic Control")

Middle managers suffer the fast obsolescence of the performance measurement system. The obsolescence of the system deprives them of clear guidelines and does not evaluate the tasks they actually perform (that are outside the forms systems) to answer to their bosses. They call for a functioning formal system that may increase compliance with rules and provide clear goals (*values*).

The lack of validity of the formal performance measurement system causes *ambiguity* in terms of unclear goals and tasks. A top manager explains:

> The performance measurement system includes formal goals that tend to become less important during the year. There could be urgencies that become new priorities and more important than the formal goals previously assigned to and shared with the employees.
>
> (Direction "Organisation and Resources")

The warrant underlining the *claim "urgencies becoming new priorities and more important of the formal goals previously assigned and shared with the employees"* is that not all events can be formalised; instead, new events escaping from the performance system become more important and should be pursued outside their formal representation. This top manager argues that in order to make *possibilities* also *factual*, there is a need to adopt less formalisation and greater ambiguity.

Top managers in order to pursue their *value* of flexibility (not represented in the formal system) are inclined to use an informal system. Hence, whereas for middle managers ambiguity is the main difficulty in performing their job effectively, top managers seem to benefit from it because it allows them to adapt their requirements according to the changeable desiderata of politicians.

The positions that these actors occupy in the hierarchy and their tasks play crucial roles. Middle managers, who perform routine operational tasks, feel that formalising all their work is particularly important and ask for a performance measurement system as a tool through which to demonstrate their efforts and results. Accordingly, middle managers perceive political influence as negative and pursue the *value* of autonomy from politicians. However, the fact that they are accountable to top managers creates high ambiguity.

On the contrary, top managers make strategic decisions and know that their performance will be evaluated by politicians according to their capability of driving the organisation toward the political agenda. Therefore, despite suffering the instability created by political influence, they accept less formalisation of performance and compliance with politicians. In this respect, the argument of this top manager is interesting:

> Probably I know that I say something . . . but probably a discretionary evaluation of politicians on our work . . . if politicians, how to say,

exercise this evaluation properly, if they exercise it in an appropriate manner, it could also be a keystone; not everything can be formalized.

(Direction "Presidency bureau")

This top manager claims two aspects: not everything can be formalised and there is a need for discretionary evaluation from politicians. The implicit warrant is that in a changing environment, the organisation can survive and realise *factual possibilities* with less formalisation and greater political discretionary evaluation of the work. Two implicit *values* can be individuated: compliance with politicians and ambiguity.

Overall, the divergence of opinions concerning the desirability of a politics-administration dichotomy (Svara 1985; Wilson 1887; Svara 1999) shows lack of integration of *values* between top and middle managers. This divergence shows that middle and top managers' *realities* are not integrated, not only because of their conflicting *values* but also because of the invalidity of the performance measurement system in terms of its inability to represent *facts* and support the pursuit of common *values*.

Furthermore, our analysis suggests that the implementation of an unsuitable performance measurement system may incentivise the development of a 'tick box mentality' (Lapsley 2009), meaning that individuals are moved only by extrinsic motivation (Ryan and Deci 2000). In this specific case, formalised performance appraisal objectives act as motivators for middle managers, but they weaken the managers' commitment to carry out other informal tasks that fall outside the formalised performance evaluation. This confirms the performativity of performance information, that is, its ability to affect the behaviour of individuals.

Discussion and Conclusions

The analysis conducted in TRA according to the PC approach delivers the picture of a reality disaggregated among the actors and, as a consequence, *factual possibilities* are denied.

The first reason is that *values* are so divergent that integration is not possible. Second, invalidity of the performance measurement system contributes to enhancing the divergence between top and middle managers and keeps them from achieving their values, given that they are not represented in the system. The rigidity of the performance management system clashes with the desire of top managers to assess the flexibility of middle managers for complying with politicians. The formal performance measurement system cannot capture and formalise measures of these behaviours; thus, they can be assessed only by an 'informal' system. By contrast, middle managers who are required to be flexible find that this required behaviour is not represented in the performance measurement system, and according to their *value* of compliance with rules, face difficulties in their work.

These circumstances contribute to feeding the ambiguity of the environment in which the TRA actors operate. Ambiguity allows top managers to deal with the changing environment and the requirements of politicians. Informal assessment can thus replace the formal performance management system in measuring this managerial ability.

The following picture represents the disaggregated reality in TRA, as resulting from our research (Figure 9.1).

Given these findings, this chapter contributes to a deeper understanding of ambiguity in public organisations and the role played by performance measurement in this context (Vakkuri and Meklin 2006).

Application of the PC approach shows that ambiguity can be caused by three main interlinked issues: a changing and complex environment determined by politicians who change goals quickly; invalidity of the performance measurement system; and misalignment between top and middle managers' *values*. First, the changing environment causes ambiguity because goals change continuously and make the formal performance measurement system obsolete rapidly, thus leaving actors without a guide for decision-making. Second, goal and role ambiguity also derive from the invalidity of the performance measurement system that does not incorporate actors' reality in the information it provides. It is divergent from actors' *topoi* and causes the emergence of an informal system. In fact, the system is slow compared to the speed of the changing environment and provides goals that are not representative of actual work activities. The slowness (and rapid obsolescence) of the system contrasts with the *values* of top managers and deprives middle managers of the precise rules and procedures they require in

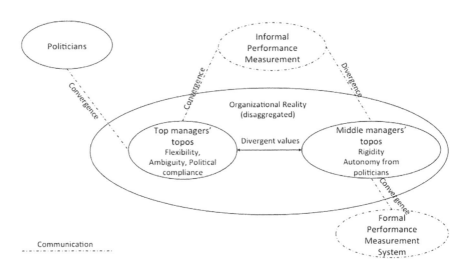

Figure 9.1 A Representation of Reality in TRA

their work according to their *values*. Third, the misalignment between top and middle managers values, worsened by the invalidity of the performance measurement system, increases ambiguity as conflicting values (and goals) cohabit, while a common organisational vision does not exist.

In this empirical setting, ambiguity plays a role in making at least part of the organisation (the top managers) more comfortable in coping with an uncertain environment. In this sense, ambiguity allows top managers to informally apply flexibility, which is better than fixed rules, to face an uncertain environment. Top managers seem to feel comfortable with ambiguity. They think that pre-defined and clear goals do not suit the changing environment in which they operate; instead, they ask for less formalisation and, in this way, greater ambiguity to be better compliant with politicians' aims. In this sense, ambiguity seems to become a *value*.

Our findings also suggest that the existing diverging *values* may depend on the actors' positions in the organisational hierarchy and the tasks that top and middle managers perform. The managers serve different conflicting interests and are expected to comply with divergent requirements. Politicians exercise their power over top managers by asking them to comply with a changeable political agenda. In turn, knowing that their careers and appointments depend on the willingness of politicians, top managers try to shape their organisation in a way that meets the political desiderata. Furthermore, top managers are devoted to strategic non-routine activities. Accordingly, their position asks for flexibility to build a fast and responsive organisation that can deal with a changeable and unstable environment and non-routine activities. However, the translation of this design into practice encounters resistance from middle managers.

Middle managers are devoted to routine activities and are appointed by public competition. Accordingly, they do not accept the power exercised by politicians and call for greater autonomy and independence. However, they are accountable to top managers, and the contrast between their values and those of top managers makes difficult their work and creates ambiguity.

The use of PC to analyse the TRA context suggests that a few values are somewhat "floating" according to the context. The *values* of top managers are floating in the sense that they exist also because of being determined by a certain context: flexibility and ambiguity for compliance with politicians is not likely to be a *value* embedded in the actors' minds but rather a *value* induced by emerging *facts* (political influence and changing environment).

However, top managers find themselves in conflict with the *values* of compliance with rules and with the claim of autonomy from politicians pursued by middle managers. The *values* of middle managers are not floating but are in contrast with the context. In this respect, the values of middle managers seem stronger than those of top managers. Their *values* contrast with the changing environment, and they ask for a solution to the problem of ambiguity and need precise goals and pre-defined procedures.

The findings of this research provide some insights for overcoming the ambiguity highlighted in the case study. The PC approach suggests that the first step towards reducing ambiguity is integration between the top and middle managers' *topoi*, as it can contribute to creating a common organisational vision by supporting the existence of shared, instead of conflicting, *values*.

When identification of shared values is difficult, a leading position should be played by accounting that should assume the role of media of cooperation. In fact, after identification of the prevailing *values*, PC suggests that effort for creating coherence between those *values* and representational practices is required. As shown in the case, *values* can be very divergent, and a common group of *values* can be difficult or impossible to create. Accounting may have the power to act as a moderator between conflicting *values* by supporting the search for agreements between them, thus stimulating actors to collaborate towards a common objective. Thus, rethinking the approach to management accounting design and implementation and the choice of adequate tools and measures can help in these settings. The adoption of participative approaches such as the involvement of actors in identification of measures and meetings to discuss objectives can stimulate communication between actors finalised to find agreements. The identification of adequate measures such as incentives for goal achievement or design of interdepartmental indicators might help integrate conflicting *topoi* (Lascu et al. 2006). Politicians should also be involved in this process: they are required to disclose their *topoi* and search for a convergence with other actors in the organisation.

Finally, this research illustrated the utility of Toulmin's model as a tool for investigating the dimension of actors' *communication* and access to the other dimensions of PC, thus providing a path to operationalize PC in an empirical setting. The argumentation analysis, supported by Toulmin's model of argumentation (2003), proved to be particularly useful in discovering *facts* and *values* through the analysis of *communication*. However, qualitative research is not pre-defined, and several attempts and revisions are required until the analysis suits the research objectives. Although we argue that the proposed tool can be very useful for investigating actor's *topoi*, the analysis always remains subjective, in so far as the investigation of actors' *topoi* requires interpretation. The reflexivity that characterises this kind of interpretative research may constitute a limitation of the current study. In this respect, the use of Toulmin's model may offer a reliable interpretation scheme to reduce arbitrariness of the analysis.

References

Arnaboldi, Michela, and Irvine Lapsley. 2009. "On the implementation of accrual accounting: A study of conflict and ambiguity." *European Accounting Review*, 18 (4): 809–836.
Arnaboldi, Michela, and Tommaso Palermo. 2011. "Translating ambiguous reforms: Doing better next time?" *Management Accounting Research*, 22 (1): 6–15.

Auerbach, C., and L.B. Silverstein. 2003. *Qualitative Data: An Introduction to Coding and Analysis.* New York: New York University Press.

Baldwin, J. Norman. 1987. "Public versus private: Not that different, not that consequential." *Public Personnel Management*, 16 (2): 181–193.

Brignall, Stan, and Sven Modell. 2000. "An institutional perspective on performance measurement and management in the 'new public sector'." *Management Accounting Research*, 11 (3): 281–306.

Cavalluzzo, Ken S., and Christopher D. Ittner. 2004. "Implementing performance measurement innovations: Evidence from government." *Accounting, Organizations and Society*, 29 (3): 243–267.

Chenhall, Robert H. 2003. "Management control systems design within its organizational context: Findings from contingency-based research and directions for the future." *Accounting, Organizations and Society*, 28 (2): 127–168.

Covaleski, Mark A., and Mark W. Dirsmith. 1981. "MBO and goal directedness in a hospital context." *Academy of Management Review*, 6 (3): 409–418.

Davis, Philip J., and Reuben Hersh. 1986. *Descartes' Dream: The World According to Mathematics.* San Diego: Harcourt Brace Jovanovich.

Henriksen Lars B., Lennart Nørreklit, Kenneth M. Jørgensen, Jacob B. Christensen, and David O'Donnell. 2004. *Dimensions of Change—Conceptualising Reality in Organisational Research.* Copenhagen: Copenhagen Business School Press.

Hopwood, Anthony G. 1972. "An empirical study of the role of accounting data in performance evaluation." *Journal of Accounting Research*, 10: 156–182.

Humphrey, Christopher, Peter Miller, and Robert W. Scapens. 1993. "Accountability and accountable management in the UK public sector." *Accounting, Auditing & Accountability Journal*, 6: 3.

Kaplan, Robert S. 2001. "Strategic performance measurement and management in nonprofit organizations." *Nonprofit Management and Leadership*, 11 (3): 353–370.

Kim, Dongmin, and Izak Benbasat. 2006. "The effects of trust-assuring arguments on consumer trust in Internet stores: Application of Toulmin's model of argumentation." *Information Systems Research*, 17 (3): 286–300.

Klott, Louise. 2002. "Performance management and measurement in universities: A case study." Paper presented at the 25th annual congress of the European Accounting Association, Copenhagen, Denmark.

Kurunmäki, Liisa, and Peter Miller. 2006. "Modernising government: The calculating self, hybridisation and performance measurement." *Financial Accountability & Management*, 22 (1): 87–106.

Lapsley, Irvine. 2001. "Accounting, modernization and the state." *Financial Accountability and Management*, 17 (4): 201–207.

Lapsley, Irvine. 2009. "New public management: The cruellest invention of the human spirit?" *Abacus*, 45 (1): 1–21.

Lascu, Dana-Nicoleta, Lalita A. Manrai, Ajay K. Manrai, and Ryszard Kleczek. 2006. "Interfunctional dynamics and firm performance: A comparison between firms in Poland and the United States." *International Business Review*, 15 (6): 641–659.

Malterud, Kirsti. 2001. "Qualitative research: Standards, challenges, and guidelines." *The Lancet*, 358 (9280): 483–488.

March, James G., and Herbert Alexander Simon. 1958. *Organizations.* Oxford: Blackwell.

Matland, Richard E. 1995. "Synthesizing the implementation literature: The ambiguity-conflict model of policy implementation." *Journal of Public Administration Research and Theory*, 5 (2): 145–174.

Modell, Sven. 2003. "Goals versus institutions: The development of performance measurement in the Swedish university sector." *Management Accounting Research*, 14 (4): 333–359.

Modell, Sven. 2004. "Performance measurement myths in the public sector: A research note." *Financial Accountability & Management*, 20 (1): 39–55.

Nørreklit, Hanne, Lennart Nørreklit, and Falconer Mitchell. 2010. "Towards a paradigmatic foundation for accounting practice." *Accounting, Auditing & Accountability Journal*, 23 (6): 733–758.

Nørreklit, Lennart. 2014. "Reality as a construct: Outline of a pragmatic constructivist perspective." *Proceedings of Pragmatic Constructivism*, 3 (2): 57–66.

Nørreklit, Lennart. 2017a. "Actor reality construction." In *A Philosophy of Management Accounting: A Pragmatic Constructivist Approach*, edited by Hanne Nørreklit. Chapter 2, this volume. New York: Routledge.

Nørreklit, Lennart. 2017b. "Epistemology." In *A Philosophy of Management Accounting: A Pragmatic Constructivist Approach*, edited by Hanne Nørreklit. Chapter 3, this volume New York: Routledge.

Nørreklit, Lennart, Hanne Nørreklit, and Poul Israelsen. 2006. "The validity of management control *topoi*. Towards constructivist pragmatism." *Management Accounting Research*, 17: 42–71.

Otley, David. 1999. "Performance management: A framework for management control systems research." *Management Accounting Research*, 10 (4): 363–382.

Ozkan, Betul C. 2004. "Using NVivo to analyze qualitative classroom data on constructivist learning environments." *The Qualitative Report*, 9 (4): 589–603.

Pandey, Sanjay K., and Bradley E. Wright. 2006. "Connecting the dots in public management: Political environment, organizational goal ambiguity, and the public manager's role ambiguity." *Journal of Public Administration Research and Theory*, 16: 511–532.

Poister, Theodore H., and Gregory Streib. 1995. "MBO in municipal government: Variations on a traditional management tool." *Public Administration Review*, 55: 48–56.

Puxty, Anthony G. 1993. *The Social and Organizational Context of Management Accounting*. London: Academic Press.

Rainey, Hal G. 1983. "Public agencies and private firms incentive structures, goals, and individual roles." *Administration & Society*, 15 (2): 207–242.

Rainey, Hal G. 1993. "Toward a theory of goal ambiguity in public organizations." *Research in Public Administration*, 2: 121–166.

Rizzo, John R., Robert J. House, and Sidney I. Lirtzman. 1970. "Role conflict and ambiguity in complex organizations." *Administrative Science Quarterly*, 15: 150–163.

Ryan, Richard M., and Edward L. Deci. 2000. "Intrinsic and extrinsic motivations: Classic definitions and new directions." *Contemporary Educational Psychology*, 25 (1): 54–67.

Schmidt, David P. 1986. "Patterns of argument in business ethics." *Journal of Business Ethics*, 5 (6): 501–509.

Scott, W. Richard. 1995. *Institutions and Organizations: Foundations for Organizational Science*. London: Sage.

Seal, Will, and Ruth Mattimoe. 2014. "Controlling strategy through dialectical management." *Management Accounting Research*, 25 (3): 230–243.

Simons, Robert. 1991. "Strategic orientation and top management attention to control systems." *Strategic Management Journal*, 12 (1): 49–62.

Svara, James H. 1985. "Dichotomy and duality: Reconceptualizing the relationship between policy and administration in council-manager cities." *Public Administration Review*, 45: 221–232.

Svara, James H. 1999. "Complementarity of politics and administration as a legitimate alternative to the dichotomy model." *Administration & Society*, 30 (6): 676–705.

Toulmin, Stephen E. 2003. *The Use of Argument: Updated Edition.* Cambridge: Cambridge University Press.

Vakkuri, Jarmo, and Pentti Meklin. 2006. "Ambiguity in performance measurement: A theoretical approach to organisational uses of performance measurement." *Financial Accountability & Management*, 22 (3): 235–250.

Weiss, Janet A. 1996. "Psychology." In *The State of Public Management*, edited by Donald F. Kettl and H. Brinton Milward, 118–142. Baltimore, MD: Johns Hopkins University Press.

Wilson, Woodrow. 1887. "The study of administration." *Political Science Quarterly*, 2 (2): 197–222.

Wright, Bradley E. 2001. "Public sector work motivation: Review of current literature and a revised conceptual model." *Journal of Public Administration Research and Theory*, 11 (4): 559–586.

Wright, Bradley E. 2004. "The role of work context in work motivation: A public sector application of goal and social cognition theories." *Journal of Public Administration Research and Theory*, 14 (1): 59–78.

Wright, Bradley E. 2007. "Public service and motivation: Does mission matter?" *Public Administration Review*, 67 (1): 54–64.

Yin, Robert K. 2013. *Case Study Research Design and Methods.* Thousand Oaks, CA: Sage.

Part III
Research Approaches and Reality Constructions

10 Language Games of Management Accounting—Constructing Illusions or Realities?

*Nikolaj Kure, Hanne Nørreklit
and Morten Raffnsøe-Møller*

Introduction

Broadly speaking, current management accounting research is dominated by two opposing views on language: on the one hand, a realist stance that perceives language as a tool for representation and, on the other, a constructivist perspective that sees language as a lens through which various realities emerge (Chua 1986; Tinker 1991). In the realist view, an objective world exists 'out there' for language to describe, whereas constructivist researchers argue that no external point of reference can be used to evaluate whether a statement is true or not.

From the perspective of Pragmatic Constructivism, both of these positions are charged with a set of problems that obscure one of the core tenets of management accounting, namely enabling actors *in situ* to construe successful intentional activities. In the view of pragmatic constructivism, language, including accounting, plays a crucial part in the construction of functioning practices. But what should characterise management and accounting language if it is to contribute to successful reality constructions? The ambition of this chapter is to discuss this question. To do so, we shall briefly discuss the two extreme positions of realism and constructivism—and their limitations—before turning to pragmatic constructivism in order to describe which linguistic characteristics must be in place if language is to function as a resource for successful reality construction.

The Realist vs Constructivist Cleavage in Accounting

The Realist Position

The realist position is built on two core assumptions. First, it is believed that the world exists independently of thought and observation. There is an objective world 'out there' that remains unchanged by how people describe and conceptualise it. Second, it is believed that language is a means to reflect the world. The basic linguistic element, the sign, is given its meaning through reference to a specific phenomenon in the world, allowing people to label and picture the world (Wittgenstein 1921). In this perception, then, the world and language are two separate systems: the world exists independently of language, which is simply a tool for representation. Consequently, the goal of science, and in the context of this book: management accounting, is to describe the world as neutrally and precisely as possible. The central task of management accounting is to make distinctions between true or false: does the account reflect reality (in which case it is true) or does it obscure reality (in which case it is false)?

As it is, much conventional accounting wisdom originates from the realist paradigm (Simons and Karrenbrock 1964; Chua 1986; Tinker 1991). For instance, the much-read accounting scholar Solomons argues that "the task of accountants is to provide information as free from bias as possible that will be useful to decision makers (. . .) Though accountants sometime fail to achieve the faithful representation of economic phenomenon, that should be their goal" (Solomons 1991, 287), whereas another accounting scholar, Horngren, sees management accounting concepts and techniques as "neutral devices" (Horngren 1995, 281). The realist assumption also permeates Cooper and Kaplan's (1988) classical study of costing and decision-making in which they contend that activity-based costing is a neutral medium to "Measure Costs Right" and to "Make the Right Decisions". All in all, there can be no doubt that realism is embedded in a large stream of positivistic management accounting research (see e.g. Langfield-Smith 1997; Chenhall 2003; Ittner and Larcker 2003).

The Constructivist Position

The constructivist camp, on the other hand, contends that reality and language are two highly intertwined phenomena. Paradoxically, this argument emanates from Ferdinand de Saussure's (1983) structuralist account of language in which he essentially separates language from the external world. In a nutshell, Saussure argues that the meaning of a sign is not the result of its reference to a phenomenon in the world; rather, meaning is established through its relations to other signs in the sign system (*la langue*). The sign 'chair' is given its meaning through the way it differs from other signs (e.g. 'table', 'bench' etc.) in the sign system, not through its reference to the empirically observable chair. Whereas this proposition sheds light on how meaning is established, it also raises a new fundamental question: if language does not reflect the world, then what role does it play? An influential group of thinkers, later known as social constructivists or post-structuralists, suggests that language plays a pivotal part in the *construction of reality*. In a post-structuralist view, reality is never simply 'out there' as an a priori fact; it is construed as a result of complex linguistic processes in which reality emerges. In this sense, Saussure's theory paves the way for an abundance of social constructivist theories, all tied together by the basic assumption that language is not a neutral medium that allows the world to present itself as it is; rather, language shapes how reality becomes visible to social actors.

Like many other social sciences, accounting has been an arena for the proliferation of theories of a social constructionist slant (generally known as the linguistic turn). Tinker, for one, sets the tone by explicitly referring to Saussure's conceptualisation of the sign, leading him to conclude that "the search for representational faithfulness is futile, because there is nothing to seek!" (Tinker 1991, 303). Inspired by the philosophical thoughts of critical Marxism, he goes on to argue that accounting numbers are shaped through dialectical social forces that mask the true economic reality and thus have no final authority. In the words of Baudrillard (1981), the sign (or in this case: the number) is a simulation of reality. In fact, some accounting scholars even take the argument a step further in arguing that accounting may be considered a simulacrum, which is Baudrillard's concept for a sign that has no relation to reality at all. For instance, Macintosh et al. (2000, 13) argue that we are witnessing an increasing number of accounting concepts that do not refer "to any objective reality but instead circulate[s] in a 'hyperreality' of self-referential models" (Macintosh et al. (2000, 13).

In the specific context of management accounting, Michel Foucault (1970) plays a particularly significant role. Inspired by Saussure's view on language, Foucault develops a set of analytics to unravel how discourses create lines of actions, so-called *dispositifs*. For instance, Foucault analyses how different historical epochs are governed by discourses that not only describe human behaviour but also shape it (Foucault 1970). In this sense, Foucault's overarching project can be seen as a general attack on the dominating humanistic or anthropocentric mindset that situates the human being at the centre of thought. By focusing on how discourses constitute a context that facilitates, but also limits, how human beings think and act, Foucault turns the analytical lens upside down. To him, the discourse has primacy, not the actor. In management accounting, a critical movement that draws on Foucault has been initiated by Miller and O'Leary (1987), emphasising that discourses external to local practices govern the production of accounting numbers and knowledge structures. In this sense, the standard costing methods introduced and proliferated should not be understood as tools that produce objective information about local practices. Rather, they should be seen as a way of governing and forming organisational actors by means of measurements, comparisons, differentiations, rankings and exclusions, ultimately with the aim of installing a form of bio-politics in the organisation.

Problems of the Realist vs Constructivist Position

From a pragmatic constructivist perspective, however, both of these views on the relation between language and reality implicate a number of important problems. In accordance with Wittgenstein's view (1953), the realist perspective has at least two major flaws. First, it implies a basic language philosophical problem: as described above, the realist position contends that the primary function of language is to name or picture phenomena in the world. Yet, as Wittgenstein points out, not all signs are names. Any language consists of numerous signs, which are undoubtedly meaningful yet do not make reference to phenomena in the world, for instance the signs 'there', 'but', 'so', 'on', 'grief' and 'it itches'. It seems that the realist theory of language only works when it comes to nouns (and, to a lesser extent, verbs) and, consequently, seems inadequate as a basis for a general theory of meaning (Wittgenstein 1953). Hence, Wittgenstein, along with speech act theorists such as Austin (1962) and Searle (1975), points out that every-day language practices include referential, communicative and expressive dimensions, which are interwoven to establish successful human practices.

Second, the realist position is ridden with the basic epistemological problem that the human perception system does not represent reality in a 1:1 relation. For instance, Bohr's quantum physics illustrates how light is not simply light but appears to us either as a particle or a wave depending on how it is observed. Or, in Wittgenstein's analogy: when we observe a tree, the observation of the tree is ultimately made possible by a set of external criteria that define what a tree is and thus allow us to observe the tree as a tree. The essential element of realism, the question of correspondence between language and reality, therefore, is not simply a question of correspondence between words and objects but rather a question of how language is interwoven into concrete human practices. This further implies that knowledge interests, as well as criteria of truth and correspondence, are relative to human projects and knowledge already established. Hence, the relevant 'independent reality' to be mirrored by language is not just there as an *a priori* fact; rather, it is co-constituted by linguistic practices and actors' intentions of realising specific goals in the world.

Whereas this type of criticism poses an epistemological challenge to the realist camp, it also has a more practical consequence. By insisting that *nothing* is constructed, management accounting of a realist slant runs the risk of losing sight of what is the main task of management accounting, namely to facilitate and control how organisational actors construct profitable business activities. Thus, to our minds the important question is not whether or not an accounting system reflects reality in a 1:1 relation; rather, the crucial question is whether or not it stimulates organisational actors to engage in successful reality constructions—a perspective that realist management accounting disregards entirely.

Whereas the realist position thus implicates a number of important limitations, the social constructivist position appears to solve these issues. By assuming that language is a set of socially constructed categories that allow different versions of reality to emerge, social constructivist theories stimulate researchers to examine how different accounting systems favour specific realities and power relations. However, in doing so social constructivist theories seem to embed themselves in yet another problem, namely one of relativism. More specifically, the critical potential of social constructivism is to show how some voices are privileged/suppressed when reality is constructed in certain ways, yet it remains impossible to develop criteria that enable distinction between good and bad reality constructions. By insisting that *everything* is a construction, the criteria themselves are reduced to constructions, in which case they are robbed of their ability to function as stable benchmarks for criticism. As a result, the social constructivist perspective runs the risk of being reduced to an analytical strategy (albeit an interesting one) that may be able to describe how the world is constructed but is essentially unable to move beyond a descriptive criticism. In fact, the social constructivist strategy may even work in favour of the powerful, despite an explicit intention to do the opposite. If indeed no normative critique can be established by researchers, the logical conclusion is that the existing power configurations may be just as good as alternative ones, essentially defusing the critical ambition of the post-structuralist camp.

Furthermore, social constructivism seems to underestimate the reflexive element in language which, without criteria of knowledge, might result in people speculating against each other. If indeed language games are governed by a "hermeneutics of suspicion" due to the (often very realistic) assumption that all (or most) actors are engaging in strategic language practice, then our ability to establish realistic or veridical predictions about our common future is essentially hampered. The ability to engage in communal projects of reality construction is heightened by a certain level of trust in the intentions of the parties involved. And, in particular, management accounting relies rather heavily on certainty in the function of specific language games.

In a response to this type of problems, pragmatic constructivism sets out to develop a middle ground, arguing that organisational actors construct their relationship to the world. However, at the same time it holds realism as the pragmatic criteria of successful outcome of the organisational actors' construction. It emphasises that language must possess a set of specific qualities to facilitate a successful construction. The position is further explained below.

The Pragmatic Constructivist View on Language

Pragmatic constructivism holds that people are (and want to be) actors who construct their relationships to the world in which they operate. As opposed to the pure constructivist position, actors do not act in a void governed by linguistic practices determined outside of their local practices. Rather, they always act under presumption of a specific relation to phenomena in the world, which they continuously construct, adjust and reconstruct in light of new experiences, contexts and communication. The outcome of the process is a reality construction. For the construction to be a success, organisational actors must establish a joint set of functioning activities, producing certain intended outcomes. In other words, the actors should make construct causality, which requires a pragmatic integration of the four dimensions of reality to be made for each activity in interaction with other activities. Thus, in contrast to the pure constructivist position, pragmatic constructivism contends that there are ways of distinguishing between good and bad constructions (or, in this case: between good and bad accounting). The key to this distinction is the degree to which the constructions *function successfully*. From a pragmatic constructivist position, thus, the essential question is not whether or not reality is a construction. The crucial question is: does the accounting language *facilitate a successful, functioning reality construction or an illusionary one?* Below, we aim to deal with this question, first by describing how pragmatic constructivism draws on the language philosophy of the late Wittgenstein, and then by outlining the criteria that must be met if a particular language game (e.g. an accounting system) is to be workable (Nørreklit et al. 2016).

Language Games

In *Philosophical Investigations*, Wittgenstein (1953) argues that the question of meaning cannot be answered within the context of a purely referential understanding of language. In Wittgenstein's analysis, the referential theory is too simplistic to grasp the complexity of language; instead, he proposes that meaning in language must be found in its use. Meaning is not given by any external referent but by the practical usage of language in specific social settings. Language, in this understanding, does not consist of one overarching stable system (as proposed by Saussure) but rather by a multitude of locally constituted *language games* in which meaning is constructed, negotiated and learned.

The classic example of a language game is the 'builder's language' where a builder needs his assistant to bring him various building materials. For this purpose, they develop a language consisting of the words 'block', 'pillar', 'slab', 'beam': the builder calls them out, and the assistant brings the stones he has learned to bring at such-and-such a call (Philosophical Investigations § 2). In other words, when exclaiming 'block!' the builder does not simply point to the physical block; he actually asks his assistant to bring him the block. Thus, in our practical use of language a number of social actions are performed (orders, jokes, bullying, etc.), in effect constituting various *life forms*. In this sense, language is not external to the world; on the contrary, it is used as a toolbox by actors operating in specific situations to construe particular ways of life.

Pragmatic constructivism agrees with Wittgenstein's (1953) rejection of the realist assumption that a concept has one universal or intrinsic meaning that can be established across time and space. Furthermore, it shares the Wittgensteinian idea that people use local language games to create social actions and intentions. However, pragmatic constructivism also argues that if language is to generate specific, intended actions and outcomes, a set of relevant human intentions and factually possible conditions are required

(Nørreklit 2011; Nørreklit et al. 2016). From a pragmatic constructivist perspective, the crucial question is whether these life forms—these social practices that are generated in language games—allow people to function as actors, i.e. whether they are supportive of people's ability to develop construct causality. Yet, pragmatic constructivism also acknowledges that practices are sometimes governed by constructions that produce illusions in which case it is virtually impossible for organisational members to function as actors. In this chapter, we shall refrain from discussing how this works in general and limit our discussion to the role language plays in this regard. The question that we aim to address is this: given that pragmatic constructivism follows the late Wittgenstein in conceptualising language as a toolbox for the construction of realities, which characteristics must local language games display if they are to be considered supportive for the organisational actors in building construct causality?

Criteria for Pragmatically True Language Games

In order for organisational actors to control and coordinate actions in an effort to create meaningful and functioning practices, they need to establish a system of concepts that facilitates the social coordination of a multitude of activities. Concepts are not the phenomena themselves, yet effective concepts enable actors to develop and control life forms or practices. Below, core aspects of establishing effective concepts are explained based on the analysis of pragmatic constructivism (for a more detailed description see Chapter 3 of this volume [Nørreklit 2017] and Nørreklit et al. 2016). In particular, we discuss: i) how the structure of concepts must be outlined to effectively determine their meaning, including how new concepts are developed and formatted; ii) how the four dimensions of reality construction must be reflected as layers in the conceptual content; and iii) how to perform a pragmatic test of whether the claims established by the concepts facilitate an effective reality construction or an illusionary one.

The Structure of Concepts

Pragmatic constructivism argues that the meaning of any concept is relative to its actual *pragmatic function*. Therefore, to understand a specific concept we need to understand the role of the concept in a concrete social context. For instance, understanding the concept of rain depends on whether it is used by climatologists to understand climate change or by farmers to plan harvesting. Similarly, in management accounting the concept of 'costs' has a multitude of meanings depending on the functional context in which it is used. Costs that are relevant to decision-making are not the same as those that are relevant to control. And costs that are relevant to short-term pricing decisions are not the same as those that are relevant to long-term pricing decisions. It should be mentioned that this notion of purpose dependent meaning of costs is in fact taken into account by conventional knowledge within management accounting.

When organisational actors develop concepts to construe functioning realities, they draw on their linguistic toolboxes. But for language games to function in a specific practice, actors need to develop and adjust the meaning of the concepts. This, however, is not a simple matter. Actors need to engage in a reflective and dialogical process to reconceptualise the concepts and establish what a particular concept means in a particular reality construction. Drawing on philosophical insights on how concepts work (Nørreklit et al. 2016), we argue that if actors are to determine the meaning of a particular concept in relation to a context specific purpose, an alignment of *three structural dimensions of meaning* must be in place: abstract meaning, criteria and exemplary reference.

First, the sign must be given an *abstract meaning*. Drawing on their linguistic toolbox, actors must outline the abstract idea of the concept by defining its *content*. This enables people to determine the exemplary reference of the concept, and thereby it can be used to draw lines between that which is and is not characterised by the concept. For instance, the conceptual content of rain is associated with the idea of 'drops of water falling from clouds in the sky'. Within management accounting, the abstract meaning of the concept 'variable costs' might be delineated by costs that change in total in proportion to changes in manufacturing volume over short periods of time. And likewise in economics, actors must agree that the concept of 'recession' refers to the idea of 'a noticeable downturn in economic activity'.

However, relating a concept to an abstract idea is not always sufficient for the concept to work in practice. For instance, everyone agrees that the concept of 'rain' is related to the idea of 'drops of water falling from clouds in the sky', yet people may have difficulties determining when it actually rains. Therefore, a concept must be given a supplementary *criterion-based meaning*. Criteria have the ability to overcome issues of subjectivity by transforming the qualitative basis of the conceptual content into numbers. For instance, the concept of rain may be defined by the size and density of the drops of water; variable costs might be defined by degree of proportionality and number of days or weeks; and an economic recession may be defined by means of the criterion 'a decrease in the GDP for at least two quarters in a row'. Notice that these criteria are contingent and thus do not reflect an intrinsic meaning of any particular concept. For instance, a recession could be defined in much broader terms than the ones economists have currently decided to use. In our view, the criteria should be chosen in accordance with the pragmatic use of the concept in question. Thus, a concept with loose criteria may be useful in contexts where individuals' actions are based on individual judgement, whereas a tighter use of criteria is required when actions are externally restricted.

Finally, actors need to agree on a specific set of *exemplary references* that establish a shared horizon of understanding and thereby add meaning to the concept. For instance, in a specific practice of accounting, actors might agree that variable costs signify payments to individual employees for piece-work and raw material costs. Similarly, actors must agree that the occurrence of a recession may be exemplified by pointing to the historical events of the Great Depression in the 1930s, the mid-1970s recessions, the late 2000s financial crisis etc. When doing so, the concept of a recession is not only given meaning by its abstract idea or by a set of criteria but also by drawing on the immense set of phenomenological experiences that are condensed in these examples. For instance, when pointing to the recession in the 1930s, we all know what a recession involves because it activates collective memories and emotions.

In a dynamic world, our concepts need to be dynamic, too. When new practices unfold, it is imperative that the local language is open to the development of new concepts in order to allow actors to manage and control new practices. For instance, activity-based costing may be seen as a new concept developed to handle contemporary accounting issues more effectively. The formation of new concepts may happen through actors' re-formation of already existing concepts by changing their logic in relation to other concepts. The development of new concepts seems to happen more intuitively within some fields of practice than others. For instance, artists seem to display a high degree of sensibility to grasping new practices through metaphorical and imaginary language. However, to make accounting and performance management concepts work in a specific practice, their content and criteria have to be delimited and anchored through actors' reflective and analytical reasoning in local interactions. For example, many companies have introduced the notion of 'lean' as a new management philosophy; however, the concept is extremely open to interpretation, making the establishment of construct causality difficult.

The development of new concepts, thus, is not a purely individual accomplishment; rather, it is the result of an institutionalisation process in which logics of interaction and justification are used by individuals and groups of actors (Boltanski and Thévenot 2006) to interpret, produce, reconfigure and develop new concepts (Nørreklit et al. 2016). Thus, the ongoing creative and reflective skills of individuals and collective actors form the basis for the (re)construction of institutionalised discourses. Consequently, such institutionalised discourses may be much more heterogeneously and unevenly distributed and interpreted than suggested by for instance Foucault (1976) and Giddens (2013).

Linking Concepts to the Four Dimensions of Reality Construction

So far we have discussed the structural dimensions of a well-functioning concept. However, it is crucial that the four dimensions of reality construction (facts, possibilities, values and communication) are reflected as layers in the concept, too (see Chapter 4, this volume [Nørreklit et al. 2017], Chapter 6, this volume [Mitchell et al. 2017] and Chapter 8, this volume [Trenca and Nørreklit 2017] for a more detailed explanation of how companies might work with such integration in relation to planning and control). First and foremost, this means that a good concept must provide possibilities that are based on facts. This implies that the concept should be identifiable by its schemata of appearance and in relation to the possibilities and necessities that define its potentials and causal properties. For instance, what makes a person a customer is not that they look like a customer but that they are actually capable of buying products. A person may look like a customer but simply be a window shopper. Similarly, an account in our bookkeeping may look like an accountant receivables, but whether it is actually an account receivables depends on whether or not an actual debtor has received some products or services and that they can actually make the payment. Thus, the relation between the identifying schemata of appearance and the functionalities is the basic relation between appearance and reality. And, clearly, the borderline that determines what does and does not fall under the concept should be the functional aspects and not the appearance.

Additionally, the conceptual content must be linked to the sets of values that belong to individuals and groups of actors. To facilitate action, actors in specific local contexts must agree on the function of the concept. It is not enough that the customer is capable of buying a product; they should be willing to do so because the products are considered valuable. And, similarly, it is not enough that the debtor is capable of paying; they should be willing to pay because it is considered valuable to do so. Finally, the practical meaning of a concept must be communicated and understood by the actors in question.

Pragmatic Testing of Concepts

The final test of effectively constructed concepts is related to whether or not the expectations created by the communication are fulfilled. Accordingly, it is only through its application in actual practices that a conceptual model may be tested. Importantly, the degree of truth and reliability of the applied concepts is not an a priori issue but a purely pragmatic one. If the concepts work, i.e. the expectations created by the communication are fulfilled, the statements are true. The pragmatic test can be made by continuously comparing the pro-active truth claims of the conceptual framework regarding expected outcome of action, and the pragmatic truth as the actual result of action (Nørreklit et al. 2007).

Characteristics of Illusionary Language Games

Whereas the above criteria should pave the way for a well-functioning accounting language, there is always the risk that illusionary language games may occur. This type of language game is characterised by conceptual inconsistency and confusion, generated through the use of equivocal, ambiguous and empty signifiers (Laclau and Mouffe 1985), and the existence of loose relationships between terms. Generally speaking, when links between the function of the concept and the three dimensions of meaning are uncertain or false, illusions are the likely result (Nørreklit 1986).

Throughout contemporary society, we witness many cases of highly 'politicised' language games that socialise actors in using unrealistic or illusionary concepts, as was the case in the American housing market before the crash (Raffnsøe-Møller 2015). Also, it seems that illusionary language games appear in the management accounting field to an increasing degree. For instance, a performance measurement package can be ripe with conceptual confusion (Nørreklit et al. 2012). This is supported by a recent study of performance contracts in universities (unpublished) which shows how a key indicator for the performance of universities is the concept of 'quality', yet 'quality' is defined with reference to quantitative terms, such as more student satisfaction, more top journal publishing etc. There is no outline of the content of quality and no clear explanation as to the role of quality in the reality construction. Thus, the concept of quality may mean one thing to the university board and another to the lecturers. Also, teaching quality has the potential to mean both knowledge creation and intellectual capabilities and teaching abilities. Finally, quality might be intended to explain the totality of university activities and output. Because the conceptual content of quality is missing or unclear, people would be inclined to understand quality according to how it is used in their local language games (definition in use). Some might perceive university quality as a matter of advanced knowledge and reflective intellectual capabilities whereas others may perceive it as the mere production of knowledge. All this may lead to argumentation *ad absurdum*, which means that the accomplishment of organisational goals becomes difficult or even impossible.

Of course, the realist language form, which in particular has shown its pragmatic use within the natural science domain, may also take the form of an illusion. Because the natural sciences do not have to take into account how humans construct possibilities and motivational values, it is sufficient to operate with a single dimension in the conceptual content. Yet, when this logic is transposed to the realm of human beings, for instance when people try to define university quality in terms of quantitative criteria, problems begin to occur. It is always contentious when numbers are created to reflect concepts such as university quality. Nevertheless, direct references to the authority of scientific realism are manifold in both performance measurement models and quantitatively based management accounting research, where the subjective and complex aspects of the phenomenon are replaced by 'objective' measures that reflect the observed phenomenon very poorly. Thus, the scientific ideal of the natural sciences dominates organisational accountability under the banner of scientific objectivity, but as quantitative objectivity is an ideal rather than a real occurrence, it runs the risk of forming an illusionary norm.

222 *Nikolaj Kure, et al.*

The impact of the quantitative norm may, apart from the status of natural science itself, be due to certain domination ideologies of social cooperation, the motives and values of organisational actors, and the role of management in organisations (Bourguignon et al. 2004; Raffnsøe-Møller 2015). Hence, the ideas that organisational actors are primarily governed by institutional self-interest or preference maximisation; that social cooperation is a strategic game; and that only top management should therefore monitor and coordinate organisational cooperation, also constitute immense drivers for the establishment of 'objective figures' on the basis of which rewards and punishment may be distributed. In stark contrast to this perspective, it is the fundamental view of pragmatic constructivism that actors have a fundamental interest in co-authoring a shared valuable future, which sets basic different criteria for the function and applicability of quantitative performance measures and accountability (Kristensen et al. 2011).

Conclusion and Discussions

This chapter has been written as a response to the conceptual inconsistency and confusion that seems to pervade much current management accounting theory and practice. In Baudrillard's terms, the field of management accounting is ridden with simulations of reality or even pure simulacra with no resemblance to reality at all (Baudrillard 1981). We believe this is a problem of immense proportion as it paves the way for illusionary language games that rob the individual actor of the opportunity to create functioning realities, as well as undermining the collective opportunity of successful organisational creation of construct causality. This paper, thus, should be seen as an initial effort to explore new ways of developing functional concepts.

First, we have introduced two polarised views on language in management accounting research: on the one hand, a realist stance that perceives language as a tool for representation and, on the other, a constructivist perspective that sees language as a lens through which various realities emerge. We have then described how pragmatic constructivism provides a mediating model by drawing on the late Wittgenstein's concept of language game. Consequently, we have tried to outline a set of criteria for well-functioning concepts, i.e. concepts that may be used to build construct causality. The starting point is that a concept does not have one unified semantic meaning. Instead, the meaning of a concept is to be understood and developed in relation to its function in a concrete local setting. In this sense, concepts are constructs. This does not mean, however, that *anything goes*. Thus, it is our contention that a well-functioning concept must be agreed upon on the basis of three structural dimensions: an abstract level, a criteria-based level, and finally a level of exemplary references. If these conceptual levels are aligned, the risk of building illusions is reduced. Or, in Eco's words, being has lines of resistance (Eco 2000) and so we need to build a language that does not conflict with these lines. This involves factual possibilities that are integrated when concepts are used, and that these processes allow for the value of organisational actors to be manifested. The extent to which accounting facts and numbers are given 'global meaning' or established in a 'universal language' must be evaluated relative to how they facilitate more global aims and values of meaningful social cooperation and reality construction, and not from the rather restricted aims of monitoring and controlling management or shareholders.

References

Austin, John L. 1962. *How to Do Things with Words*. Oxford: Clarendon Press.

Baudrillard, Jean. 1981. *Simulacres et Simulation*. Paris: Éditions Galilée.

Boltanski, Luc, and Laurent Thévenot. 2006. *On Justification: Economies of Worth*. Princeton, NJ: University Press.

Bourguignon, Annick, Veronique Malleret, and Hanne Nørreklit. 2004. "The American balanced scorecard versus French Tableau de Bord: The ideological dimension." *Management Accounting Research*, 15 (2): 107–134.

Chenhall, Robert H. 2003. "Management control systems design within its organizational context: Findings from contingency-based research and directions for the future." *Accounting, Organizations and Society*, 28 (2–3): 127–168.

Chua, Wai F. 1986. "Theoretical constructions of and by the real." *Accounting, Organizations and Society*, 11 (6): 583–598.

Cooper, Robin, and Robert S. Kaplan. 1988. "Measure costs right, make the right decisions." *Harvard Business Review*, Sept.–Oct.: 96–103.

Eco, Umberto. 2000. *Kant and the Platypus: Essays on Language and Cognition*. Boston: Houghton Mifflin Harcourt.

Foucault, Michel. 1966 (1970). *The Order of Things—An Archaeology of the Human Sciences*. New York: Pantheon Books.

Foucault, Michel. 1976 (1990). *The History of Sexuality (Histoire de la Sexualité)*. Translated by Robert Hurley. New York: Random House.

Giddens, Anthony. 2013. *Sociology*. Cambridge: Polity Press.

Horngren, Charles T. 1995. "Management accounting: This century and beyond." *Management Accounting Research*, 6 (3): 281–286.

Ittner, Christopher D., David F. Larcker, and Taylor Randal. 2003. "Performance implications of strategic performance measurement in financial services firms." *Accounting, Organizations and Society*, 28 (7–8): 715–741.

Kristensen, Jens Erik, Hanne Nørreklit, and Morten Raffnsøe-Møller. 2011. *University Performance Management at Danish Universities*. Copenhagen: DJOEF.

Laclau, Ernesto, and Chantal Mouffe. 1985. *Hegemony and Socialist Strategy: Towards a Radical Democratic Politics*. London: Verso.

Langfield-Smith, Kim. 1997. "Management control systems and strategy: A critical review." *Accounting, Organizations and Society*, 22 (2): 207–232.

Macintosh, Norman B., Teri Shearer, Daniel B. Thornton, and Michael Welker. 2000. "Accounting as simulacrum and hyperreality: Perspectives on income and capital." *Accounting, Organizations and Society*, 25: 13–50.

Miller, Peter, and Ted O'Leary. 1987. "Accounting and the construction of the governable person." *Accounting, Organizations and Society*, 12 (3): 235–265.

Mitchell, Falconer, Hanne Nørreklit, and Lennart Nørreklit. 2017. "The validity of financial statement measurement." In *A Philosophy of Management Accounting: A Pragmatic Constructivist Approach*, edited by Hanne Nørreklit. Chapter 6, this volume. New York: Routledge.

Nørreklit, Hanne, Falconer Mitchell, and Lars B. Nielsen. 2017. "Reflective planning and decision-making." In *A Philosophy of Management Accounting: A Pragmatic Constructivist Approach*, edited by Hanne Nørreklit. Chapter 4, this volume. New York: Routledge.

Nørreklit, Hanne, Lennart Nørreklit, and Falconer Mitchell. 2007. "Theoretical conditions for validity in accounting performance measurement," In *Business Performance Measurement - Frameworks and Methodologies*, edited by Andy Neely, 179–217. Cambridge: Cambridge University Press.

Nørreklit, Hanne, Lennart Nørreklit, and Falconer Mitchell. 2016. "Understanding practice generalisation—Opening the research/practice gap." *Qualitative Research in Accounting and Management*, 13 (3): 278–302.

Nørreklit, Hanne, Lennart Nørreklit, Falconer Mitchell, and Trond Bjørnenak. 2012. "The rise of the balanced scorecard! Relevance regained?" *Journal of Organizational and Accounting Change*, 8 (4): 490–510.

Nørreklit Lennart. 1986. *Formale strukturer i den sociale logic*. Aalborg: Aalborg Universitets Forlag.

Nørreklit, Lennart. 2011. "Actors and reality: A conceptual framework for creative governance." In *An Actor's Approach to Management: Conceptual Framework and Company Practices*, edited by M. Jakobsen, I.L. Johanson and Hanne Nørreklit, 7–37. Copenhagen: DJOEF.

Nørreklit, Lennart. 2017. "Epistemology." In *A Philosophy of Management Accounting: A Pragmatic Constructivist Approach*, edited by Hanne Nørreklit. Chapter 2, this volume. New York: Routledge.

Raffnsøe-Møller, Morten. 2015. "Dimensions of freedom: Axel Honneth's critique of liberalism." In *Recognition and Freedom: Axel Honneth's Political Thought*, edited by J. Jakobsen and O. Lysaker, 101–123. Leiden: Brill.

Saussure, Ferdinand. 1983. *Course in General Linguistics*. La Salle, IL: Open Court.

Searle, John. 1975. "The logical status of fictional discourse." *New Literary History*, 6 (2): 319–332.

Simons, Harry, and Wilbert E. Karrenbrock. 1964. *Intermediate Accounting*. Cincinnati, OH: South-Western Publishing Co.

Solomons, David. 1991. "Accounting and social change: A neutralist view." *Accounting, Organizations and Society*, 16 (3): 287–295.

Tinker, Anthony M. 1991. "The accountant as partisan." *Accounting, Organizations and Society*, 16 (3): 297–310.

Trenca, Mihaela, and Hanne Nørreklit. 2017. "Actor based performance management." In *A Philosophy of Management Accounting: A Pragmatic Constructivist Approach*, edited by Hanne Nørreklit. Chapter 8, this volume. New York: Routledge.

Wittgenstein, Ludwig. 1921. "Tractatus logico-philosophicus." *Annalen der Naturphilosophie*, 14: 85–262.

Wittgenstein, Ludwig. 1953. *Philosophical Investigations*. Translated by G.E.M. Anscombe. Oxford: Basil Blackwell.

11 Actor Reality Construction, Strong Structuration Theory and Organised Crime

Lisa Jack

Introduction

Pragmatic constructivism, on which the actor reality construction (ARC) model is based, provides a conceptual methodology with which to examine how organisational realities are constructed and the extent to which they are based on illusion. Once realities are constructed and attain some longevity, one would expect to see a degree of institutionalisation of practice. Conversely, realities are constructed within the constraints and parameters of existing institutions and practices. One criticism of ARC in its current development is that it does not sufficiently address questions of institutionalisation, being often an analysis of a particular organisational topos at a particular time. Pragmatic constructivism looks at how individual human actions happen in an orientation to the other and the structure. Functioning practice is produced as people author and co-author their practices as individuals and within groups: integration results from interactions between people in certain times and localities. The processes by which integration and relational structure occur and endure across longer time spans and wider spaces deserves further consideration.

The creation of narratives in ARC, discussed in the introduction to this book, has some similarity to ideas of structuration, and I was drawn into the study of ARC because of its potential to address one of the weaknesses in structuration theory, which is its development of an epistemology to go alongside the ontological arguments associated with Giddens's structuration theory and Stones's strong version of the theory. One thing that makes Stones' version 'strong' is that it synthesises the criticisms of Giddens's indifference to epistemology and develops concepts of agent's conduct and agent's context analysis that can be applied in research design. These, in turn, draw on reflexivity and knowledge to provide an epistemological conceptual methodology for the analysis of structuration processes.

An immediate confusion of terms is apparent but can be understood by referring back to Chapter 2 of this volume (Nørreklit 2017). The use of actor in pragmatic constructivism and the use of agent in Giddens's structuration theory are effectively synonymous and imply intentionality. Here, 'agent' will be used when citing specific definitions within structuration theory, but otherwise, actor will be used in alignment with the theme of this book.

The aim here is to investigate whether strong structuration theory offers a sound complementary theory to use in analysis of organisational groups alongside ARC. And conversely, does ARC offer structuration theory a relevant way of extending its epistemology? In order to explore this, I am going to draw on the literature around organised crime groups that, ostensibly, demonstrate longevity and institutionalisation of practice based on what might be regarded as illusory realities. Therefore, the chapter is organised in two sections. The first provides a rationale for using actor reality construction and strong structuration theory in conjunction. The second applies the conceptual methodology that emerges to the organisational realities of organised crime. The chapter concludes with a brief discussion on the opportunities for further research in this area.

Theoretical Discussion

Amalgamating Strong Structuration Theory and Actor Reality Construction

Although there are differences in the methodologies, there is a point of contact in that both actor reality construction and structuration theory draw on pragmatic traditions of thought in philosophy (Bacon 2012) which determine validity through what is tangible and practical. Truth is demonstrated through tangible differences in behaviour and what everyone recognises rather than positivist objectivity or platonic form. Rutherford (2013, 200), applying the notion of pragmatic enquiry to financial accounting, offers this explanation:

> Characteristic maxims of pragmatism are that what works most effectively in practice provides a standard for determining truth in statements, rightness in actions, and valuation in appraisals; that the meaning of a concept is to be sought in the experiential or practical consequences of its application; and that we should be prepared to regard the best that can be done as good enough . . . Philosophical pragmatism entails that 'what works' must work in the large, consistently, systematically, durably and across society.

Giddens's structuration theory descends from similar hermeneutic roots in philosophy via German writers such as Dilthey (Joas 1993), although he developed his theory independently of pragmatism (Kilpenen 2015) and it is often classified as a realist ontological approach. Interactionist theorists have recognised his approach as fundamentally pragmatic (Joas 1993). This is based on the understanding that in studying institutional structure, Giddens is really asking what practices, beliefs and so on should be institutionalised and what it is that would make a better society. For one of the early philosophers in this field, William James, pragmaticism involved hypothetical questions such as: "What differences would arise if this line of action as opposed to this or that alternative were invoked"? (Prus 1996).

As we have seen throughout this book, the ARC model demonstrates how creative governance in organisations can be achieved that, in pragmatic terms, turns possibilities for more equitable, productive working environments into realities. The model is an analytical methodology that enables researchers to examine empirical data from cases to show why some organisational environments are based on fictions and illusions, and over time, fail to create governance that contributes to the well-being of its employees and society.

Organised crime has the fascination that it mirrors other, legitimate, corporate practices. Criminal markets have similar patterns to non-criminal ones; groups have rules, routines, management controls and cultures. There is a tangible reality to their activities. Therefore, they should make an interesting case study for actor reality construction in contemporary organisations, in which "the lead-actor communication aims at creating a topos with which to enact employees so that they become powerful and committed actors realising the strategy of the company" (Nørreklit 2011, 10). Criminally run organisations are disturbingly successful.

Organised crime makes profits from illegitimate activities and financial crime. The illegitimate activities are run as businesses, and are coherent, integrated and based on long-established values and relationships. Criminal markets are efficient and are studied in much the same way as legitimate markets. Furthermore, the proceeds of organised crime are often laundered into legitimate businesses that operate, apart from the initial capital, on normal business practices and may exhibit signs of good governance. Organised crime offers a deviant viewpoint on fact and fiction, creative governance and pragmatic construction in organisations.

The underlying concern here is the social problem of organised crime: it apparently works 'in the large, consistently, systematically, durably and across society', however it might be viewed as abhorrent. What alternative structures or actions are required to eliminate organised crime? An understanding of ARC might help to understand the extent to which organised crime is based on fact or illusion; how members author themselves and others as professional criminals; why groups persist, and indeed, whether the ideal of eliminating such crime is based on fact or illusion. However, I contend that the additional concept of structuration processes is needed to provide the conceptual methodology for the analysis of longevity.

The Frameworks

Stones (2005, 7) explains the purpose behind his strong version of structuration theory in this way:

> As I see it, a key advantage of the strong theory of structuration . . . is its refusal to remain focused upon only the philosophical level, to the

neglect of the conceptual and methodological links between the abstract and the particular.

More recently, he explains how strong structuration can be viewed as a conceptual methodology that bridges the divide between ontological concepts and empirical research that focuses firmly on people in situations, and how they reflexively (re)produce structure through action based on their knowledge of themselves, the situation and external structures as they perceive them (Stones and Jack 2016).

It is this development of an ontology-in-situ that that led Bryant and Jary (2011, 444) to say that "In . . . *Structuration Theory* (2005), Stones sets out the most important development of structuration theory since Giddens himself turned to other matters". Englund et al. (2011) and Englund and Gerdin (2014) provide an insightful analysis of the use of structuration theory in accounting literature and directions for future research. They also observe that the community of accounting scholars has scarcely begun to exploit the theory's full potential. One of the threads to emerge from their work concerns the paucity of accounting researchers who engage critically with structuration theory. By this they mean that researchers are insufficiently reflexive in their treatment of the theory and do not explore or challenge its assumptions. They find exceptions in the work of Jack and Kholeif (2008) and Coad and Herbert (2009), which use strong structuration theory (Coad et al. 2015).

Stones (2005) provides three main tools for empirical research:

- The ontological sliding scale for locating the level of abstraction in the analysis undertaken;
- The quadripartite model of structuration as shown in Figure 11.1.
- The concept of agent-in-focus as the unit of analysis in a study.

These concepts which are further explained in an accounting and management context in Jack and Kholeif (2007) and Coad et al. (2015), are tools.

The main conceptual methodology offered by strong structuration is the use of agent's conduct and agent's context analysis, which is achieved through methodological bracketing. Starks and Trinidad (2007, 1376) describe the purpose of bracketing where the researcher "must be honest and vigilant about her own perspective, pre-existing thoughts and beliefs, and developing hypotheses . . . engage in the self-reflective process of 'bracketing', whereby they recognize and set aside (but do not abandon) their a priori knowledge and assumptions, with the analytic goal of attending to the participants' accounts with an open mind". Giddens uses strategic conduct and institutional analysis as brackets. One must suspend investigation into institutions and vice versa, in order to understand the one without pre-existing notions of the other. In practice, this means analysing one or the other at a time: if you are looking at strategic conduct of actors, then institutional analysis is set to one side and vice versa. Englund and Gerdin

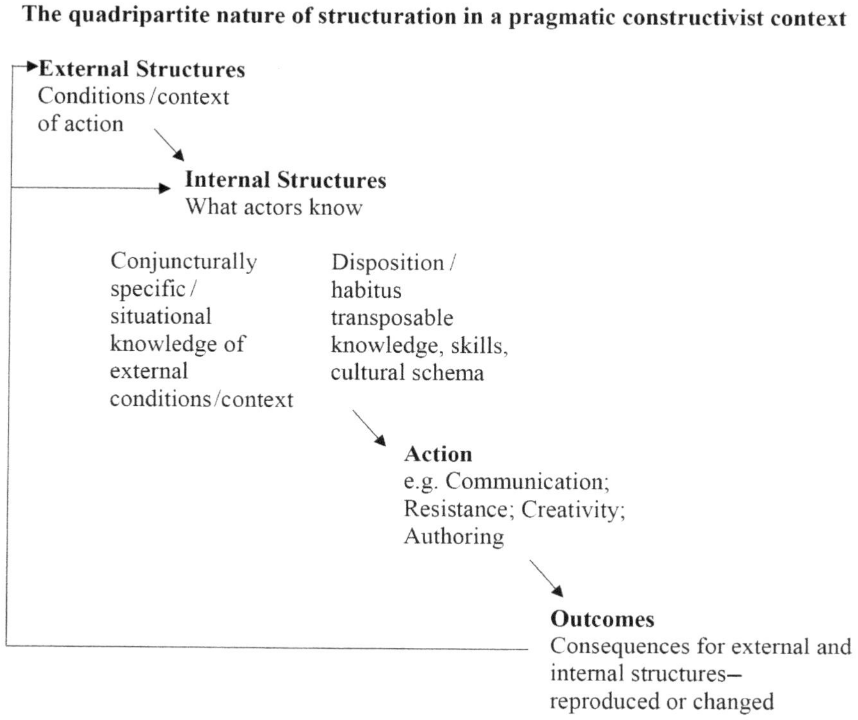

The quadripartite nature of structuration in a pragmatic constructivist context

External Structures
Conditions/context
of action

Internal Structures
What actors know

Conjuncturally
specific/
situational
knowledge of
external
conditions/context

Disposition/
habitus
transposable
knowledge, skills,
cultural schema

Action
e.g. Communication;
Resistance; Creativity;
Authoring

Outcomes
Consequences for external and
internal structures—
reproduced or changed

Figure 11.1 The Quadripartite Nature of Structuration

(2014) identify a common problem with accounting studies—we tend to only carry out institutional analysis, a point backed up by Roberts (2014).

One of the issues with strategic conduct analysis, however, is that Giddens does not explain what a researcher might be looking for in empirical work or give a detailed understanding of knowledge in this area. This is usually explained by noting that many of his analyses were at a macro-level of abstraction, and did not require an understanding of the behaviours of individual or small groups of actors. Taking this starting point, Stones developed an empirical, epistemological approach to strategic conduct analysis (Stones 2005, 2015; Stones and Jack 2016) that takes agent(s)-in-focus as the starting point of any analysis of the structuration process.

The concepts of agent's context analysis and agent's conduct analysis are closer to the ontic level of examination.

For Stones (2005, 121–122) "agent's *conduct* (original italics) analysis draws upon the ontological category of knowledgeability" and "attention becomes focused on the agent's critically reflective and pre-reflective processes of sifting and sieving". Most importantly, "it is this process of negotiation and reconciliation—pragmatic or otherwise—that produces the conduct of the agent and that can, in a range of circumstances, lead to an attenuation of the agent's general-dispositional frame". In contrast, agent's context analysis "draws on the notion of knowledgeability', that is conjuncturally-specific internal structures, related to the situation (conjuncture) in which the agent-in-focus finds herself. In other words, we examine the "social nexus of interdependencies, rights and obligations, asymmetries of power and the social conditions and consequences of action" in which the agent must act. Importantly:

> Agent's context analysis can be used to analyse the terrain that faces an agent, the terrain that constitutes the range of possibilities and limits to the possible.
>
> (Stones 2005, 121–122)

And

> Without agent's context analysis the researched agent would be deracinated and condemned to be turned inwards upon herself, cut off from any account of her hermeneutic and practical engagement with external structures.
>
> (Stones 2005, 121–122)

Such analyses of conduct, context and knowledgeability provide a stronger epistemological focus than offered by Giddens, and we can begin to see how these concepts might resonate for the actor reality construction researcher.

It is quite easy to map actor reality construction terms and concepts onto a strong structuration model. From this point, the term actor will replace the term 'agent-in-focus'. Therefore, actors would be located within a topos at micro- or meso-levels of analysis (with the smallest topos being the individual and their immediate environment in the situation under investigation, and meso-level being at say, a division or organisation or professional field viewed abstractly as a cluster or group). Actors' general dispositions and conjuncturally-specific (or situationally-specific) knowledge could be analysed further to facts, possibilities and values. The same for external structures and the actors ' knowledge of them—it is about the researcher coming to understand the actors' understanding of situations, what Giddens (1984) termed the *double hermeneutic*.

For clarification at this point, actors can be distinguished from adaptors in that "an actor engages in activities with the intention of being a part of creating the world we live in. The adaptor, on the other hand, is passive and merely aligns with the management or the social flow without intending to influence their direction" (Nørreklit et al. 2017, Chapter 1, this volume). Agents in pragmatic constructivism are those acting on behalf of others, as in economic agency theory. In strong structuration theory the term agent would cover all of these positions and practices: agency is in the choice to play a role, to not act or to do otherwise based on the agent-in-focus' reflexive knowledge of their situation. Active agency, paradoxically, may be the choice to be passive. Thus, the term agent is strong structuration theory is more or less synonymous with that of actor in pragmatic constructivism as described earlier by Nørreklit (2017, Chapter 2, this volume): "An actor is not only playing a role, she is the source of her intentions and activities, and she needs to be co-author of her roles. She not only accepts and plays a given role based on her interpretation, she also moulds it and participates in construction of the role system and the plot in the construct."

Following from this, Stones (2005, 117) shows that:

> a focus on conjuncturally-specific internal structures would allow one to begin to gain purchase on strategic, practical, political (in the widest sense), *in-situ*, questions and issues regarding the range of possibilities for action and the potential consequences of such action . . . Such a focus would allow one to look at conjunctural constraints, probable sanctions, opportunities, impossibilities and possibilities.

Which echoes the claims in actor reality construction that:

> An infinite array of possibilities are disclosed as soon as reflection 'challenges' the facts and envisions possible alternatives.
>
> (Nørreklit 2011, 27)

This reflection on internal and external structures and possibilities of action creates this central point of strong structuration theory, its concept of active agency. Here we have an important point when studying accounting in particular. Active agency is 'what is done' as shown in Figure 11.1 but more importantly, we need to see how communication can be 'what is done'. It is not just that there is a report or transaction processed or email sent, it is the choice of words, the ongoing dialogue, the visual symbols displayed, the unwritten codes embedded in body language, the attempt to persuade, the mode of decision-making adopted—the activity of communication (Coad and Glyptis 2014; Coad et al. 2016; Harris et al. 2016). All the discussions, actions, rules, routines, symbols and so on that create and maintain integration of reality within a topos. In turn, authoring and co-authoring that leads to integration could be termed active agency and from this point, we will refer to authoring rather than active agency.

A study in strong structuration incorporating concepts from actor reality construction would allow us to extend beyond a classification of the elements of pragmatic constructivism to study the dynamics of how creative governance is actively structured and what it takes for those structures to persist. This is because:

- SST requires greater attention to the conduct of actors 'in situ' (meso- and micro- level analyses)
- It concentrates on how actors reflexively monitor what they do in inter-action with others
- Such studies require a sophisticated account of motivation, which avoids impoverished descriptions of actors' knowledgeability, and require an interpretation of the dialectic of control where actors are studied in relation to other actors and institutionalised practices (Stones 2005).

Actor reality construction in turn, adds a layer of analysis to strong structuration theory not covered by Stones to any great extent. This is the concept of whether the reality created is based on fact or illusion. One could call this the validity of the situation in hand. Once integration takes place, one would expect a constructed actor reality to settle into rules and routines, taken-for-grantedness—hopefully, a state of creative governance. In other words, there is a lack of resistance or need to do otherwise. The longer the circumstances persist, then the greater the pragmatic validity of the reality constructed. At least, this perception of validity may be the case within the organisation—the test, maybe, is the wider community or society recognition of the per-sistent entity. To explore longevity, the concepts of resistance and possibility are linked to show why structures and actions become reproduced by agents in certain positions at certain times and within certain social spaces. Our exploration of organised crime in the following section questions what we mean by validity, fact and fiction. Some groups have longevity and the fact of their success shows that a reality has been constructed. Is it based on illusion, and if so, does the illusion lie in the topos of the crime group and its actors, or within the law enforcement groups seeking to contain crime?

Building Counter-Structures

Structuration theory has been used in criminology to study desistance from crime. This tends to be studies of younger men on probation and the struc-tures and agencies that enable them to choose to do otherwise than return to crime: relationships, work, financial commitments for example. However, it has also been used in criminology to study the effectiveness of prisons and sentencing, although Vaughan (2001) questions the usefulness of Giddens's structuration theory in this respect. Most of his criticisms relating to the central notion of duality and the claims of critical realism are dealt with by Stones (2005) in his strong version of the theory, which we are using here. I think the key to studying desistance and the effectiveness of counter crime structures is in the way in which Stones (2005) develops from the concept of position-practices, concepts of resistance that build on Giddens's (1984) ideas of the dialectic of control. Stones explicates this more fully in terms of analysing the position-practice relationships between actors. Resistance requires actors to have three properties (Stones 2005, 115, *original italics*):

1) *adequate power* to resist *without* endangering the conditions of possibility for the realisation of core commitments;
2) *adequate knowledge* of alternative possible courses of action and their probable consequences;
3) *adequate critical distance* in order to take up a strategic stance in relation to a particular external structure and its 'situational pressures'.

This list of properties becomes part of the analysis of conduct and context analyses, and provides a useful tool to make a fine-grained assessment of the reasons why change may or may not have happened. The actors' ability to bring about change represents the ability to choose between alternative sets of structures (Kilfoyle and Richardson 2011). It demonstrates reflexivity in structuration processes. This suggests that co-authoring and creation of narratives in pragmatic constructivism could benefit from this more nuanced analysis. The causalities constructed around domination and oppression within an organisational unit can be drawn in terms of resistance. For example, actors who resist need perceived power or capability in relation to other actors, adequate knowledge of relevant external structures and requisite reflective distance. Then, "all things being equal, the greater the possession of these properties the greater the actors ability to regulate, modulate, deflect or erase specific aspects of . . . external demands and pressures" (Stones 2005, 115). Therefore, we can consider here aspects of longevity as to why criminals choose to act in ways that resist the law; why some may choose to resist (or not) the crime group to set up alone or 'go straight'; why enforcement bodies, governments and individuals choose to challenge (or not) existing groups.

Summary

There is some correspondence between strong structuration theory and actor reality understanding of pragmatic constructivism that provides a suitable conceptual methodology to guide interpretative empirical research into the longevity of organisational forms. Epistemologically, the actor's knowledge of the facts, possibilities and values in their internal structures and in their perceptions of external structures leads to reflexive action that can be analysed. I argue that we should see communication as intentional acts and integration as an outcome in our analysis, to provide a more dynamic account of how creative governance, in particular, is achieved. The concepts of structuration and institutionalisation allow us to evaluate the longevity of organisational forms in a way that is not readily available in actor reality construction—once reality is constructed the question is one of reproduction and maintenance over time and space. On the other hand, actor reality construction brings concepts of fact and illusion in the analysis of the reality created and maintained. How long can a structure based on illusion or one that is harmful in its social context, last?

Organised Crime Groups and their Management as a Situation for Study

The following section is an initial attempt to apply this question to organised crime where there is integration within topoi, longevity and social harm. However, illusion is difficult to analyse without applying value judgements. That organised crime can be lucrative and successful is a fact, as is the existence of long-lasting groups. That crime prevention in this field lacks resources and sufficient deterrents is also factual. The chapter concludes with an outline of what needs to be investigated in order to provide an appropriate analysis based on these questions.

Defining Organised Crime

Although popular notions of organised crime focus on film representations of mafia groups (*The Godfather* or *The Sopranos* for example), there are no set definitions of organised crime in law or academic research. Activities associated with organised crime are clearly crime—murder, theft are accepted crimes (*mala in se*) and embezzlement, prostitution and corruption are proscribed (*mala prohibita*) and criminal activities. The problem is not listing crimes that take place which are attributable to organised crime groups. It is just that these crimes could be as easily committed by individuals. The problem is defining the term organised (Finckenauer 2005; Lusthaus 2013) and placing the activities in a social context. It may be related to family, networks, ethnicity but again, in themselves the terms do not define organised crime (Finckenauer 2005). The keys seem to be the element of business-like activity, profit-making and systematic use of violence. Finckenauer (2005, 81–82) provides the following summary:

> The attributes of the criminal organizations that make the crimes they commit organized crime include criminal sophistication, structure, self-identification, and the authority of reputation, as well as their size and continuity. These criminal organizations exist largely to profit from providing illicit goods and services in public demand or providing legal goods and services in an illicit manner . . . What is essential to the definition of organized crime is the ability to use, and the reputation for use of violence or the threat of violence to facilitate criminal activities, and in certain instances to gain or maintain monopoly control of particular criminal markets. Also essential is that organized crime employs corruption of public officials to assure immunity for its operations, and/or to protect its criminal enterprises from competition.

Traditionally, a Chicago School-style definition of organised crime has tended to be accepted, such as that put forward by Cressey (1969, 72)

> The organized criminal, by definition, occupies a position in a social system, an 'organization' which has been rationally designed to maximize profits by performing illegal services and providing legally forbidden products demanded by the broader society within which he lives.

But this is problematic when discussing certain forms of non-racially aligned, non-mafia type and seemingly irrational groups. The main danger is that one overplays or valorises just how organised and business-like such illicit activities are or could be.

I am going to take Petter Gottschalk's book *Entrepreneurship and Organised Crime: Entrepreneurs in Illegal Business* (2009)—the basis for that article—as my main source for the organisational nature of organised crime. Gottschalk has written extensively on the theorisation of financial crime from a management point of view, and draws widely on related literature in criminology. His methodological position is one of structural-functionalism with its roots in the Chicago school of sociology and management studies, whereas here we look at how pragmatic constructivist approach might deal with the same ideas.

Gottschalk's thesis that organised crime consists of highly entrepreneurial business empires is not new. Merton's (1938) theory of anomie recognises that individuals adapt to that phenomenon using different strategies, one of which is innovation in the form of deviant, criminal behaviour (the other strategies are conformity, ritualism, rebellion and retreatism). Taylor et al. (1973) defined innovation as "the adoption of illegitimate means to pursue and obtain success." But because 'routine' pedestrian criminal acts do not lead to any significant level of economic success, true innovation is the adoption of criminality that is sophisticated, well-planned, skilled and organised.

Gottschalk (2009) applies stages of growth models taken from strategic management theory to organised crime. He suggests that criminal careers can begin with gangs of friends engaged in what Junninen (2009) refers to as 'group criminality', led by the most innovative and entrepreneurial member of the gang. This then leads to trouble making, where gang members challenge each other to more daring crimes and then as competence is gained, profit-seeking behaviour takes over from loyalty to create first a criminal network and then an established gang with structures, values, rules and routines. Other routes are for the individual to build their own gangs around their business, being the planners who recruit others to commit the actual crimes. In the terminology of pragmatic constructivism the leaders of such gangs and networks are authoring a narrative of organised crime, and constructing a local reality of an organisation with career paths, hierarchies and strategies.

The gang itself can go through stages of growth. They may start out as 'opportunity-based criminal organisations' and then mature into 'activity-based', then 'knowledge-based' and finally 'strategy-based' organisations. Gotteschalk draws on the example of the Sicilian mafia where "violent activity at Stage 2 was typical in 1870, running local communities at Stage 4 became the norm a few decades later" (2009, 28). This model is then extended, with activity-based being Level 1 and value-based being Level 4. These last are the ones that intrigue: the shared values of say, mafia groups or Hell's Angels that allow tensions between loyalty and hierarchical control, and local autonomy, also contribute to longevity. Are these stable organisations, or cultural phenomena, or both?

Gotteschalk attempts to benchmark the stages of growth, drawing on United Nations' data, with value-based organisations demonstrating organisational values, hierarchical structures, shared vision, knowledge specialisms, leadership led communications, charismatic leadership, and continuous corruption. Hagan (2006), in contrast, sets out more generic characteristics of organised crime groups, classifying them according to the extent of ideology, threat of violence, illicit services, immunity, corruption and intimidation (primary characteristics) and the extent of structured hierarchy, rules and codes of secrecy and initiation/exclusivity (secondary characteristics). All this can be applied to what people generally perceive as organised crime—an established gang with a recognised leader such as the New York mafia or the Adams family in the UK. However, in the twenty-first century, there are shifts whereby associations and co-offending between organised individuals are discernible rather than organisations (Gottschalk 2009, 93, based on Europol data). There is a globalised nature to organised crime, and a far greater blurring of the line between legitimate and illegitimate business activity. Recognising this crucial observation, nevertheless, here I am going to take a simpler model of a local organised crime group engaged in supplying illegal goods and services who use violence and corruption of local law enforcers to protect their business interests, to explore the application of the concepts discussed in part one of this chapter.

Internal and External Structures—Facts, Possibilities, Values

Organised crime exists because there are markets (criminal markets) for illicit goods and services, and they are profitable. This provides the basic analysis for the facts and possibilities associated with organised crime. For example, Morselli et al. (2010) examine the factors behind the movements of organised crime groups, which they argue is based on finding markets in which such groups can establish themselves. Push factors refer to forces which drive criminal groups away from a setting. Pull factors refer to forces which draw criminal groups to a setting, which could be renamed as facts and possibilities (Morselli et al. 2010, 6). Bagley (2004) also addresses the pull factors that explain why criminal groups emerged in certain settings.

His article addresses the possible involvement of Russian criminal groups in illicit activities in a number of Latin American and Caribbean countries. The presence of Russian organised crime groups in diverse countries illustrates the importance of local contextualities. Possibilities (or pull factors) vary from one country to the next. Central America provides a workforce (poverty); Colombia provides a product; Mexico provides connections to influent individuals involved in drug trafficking; Brazil provides a strong demand. A second finding concerns Cuba. Russian criminal groups were incapable of seizing illicit market possibilities even after the illicit drug market emerged and the Cuban navy could not afford to effectively patrol their waters. Bagley attributes this to the highly centralised regime, embargo issues and resentment toward Russians in Cuba.

Say we were to take a leader or coordinator in local organised crime group as the main actor for a study. Our research purpose in hand (Stones and Jack 2016) might to understand the strategic, operational and/or tactical management controls put in place by this actor and their role in establishing a long-lasting entity. This would include investigating their understanding and navigation of the opportunities offered locally for black or grey market goods and services, as well as the opportunities for laundering money through legitimate businesses. We could examine their understanding and interpretation of the push and pull factors, and the attempts made to exploit the possibilities open to them in terms of business transactions.

Our conduct and context analyses would examine knowledge of local rivals, the venality of individual enforcement officers and local government officials and the logistics of selling goods and services in their environment. Not all opportunities and possibilities are positive: professional criminals, as Gottschalk (2009) and Junninen (2009) find, treat capture and imprisonment as occupational hazards. Although for some, corruption of the police and judiciary means there is nothing to fear from arrest. For others, lenient sentences mean that prison stays may be short and, actually, offer possibilities of building and strengthening criminal networks, devising new crimes and continuing to direct operations through communications allowed in prison.

The values we might investigate should take into account the actor's view of criminality. Both Gottschalk (2009) and Junninen (2009) find that the main beliefs of members in organised crime groups centre on their professionalism. Through qualitative empirical work, Junninen (2009, 491) found that professional criminals in Finland describe themselves as having the capacity for "1) demanding, profitable crimes, 2) committing crimes is exercising a profession, and 3) right and smart attitude, i.e. planning and inventing new forms of crimes, and good manners". New organised crime units are established by such innovative individuals and the leaders of mature organised crime gangs recruit such individuals to extend operations.

Taking this outline of the more or less knowledge our actor has of their context, we can already see that certain elements of conduct begin to flow.

The choice of business activity, the establishment and management of that activity and those involved in it, the protection of themselves and those in their employ, the way in which they enact professionalism. Successful outcomes in the form of profits, silences, increased business and establishment of a perhaps feared identity in the community would lead to reproduction of structures in terms of rules, routines, rituals and values for the group, and the continuation of the social effects of their activities. It is an integration of facts, possibilities and values into a well-governed organisation of people. However, what we are missing so far is the crucial element of active agency and the role of communication.

Communication as Active Agency or Intentional Action

Our actor will be required to communicate on a number of different levels. There is the choice of words used to persuade people to buy goods and services, to act in an employed capacity (say as runners or drivers), or simply to keep quiet. There are signs, symbols and messages to be chosen and continually reinforced in order to keep enforcement officers at bay or on side. There is the spreading of myths and stories to support the image the actor might wish to portray of their activities. There are the visual clues of success in terms of clothes, houses and cars—or their counterparts to enable concealment. In other words, the building and reproduction of structure through words, actions that have visual or visceral impact, and symbolic gestures as continual active agency.

Following Gottschalk (2009), an investigation of how our actor thinks, talks and acts in the stages of moving from 'opportunity-based' to 'activity-based', then 'knowledge-based' and finally a 'strategy-based' organisation would be interesting. Who was convinced to join, and how, by the agent-in-focus? How is the strategy conveyed to maintain the high level organisation: value-based, demonstrating organisational values, hierarchical structures, shared vision, knowledge specialisms, leadership led communications, charismatic leadership, and continuous corruption. Or is our local group not quite yet at that level?

Recent work on organised crime has touched on structuration, as for example in Densley and Stevens (2014). In particular, this work looks at the use of violence (which Finckenauer (2005) identifies as a defining element of organised crime) to consolidate identity and structure, and to drive action. In other words, this is violence as a means of communication to members of the group and to those trying to eliminate them. The requirement to be violent is also intrinsically part of the values held by the actors involved. The following quote is given in full as it illuminates the extent to which the actions of organised criminal entities are based on enduring structures. The paper concerns Eastern European mafia and Chinese triads, and in particular, Albanian organised crime:

The use of violence has been always highly influenced by the ancient creeds and it represented an archetype of social control. Therefore, historically the 'violent' behaviour of the ethnic Albanians has not been based primarily on a personal emotional drive and individual rational interests. For example, although the blood feuds have been seen literally as a matter of life and death, they are in fact strangely impersonal or abstract tragedies, where the actors attract no personal guilt. Blood feuds have to be regarded as collective acts involving the community. As Allcock explains, 'far from representing the breakdown of order, the feud is the expression or implementation of order, not the decay of structure but the process of structuration itself'.

(Arsovska and Craig 2006)

Violence used as a means of implementing order, points to how values are used in the co-authoring of what it means to govern an organised crime group in a particular locality and those who might oppose their practices and presence.

Empirical Studies of Organised Crime

In an interview in 2016, Rob Stones explains how conduct analysis is about getting inside the head of the agent-in-focus/actor and understanding their actions from an analysis of the knowledge that they have of their context. Strong structuration lends itself to fine brushstrokes in case analysis and the careful mapping of who, what, why, where, when and how (Stones 2005, 127; Stones 2015; Coad et al. 2016). However, this type of analysis in crime is obviously a dangerous and ethically fraught research activity.

There are studies in which researchers have interviewed members of organised crime groups. In his work on Finnish criminal organisations in the 1990s, Junninen (2008, 2009) found that only three of his sets of interviewees approached what might be called fully-fledged organised crime enterprises, that might be defined by Gottschalk as strategy- or value-based organisations, although none had the status of mafia-type organisations in other countries. Five of the 14 groups were better characterised as being involved in group criminality whereas the remainder were in varying degrees, semi-organised crime groups Junninen (2009). He comments that part of the value of his study is to test the extent to which definitions of organised crime were valuable in reality, implying that much organised crime is not mafia-based but in more loosely connected groups. This is interesting for this discussion, because applying pragmatic constructivism allows us to examine degrees of integration and reality construction, and to critique more colourful depictions of organised gangs as 'bands of (criminal) brothers'.

However, there is an argument for using fiction or autobiography, or even so-called faction such as the true crime genre as a basis for analysis to understand how the conceptual methodology might operate. Asked why he draws on so many works of fiction in his books on structuration theory, Stones responded that:

> Literature is extremely useful for respecting the hermeneutic dimension of social life, because novels look inside the heads of people. Not all novels, but a lot of novels follow people's streams of consciousness, their internal life, what Margaret Archer would call their internal conversations, their emotions, their reasoning, and the interweaving of these. They're *in situ*—you know a lot about these people's lives in quite some depth, and then you have the interaction between different characters in the contextual field. Because of this, the depth of hermeneutic-structural purchase that you have from novels is much greater than you can get from almost any social science literature.
>
> (Stones and Jack, 2016, 1147–1148)

Playing with this idea, we could take the twenty-first century police procedural novels of Graham Hurley (2004 and others) set in Portsmouth to illustrate what Stones is speaking about. Although not so widely known outside the South of England (my current university appears regularly as an incidental player which helps to gain a readership among staff and students), Hurley had inside access to the police detective unit over several periods of time when carrying out his background research, and his books have been endorsed at least by Hampshire police as being close, recognisable portraits of the problems that they face with local low level crime, occasional murders and the growing drugs trade, and of the way in which the police think and act. There are 12 books in the series and gradually the figure of Barry Mackenzie emerges as the untouchable local crime lord whose business is an organised drugs trade. His trajectory from local, opportunistic thug (despite having been to a good school) to entrepreneurial, strategic mastermind outwitting the police follows the pattern identified by Gottschalk (2009).

The key to understanding how empirical work using structuration theory might be carried out is to understand that the actor is carrying out conduct and context analysis continually on other situations and actors before they act in ways which reproduce or alter structure. At the same time, our actor is the subject of other people's context and conduct analysis. Each provides external constraints and enablers for the other. A police novel sets this out well. Police work, by its nature, is about understanding and acting reflexively on knowledge of the criminal's situation, their actions, whether they can exercise power and on how they operate. They need to get into the mind of the criminal and pre-empt their next move, as well as being conscious of the constraints of legislation and police guidelines on their actions. Dramatically, Hurley has one central character (DI Joe Faraday) who works within the rules, and another (Paul Winter) who knows but habitually breaks the rules. The more thoughtful criminals like Mackenzie carry out their own detailed context and conduct analysis of the police in assessing what crimes they can, and cannot, get away with. The novelist is then allowing the reader to carry out their own analysis of the police or criminal (as the main actor) conduct and context to understand the plot, and to critique the author's analytical portrayal of the situation.

Stones (2015, 59–93) maps out just such an exercise in his dissection of the television political drama *Borgen* in the book *Why Current Affairs Needs Social Theory*. To apply the same approach but in brief, one of Hurley's novels (2004) involves a police operation to entrap Mackenzie. The topos is the small team put together for the operation, drawn from different parts of the police force. Taking this team as the main actors, they co-author an identity which is secretive, closed and highly professional in terms of diligence of data gathering and the setting up of an undercover policeman posing as a buyer for property that Mackenzie is also interested in buying. In terms of context, they have to understand the values, facts, possibilities and communications available to themselves, and those of Mackenzie. The painstaking gathering of forensic accounting information and local intelligence, and the endless discussions and planning meetings are a process of structuration. The team understands how they can operate within the rules of policing and the other external pressures to be seen to be tackling drug crime in the city. In terms of conduct, they build up a picture of situationally-specific knowledge which can be seen to encompass facts (knowledge of the assets owned by Mackenzie, for example or even the lack of knowledge about the money laundering exercises involved), possibilities (that Mackenzie might reveal incriminating evidence in discussions with the undercover policeman) and values (to work within the law). Re-iteration through verbal communication within the team and to the chief officer involved of this knowledge reinforces the group identity and the way in which it is governed. Integration takes place and the active agency of mounting the trap consolidates the structures in place.

It turns out to be illusory. Mackenzie, through his own context and conduct analysis, turns out to be following the operation. Without giving away the plot too much, the drug lord's authored reality is well-integrated and, ironically, seems factual rather than fiction. He is able to communicate to the police that his position is impregnable, that the structures of his organisations and finances are institutionalised in ways that mean that money in his name is laundered and untraceable, and that there is governance in place over his own operations which will continue in terms of drug supply and violent reprisals. This is only a sketch but indicates that longevity of groups is linked to the way in which they not only integrate and construct causality but in which this integration is also a structuration process which embeds the strategic governance of organised crime.

Concluding Comments

There is further work needed to consolidate the arguments put forward in this chapter. Arguments for aligning actor reality construction and strong structuration theory need to take into consideration questions of ontology as well as epistemology. It appears initially that the two approaches are complementary. ARC offers a way of analysing organisational groups within strong structuration theory that would emphasise aspects of authoring and co-authoring as well as the dimensions of ARC. Strong structuration extends the epistemology of ARC through further consideration of processes of structuration across time and space. There also needs to be further analysis of the extent to which the concepts of resistance discussed above might lead to a more nuanced understanding of what is in the minds of people as they co-author an organisational group. A study of organised crime has potential for in-depth analysis of both criminals and law enforcement, and their analyses of each other.

References

Arsovska, Jana, and Mark Craig. 2006. "Honourable behaviour and the conceptualisation of violence in ethnic-based organised crime groups: An examination of the Albanian kanun and the code of the Chinese triads." *Global Crime*, 7: 214–246.

Bacon, Michael. 2012. *Pragmatism: An Introduction*. Cambridge: Polity Press.

Bagley, Bruce. 2004. "Globalisation and Latin American and Caribbean organised crime." *Global Crime*, 6: 32–53.

Bryant, Christopher G.A., and David Jary. 2011. "Anthony Giddens." In *The Wiley-Blackwell Companion to Major Social Theorists*, edited by George Ritzer and Jeffrey Stepnisky, 432–463. Malden, MA: Wiley-Blackwell.

Coad, Alan F., and Loukas G. Glyptis. 2014. "Structuration: A position–practice perspective and an illustrative study." *Critical Perspectives on Accounting*, 25 (2): 142–161.

Coad, Alan F., and Ian P. Herbert. 2009. "Back to the future: New potential for structuration theory in management accounting research?" *Management Accounting Research*, 20: 177–192.

Coad, Alan F., Lisa Jack, and Ahmed Kholeif. 2015. "Structuration Theory: Reflections on Its Further Potential for Management Accounting Research. *Qualitative Research in Accounting and Management*. 12 (2): 153–171.

Coad, Alan F., Lisa Jack, and Ahmed Kholeif. 2016. "Strong structuration theory in accounting research." *Accounting, Auditing & Accountability Journal*, 29: 1138–1144.

Cressey, Donald R. 1969. *Theft of the Nation: The Structure and Operations of Organized Crime in America*. New Brunswick, NJ: Transaction Publishers.

Densley, James A., and Alex Stevens. 2014. "'We'll show you gang': The subterranean structuration of gang life in London." *Criminology and Criminal Justice*, 15: 102–120.

Englund, Hans, and Jonas Gerdin. 2014, "Structuration theory in accounting research: Applications and applicability." *Critical Perspective on Accounting*, 25: 162–180.

Englund, Hans, Jonas Gerdin, and John Burns. 2011, "25 years of Giddens in accounting research: Achievements, limitations and the future." *Accounting, Organizations and Society*, 36: 494–513.

Finckenauer, James O. 2005. "Problems of definition: What is organized crime?" *Trends in Organised Crime*, 8: 63–83.

Giddens, Anthony. 1984. *The Constitution of Society: Outline of the Theory of Structuration*. Berkley, CA: University of California Press.

Gottschalk, Petter. 2009. *Entrepreneurship and Organised Crime: Entrepreneurs in Illegal Business*. Cheltenham: Edward Elgar Publishing.

Hagan, Frank E. 2006. " 'Organized crime' and 'organized crime': Indeterminate problems of definition." *Trends in Organized Crime*, 9: 127–137.

Harris, Elaine P., Deryl Northcott, Moataz Moamen Elmassri, and Jari Huikku. 2016. "Theorising strategic investment decision-making using strong structuration theory." *Accounting, Auditing & Accountability Journal*, 29: 1177–1203.

Hurley, Graham. 2004. *Cut to Black*. London: Orion Publishing Group.

Jack, Lisa, and Ahmed Kholeif. 2007. "Introducing strong structuration theory for informing qualitative case studies in organization, management and accounting research." *Qualitative Research in Organizations and Management: An International Journal*, 2: 208–225.

Jack, Lisa, and Ahmed Kholeif. 2008. "Enterprise resource planning and a contest to limit the role of management accountants: A strong structuration perspective." *Accounting Forum*, 32: 30–45.

Joas, Hans. 1993. *Pragmatism and Social Theory*. Chicago: University of Chicago Press.

Junninen, Mika. 2008. "Depth-interviewing Finnish professional criminals." *Trends in Organized Crime*, 11: 59–69.

Junninen, Mika. 2009. "Finnish professional criminals and their organisations in the 1990s." *Crime, Law and Social Change*, 51: 487–509.

Kilfoyle, Eksa, and Alan J. Richardson. 2011. "Agency and structure in budgeting: Thesis, antithesis and synthesis." *Critical Perspectives on Accounting*, 22: 183–199.

Kilpinen, Erkki. 2015. "Social Theory." In *The Bloomsbury Companion to Pragmatism*, edited by Sami Pihlström. London: Bloomsbury Press.

Lusthaus, Jonathan. 2013. "How organised is organised cybercrime?" *Global Crime*, 14: 52–60. doi:10.1080/17440572.2012.759508.

Merton, Robert K. 1938. "Social structure and anomie." *American Sociological Review*, 3: 672–682.

Morselli, Carlo, Mathilde Turcotte, and Valentina Tenti. 2010. *The Mobility of Criminal Groups*. Report No.004 for Research and National Coordination Organized Crime Division Law Enforcement and Policy Branch Public Safety Canada.

Nørreklit, Hanne, Falconer Mitchell, and Hanne Nørreklit. 2017. "Introduction." In *A Philosophy of Management Accounting: A Pragmatic Constructivist Approach*, edited by Hanne Nørreklit. Chapter 1, this volume. New York: Routledge.

Nørreklit, Lennart. 2011. "Actors and reality: A conceptual framework for creative governance." In *An Actor's Approach to Management: Conceptual Framework and Company Practices*, edited by Morten Jakobsen, Inga-Lill Johansson, and Hanne Nørreklit, 7–38. Copenhagen: DJØF Publishing.

Nørreklit, Lennart. 2017. "Actor reality construction." In *A Philosophy of Management Accounting: A Pragmatic Constructivist Approach*, edited by Hanne Nørreklit. Chapter 2, this volume. New York: Routledge.

Prus, Robert C. 1996. *Symbolic Interaction and Ethnographic Research: Intersubjectivity and the Study of Human Lived Experience*. Albany, NY: SUNY Press.

Roberts, John. 2014. "Testing the limits of structuration theory in accounting research." *Critical Perspectives on Accounting*, 25: 135–141.

Rutherford, Brian A. 2013. "A pragmatist defence of classical financial accounting research." *Abacus*, 49: 197–218. doi:10.1111/abac.12003.

Starks, Helene, and Susan B. Trinidad. 2007. "Choose your method: A comparison of phenomenology, discourse analysis, and grounded theory." *Qualitative Health Research*, 17: 1372–1380.

Stones, Rob. 2005. *Structuration Theory*. Basingstoke: Palgrave Macmillan.

Stones, Rob. 2015. *Why Current Affairs Needs Social Theory*. Basingstoke: Palgrave Macmillan.

Stones, Rob, and Lisa Jack. 2016. "The bridge between ontological concepts and empirical evidence: An interview with Rob Stones." *Accounting, Auditing & Accountability Journal*, 29: 1145–1151.

Taylor, Ian, Paul Walton, and Jock Young. 1973. *The New Criminology*. London: Routledge and Kegan Press.

Vaughan, Barry. 2001. "Handle with care: On the use of structuration theory within criminology." *British Journal of Criminology*, 41: 185–200.

12 A Comparison of Pragmatic Constructivism and Actor Network Theory

Morten Jakobsen

Introduction

Since Burrell and Morgan (1979) introduced their framework to classify research within sociology, the framework has been widely used to categorise assumptions for management accounting research (e.g. Hopper and Powell 1985; Chua 1986). Thereby, Burrell and Morgan's work has had a huge impact on our understanding and classification of research paradigms within the field of management accounting (Justesen and Mouritsen 2011). However, these four box frameworks and their paradigms have a tendency to turn the world into a dualistic setting due to the dichotomy assumptions of the frameworks. In the research field of management accounting there is no open war between different streams of research (e.g. Lukka and Granlund 2002). The different streams seem to coexist in a form of silent ceasefire, but for the moment it seems as if the mainstream accounting paradigm is the dominating paradigm (Macintosh 2004; Lukka 2010). Merchant (2010) argues that the pendulum will swing back. But back to what? Going to the other extreme of Burrell and Morgan's framework will not in itself provide us with richer insights into the field of management accounting, because entering the interpretive paradigm may open other perspectives, but also shut down others. What pragmatic constructivism with its integration of the four dimensions of reality suggests is a research approach that spans several methodologies as also suggested by Goles and Hirschheim (2000), Davila and Oyon (2008) and Malina et al. (2011). So despite us seeing reality as a construction, pragmatic constructivism is open to most methods if these methods make sense in order to shed light on the actual situation. For instance, statistical methods can be very helpful in order to make an informed factual basis for decision-making. Not as truth-generating machines, but as well-arranged facts based on valid data that can form the foundation for human judgement. Hence, choice of method must be driven by pragmatism. The criterion for choosing and using methods is that the method makes sense for the actor, and that the method will contribute positively to the creation and integration of reality for the actor.

Within the field of management accounting research, Actor Network Theory (ANT) also attempts to reveal the weaknesses of positivistic research that is unaware of own paradigmatic conditions (e.g. Latour 2005), and the ANT framework has been used as a platform for developing a powerfully-positioned stream of research within the management accounting research field (e.g. Lowe 2001; Mouritsen et al. 2001; Busco et al. 2007; Pipan and Czarniawska 2010). However, as will be shown, the research ambition of ANT is mainly to describe reality, whereas pragmatic constructivism has the ambition to understand, interpret and guide the reality construction of actors. Thereby ANT and pragmatic constructivism may not be allied. On the other hand, ANT and pragmatic constructivism should certainly not be opponents due to our common objective of broadening our understanding and acceptance of different methodologies.

The ambition of this chapter is to analyse the similarities between Pragmatic Constructivism and Actor Network Theory. We make this analysis because it is useful to reflect upon where the two theories agree, and to shed light on where they disagree. Such reflection and the conclusion can be used to make us understand how the two theories can complement each other if possible. In addition, the chapter also attempts to discuss the kind of human realities that may be the consequence of ANT and pragmatic constructivism.

The chapter will show that despite similar ambitions, pragmatic constructivism and ANT differ substantially concerning the understanding of the actors' freedom to choose and ability to reflect. This difference is found concerning the possibility dimension, where ANT seems to subscribe to a kind of essentialism, and concerning the value dimension that seems totally absent within ANT.

Although Actor Network Theory has been developed by Bruno Latour, John Law and Michel Callon (e.g. Hansen 2011), Latour has been the main spokesman for ANT in the management accounting literature (e.g. Justesen and Mouritsen 2011). Therefore, Latour's texts will be the main sources for discussing ANT compared to pragmatic constructivism. The chapter is not an introduction to the ideas developed by Latour. For an introduction to these ideas we refer to Blok and Jensen (2011) and, of course, the original texts by Latour. Researchers within the accounting discipline started to get their inspiration from Latour around 1990. From then, an increasing amount of research papers seem to inform the management accounting field (Justesen and Mouritsen 2011). By far the most cited text by Latour in the accounting research is Latour's book *Science in Action* from 1987 (Justesen and Mouritsen 2011). This is actually quite interesting because the book is part of Latour's early work where his concepts and framework are still being developed. This indicates that the accounting literature seems to be stuck in the older work of Latour and thereby has missed the opportunity to benefit from the research and work done by Latour since 1987. Justesen and Mouritsen (2011) point out that much of the management accounting research done, which is based on the *Science in Action* book from 1987, has a social constructionist and institutionalist approach. This focus has ironically taken the ANT research within management accounting away from Latour's work and criticism of social science (Latour 2005, Introduction).

The analysis of and comparison between ANT and pragmatic constructivism will begin by comparing the research ambition of ANT and pragmatic constructivism. After that, the concepts of world and reality within ANT and pragmatic constructivism are discussed. Then the four dimensions of pragmatic constructivism are discussed in relation to ANT. Before the conclusion, a few selected papers published in accounting journals will be discussed in order to exemplify some of the differences between ANT and pragmatic constructivism. Finally, conclusions are drawn from the analyses made during the chapter.

Research Ambitions of ANT and Pragmatic Constructivism

The ambition of Latour is to break down the dominance of natural sciences in our society, and to provide room for other scientific fields to contribute to our understanding of the society of which we are all part (Latour 1999, 1–23). The empirical work made by Latour is primarily done on the home turf of the natural sciences, for instance in laboratories (e.g. Latour 1987) and in the wild nature where the natural scientists in the form of a pedologist and a geomorphologist colonise the wild Brazilian jungle with their methods and instruments (Latour 1999, 24–79). Latour attempts to improve our understanding of the development of knowledge within natural sciences by pointing out that research processes are not a matter of studying the world and reaching objective truths based on sterile rationales and methods of observation. Instead, Latour claims that research processes are made in chains of interactions between actants. By actant Latour refers to both human and non-human actors. The actant is identified by what the actant does. The actant is defined as a list of effects; these effects Latour labels performances (Latour 1999, 303). Latour argues that modern natural sciences seem to have forgotten that research is a knowledge construction process. In Danish and Germen this process is recognised in the daily language. Here, the researcher is called knowledge creator (e.g. Arbnor and Bjerke 2008). In English the term scientist or researcher is used to describe the person who creates knowledge. Such a person is more distant, observing and non-engaging with the phenomena about which he or she is creating knowledge. Ontologically, this makes sense if the world is out there, and we epistemologically are able to describe, measure and transform the world into portable tables on paper. At least such thinking is the dominating paradigm within natural sciences that to a large extent is dominated by repetitive studies where a theory is researched under new conditions. According to Latour, this paradigm has created neurotic scientists who he describes as brains in gaze (Latour 1999, 1–23). By this bizarre illustration, Latour indicates that the natural sciences have focused on rationale and logic and have forgotten that research happens in interaction with the reality around the researcher, and that the non-human actors interact during the research process.

ANT seeks to record and describe the actions of the actors (Latour 2005, 55, 147). "ANT is simply the social theory that has made the decision to follow the natives" (Latour 2005, 62). So basically the method of ANT consists of making dense descriptions of the actions of actants. Latour advises not to apply explanations in the form of a metatheory that can explain the behaviour of the actors. If the behaviour is unclear, the cure is more descriptions. So in a way Latour advocates a kind of grounded theory. The methodological approach by Latour is a reaction to the sociological research tradition of having certain perspectives and pre-defined categories into which the observed people are sorted. According to Latour, the actors and their reality are richer than that. Using simplistic categories in social analysis is an insult to the actors we follow. From a pragmatic constructivist point of view, such an approach seems appealing because it takes the actor and the life conditions of the actor seriously. However, it also restricts the research ambition of the study. Because ANT explicitly aims to describe the actions of the actor, it becomes very difficult to help the actor. Latour's micro-sociology and all its detailed descriptions will not provide an overview that will orientate both the actor and the researcher and thereby allow for action, transformation and future reality construction. Basically, Latour's method is related to a form of empiricism due to his focus on observing and following the natives (Krarup and Blok 2011). There is generally no focus on the reflections made by the people involved and the values of these people. Wilfrid Sellars (1956) advocates that one of the consequences of empiricism's neglect of peoples' ideological and metaphysical positions is that it will hide the motives of people and thereby make it impossible to discuss these motives. This may also be the case concerning ANT, and, consequently, it becomes difficult to criticise and discuss findings made based on the ANT method. As such, the ANT method contributes to the anything goes rhetoric that comes with the post-modern social constructivism that Latour actually wants to dispute.

The World and Reality Concepts

Within the framework of pragmatic constructivism there is a distinction between the world and reality (Nørreklit 2011; Nørreklit 2017, Chapter 2, this volume). The world is an inclusive concept, because it per definition embraces everything. It contains people, their ideas, their belongings and possibilities. The world also includes misunderstandings and illusions. The world is not an unreachable objective and static phenomenon as we know it from Kant's idea of *Das Ding an sich*. The world is the source from where we as actors mobilise elements for our construction of our reality, and as such we are able to interact with the world and make use of the world through our reality construction.

In pragmatic constructivism reality expresses a successful and well-functioning relationship between the actor and the world (Nørreklit 2011, 19). The reality is a subset of the world, and thereby the reality of the actor becomes exclusive.

In Latour's texts it is difficult to find a definition of the concepts world and reality. The chapter: "Do You Believe in Reality?" (Latour 1999) is perhaps the closest we get to an understanding of Latour's conceptualisation of reality. In that chapter Latour describes a meeting with an American psychologist, where the psychologist begins the conversation by raising the question: "Do you believe in reality?" This question initiates reflections about how the psychologist can raise such a question, because: "Is reality something we have to believe in?" (Latour 1999, 1). For Latour, reality is created by actors in a network. Actors are identified when they do something that makes a difference, their performances. Latour is not interested in things that might have happened; he is only interested in things that have actually happened or even better, when they happen, before the black box closes.

Latour does not separate reality into dichotomies such as nature versus society (Blok and Jensen 2011, 52–73). One of his major points is that reality is a hybrid between nature and society, and that reality becomes visible when nature and society interact. Things in the world that are not mobilised by an actor do not make a difference. Therefore, such things in the world are irrelevant for Latour's analyses, and perhaps this is why he does not distinguish between the world and reality. Thereby, he becomes blind for things in the world as defined within the pragmatic constructivist framework. Consequently, he excludes things that could have happened, things that pragmatic constructivism would label possibilities. Latour also excludes himself from evaluating whether the reality that his actors work within is a good reality. All he can observe is what they do, and how one actor is able to influence the actions of the other actors in the network.

Facts

Within pragmatic constructivism we take facts very seriously. Facts are the stepping stones that allow us to walk through life and to act in a social context. Facts are a kind of condition of living that we have learned will not harm us through personal or common experience. Thereby, facts point into the past. Pragmatic constructivism does not subscribe to an idea of the world consisting solely of brute facts. Anscombe (1958) discusses brute facts using an example of a person to whom a grocer has delivered potatoes. Under normal circumstances it would be a fact that this delivery implies that the customer owes the grocer money. However, the circumstances could be different, whereby the customer may not owe the grocer money despite the fact that the customer had the potatoes delivered. The point is that facts cannot stand alone. Facts require an explanation and a context in order to be valid, and the explanation and context must be generally accepted among people. For pragmatic constructivism it is important to know what facts are constituted for the actor. It is important to know whether these facts are valid and thereby correspond to phenomena in the world. The facts also have to be reliable so that other actors have similar perceptions of the phenomena in the world.

When Latour is interested in facts, then it is in the fact-construction process, specifically in the construction of scientific facts (Blok and Jensen 2011, 26–51). Facts are not absolute and eternal truths. For Latour, facts become facts when they are stabilised in networks, and then he uses the concept factish. Factish is an amalgamation of the two words Fact and Fetish. When Latour speaks of facts in this relation, facts are similar to brute facts. Fetish: "implies that believers have simply projected onto a meaningless object their own beliefs and desires" (Latour 1999, 306). Latour states that both facts and fetishes are fabricated. Fabricated must be understood in the way that when facts are well fabricated, facts are autonomous; and when fetishes are well fabricated, they are what make us act rightly (Latour 1999, 274). Such description is very much in line with how facts within the pragmatic constructivist framework are used to help the actor to construct a reality that works. Latour makes a huge effort in order to distance himself from post-modernism, which in Latour's words would claim: "Yes, of course construction and reality are the same thing; everything is just so much illusion, storytelling and make believe" (Latour 1999, 275). In response to this, Latour states: "The factish suggests an entirely different move: it is because it is constructed that it is so very real, so autonomous, so independent of our own hands" (Latour 1999, 275). But where pragmatic constructivism insists on a pragmatic truth, that a functioning link exists between world phenomena and the reality we as actors work within, and that we constantly challenge this link in order to make sure that it actually works, such forward-looking reassurance is not part of Latour's theories. In order to support his fact, fetish and factish theory, he uses an anecdote where Jagannath wants to reveal that the holy stone, saligram, is nothing but a stone. Jagannath's attempt to reveal this illusion fails. Latour sees this as example of how the fetish related to the stone is so strong that it becomes not a fact but a factish because it is a fabricated truth. Latour stops here. Pragmatic constructivism, on the other hand, has the intention to continue and, in this case, help Jagannath reveal the illusion into which his fellow actors seem to be trapped.

Possibilities

For pragmatic constructivism possibilities are potential actions that the actor can choose to make. Within pragmatic constructivism things in the world contain possibilities for the actor to act in certain ways. But it is the actor that chooses to use the possibility for what it most obviously is intended. For instance, a cup contains the possibility for the actor to drink from the cup. However, the cup can also be used for other purposes. Latour has a much more strict view on things. Latour would say that the performance of the cup is that it makes humans drink from it. Thereby, things are made able to influence action to such an extent that he equates human actors and things, which he then labels non-human actors.

One problem with Latour's understanding of the nature of non-human actors is that it degrades human beings into a kind of robot that simply responds to the instruction given by the thing. Thereby the reflectiveness of humans is not taken into account, because the potential actions of humans are defined by the actions of the non-actors. Such relationship between humans and non-human actors could be interpreted as a kind of essentialism. However, traditional essentialism is probably also a too simple way to categorise Latour's ideas. Artifacts: "deserve to be housed in our intellectual culture as full-fledged social actors. Do they mediate our actions? No they are us." (Latour 1999, 214). This quote only gives some kind of meaning when it is seen in relation to the ambition of Latour, which is to show that the world is not object or subject, it is both (Blok and Jensen 2011). Thereby things (object) that we invent are constructed by humans (subject), and the shape, functionality and limitations of the thing contain some human elements, that is, a hybrid.

The idea of a hybrid ontology is also the reason why we cannot just reduce Latour's ideas to traditional essentialism because the characteristics of an artifact are constructed by humans, and the strength of the artifact is also defined by humans due to the strength of the network related to the artifact. This way of reasoning may also by the reason why Justesen and Mouritsen (2011) label Latour as anti-essentialist. However, whether the performance of an artifact is determined by the inner nature of an artifact or by humans in other parts of a network really makes no difference seen from a pragmatic constructivism point of view. The implication of both understandings is that the actor is limited in the usage of the artifacts. Later in their text Justesen and Mouritsen (2011, 169) contradict themselves by stating that: "The specific Latourian twist is provided by adding to the anti-essentialist approach a strong emphasis on the question of how specific technologies and inscription devices forge new linkages and enable certain kind of action and new practices." This is not how we within pragmatic constructivism understand how things provide possibilities for actors. If we return to the cup mentioned above, clearly, most cups are excellent to drink from. But for the entrepreneurial actor cups contain many other possibilities. If you take a cup and put flour, cacao powder, baking powder, melted butter, milk and chocolate into it, and put it all into a microwave oven for 2 minutes, then you have used your cup, not to drink from, but for baking a cupcake. Analysing the invention of cupcakes is, of course, possible by the use of ANT. Such an analysis would contain cups, different ingredients and microwave ovens. But the analysis would probably not grasp how these artifacts meet and become something new. Pragmatic constructivism would probably grasp it, because of the explicit focus on possibilities and how the innovative actor makes use of things in ways for which they may not originally have been meant.

Values

Latour does not explicitly mention values, so here we find a huge difference between ANT and pragmatic constructivism. For pragmatic constructivism, the values of the actor are central because the values are the basis for the actor to choose among different alternative possibilities and thereby construct the reality of the actor.

When Latour touches upon values, it is often in relation to concepts like subject and politics, e.g. Blok and Jensen (2011, 75–101) and Latour (1999, 174–215). Due to Latour's hybrid thinking, values are embedded in the things or artifacts in focus. This is actually quite peculiar, because how can a thing have an embedded value in itself? One explanation to this may be that Latour wants to distinguish his thinking from many post-modern sociologists who would claim that everything is socially constructed whereby we can disregard any coupling between the social and the world. Another explanation can be that Latour in his analyses is uninterested in values. Latour is interested in what humans or things do, their actions and performativity (Latour 2005). The consequence of this focus is that the ANT analyses are unable to provide answers to questions starting with why. ANT can reveal who and what. Such questions are suitable for the purpose of descriptive analyses. But if we truly want to understand people, then we need concepts that we can use to get access to the motives and values of people.

Krarup and Blok (2011) also reflect upon the lack of values in Latour's thinking. They argue that as consequence of Latour's ambition to trace the links between subject (humans) and object (non-humans), human morality is neglected. In order to compensate for this, Krarup and Blok introduce the concept quasi-actants in order to contribute to the ANT theory. Strangely enough, Krarup and Blok do not come up with a clear definition of what this concept is. From their text it seems as if quasi-actant is a phenomenon that informs the human actors in their formation of networks with non-human actors. This reconstruction of our understanding of how networks in an ANT setting are formatted contributes to the theory, by adding a moral aspect. But it still seems peculiar that morality is something external to the human actors. For pragmatic constructivism, values, including moral stands, are central for the way actors construct their reality. It is the values that guide our choices in life. Therefore, values cannot be seen as something quasi. It is central for human actors.

Communication

In pragmatic constructivism, communication happens between the actor and the world. For ANT, communication is termed Translation. Translation as communication is not only a matter of two people talking together. Latour defines the term as:

> Instead of opposing words and the world, science studies, by its insistence on practice, has multiplied the intermediary terms that focus on the transformations so typical of sciences; like inscriptions or articulation, translation is a term that crisscrosses the modernist settlement. In its linguistic and material connotations, it refers to all the displacements through other actors whose mediation is indispensable for action to occur. In place of a rigid opposition between context and content, chains of translation refer to the work through which actors modify, displace, and translate their various and contradictory interests.
>
> (Latour 1999, 311)

There is a problem about this understanding of translation, and the problem boils down to the method of following the actions of the actors, and a lack of validity criteria for actions. All actions are equally good, according to Latour. If we use the example of language translation, then it will be very difficult to make a translation that makes sense if you do not know the phenomenon in reality that is referred to by a specific concept in one language in order to convert it into another concept in another language. If you are unable to make such reality verifications, then there is a huge risk that the message will change into a totally different meaning than the original. The American philosopher John Searle has an example he calls the Chinese Room (Searle 1984). In this room a man has been placed in total isolation. All he has is a number of dictionaries that allows him to translate texts from one language to another. Due to his lack of contact to the world, there is no reference from the words in the dictionaries to the world/life phenomena they ought to represent. Thereby, all he can do is to produce symbol manipulation. Like Google translate, it sometimes works. But often, such symbol manipulation produces gibberish. They are combinations of words that make no sense because they are out of touch with reality. Such a situation is what pragmatic constructivism would label an illusion. Latour's concept of translation has no built in reality verification, and may lead to the construction of illusions.

Latour surrounds himself with concepts that are weakly defined, slippery and even metaphorical (Blok and Jensen 2011, 18). For instance: inscription, performativity and calculative spaces. These concepts are reformulations of established concepts, and in many cases these reformulations add to conceptual ambiguity. If we take the concept inscription, Latour defines the concept as: "A general term that refers to all types of transformations through which an entity becomes materialised into a sign, an archive, a document, a piece of paper, a trace. Usually but not always inscriptions are two dimensional superimposable and combinable." (Latour 1999, 306). First of all, he indicates that the concepts contain both action (transformations, becomes) and a specific phenomenon (materialised, document, piece of paper etc.). So what he is talking about on a superficial level: is inscription a verb or a noun? On a deeper level he creates uncertainty by talking about transformation that often appears erratically. This transformation manifests in the inscription that in the ordinary use of the noun it most often refers to signs or messages that are made durable by engraving these into solid materials like stone or metal—that is, durable materials. Latour may want to emphasise his ambition about emphasising his message about reality as a hybrid. However, this ambiguity also makes Latour's texts wide open for interpretation, allowing a torrent of words that may sound full of insight, but also too undiscussable, to stand valid. This means that we can easily end in metaphysical rhetoric.

The Use of ANT in Management Accounting Research

Justesen and Mouritsen (2011) provide us with a notable literature review of the effects of Actor Network Theory in accounting research. They show that ANT has been used for analysis of accounting change, where ANT has contributed by focussing on the historical processes, often through unforeseen actors and translations. Another contribution to our understanding of accounting provided by the use of ANT is by pointing at accounting and management control as non-human actors that enable action at the distance. In this section three papers published in AOS or MAR will be discussed. The papers are selected because they represent specific examples of the general differences between ANT and pragmatic constructivism discussed in prior sections.

Justesen and Mouritsen present statistics concerning the publication of ANT-inspired articles in top ranking accounting journals (AOS, AAAJ, MAR and CPA). In the period 1988 to 2008, around 170 articles referring to Latour have been published in the journals mentioned. What is interesting is that the dominant reference is made to the book *Science in Action* from 1987 (Justesen and Mouritsen 2011, Figure 2), which represents the early and perhaps less-developed work of Latour (Blok and Jensen 2011). This indicates that the usage of the conceptual framework provided by Latour may not have been mobilised in the more recent articles published. Therefore, Justesen and Mouritsen (2011) also conclude that new inspiration for accounting research can be found in the more recent texts, although they do not elaborate further on this.

According to Justesen and Mouritsen (2011), Peter Miller's article from 1991 *Accounting innovation beyond the enterprise: problematizing investment decisions and programming economic growth in the U.K. in the 1960s* is one of the agenda-setting articles for ANT research within accounting. Miller (1991) describes how the debate concerning the use of discounted cash-flow techniques has been problematised, and how the interest and acceptance of discounted cash flow has increased. Miller makes a straightforward ANT analysis of the debate and the progression of this debate. In that sense, the paper is basically a replication study of Latour's analyses made in laboratories in an accounting setting. From a pragmatic constructivist point of view, especially, the possibility dimension is absent. One obvious explanation that could have been discussed was the development and rising possibilities for calculating and using discounted cash flows due to increased computer power. Another explanation could have been that people should start seeing the possibilities from the discounted cash-flow technique. However, this is not done, and the study is therefore rather descriptive. As such, it can serve as an example of the limited possible research ambition that ANT contains.

Another article that addresses accounting change is Quattrone and Hopper's article: *What does organizational change mean?* The paper is methodologically inspired by sociology of translation whereby they indicate use of not only Latour but also Callon (e.g. Callon 1984) in their interpretation of ANT. Quattrone and Hopper criticise both rationalism and social constructivism because: "Both assume a unique external reality, socially constructed or real, and a linear view of space and time. Both essentially explain processes towards stability" (Quattrone and Hopper 2001, 406). So here there is a clear link to Latour's criticism of existing research paradigms. Their paper analyses two case studies of the large SAP-system implementation. This system contains many possibilities, and in most cases these possibilities are difficult or even impossible to foresee before people in the organisations start working with the system and become familiar with the different functionalities. In that sense it does make sense that Quattrone and Hopper abandon the idea of a unique external reality. What becomes problematic in their analysis is that they decouple the reflective actors by introducing their drift concept whereby the actor is reduced to a log that floats around in the water. This seems peculiar, because the statements made by the actors interviewed in the case companies point to the fact that these actors start seeing possibilities in the SAP system and actively begin to integrate these in their construction of a new reality including the possibilities of SAP (Quattrone and Hopper 2001, 417). This indicates that pragmatic constructivism perhaps could have enriched the analysis, because pragmatic constructivism enables the researcher to go beyond the surface of what is directly visible. This is due to opening the dimension of values and possibilities. In this specific case the logs drifting around may have turned out to be small canoes skilfully steered based on values in a stream of troubled water made out of the many new possibilities from SAP.

The final article to be discussed is Mouritsen et al. (2001): *Intellectual capital and the 'capable firm': narrating, visualising and numbering for managing knowledge*. In this article they propose a framework for managing knowledge in companies. They define a concept of knowledge by combining ideas from Foucault, Lyotard, Giddens and Latour (Mouritsen et al. 2001, 739). The knowledge concept they define has similarities to the fact dimension from pragmatic constructivism. First, knowledge is not a stock; it is involved in the production of problems and solutions. Second, "Knowledge exists in relation to certain practices" (Mouritsen et al. 2001, 739). Third, it is related to processes. The starting point of the intellectual account is the knowledge narrative, which is the: "story about how the firm's intellectual capital is related to a specific kind of organizational identity and a form of management which enables the firm to be competitive in an uncertain knowledge based future and to be a capable firm" (Mouritsen et al. 2001, 745). So taken at face value, the knowledge narrative has some similarity to the topos concept from pragmatic constructivism. From the knowledge, narrative themes of representations and knowledge indicators are to be developed, and it is based on these that knowledge is supposed to be managed at the distance. The empirical foundation of the paper is 17 companies. Of these 17 companies, three companies are described in detail, and the specific intellectual capital indicators are shown for the three companies. Common for all of the indicators is that they are very general and lack a referent, or the referent is very diffuse. For example one of the companies uses an indicator: average hour. One can have an idea of what that is. Most people would probably use a chronometer to measure this phenomenon. But when, where and why should we measure, and for what purpose? It is impossible to say for people outside the group that has worked with the intellectual capital statement. Another of the case companies—a software company—used an indicator called Cola-index (Mouritsen et al. 2001, 753). Again, one may have an idea of what a cola is, but one will not know what cola has to do with the development of software. Using Latour's definition of knowing, it is even questionable whether the indicator actually represents knowledge. "To know is not simply to explore, but rather is to be able to make your way back over your own footsteps, following the path you have just marked out" (Latour 1999, 74). Because managing knowledge, according to Mouritsen et al., is about acting at the distance in space and time, Latour's quote probably has to be taken more seriously. This could have been done by means of pragmatic constructivism using the concept of construct causality that could have addressed more specifically and explicitly the relationships between the indicators and their contribution to the knowledge narrative.

Concluding Comments

ANT and pragmatic constructivism seem to share the same ambition: to help the positivistic research tradition down from its pedestal. We do not want to disregard the positivistic research tradition, because for many of the problems that we face in our society, natural sciences can actually bring forward good solutions. What we want to bring into play is that positivistic research cannot stand alone. The consequence of positivistic research standing alone is that it becomes an amputated body part out of reach for reality, and thereby unable to take part in reality. This situation is what Latour describes as brains in gaze. Pragmatic constructivism is more concerned with situations where positivistic research traditions are used within social sciences and embedded in management models. We often see that these models create illusions because they are not paying sufficient respect to the actor. But where Latour only points at these problems, pragmatic constructivism attempts to help the actor to construct realities that work.

On an ontological level there seem to be a huge difference. Pragmatic constructivism distinguishes between the world and reality. Latour only operates with reality. He thereby neglects the possibilities that lie in all the things in the world. Reading his texts, one gets the impression that the non-human actors play the main character, and that the human actors are more responsive, supporting actors. As such, the human actors' free will seems rather limited. Consequently, Latour's ideas disable actors from being actors because the possibilities at hand are narrowly outlined and defined by the non-human actors. In pragmatic constructivism, we focus on people's ability to realise opportunities and to use possibilities in a creative way in order to develop and construct a reality that is factually possible.

Empiricism seems to drive ANT. As Sellars (1956) points out, empiricism with its avoidance of discussing the underlying assumptions of the researcher makes it impossible to discuss possible agendas of research. This may be less important when science studies within the natural sciences are conducted as originally done by Latour. But when we start employing ANT within social sciences the problem of hidden assumptions becomes a problem that probably needs more careful attention than what is currently the case. Here, pragmatic constructivism certainly has a contribution to make due to its explicit focus on the actor and the values of him or her.

References

Anscombe, Gertrude Elizabeth Margaret. 1958. "On brute facts." *Analysis*, 18 (3): 69–72.
Arbnor, Ingeman, and Bjorn Bjerke. 2008. *Methodology for Creating Business Knowledge*. Thousand Oaks, CA: Sage.
Blok, Anders, and Torben Elgaard Jensen. 2011. *Bruno Latour: Hybrid Thoughts in a Hybrid World*. London: Routledge.
Burrell, Gibson, and Gareth Morgan. 1979. *Social Paradigms and Organizational Analysis: Elements of the Sociology of Corporate Life*. London: Heinemann Educational.
Busco, Cristiano, Paolo Quattrone, and Angelo Riccaboni. 2007. "Management accounting: Issues in interpreting its nature and change." *Management Accounting Research*, 18 (2): 125–149.
Callon, Michel. 1984. "Some elements of a sociology of translation: Domestication of the scallops and the fishermen of St. Brieuc Bay." *The Sociological Review*, 32 (S1): 196–233.

Chua, Wai Fong. 1986. "Radical developments in accounting thought." *Accounting Review*, 61 (4): 601–632.

Davila, Tony, and Daniel Oyon. 2008. "Cross-paradigm collaboration and the advancement of management accounting knowledge." *Critical Perspectives on Accounting*, 19 (6): 887–893.

Goles, Tim, and Rudy Hirschheim. 2000. "The paradigm is dead, the paradigm is dead . . . long live the paradigm: The legacy of Burrell and Morgan." *Omega*, 28 (3): 249–268.

Hansen, Allan. 2011."Relating performative and ostensive management accounting research." *Qualitative Research in Accounting and Management*, 8 (2): 108–138.

Hopper, Trevor, and Andrew Powell. 1985. "Making sense of research into the organizational and social aspects of management accounting: A review of its underlying assumptions." *Journal of Management Studies*, 22 (5): 429–465.

Justesen, Lise, and Jan Mouritsen. 2011. "Effects of actor-network theory in accounting research." *Accounting, Auditing and Accountability Journal*, 24 (2): 161–193.

Krarup, Troels Magelund, and Anders Blok. 2011. "Unfolding the social: Quasi-actants, virtual theory, and the new empiricism of Bruno Latour." *The Sociological Review*, 59 (1): 42–63.

Latour, Bruno. 1987. *Science in Action: How to Follow Scientists and Engineers Through Society*. Cambridge, MA: Harvard University Press.

Latour, Bruno. 1999. *Pandora's Hope: Essays on the Reality of Science Studies*. Cambridge, MA: Harvard University Press.

Latour, Bruno. 2005. *Reassembling the Social: An Introduction to Actor-Network-Theory*. Oxford: Oxford University Press.

Lowe, Alan. 2001. "Accounting information systems as knowledge-objects: Some effects of objectualization." *Management Accounting Research*, 12 (1): 75–100.

Lukka, Kari. 2010. "The roles and effects of paradigms in accounting research." *Management Accounting Research*, 21 (2): 110–115.

Lukka, Kari, and Markus Granlund. 2002. "The fragmented communication structure within the accounting academia: The case of activity-based costing research genres." *Accounting, Organizations and Society*, 27 (1): 165–190.

Macintosh, Norman B. 2004. "A comment on "Recovering Accounting." *Critical Perspectives on Accounting*, 15 (4): 529–541.

Malina, Mary A., Hanne Nørreklit, and Frank H. Selto. 2011. "Lessons learned: Advantages and disadvantages of mixed method research." *Qualitative Research in Accounting and Management*, 8 (1): 59–71.

Merchant, Kenneth A. 2010. "Paradigms in accounting research: A view from North America." *Management Accounting Research*, 21 (2): 116–120.

Miller, Peter. 1991. "Accounting innovation beyond the enterprise: Problematizing investment decisions and programming economic growth in the UK in the 1960s." *Accounting, Organizations and Society*, 16 (8): 733–762.

Mouritsen, Jan, Heine T. Larsen, and Per N.D. Bukh. 2001. "Intellectual capital and the 'capable firm': Narrating, visualising and numbering for managing knowledge." *Accounting, Organizations and Society*, 26 (7): 735–762.

Nørreklit, Lennart. 2011. "Actors and reality: A conceptual framework for creative governance." In *An Actor's Approach to Management*, edited by Morten Jakobsen, Inga-Lill Johansson and Hanne Nørreklit, 7–38. Copenhagen: DJØF Publishing.

Nørreklit, Lennart. 2017. "Actor reality construction." In *A Philosophy of Management Accounting: A Pragmatic Constructivist Approach*, edited by Hanne Nørreklit. Chapter 2, this volume. New York: Routledge.

Pipan, Tatiana, and Barbara Czarniawska. 2010. "How to construct an actor-network: Management accounting from idea to practice." *Critical Perspectives on Accounting*, 21 (3): 243–251.

Quattrone, Paolo, and Trevor Hopper. 2001. "What does organizational change mean? Speculations on a taken for granted category." *Management Accounting Research*, 12 (4): 403–435.

Searle, John R. 1984. *Minds, Brains, and Science*. Cambridge, MA: Harvard University Press.

Sellars, Wilfrid. 1956. "Empiricism and the philosophy of mind." *Minnesota studies in the Philosophy of Science*, 1 (19): 253–329.

13 A Pragmatic Constructivist Perspective on Sensemaking in Management Control

Will Seal and Ruth Mattimoe

Introduction

In a famous story told by Weick (1995), a small military unit got lost in the Swiss Alps. As panic set in they found a map which calmed them down as they plotted a route back to their base. Finding that the map did not match landmarks and obstacles, they used other information such as advice from villagers. When they eventually got to their base camp, they discovered that the map was of the Pyrenees and not the Alps. But, as Ancona put it: "When you're tired, cold, hungry, and scared, any old map will do" (2012, 6). Building on this story, this chapter deploys a pragmatic constructivist (PC) perspective to critically examine the notion that "any old map will do". We consider that the map metaphor may be actually be a very useful way of conceptualising a management control package just as it can be for explaining the role of theoretical models in social science for as Joan Robinson (1962, 33) so famously put it: "A model which took account of all the variegation of reality would be of no more use than a map at the scale of one to one." Similarly, a management control package need not try to represent the totality of organisational detail even if we knew what that was. We also find that the map metaphor has a number of different aspects: how are maps made; how are these used; and what constitutes a 'good map'? But drawing on the PC approach, we also find that the map metaphor has limitations in comparison with a multi-dimensional perspective based on facts, logics, values and communication (Nørreklit et al. 2006; Nørreklit 2011; Cinquini et al. 2013).

In the next section, we review some of the key insights of sensemaking that have influenced the management accounting and control literature. In the following sections we use pragmatic constructivism to point out some of the weaknesses of the sensemaking concept and how pragmatic constructivism can contribute to the use of sensemaking in a management control context.

Some Possible Contributions of Sensemaking and Sensegiving Methods to Management Control and Accounting

In sensemaking, members of organisations extract cues to action from the changing environment in which the organisation finds itself. What is seen as significant will vary, and is influenced by previous experiences and underlying values. The action that occurs as a result of these cues, will, in turn, change the environment within the organisation and will play a part in determining which cues are noticed in future. This process is circular. In other words, the beliefs that people hold about what their role is, will determine which cues they notice in the world around them; this in turn, will determine how they behave. How they behave will change the environment in which they are working, and will affect which cues they notice in the future as well as their beliefs about their role. As Arbnor and Bjerke put it:

> Sensemaking is a process where people try to *make sensible explanations* of experienced situations. It is concerned with the future, but is retrospective in nature, and is based on earlier sensemaking in an *ongoing flow*.
>
> (original emphasis 2009, 403)

According to Tillmann and Goddard (2008), the concept of sensemaking has been extensively discussed in diverse organisational fields, but relatively rarely in the accounting literature. Tillmann and Goddard's (2008) paper explores what is meant by sensemaking and how management accounting is used to assist that process. Earlier researchers argue that accounting is "one of the major formal sets of symbols available to organisational actors for ordering and interpreting their experience" (Boland and Pondy 1983, 224). Serving "as a bridge in the establishment of a common interpretive scheme" (Jönsson 1987, 290), accounting texts "give meaning to an organisation and its history, but they also use them to give meaning to their own selves and worlds" (Boland 1993, 140). In their study, Tillmann and Goddard (2008) used a case study methodology to demonstrate how management accountants were called upon to assist an organisation to understand a situation and to make it more transparent when faced with a decision of a strategic nature—in other words accounting was perceived as an important sensemaking tool.

One of the key insights of sensemaking is that effective managerial action does not necessarily depend on the accuracy of management accounting information. Swieringa and Weick (1987) argue that management accounting academics can over emphasise the analytical and decision-making aspects of management accounting to the neglect of cognition, motivation and commitment. One result of the traditional focus is that researchers may underestimate the effect of action in creating order. Arguing that order may be constructed by managers if, by acting *on a presumption of order* "action implants the rationality that was presumed" (304). As Swieringa and Weick put it:

> Biased, incomplete analyses may mobilize strong action which, because of its strength, may often change situations so that they, in fact, eventually validate the incomplete presentation that first stimulated the action.

Self-validating action stimulated by relatively crude accounting approaches may be a common though neglected pathway by which management accounting affects organizations.

(1987, 293)

Swieringa and Weick use ROI to illustrate their argument. It is not the theoretically best method of either appraising investments or monitoring divisional performance (Seal 2010), but it may have better sensemaking properties especially if *non-accountants* in the organisation accept and understand it. In short, ROI has the capacity to *give* as well as *make* sense.

Gioia and Chittipeddi (1991) combine sensemaking and sensegiving as a way of understanding an organisation undergoing strategic change. They see the relationships between action and cognition as taking on a cyclical nature as shown in Figure 13.1. The diagram evokes different phases of convergent and divergent thinking and action. Initially, sensemaking draws on a number of organisational members to help leaders gain an understanding the issues. The final implementation phase represents the diffusion of the resulting plan to organisational members. These cycles need not be a one-shot phenomenon and they may involve several iterations. Alternatively, if as Mintzberg (1978) argues, strategy is inherently emergent, then the cycle will just go on continuously as an organisational routine.

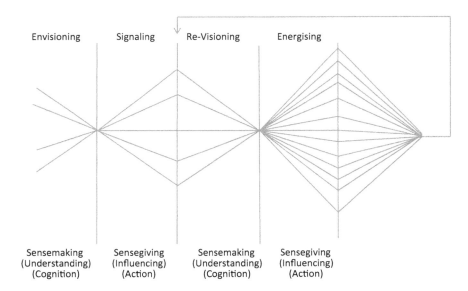

Figure 13.1 Strategic Initiation and Implementation: a Sensemaking and Sensegiving Perspective (Republished with permission of John Wiley and Sons, Inc. from Strategic Management Journal, Gioia, D. and Chittipeddi, K., 12, 433–448 (1991); permission conveyed through Copyright Clearance Center, Inc.)

Some Limitations to the Map Metaphor from a PC Perspective

In our introduction we deployed the famous 'map story' that has been used to illustrate some key aspects of sensemaking. We may also use the map metaphor as a way of comparing and contrasting PC with sensemaking. In the latter, the key concept is not the map *per se* but the *process* of cartography. As Ancona puts it:

> Maps can provide hope, confidence, and the means to move from anxiety to action. By mapping an unfamiliar situation, some of the fear of the unknown can be abated. By having all members of a team working from a common map of 'what's going on out there,' coordinated action is facilitated. In an age where people are often anxious about their circumstances, mapmaking becomes an essential element of sensemaking and leadership. In a world of action first, sensemaking provides a precursor to more effective action.
>
> (2012, 6)

If actors find themselves in unfamiliar circumstances, such as managing a new business, they will tend to draw on explanations and plan actions based on their experience in different, but nevertheless, familiar business settings. Yet, as with our military unit, their organisational 'map' may actually be a map of a different mountain range and, although enabling initial action, it will have to be accompanied by a capacity to react to obstacles that were not marked on the map. The soldiers had a map, but it was clearly an illusion, because it was not a map of the Alps, it was a map of the Pyrenees. The soldiers were also reflective actors, because they started to realise that something was wrong, and they started to look for new possibilities through communication with the villagers.

These issues can be conceptualised using the PC framework because, unlike a two-dimensional map, the defining characteristic of the PC approach is that it construes empirical material in a framework constructed out of a *multi-dimensional organisational reality* (Nørreklit et al. 2006; Jakobsen et al. 2011). More specifically, managerial reality is constructed through a synthesis of logics, facts, values and communication (Nørreklit et al. 2006). In their original exposition of PC, Nørreklit et al. (2006) used the dimension of *logics*, arguing that these were the basis of individual and organisational *possibilities*. Nørreklit et al. argue that there is no set of general principles that integrate their four dimensions of reality, rather it is a question of finding "a company-specific *topos*, where *topos* refer to the concepts and arguments applied in a specific setting" (2006, 43). The basic PC model is illustrated in Figure 13.2 below. Although for each organisational setting the dimensions and the modes of integration will be very specific, the basic structure of the model remains the same. As we shall see later, this stability of structure enables us to compare different organisations and to search for possible innovations.

The PC model is essentially a heuristic device. The map metaphor is also a heuristic device, but it has some significant limitations from a management control perspective. A map is depicting some directly observable empirical phenomenon of the world, whereas a management control system such as an accounting system is a logical conceptual model (Nørreklit et al. 2010), which cannot be verified or tested as easily as a map.

But PC is not just a way of modelling organisational settings or researchers' reality. It is primarily a way of developing good managerial practice or, more specifically, creative governance based on the criterion of practical validity (Nørreklit 2011; Nørreklit 2017, Chapter 2, this volume). A management control approach which fulfils the criterion of practical validity is characterised by an avoidance of possible illusions of management control. Dermer and Lucas argue that the illusion of control "fosters the belief among managers that conventional controls such as operating standards, profit targets and budgetary criteria accurately and validly measure, and thereby

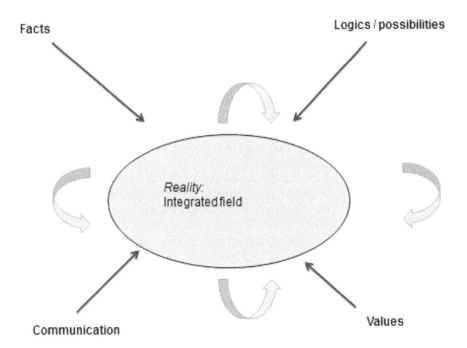

Figure 13.2 Pragmatic Constructivism (Reprinted from *Management Accounting Research*, 17 (1), Nørreklit, H., Nørreklit, L., and Israelsen, P. "The validity of management control topoi: Towards constructivist pragmatism", 42–71 (2006), with permission from Elsevier)

control behaviour" (1986, 471). According to PC, managerial control illusions may be avoided by the construction of a valid organisational *topos* that follows an actor-based approach to management. The PC framework argues that a successful management control *topos* will succeed because it is based on reality rather than illusions—it has *practical validity*. In PC, a concept of organisational/management reality is based on the Germanic premise of *wirklichkeit* or reality is 'that which works' (Nørreklit 2011). Although it shares a constructivist ontology with sensemaking, PC rejects extreme forms of social constructivism which deny the existence of an external objective reality. In PC, facts are a dimension of reality and are constructed through a relationship between the actor and the world. In short, PC has an empirical dimension which offers a way of checking the validity of constructions such as a management control model. In PC, fictions may play a role in the construction and communication of a management control *topos* but they must, at least in principle, be checked against a reality that, although a construction, have some basis in an external world (Nørreklit 2011).

Making a Better Map: Pragmatic and Pro-Active Truth

The appeal to facts may suggest that PC has a less forgiving attitude to management control packages than sensemaking. In other words, the specific characteristics of the organisational *topos* may be subject to a more careful scrutiny than it might under sensemaking criteria. Or to reprise the famous story, any map may be better than no map *but some maps are better than others*. As a way of evaluating management control models/organisational maps, PC proposes a concept of pragmatic truth. For example, the London Tube map may have a very poor correspondence with reality but it meets the criterion of pragmatic truth (Mitchell et al. 2008) in that it has enabled millions of passengers to successfully navigate their way around the London tube system. As argued above, a map is quite easy to test by comparing it with easily observed empirical facts. In comparison, a management control system based on accounting principles is much more ambiguous and much more difficult to interpret and test. For this reason, PC proposes that action be based on a pro-active concept of truth. As Nørreklit et al. point out:

> A problem with this pragmatic concept of truth is that one can only know the truth after events have proven whether the expectations were met. Since it is absurd to wait for ex-post testing of all statements and especially of strategic statements, a concept of preliminary truth, pro-active truth similar to the correspondence notion of truth, is needed to provide a basis for action.

(2008, 21)

Nørreklit et al. have set out the processes by which actors create a practical valid reality in terms of pro-active truth as follows:

> in order to apply the pragmatic notion of truth one needs an idea of truth based on the present. This is *pro-active truth*. This pro-active truth is then subject to a continuous process of improvement which identifies and diminishes the difference between the pragmatic truth as the outcome and with pro-active truth.
>
> (2008, 21–22)

The difference between pro-active and pragmatic truth opens up the possibility that actors can engage in a learning process termed the "pragmatics of truth" (Nørreklit et al. 2007, 197). Over time, organisational actors compare pro-active truth claims with actual outcomes, that is, with pragmatic truths in order to test whether their expectations—perhaps based on theories derived from their institutional and organisational environment—accorded with their experiences in their own organisation. As we shall see below, case study respondents who engaged in these sorts of learning behaviours did not just reflect on the pragmatic outcomes of their existing management control systems, but checked to see whether the systems could be improved on the basis of orthodox but, as yet, untried accounting principles. With a pro-active truth perspective on management control, the map metaphor begins to show some limitations, as creating a map is not the same as planning a journey. Here, PC is undoubtedly more productive with its stress on integration between values, possibilities, logics and communication. The PC framework for creative governance (Nørreklit 2011) promises to go beyond retrospective sensemaking by offering a recipe for the future; an approach that enables strategic performance control (Mitchell et al. 2013; Seal and Mattimoe 2014).

In sum, PC proposes that new business models may be developed by closing the gap between pro-active and pragmatic truth. Pro-active concepts may be based on prior experience and/or by drawing on existing theories in the management literature. This process may be illustrated empirically in case 1. As the discussion of co-authorship in case 1 shows, recommendations based on PC derive their power from a holistic approach to managerial problems with an emphasis on empathy rather than direction. Change comes through greater awareness and understanding by organisational members, which enables better integration between the dimensions of their management control *topoi*. The notion of management change as therapy and empathy is also consistent with sensemaking which sees this process change as an ongoing and recursive accomplishment. PC emphasises *learning* rather than sensemaking; in particular closing the gap between pro-active truth and pragmatic truth. Nørreklit et al. argue that:

> the learning perspective becomes the objective of installing management accounting systems. The deviation is information about differences

between the reality of the firm and the observed and controlled firm. Analysis of the control system should lead to improvements in the control system. The dynamics of the world will always tend to make proactive and real truth drift apart. The implemented learning process counters this problem.

(2007, 213)

The learning perspective on management control is also illustrated empirically in case 2 below, which, in contrast to case 1, describes a long-established and successful business model.

Case 1: Countryhouse Hotel

The *Countryhouse* hotel was located around a country house set in attractive grounds. It had been used as a conference centre but had recently been acquired by a local company whose background was in car repairs. In short, the new owners and their accounting staff had no previous experience in running a hospitality business. As well as re-furbishing the hotel on a piecemeal basis, the owners were keen to build it up as a wedding venue. They had had some success but they were troubled by the seasonal and in-week variation in bookings. There were two key features of the *Countryhouse* case. First, it was a very new business and, consequently, they did not have much of a customer database or experience with which to plan. Second, the senior management and owners did not have a background in hospitality and thus 'the case' illustrates learning processes rather than examples of best practice. As a part-qualified management accountant, the financial manager was very aware of what might be regarded from a generic perspective as good practice. For example, she had considered activity-based costing, but was unsure about its operationality in a hotel context. Most of the accounting was based on their car repair rather than their hospitality business. Recognising the need to close the gap between the accounting system and the different facts and logics of the hotel business, the financial manager was keen to draw on pro-active concepts from other hotels and from other outsiders, such as visiting researchers. She also found that the hotel staff could contribute to a co-authored management control model based on closing the gap between pro-active and pragmatic concepts. For example, a dynamic pricing system could theoretically help to fill the rooms away from the wedding dates, but the data for such a system took time and experience to develop.

Case 2: Coastal Hotel

Coastal hotel contained 37 eco-friendly bedrooms and was situated in a spectacular coastal location in a part of Southwest England particularly popular with holiday makers. The hotel derived most of its revenues from accommodation, as it was a very popular destination for families. Special entertainment for adults and a dedicated area and entertainment for children were provided which proved a very positive selling point for a mid-market, family clientele. The domestic family market comprised approximately 75 percent of total revenues and business conferences and weddings comprised the remaining 25 percent. The hotel always sold a package to include dinner, bed and breakfast.

The management accountant had developed the budgeting and cost controls in two ways. First, she had introduced a special package for rostering labour, which had been very successful in reducing labour cost and in avoiding unauthorised overtime. Second, whereas in the previous year, the hotel had moved to monthly budgets from a full year's budget, it had been decided that weekly budgets were the most important. These changes reflected the realisation that the key features of the overall reporting system were simplicity and timeliness. Reflecting her enthusiasm for innovation and best practice, the FC stated that she was not entirely happy with the model and that she wanted to develop a more sophisticated customer profitability analysis. This analysis would establish how profitable conference and banqueting clients were to the hotel, especially during the busy season, where some rooms could have been sold to non-conference/non-banqueting clients. Overall, the *Coastal* case indicated a close alignment between the business model, the management control framework and the material factors in the case, notably the location of the hotel. Given the settled nature of the hotel's business model, the management accountant seemed to have considerable capacity for both sensemaking and sensegiving. In other words, if a significant change in the business environment affected *Coastal*, then we would expect the hotel's leadership to recognise the new problems and mobilise the organisational actors in an effective manner. There was also evidence of a high level of social integration, whereby accounting data was both understood and authored by non-accounting actors. Action was stimulated through accounting-based cues, such as the flash reports. This latter property was the outcome of a successful process of sensegiving in which the management accounting reports played a key role.

Comparing the Cases

In *Coastal*, with a settled business model and a routinised management control framework, the accountant drew on rationalistic sensemaking. At the other extreme, in *Countryhouse*, the accountant was trying to make sense of her role through reflecting and conversing with external actors. In the latter case, there was a sense of the unexpected, as the new hotel and new managers sought to survive and grow the business. In *Coastal*, the financial manager anticipated few surprises and saw innovations such as customer profitability analysis from an almost playful perspective.

The main weakness in the sensemaking approach is that it focuses on the relationship between cognitive processes and action, but lacks a comprehensive and robust model with which to compare *all* the issues affecting the success of the businesses. In contrast, the PC framework offers a rich and robust structure into which business specific data may be inserted. 'Brute facts' (such as the location and the architecture of a hotel) are important in the PC interpretation but the concept of management control *topoi* captures far more than just physical features. The PC framework acknowledges both the socially constructed nature of reality and the impact of discourse on the selection and omission of facts. Furthermore, values and communication are also part of the hotel's *topos*. Values are not assumed. A hotel may pursue profit but this goal has to be empirically established and cannot be assumed on some notion of *Economic Man*. Similarly, a budget may be seen as an important form of communication in a particular *topos* (Nørreklit et al. 2006), but it can also be interpreted as a mechanism for *constituting* rather than just representing 'business facts'.

Unlike some of the general mechanical models often advocated in the management accounting literature, the PC approach argues that a successful management control *topos* has to be business specific and co-authored with contributions from participants both inside and outside the organisation. Sensemaking and PC research methodologies both encourage reflexivity in which the researchers explicitly explore not just the positions of their interviewees but their own position and reactions. The creation of business knowledge is seen as a co-production between the researchers and the researched as they share concepts and reflections during the field work process. The PC framework has the considerable merit in that it is not laden with pre-conceived values or specific logics. It is open to different values and to a variety of different theories that may emerge both from the other texts and from the empirical findings. In this respect, the framework allows the empirical work to 'speak to' researchers. The metatheory of PC is based on a multi-dimensional view of reality. In contrast, the prescriptive theories that are applied abductively are both abstract and intentionally reductivist with a focus on the factual and logical dimensions of managerial reality. In PC, management control practices are evaluated on the criteria of practical validity, which is premised on an ability to differentiate between fact and fiction. In contrast, in sensemaking research, the main criteria is to assess whether the management control package generated individual and organisational action and enabled actors to reflect on their actions.

Conclusions

Overall, it would seem that in terms of the production of management control knowledge, PC and sensemaking have many overlaps and complementarities. Yet, when it comes to the linking of theory and data and the production of valid management control knowledge, the PC approach provides a vital set of criteria against which we can evaluate the stories of practitioners on the basis of 'does it work?' Given the ambiguity of what constitutes organisational success, it may be hard to test whether a particular management control framework embeds illusions of control; we should at least prefer a research framework that requires that the management control package does not just promote organisational action but, additionally, evaluates that action according to some notions of organisational success. Any map may work in the sense that it overcomes despair and lethargy with PC, but we are urged to explore the characteristics of a good map.

As we argued earlier, sensemaking focuses on cartography—the process of mapmaking. In contrast, we submit that PC has a set of concepts with which a specific map can be evaluated in detail. For example, it can be used to ask fine-grained questions concerning the relationship between the actor and the world in the construction of facts. The PC concern with facts can be used to ask critical questions about the completeness of specific performance indicators. PC does not expect a map to represent some notional reality, but it can be used to analyse the technical basis of representation.

Yet, it would be wrong to present PC and sensemaking in some sort of notional competition. Although they focus on different aspects of management control and accounting, they both share an interest in performativity. In short, both approaches either explicitly ask: how is a map used and how does it relate to individual and organisational action? In sensemaking, the great fear seems to be inaction induced by organisational paralysis; in PC, the great fear is not organisational inaction, but rather a concern that actors, particularly senior managers, are suffering from the illusion that the system of control that they impose on an organisation necessarily, enables successful outcomes.

References

Ancona, Deborah. 2012. "Sensemaking: Framing and acting in the unknown." In *The Handbook of Teaching Leadership*, edited by S. Snook, N. Nohria and K. Rakesh, 3–20. Thousand Oaks, CA: Sage.

Arbnor, Ingeman, and Björn Bjerke. 2009. *Methodology for Creating Business Knowledge*. 3rd ed. Thousand Oaks, CA: Sage.

Boland, Richard. 1993. "Accounting and the Interpretive Act." *Accounting, Organizations and Society*, 18 (2–3):125–146.

Boland, Richard J., and Louis R. Pondy. 1983. "Accounting in organizations: A union of natural and rational perspectives." *Accounting, Organizations and Society*, 8 (2–3): 223–234.

Cinquini, Lino, Falconer Mitchell, Hanne Nørreklit, and Andrea Tenucci. 2013. "Methodologies for managing performance measurement." In *The Routledge Companion to Cost Management*, edited by Falconer Mitchell, Hanne Nørreklit and Morten Jakobsen, 360–380. London: Routledge.

Dermer, Jerry D., and Robert G. Lucas. 1986. "The illusion of managerial control." *Accounting, Organizations and Society*, 11 (6): 471–482.

Gioia, Denis, and Kumar Chittipeddi. 1991. "Sensemaking and sensegiving in strategic change initiation." *Strategic Management Journal*, 12: 433–448.

Jakobsen, Morten, Inga Johansson, and Hanne Nørreklit (Eds.). 2011. *An Actors Approach to Management*. Copenhagen: Djof Publishing.

Jönsson, Sten. 1987. "Frame shifting, sense making and accounting." *Scandinavian Journal of Management Studies*, 3 (3): 255–298.

Mintzberg, Henry. 1978. "Patterns in strategy formation." *Management science*, 24 (9): 934–948.

Mitchell, Falconer, Lars Nielsen, Hanne Nørreklit, and Lennart Nørreklit. 2013. "Scoring strategic performance: A pragmatic constructivist approach to strategic performance measurement." *Journal of Management and Governance*, 17: 5–34.

Nørreklit, Hanne, Lennart Nørreklit, and Falconer Mitchell. 2007. "Theoretical Conditions for validity in accounting performance." In *Business Performance Measurement*, edited by Andy Neely, 179–217. Cambridge: Cambridge University Press.

Nørreklit, Hanne, Lennart Nørreklit, and Falconer Mitchell. 2010. "Towards a paradigmatic foundation for accounting practice." *Accounting, Auditing and Accountability Journal*, 23 (6): 733–758.

Nørreklit, Lennart. 2011. "Actors and reality: A conceptual framework for creative governance." In *An Actor's Approach to Management*, edited by Morten Jakobsen, Inga-Lill Johansson and Hanne Nørreklit, 7–38. Copenhagen: DJØF Publishing.

Nørreklit, Lennart. 2017. "Actor reality construction." In *A Philosophy of Management Accounting: A Pragmatic Constructivist Approach*, edited by Hanne Nørreklit. Chapter 2, this volume. New York: Routledge.

Nørreklit, Lennart, Hanne Nørreklit, and Poul Israelsen. 2006. "The validity of management control *topoi*. Towards constructivist pragmatism." *Management Accounting Research*, 17: 42–71.

Robinson, Joan. 1962. *Essays in the Theory of Economic Growth*. London: Macmillan.

Seal, Will. 2010. "Managerial discourse and the link between theory and practice: From ROI to value-based management." *Management Accounting Research*, 21 (2): 95–109.

Seal, Will, and Ruth Mattimoe. 2014. "Controlling strategy through dialectical management." *Management Accounting Research*, 25 (3): 230–243.

Swieringa, Robert, and Karl E. Weick. 1987. "Management accounting and action." *Accounting, Organizations and Society*, 12 (3): 293–308.

Tillmann, Katja, and Andrew Goddard. 2008. "Strategic management accounting and sense-making in a multinational company." *Management Accounting Research*, 19 (1): 80–102.

Weick, Karl E. 1995. *Sensemaking in Organizations*. Thousand Oaks, CA: Sage.

Weick, Karl., Kathleen Sutcliffe, and David Obstfeld. 2005. "Organizing and the process of sensemaking." *Organizational Science*, 16 (4): 409–421.

14 A Pragmatic Constructivist Approach to Studying Difference and Change in Management Accounting Practice

Falconer Mitchell

Introduction

The study of difference and change in practice has long occupied a leading position in empirical management accounting research. This is not surprising as the forces that determine the discipline will be most apparent when the discipline is diverging and developing. In this chapter, a pragmatic constructivism framework (Nørreklit et al. 2006; Nørreklit 2017, Chapter 2, this volume) is used to explore the extent to which this approach can aid the explanation and understanding of these two aspects of practice.

The different forms evident in management accounting practice in the real world and the way in which practice evolves over time have attracted varied research interest. A broad range of theories have been employed to study them. Most prominent have been contingency theory to explain difference and institutional and diffusion of innovation theory to explain change. Results to date indicate that both of these aspects are related (the form of practice at any given point in time is the result of prior change) but complex and whereas considerable light has been shed on how and why practice develops (and develops differently in different settings), it is also clear that general and definitive answers have not been found (Busco et al. 2007). What is clear, however, is that for practice difference and change to be explained convincingly, a focus has to be placed on the people involved in these processes. Management accounting is a human creation. Only people can determine the form management accounting takes in practice and the changes by which it arrives at its various forms.

Given the centrality of participants' behaviour, pragmatic constructivism holds considerable potential as a research framework in these areas. Its focus is on how people relate to the reality to which they are exposed before they engage in meaningful action (e.g. practice). Thus, the analysis in this chapter is based on the four component dimensions of pragmatic constructivism (facts, possibilities, values and communication) as a means of exploring how people have created different management accounting systems that have changed and evolved over time. This is followed by a discussion of the implications of the analysis for the practice of and research in management accounting. Finally, some conclusions and suggestions for research are made.

Analysis of the Four Dimensions of Pragmatic Constructivism

Facts

The world comprises a myriad of facts. They exist in infinite number. They surround people. It is through recognition of facts that people begin to define the reality in which they operate. Given the scale and dynamism of their factual context, people have to be selective in respect of the facts that they recognise and use. Each individual or group has to engage in a search and selection process to ascertain the facts that they will relate to in deciding on action. However, people are different and are likely to view the significance that facts hold for them differently. The significance of facts will be determined by many factors including education, prior experience, personality, role or functional specialism. Consequently, different arrays of facts will face those involved in practice decisions at different times and in different settings. Indeed, even at the same time and setting, different people will have different conceptions of the significant facts. As a result, the facts upon which a practice such as management accounting is ultimately based will be different for different people. This means that the factual base for action represents a key source of difference and change in management accounting practice. Strong support for this proposition is evident in the failure of prior attempts to bring uniformity to the practising of the discipline (Walker and Mitchell 1996; Mitchell and Walker 1997).

The factual basis of the practice setting is made more complex by the dynamic nature of its factual content. In management accounting, many facts will frequently change both in their absolute and relative importance, in their recognition, in their interpretation and in their form and existence. For example, the fact of spare capacity can change to a capacity shortage, plentiful resources can become limited, reliable suppliers can become unreliable, competition can become more or less intense and organisational objectives can be modified etc. The involvement of different people can also lead to changes and differences in practice. The facts may be revised when the realisation of practice errors occurs or when new methods emerge. The popularity of ABC can be traced to the recognition that overhead costs had, in many organisations, changed both in their importance as a cost component and in their constitution.

In all of these ways, the factual basis upon which people predicate their actions provides an important source of the difference and change that is found in management accounting practice.

Possibilities

Whereas facts provide one foundation upon which action is based, the nature of an action response is dependent on the possibilities for action that are inherent in the facts. People confronted with the facts have to identify these possibilities before action can occur. In management accounting, the fact that fixed and variable costs exist creates the possibilities of valuing inventory and measuring profit on either a full cost or variable cost basis. This fact also creates different possibilities for action in respect of pricing methods, decision and planning support models and the design of control systems. People may identify and favour different possibilities even from the same set of recognised facts. Possibilities, therefore, intensify the level of complexity and the potential for difference and change that facts initially establish for practice.

Whereas facts and their related possibilities can underpin the features of management accounting practice, facts and possibilities may also be created through the operation of a management accounting system. A favourable budget variance may be a fact generated in this way. Again, this type of practice-based fact gives rise to any or more than the following possibilities for action: a cut in the subsequent budget; a reward for the people responsible; a source of extra resource for another project; a re-organisation of other parts of the business to promote similar performance; or a decomposition of the variance to create more facts that can better direct action. Thus, possibility identification can build cumulatively on facts and can relate to the information production practices of management accounting and to information interpretation and use aspects as well.

The possibilities for management accounting practice increase over time as new methods are developed and tested. A practice, not so long ago, described as static for the best part of a century (Johnson and Kaplan 1987) has, in recent decades, become much more innovative. This has been due to developments in technology (where, for example, spreadsheets have facilitated sensitivity analyses in decision-making and ERP software has enhanced resource acquisition and use) and in practice methods (where, for example, a much wider choice of performance measurement packages, costing systems and strategy support information has emerged). These are all factors which have extended the possibilities inherent in the type of facts that management accounting practitioners recognise. Consequently, they have increased the potential for practice difference and change.

Values

Action (in the case of management accounting its practice) is derived from the multiple pathways that facts and their possibilities create. The choice of actions from the array of possibilities that confronts people depends on the values they hold. The possibilities for action that are judged to best meet these values are those which are selected.

Three types of value apply to an information provision and use practice such as management accounting. First are a set of values considered related to the virtuous qualities of information provided by management accountants. True, objective, fair and neutral information provided in an ethical manner encompasses some of the key perspectives falling within this category. These are broad behavioural values that can guide accounting practice in a general way. However, second, these need to be supplemented by technical values that will also drive method and information use choices. The value of technical appropriateness has to be applied if practice is to be the best that it can be. Management accounting methods selected must be suitable for purpose i.e. the use for which they are intended. User decision and control needs need to be met from technically relevant and reliable practice. Third, the values appropriate to the organisation within which practice exists must also be met. If the objective of the organisation is an economic one, such as the pursuit of profit for owners, then that quality has to be impounded in management accounting practice. If a wider stakeholder perspective has been adopted then practice should involve information that reflects the interests of employees, suppliers, customers, government. If externalities are an issue, then environmental concerns may influence the management accountants' practices.

This range of values allows for, and may often foster, differences in practice. People and organisations will hold different value sets. The virtuous qualities of such as truth or objectivity are open to different interpretation as are, in many circumstances, the technical suitability of methods for any given situation. In addition, organisational objectives both differ and change. The establishment of values will therefore be both individual and organisationally specific to some extent and so help to create the differences and change found in management accounting.

Communication

People do not only act as individuals operating in isolation. In reality they normally interact with others. The role of the management accountant involves not only interaction among accountants but also with all of the functional specialists within the organisation. In order to reflect this characteristic of humans, as they relate to their reality, one further dimension (i.e. communication) has to be added to the pragmatic constructivist framework as an additional precursor to action.

In an information supply practice such as management accounting, communication is a central feature of practice. Accountants have to communicate with those responsible for providing data to them and with those who will use the information that they generate. The importance of communication of this type is inherent in the management accountant business partner role which has been so heavily advocated in recent years. Communications over the ascertainment of facts, possibilities and values are necessary. Operating as a business partner is likely to make these types of communication both easier and more effective. In a sense communication is not simply an input preceding action but also an action output in its own right as reports, circulars, interpretations and presentations are given.

Communication is, therefore, a component of management accounting practice. As such it can take many forms e.g. face to face discussions, group or individual presentations, hard copy or computer access, detailed or summarised, raw information or analysed and interpreted information. The scope for variety and development is large and, so, the communication dimension provides another source of the difference and change in a practice such as management accounting.

Implications

The above analysis indicates the potential of using a pragmatic constructivist perspective to undertake novel research on the different forms management accounting practice can take in different organisations and the manner in which it changes over time. Each of the four dimensions of management accounting represents a focus for this type of research. What are the facts used by practising management accountants in their work? What are the action possibilities that they derive from them? What values do they employ in selecting the possibilities for action that are realised by them? What communication is needed in the generation and use of management accounting information? Why and how do answers to these questions differ across organisations and how do the dimensions of pragmatic constructivism alter to create change in practice? Undertaking the research which answers these questions will contribute significantly to the understanding we have of management accounting practice.

In addition to providing its own framework for research, pragmatic constructivism can also be used as part of a mixed methods research design. Its focus on the actions of the people involved in creating difference and change in management accounting fosters this possibility as it can provide new information on the operation of many of the variables involved in other behavioural theories. For example, contingency theory-based research may establish statistical associations between contingent variables and aspects of practice. However, the methods by which and the reasons why contingencies influence (or do not influence) practice is not well explained by the theory. Pragmatic constructivism can, therefore, when used in conjunction with another theory such as contingency theory, provide a complementary approach to enable insight to be gained on how and why people respond (or do not respond) to contingent variable stimuli when carrying out the practice of management accounting.

Finally, the gap that exists between research and practice in management accounting has long been recognised and debated (Scapens 1994; Mitchell 2002; Tucker and Lowe 2014). Research on this topic utilising a pragmatic constructivist approach can contribute to the explanation of this gap in two ways. First, it can provide a rich descriptive analysis of how people in practice operate (Nørreklit et al. 2016). This will facilitate an understanding of their research needs and so demonstrate why so little of the research undertaken in management accounting is found useful for practice. Second, the pragmatic constructivist approach can also be applied to studying practice in the research community. This will indicate how their reality differs from that of practitioners and so reveal why research for practice is not a significant feature of the management accounting discipline.

Conclusion

An important conclusion can be drawn from this analysis of the potential for applying the pragmatic constructivism perspective to management accounting. It is a conclusion directed to the profession of management accounting which, at a central level, has the responsibility of defining, justifying and defending management accounting practice in its societal context. One key way in which this can be done is through the construction of a conceptual framework for practice (and this is exactly what the UK's specialist professional body in management accounting has recently attempted). Pragmatic constructivism can provide a structural basis for doing this because it reveals how action (practice) happens in relation to its real world context (Norreklit et al. 2010). It can demonstrate that management accounting is a fact-based practice, that its boundaries are established in selected facts and their related possibilities for action that are recognised by the profession, that it has established values to guide such recognition and that it is based on developing and fostering methods of communication that can achieve the desired professional values through the practices adopted in producing and using management accounting information.

References

Busco, Cristiano, Quattrone Paolo, and Angelo Riccaboni. 2007. "Management accounting. Issues in interpreting its nature and change." *Management Accounting Research*, 18 (2): 125–149.

Johnson, H. Thomas, and Robert S. Kaplan. 1987. *Relevance Lost: The Rise and Fall of Management Accounting*. Boston: Harvard Business School Press.

Mitchell, Falconer. 2002. "Research and practice in management accounting: Improving integration and communication." *European Accounting Review*, 11 (2): 277–289.

Mitchell, Falconer, and Steven P. Walker. 1997. "Market pressures and the development of uniform costing in the UK printing industry." *Management Accounting Research*, 8 (1): 75–101.

Nørreklit, Hanne, Lennart Nørreklit, and Falconer Mitchell. 2010. "Towards a paradigmatic foundation for accounting practice." *Accounting Auditing Accountability Journal*, 23 (6): 733–758.

Nørreklit, Hanne, Lennart Nørreklit, and Falconer Mitchell. 2016. "Understanding practice generalisation-opening the research practice gap." *Qualitative Research in Accounting and Management*, 13 (3): 278–302.

Nørreklit, Lennart. 2017. "Actor reality construction." In *A Philosophy of Management Accounting: A Pragmatic Constructivist Approach*, edited by Hanne Nørreklit. Chapter 2, this volume. New York: Routledge.

Nørreklit, Lennart, Hanne Nørreklit, and Poul Israelsen. 2006. "The validity of management control *topoi*: Towards pragmatic constructivism." *Management Accounting Research*, 17 (1): 42–71.

Scapens, Robert W. 1994. "Never mind the gap: Towards an institutional perspective on management accounting." *Management Accounting Research*, 5 (3): 301–321.

Tucker, Basil P., and Alan Lowe. 2014. "Practitioners are from Mars; academics are from Venus? An investigation of the research-practice gap in management accounting." *Auditing Accounting Accountability Journal*, 27 (3): 394–425.

Walker, Steven P., and Falconer Mitchell. 1996. "Propaganda, attitude change and uniform costing in the British printing industry, 1913–1939." *Auditing Accounting Accountability Journal*, 9 (3): 98–126.

Index

284 *Index*

Plato 65; platonic form 226
political influence 197, 200, 203
politicised language game 221
Popper 74
positivism 11, 59–60
positivistic methods 8, 10
possibility/ties i, ix, 5–6, 11–16,
  29–30, 32–5, 39–43, 45, 47–8, 50,
  53–9, 63–4, 66, 68, 69n5, 73, 78–9,
  81, 84–5, 88, 90, 99–102, 104–6,
  108, 11–12, 114, 117–31, 136–40,
  144, 146, 149–54, 156, 161–4,
  170–2, 174, 177, 183–5, 188, 190,
  192–201, 219–20, 221, 223, 227,
  230–3, 236–8, 241, 246, 248–52,
  255, 257, 266, 272, 274–6; abstract
  41; factual possibilities *see* factual,
  possibilities; logical 41, 42, 85, 86,
  150; real 39; technical 42; theoretical
  42; types of 5, 39, 41
post-modern 60, 248, 252
post-structuralism 212, 215
power 8, 11–12, 18, 27, 28, 33, 40,
  41, 44, 47–8, 53, 57, 59, 63, 77,
  87, 88, 124, 126, 138, 141, 144,
  149, 154–7, 159–61, 163–7, 169,
  203–4, 214, 214–15, 227, 230,
  233, 240, 266
practice i, ix, 1–4, 6–9, 11–18, 23,
  26–7, 30–5, 37–43, 48–56, 58,
  61–3, 66–8, 73–5, 77–83, 85, 87–8,
  90, 98–101, 105, 118–20, 122,
  125, 128–31, 134–6, 138–9, 141,
  144–6, 149, 152–5, 161, 163, 165,
  169–70, 172, 174, 176, 179, 182–4,
  188, 192, 199, 203–4, 211, 213–15,
  217–20, 222, 225–8, 231–3, 239,
  251, 253, 256, 264, 267–9, 272–7;
  field 174; theory 8–9
pragmatic/s 23–4, 29, 30–2, 34, 61–3,
  73–4, 78–81, 83, 87, 99–101, 102,
  104, 106; approach 73; criterion 7,
  9, 12; effect 32; integration 6, 99;
  truth *see* truth, pragmatic
pragmatic constructivism i, ix–x,
  1–10, 12–18, 23, 32, 57, 60, 64, 67,
  98–100, 102, 114, 119–20, 128–30,
  135–7, 143–4, 146, 149, 151, 155,
  170–1, 174, 188, 191, 211, 215–17,
  222, 225, 231, 233, 235, 239,
  245–57, 260, 264, 272–3, 276–7
pre-understanding 23, 80, 101,
  152–3, 166
principal-agent theory 7, 27–8, 186

profession 15, 30, 51, 58, 144, 146,
  237, 277; professional 18, 26–7, 53,
  58–9, 74, 76, 103, 146, 182, 189,
  192, 197, 227, 230, 237–8, 241, 277

questioning 107, 134, 177–81, 183,
  185

rationalism 11, 63–5, 255
rationality 10, 12, 185, 261
realism 8, 134–5, 211–15; and
  constructivism 29
reality 5–7, 23, 24–6, 29–30, 31, 248;
  coherence of – constructs 52–3;
  diffusion 49, 52; dimensions of
  reality i, ix, 5, 6, 9, 11–14, 24, 34,
  63, 99, 170–1, 184, 193, 217, 219,
  245, 263; disaggregated 15, 201–2;
  an exclusive concept 30, 249; future
  53; not multiple realities 14, 24, 49,
  51, 68; present 53, 190, 214
reality construction/construction of
  reality 23–5, 28–30, 32–4, 81–2,
  89, 103, 108, 153, 163, 171, 173–5,
  182, 184–5, 192, 211–12, 214–19,
  221, 223, 225–7, 230–3, 237, 239,
  241, 246, 248; real construction
  25, 29; *see also* actor-reality
  construction)
reason/ing/able 1, 2, 6, 12, 35, 40,
  42–3, 45–6, 64–6, 73, 80–1, 86–8,
  91, 103, 105, 111, 125, 140, 142,
  151, 153–4, 170, 172, 176–7, 183,
  193, 195–6, 198, 201, 219, 233,
  240, 251, 265, 276
reducti/onist/ve 2, 6, 11–12, 48, 65,
  67, 89, 269; of dimensions 9
reflecti/on/ve 4–5, 6–7, 11, 13–16,
  18, 23–25, 30, 39, 43–4, 50–2, 54,
  60–2, 64, 67, 73, 76–8, 81–7, 90–1,
  97, 101–3, 105, 107–9, 111–14,
  123, 125, 139, 141–3, 145, 160,
  169, 170, 173–4, 176, 178–9,
  181–5, 193, 204, 211–12, 214–15,
  217–19, 221, 225, 228–9, 231–3,
  246, 248–9, 251–2, 255, 263, 266,
  268–9, 275; actors 8; insufficiently
  228; interaction 3, 9; management
  182; methodological tools 7; practices
  5; pre- 229; self-reflective 228
representation/al 7, 8, 10, 12,
  18, 77, 78–9, 82–3, 88, 134, 138,
  143, 192, 200, 202, 204, 211–13,
  222, 234, 256, 270

For Product Safety Concerns and Information please contact our EU
representative GPSR@taylorandfrancis.com
Taylor & Francis Verlag GmbH, Kaufingerstraße 24, 80331 München, Germany

www.ingramcontent.com/pod-product-compliance
Ingram Content Group UK Ltd.
Pitfield, Milton Keynes, MK11 3LW, UK
UKHW021606240425
457818UK00018B/415